The Personal Problem Solver

CHARLES ZASTROW is Associate Professor of Social Welfare and chairperson of the department at the University of Wisconsin, Whitewater. He has had extensive experience in counseling and has published a number of articles on personality theories, therapy approaches, marriage and the family, transracial adoptions, juvenile delinquency, and social data banks.

DAE H. CHANG is Professor of Administrative Justice and chairperson of the department at Wichita State University. He is the author of four other books, including *Sociology: An Applied Approach* and *Prison: Voices from the Inside,* and has published numerous articles on juvenile delinquency, the family, and criminology.

THE PERSONAL PROBLEM SOLVER

edited by

Charles Zastrow

Dae H. Chang

A SPECTRUM BOOK

PRENTICE-HALL, INC., *Englewood Cliffs, New Jersey 07632*

Library of Congress Cataloging in Publication Data

Main entry under title:

The Personal Problem Solver.

    (A Spectrum Book)
    Includes bibliographies and index.
    1. Conduct of life. I. Zastrow, Charles.
II. Chang, Dae H.
BF637.C5P46   158'.1   76–48943
ISBN 0–13–657312–6
ISBN 0–13–657304–5 pbk.

10   9   8   7   6

Prentice-Hall International, Inc., *London*

Prentice-Hall of Australia Pty. Limited, *Sydney*

Prentice-Hall of Canada, Ltd., *Toronto*

Prentice-Hall of India Private Limited, *New Delhi*

Prentice-Hall of Japan, Inc., *Tokyo*

Prentice-Hall of Southeast Asia Pte. Ltd., *Singapore*

Whitehall Books Limited, *Wellington, New Zealand*

Dedicated to

Debbie and Seung Hi

Contents

Preface   xiii

PART ONE: EMOTIONAL PROBLEMS

The ABCs of Better Emotional Self-Control   3
    Maxie C. Maultsby, Jr.

Romantic Love vs. Rational Love   19
    Warren A. Shibles and Charles Zastrow

How to Handle Being Depressed   29
    Charles Zastrow

How to Cope with a Sense of Failure   35
    Merlin J. Manley

How to Cope with Loneliness   46
    Wanda L. Bincer

How to Adjust to the Death of a Parent, Close Relative, or Friend   54
    Jane K. Burgess

Dying as the Last Stage of Growth   66
    Mwalimu Imara

PART TWO: SEXUAL PROBLEMS

Making Your Sex Life More Rewarding   83
    Lloyd G. Sinclair, Richard L. Timmers, and Jane Rea James

Overcoming Difficulty with Erection   89
  Lloyd G. Sinclair

For Men: Controlling Premature Ejaculation   97
  Richard L. Timmers

For Women: Reaching Orgasm   106
  Jane Rea James

Protecting Yourself from Unwanted Parenthood   115
  Sol Gordon and Roger Conant

Coming Out of the Closet: Discovering One's Homosexual Identity   122
  Steven E. Webster

PART THREE: HEALTH PROBLEMS

If You Want to Give Up Cigarettes   135
  The American Cancer Society

10 Ways to Make Your Diet Work   151
  Jean Mayer

How to Adjust to a Mastectomy   156
  Hylda M. Roberts

Adjusting to a Miscarriage   160
  George C. Thosteson

When Labeled Mentally Ill   163
  Charles Zastrow

Drug Facts and Effects   170
  Wayne W. Dunning and Dae H. Chang

What to Do When You Discover Your Son or Daughter
is Experimenting with Marijuana or Other Drugs   184
  Frank E. Ladwig

How to Have an Alcoholic Admit a Drinking Problem
and Stop Drinking   188
  Ronald J. Barta

PART FOUR: INTERPERSONAL PROBLEMS

How to Handle Incidents of Racial Discrimination   197
  Marlene A. Cummings

Facing Job Discrimination: What Women Can Do   207
  Leticia M. Smith

What to Do When He Leaves You   230
  Janet Gregory Vermandel

How to Become More Assertive   236
  Charles Zastrow

Effective Communication   244
  Patricia H. Mewaldt

Getting Along When Religious Beliefs Differ   252
  Charles Zastrow

How to Be More Attractive   258
  Cathy Jensen

PART FIVE: CRISIS SITUATIONS

How to Counsel   267
  Charles Zastrow

Counseling Suicidal Persons   275
  Bernard I. Cesnick and Suzanne K. Nixon

How to Avoid Becoming a Rape Victim:
and What to Do If Rape Occurs   290
  Cathryn M. Wagner

When Premaritally Pregnant   309
  Ursula S. Myers

How to Tell Children They Are Adopted   327
  Laurie Lytle

Bankruptcy: Alternative Methods for Financial Crisis   332
  Kirk Y. K. Kim

Dignity and Welfare: Your Right to Both   338
  Ralph G. Navarre

How to Avoid Becoming a Crime Victim   347
  Dae H. Chang

How to Hire, Fire, and Pay an Attorney   358
  Joseph K. Kuemmel

PART SIX: IDENTITY

Who Am I? The Quest for Identity   365
  Charles Zastrow

List of Contributors   371

Index   375

Preface

The chapters in this book address some of the most important issues and problems facing every citizen—man or woman, young or old, rich or poor, well educated or not, urbanite or rural dweller.

Life—everything between birth and death—is fraught with challenges, crises, and problematic situations. If not resolved, misery, long-term discomfort, depression, and other emotional problems will arise.

From the first few days of birth, throughout life, continual challenges and crises arise daily. Extensive and complex demands are placed on every person. A baby faces brief periods of separation from mother, standing for the first time, learning not to touch hot objects, painful falls, being forced into toilet training, and understanding strange sounds. Equally terrifying situations are faced by adults: controlling undesirable emotions, facing a terminal illness, love relationship problems, sexual dysfunctions, depression, handling failures, drug and alcohol abuse, racial and sexist discrimination, loneliness, premarital pregnancy, death of someone close, temper outbursts, adjusting to such health problems as having a mastectomy or a miscarriage, mental illness, rape, interpersonal communication problems, suicidal desires, financial crises, and avoiding becoming a crime victim.

For many years the general public has had widespread interest in and desire for more information on how to solve personal problems by using step-by-step procedures. With this demand in mind, we have prepared *The Personal Problem Solver*. The book is designed as a step-by-step guide for solving personal problems that will be useful for many people, including readers looking for answers to their own personal problems, counselors, parents, students, teachers, and the general public.

There are three unique features of this book designed to have considerable value for a large audience:

1. The text de-emphasizes theory, instead focusing in detail on the steps recommended by recognized authorities in counseling and the helping professions for solving personal problems. The practical, jargon-free approach is used so that students, parents, teachers, and most people with problems can understand and learn from the material provided.

2. The topics to be covered were selected from questionnaries filled out by over 1,000 college students, professionals, and general citizens. They responded enthusiastically when we requested they list problems (of a personal or social nature) that they wanted more information about in order to deal with these problems more effectively in their personal and professional lives. This survey helped to assure us that the problems we cover are those that most readers want to learn how to handle.

3. Following the selection of topics, chapters were commissioned from nationally prominent scholars, practitioners, and counselors with expertise in the problem area identified. We asked them to specify their step-by-step suggestions for solving the problem. Having recognized authorities provide answers to the most pressing problems we all encounter in our daily lives gives assurance that the recommended solutions have validity.

This book does not guarantee an ironclad solution for everyone with a problem covered here. However, by having experienced scholars and practitioners give their recommendations, the reader who follows their advice can anticipate a fairly high probability of securing at least some relief, improvement, and perhaps resolution of the problem.

An encyclopedic approach was used in compiling this text in that a vast array of personal problems are covered. The coverage is, of course, not exhaustive, but our survey of college students, the general public, and professionals helps to assure that the most frequently asked concerns are discussed. We believe that the encyclopedic approach is the initial effort in the field of mental hygiene to provide a text covering a broad array of common personal problems. There are a number of books on theories of counseling that present global theoretical approaches to solving problems, but they do not explain how to solve specific problems. There are also a number of books covering specific topics — how to handle sexual problems, how to communicate more effectively, how to prevent alcohol and drug abuse, how to be more assertive, and so on. This book is unique in that a broad array of topics are covered, theory and jargon are de-emphasized, and specific "how to" recommendations by authorities are frankly and concisely stated.

The editors have respected the individual authors' views and suggestions. Our central role was to provide the opportunity for experts to contribute their works for editing purposes. Undoubtedly, some of the opinions expressed can be viewed as liberal, some even radical. Other suggestions will be regarded as conservative and perhaps ultraconservative. In any case, the suggestions are being put forth by experienced and recognized authorities. It is up to the reader to decide if the suggestions will fit his or her own particular circumstances and merit a trial effort.

Each chapter briefly covers material on the causes of the problem. The main focus, however, is to provide specific, practical suggestions for coping with and resolving the problem situation. Each chapter discusses alternative approaches for problem resolution. Specific case examples illustrating a recommended course of action are frequently given.

We feel that the personal concerns included in this text serve only a beginning. In years to come we hope to identify more areas of human concern. In this context we solicit your comments and suggestions so as to expand our horizon of knowledge.

Acknowledgments

We wish to express our deep appreciation to the people who made this book possible, the contributing authors, and the following who assisted in selecting authors for topics, critiqued chapters, distributed survey questionnaires, and were "alter egos" for conceptualizing various chapters: Carol Bier, Margaret Bostwick, Linda Brown, Holly Knuth, Debra Parkin, Barbara Radloff, Dr. Don S. Ross and Vicki Vogel. To Robert Gustafson, our illustrator, we express a special note of gratitude.

PART ONE
EMOTIONAL PROBLEMS

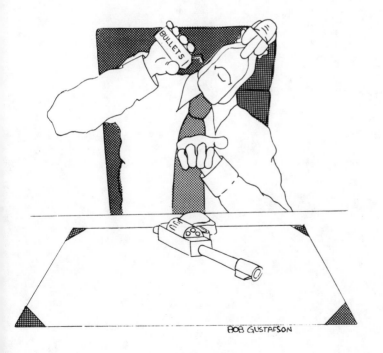

BOB GUSTAFSON

The ABCs
of Better Emotional Self-Control

Maxie C. Maultsby, Jr.

INTRODUCTION

To get the most from reading this chapter, keep an open mind and expect to learn new facts about your emotions. But don't expect these new facts to feel *right* when you first read them. They probably won't, especially if they conflict with your old feelings. Just remember, even when facts feel right or wrong, they *NEVER* are either; facts always just are. Only your beliefs about facts can be right or wrong.

A contrary belief will make a new fact feel wrong almost every time. But what you now believe about your emotions obviously is not right enough to give you the results you want. Otherwise, you wouldn't be reading this chapter. It is only logical, therefore, for you to consider alternative beliefs. That is what this chapter gives you: alternative, emotional beliefs. But to benefit from them, you must avoid the emotional trap of feeling right while thinking *wrong*.

Feeling right while thinking wrong is neither rare nor new. Less than 300 years ago it felt normal, natural, and right for many people to think: "There

This article was especially written for this book.

are witches in the world just waiting to harm me. To protect myself, I should hunt them down and burn them at the stake." Those ideas felt so normal, natural, and right that thousands of people regularly looked for witches, found them, and did, indeed, burn them at the stake. But by the twentieth century people—most people anyway—had stopped looking for witches, not because all the witches had been burned, but, more likely, because people had replaced their wrong beliefs about witches with facts. Hopefully, this chapter will help you to replace your wrong beliefs about your emotions with facts.

Don't expect these new facts to force themselves on you. They won't; to benefit from them, you must willingly learn them; then you must act on them, even though at first they may feel abnormal, unnatural, and wrong. And to make your benefit permanent, you will have to keep acting on those facts until they feel normal, natural, and right. In short, you must be willing to feel abnormally and unnaturally *less* miserable; then you must be willing to go on feeling that way until feeling more miserable feels *abnormal, unnatural,* and *wrong.* Then, feeling *less* miserable will NOT ONLY *feel* right, it will *be* right for you. If these ideas make sense, you can read on with confidence that you are going to help yourself to happiness.

A BELIEVABLE, FACTUAL, AND USEFUL SELF-UNDERSTANDING

Everybody's self-understanding is believable; otherwise they couldn't believe it. But how many people can honestly say yes to these questions: Does my self-understanding help me to feel the emotions I want to feel? Does it help me to achieve my goals today and tomorrow? Does it help avoid significant conflict with others? If your answers are NO more often than you want them to be, your self-understanding may not be worth having. You might be better off without it.

Recent research in psychophysiology shows that normal human emotions consist of perceptions, thoughts, and visceral, or gut, feelings. You experience gut feelings totally, but they are only the "feeling" part of your total emotions. It is wrong and confusing to believe that the feeling part of your emotions is the total emotion; the feeling part is only one-third of it, and the *least* important part at that. Those facts imply the following four believable, factual, and useful self-understandings.

1. Your own thoughts, attitudes, and beliefs cause your emotional feelings. In terms of the ABCs of better emotional self-control: "A" is what you notice

(for example, a barking dog); "B" is what you think and believe, or your attitude, about "A" *with reference to you* (for example, "That dog might bite me"); "C" is your emotional feeling about "A" and "B" (in this case, usually fear). It takes all three parts (A, B, and C) to make up a complete emotion.

2. Each personal attitude or belief makes you feel one of the following four types of emotions—relatively positive, relatively negative, relatively neutral, or some mixture of the three. That understanding is essential for changing an emotional feeling without alcohol or other drugs.

3. If you are healthy and not on drugs, but you are having more unwanted emotions than you would like to have, that usually means you have attitudes and beliefs that are wrong for you. You would probably be happier if you did not have them. That is true even though your attitudes and beliefs are the same as "everybody else's."

4. Without alcohol or other drugs, the only way you can get rid of unwanted emotions is to *find* and *get rid* of the wrong attitudes and beliefs that cause them.

My book, *Help Yourself to Happiness* (Maultsby, Marlborough/Herman, Boston, 1975) explains in detail why Rational Self-Analysis (RSA) is one of the most effective techniques for finding and getting rid of such wrong attitudes and beliefs. The following explanation and case examples of Rational Self-Analysis will demonstrate how easily and quickly you can learn to do it.

RATIONAL SELF-ANALYSIS (RSA)

For a self-analysis to be rational, it must obey at least three of the following five rational rules. It must:

1. be based on objective reality,
2. help you to protect your life,
3. help you to achieve your short- and long-term goals most quickly,
4. help you to avoid significant[1] trouble with other people,
5. help you to feel the emotions you want to feel.

An RSA has six parts. Each is based on the three parts (the ABCs) of a complete emotion.

---

[1]*Significant conflict* is the amount you don't want and act to avoid.

FORMAT FOR RSA

| *A*
Facts and Events | *Da*
Camera Check of A |

| *B*
Self-talk | *Db*
Rational Debate of B |

1. _____   1. _____

2. _____   2. _____

etc.   etc.

| *C*
Emotional Consequences of B | *E*
Emotional Goals and Behavioral
Goals for Similar Future Events |

THE FIVE QUESTIONS FOR RATIONAL THINKING

1. Is my thinking based on objective reality?
2. Does this thinking help me to protect my life?
3. Does this thinking help me to achieve my goals today and tomorrow?
4. Does this thinking help me to avoid significant trouble with others?
5. Does this thinking help me to feel the emotions I want to feel?

How to Do RSA

When you have any unwanted emotion (fear, anger, love, hate, depression, and so on) describe the entire event on paper. Follow the ABC order (first A, then B and C); use your everyday language and write it as soon as possible. The longer you delay, the more you forget, and the less *immediate* help your RSA will give you.

Under A (Facts and Events), simply state the facts as you experienced them.

Under B (Self-talk), write all of your thoughts, attitudes, and beliefs about A. Number each statement in order (1, 2, 3, and so on). Typical B section statements are: "I goofed it all up. Now everybody will see how stupid I am. What an idiot I am!" To show yourself how you believed each B section statement reflected on you as a person, write the word good, bad, or neutral in parentheses immediately after each statement. For example: B-1 "I goofed it up again" (bad), B-2 "What an idiot I am!" (bad). After you complete your B section, count up your goods, bads, and neutrals. Your counts will clearly show how your beliefs alone caused your positive, negative, or neutral emotions at C.

Under C (Emotional Consequences of B), write simple statements describing your emotions about A and B. For example. "I felt anxious. I was depressed. I was upset." Be specific and factual. "You scared me, it made me mad"—these are opinions about the origins of your emotions. Opinions belong in the B section of your RSA. Next, write the five questions for rational thinking immediately under the C section. Now write the D section.

The D section is divided into two parts: Da and Db. Write Da *only* after you have written the A, B, C sections and the five questions for rational thinking. Then reread the A section and apply the camera rule of thumb. That means, ask yourself: "If I had taken a moving picture of what I said happened, would I have seen and heard more or less than what I'm calling facts?" What a moving picture would have recorded is probably fact; what it wouldn't have recorded is probably personal belief, and belongs in the B section. A typical example of opinions mistaken as facts is: "She put me down." Under Da (Camera Check of A), correct such an opinion to statements of fact, such as: "She didn't put me down; she didn't even touch me. I accused her of that because I felt as if I had been put down. But my feeling was irrational, because I was standing up the whole time."

The camera rule of thumb applies *only* to external events, never to feelings. Simple statements of facts, however— "My wife (or husband) left me and I felt depressed"—can stay in the A section. If you felt depressed, that was an emotional fact, even though you could not have taken a picture of it. That is why such statements can be in the A section. Even so, you will still put "I felt depressed" in the C section.

After you complete the Da section, read the B-1 statement. Then ask yourself each of the five questions for rational thinking. If you can give an honest Yes for at least three of them, merely write: That's rational.

If you don't answer Yes at least three times, think of an alternative idea to that B statement. Make sure your new idea has these features: 1) it merits an honest Yes for three or more of the five questions for rational thinking, and 2) you are willing to accept that idea as a new *personal* belief. Then write that new way of thinking as Db-1 in the Db section. Next, debate B-2, B-3, and so on in the same way.

Under the E section, describe the new emotions and actions that you want to have in similar, future A situations. To be *rational* emotions and actions for you, they must be logical for your Db section ideas. For example: Suppose you are depressed because poor work or poor study kept you from passing this term. Under E, you would probably put: "I want to feel just enough rational irritation and dislike *for my failure* (but not for me as a person) to cause me to improve my work and avoid further failure." It probably *would not* be rational to want to be happy about your failure. Feeling happy about it might cause you to want to fail again.

An E section that reads "I want to have no feelings at all" or "No emotion" is meaningless; such states *cannot* be achieved. Your brain controls your emotional state. A physically healthy and undrugged brain forces you to have some kind of emotional feelings about everything you notice.

Some people believe that if they stop feeling miserable, they will stop feeling *altogether*—have no emotions at all. They are wrong. Learning rational, emotional control *cannot* rob you of your ability to feel. Rational, emotional control only enables you to have more of the emotions you want and less of the ones you don't want. Those facts are dramatically demonstrated in the following RSA. A college girl did this RSA during her class in rational self-counseling for normal people.[2]

WHY DOESN'T MY PERIOD COME?

A
(Facts and Events)

A. I missed my menstrual period, which has never happened to me before. I had been off the pill for several months, so I went to the doctor for a pregnancy test. He said it was too soon for that. But he gave me five pills to take and said if I was not pregnant, the pills would bring on my period within 10 days. I waited, but my period didn't come.

Da
(Camera Check of A)

Da. This is all factual.

B
(My Self-talk)

B-1   My god, I'm pregnant. (bad)

Db
(My Rational Debates of B)

Db-1.   It is true that the pills didn't bring on my period. But until I get a final

[2]For more information about courses in Rational Self-Counseling, write to Ms. Linda Carpenter, Rational Behavior Training Section, University of Kentucky Medical Center, Lexington, Kentucky 40506.

B-2. This is awful. (bad)

pregnancy test, I can't be sure I'm pregnant.

Db-2. It's not awful; it's just a missed period. Thinking it's awful just makes me feel awful about it. I'd feel better if I just deal as rationally as I can with the consequences.

B-3. This can't be happening to me! (bad)

Db-3. This obviously *is* happening to me, and it should be happening because I did everything necessary to make it happen. I made love knowing full well that I had stopped taking the pill.

B-4. I'll have to get an abortion and Mark has left me. (bad)

Db-4. I don't have to get an abortion. It's just one of two choices I have. So, I'll consider the pros and cons and make a rational decision. Yes, it's true that Mark is gone. That's an objective fact.

B-5. Where will I get the money? (bad)

Db-5. I'll start by contacting Mark since he supplied half of my problem. If he fails me, I'll try to borrow the money from my sister or the bank and pay them back with my income tax refund.

C
(My Emotions)

Anxious, scared, depressed, angry. I had five bads. That's why I feel 100 percent bad.

E
(My Emotional and Behavior Goal)

To be rationally calm and to do all the things necessary to solve this problem with the least emotional conflict.

By continuously thinking the rational ideas described in the Db section, the girl in the example began to feel calmer. That freed her to start making rational plans for an abortion. Three days later, her period came.

On the basis of that one case, an RSA is not recommended as a pregnancy test. But it is well to remember that when healthy people are rationally calm, nature usually takes its most natural course.

You now have the general idea about Rational Self-Analysis. But you will get personal benefit from your insight only if you put it into practice. To help yourself practice in the safest way possible, diligently use the following As-If RSA.[3]

---

[3]The As-If RSA is a rational growth game created and used by ART (Association for Rational Thinking). ART is a nonprofit organization of people from all walks of life whose common desire is to help make their worlds happier places to live. Their insight is: Helping others help themselves be happier, helps me. For further information, write to Ms. Wanda Wasson, Administrative Assistant, ART National Headquarters, P. O. Box 159, Lexington, Kentucky 40501.

To use an As-If RSA most diligently, you must actively use your imagination. As you read the A, B, and C sections, imagine that you are the person who wrote them. Next, fill in the blank spaces based on how you believe you would have answered the five questions for rational thinking. Finally, check your responses against those of the real person and her counselor.

THE ADOLESCENT REBEL WITHOUT A CAUSE

Cathy N., a 15-year-old ninth grader, was referred to her school psychologist after her third runaway. Psychological evaluation revealed that Cathy had average intelligence and was basically sound emotionally. Her main problem was somewhat above-average, adolescent feelings of inferiority that she tried to ignore. The more she tried to ignore them, the worse she felt. Things had begun to look hopeless, and Cathy was chronically depressed. Her depression seemed to her to be logical punishment for being an inferior person. Since her depression was real and seemed so logical and right, she did not try to fight it.

Like many depressed people, Cathy had the unnoticed attitude that if she just suffered enough, she would somehow—magically—stop being inferior. Then her depression would disappear. Of course that did not (and does not) happen. Instead, Cathy's depression caused her to lose interest in her usual daily life, both at home and at school. That, understandably, resulted in increased criticisms from her teachers and parents. But to Cathy this criticism seemed cruel and unfair. She sincerely wanted to do better; she just didn't seem able to do it. Furthermore, her painful depression seemed to her to be punishment enough for her "hopeless" state. Consequently, even the most well-intended criticism seemed to Cathy to be a vicious "kick when I'm already down." She thought: "It's dehumanizing and I can't stand it." She began to run away when she believed she could not stand it any longer.

Each time Cathy had run away, she had been caught before she had had a chance to have any negative experiences. That fact made running away seem to be both an exciting, fun thing to do and a quick solution to her depression. After three times, however, Cathy began to see that running away was probably not the best permanent solution to her problems. Still, she was convinced that running away was the best way to feel good fast, when she "just couldn't take it any more at home or at school."

The social worker at Cathy's high school taught a course in rational self-analysis. On the advice of the school psychologist, Cathy enrolled in it. When she began to feel like making her fourth runaway, she did the following RSA. Like most first attempts at RSA, this one is far from perfect. But it helped Cathy to feel better fast enough for her to postpone her fourth runaway. Feeling better fast, by just thinking better, was a new experience for Cathy. So she decided to check it out further, by presenting her RSA for class discussion.

Remember. Imagine that you are Cathy. Pretend that her feelings of inferiority are yours and you are now debating your fourth runaway. After you read her A, B, and C sections, write the five questions for rational thinking under the C section. Then fill in the blank Da section with your answer to this question: "Would a camera have recorded what I said happened?" If your honest answer is No or "not exactly," write in Da what you think a camera would have shown. Next, debate each B thought using the five questions for rational thinking. Remember, for a thought to be rational for you, it must obey at least three of the five rules for rational behavior and must be a personally acceptable new way of thinking *for you.*

CATHY'S FIRST RATIONAL SELF-ANALYSIS

A
(Facts and Events)

My mother fussed at me all day about not cleaning up my room, coming in late, my clothes, my friends—everything. Then she grounded me. I just couldn't take it anymore, so I decided to run away the first chance I got. About four hours after they went to bed, I made up my mind to go, but I decided to do this RSA first.

Da
(Your Camera Check of A)

Da.

B
(Self-talk)

1. She never lets me alone. (bad)

2. Pick, pick, pick. That's all she does. (bad)

Db
(Your Rational Debate of B)

Db-1.

Db-2.

3. What a life! (bad)   Db-3.

4. I always have to do what she wants.   Db-4.
(bad)

5. She thinks she can make me do   Db-5.
anything she tells me, and I just can't
stand it. (bad)

6. I can't take it anymore, always having   Db-6.
to jump when she says jump. (bad)

7. I'll show her that I have a mind of my   Db-7.
own. (good)

8. I'll just leave. That will show her.   Db-8.
(good)

9. She's such a witch and she deserves to   Db-9.
suffer. (good)

10. When I'm gone I'll be able to have   Db-10.
peace of mind. (good)

I had 6 bads and 4 goods. But even my
goods made me mad.

C	*E*
(Feelings)	*(Emotional Goal for Similar*
	Future Events)

Mad and wanting to run away.   Calmly to ignore her.

Fill in the five questions for rational thinking.

1. _____

2. _____

3. _____

4. _____

5. _____

Below, you will see how Cathy debated her B thoughts and how the social worker summarized the rational comments of the class. Compare your debates to Cathy's and those of the social worker. Expect most of your ideas to be different from theirs. That won't mean that your ideas are wrong; it will just mean that what is rational for you may not have been rational for Cathy. Just make sure that your responses merited an honest Yes for three or more of the five questions for rational thinking. If so, then they were rational for you.

SOCIAL WORKER'S AND CATHY'S COMMENTS

Cathy's Camera Check of A: It's all factual.

Social Worker's Comments

I seriously doubt that your A section is entirely factual. I'm sure your mother didn't fuss at you all day without stopping at all, and I'm sure she didn't fuss at you about "everything." She's only a fallible human being, so she must have missed something to fuss about. My point is, Cathy, you exaggerated the situation and then made yourself feel as if your exaggerations were objective facts. You'll have to stop exaggerating if you're going to learn to stop upsetting yourself when your mother tells you what she thinks is best for you. Even if you disagree with her, you don't have to get angry about it.

Now, let's see what could have been recorded in your case: A camera with sound would have recorded your mother telling you she disapproved of your messy room, your late hours, your clothes, and your friends. It also would have recorded your mother telling you that you were grounded. Four hours later, it would have recorded you starting to run away but deciding to do this RSA first. That's about all we would have been able to see.

Cathy's Debates to her B

B-1. She never lets me alone. (bad)
Db-1. This isn't completely true. She stops when I'm not around.

Social Worker's Comments to Db

You were exaggerating again. I'm sure she stops criticizing you sometimes, even when you two are together. But let's suppose she never stops criticizing you. That would be a bad enough situation by itself; why make yourself miserable, too? Why make an undesirable situation worse? If you were to stop upsetting yourself, you'd feel better without running away, in spite of what your mother does.

B-2. Pick, pick, pick. That's all she does. (bad)
Db-2. This isn't completely true. She does pick at me most of the time, but occasionally she stops.

14

Social Worker's Comments

Does she ever really pick at all? I mean, physically pick on you? No, of course not. All she does is say what she sincerely believes you need to hear. Her words can't hurt you, but you certainly can and do hurt yourself about them. You react as if she physically picks on you, but you and I both know that she doesn't. That's the fact you need to keep pointing out to yourself. Your mother just says things, and you upset yourself about them. You probably can't stop her from talking, but you certainly can stop yourself from being so upset about what she says.

B-3. What a life! (bad)
Db-3. True, it isn't very pleasant.

Social Worker's Comments

That's just meaningless, emotional noise made only to get yourself more upset. Your words there don't say anything logical or useful about your problem.

B-4. I always have to do what she wants. (bad)
Db-4. True.

Social Worker's Comments

That's not true! You never *have to do* what she wants unless she physically forces you. Both you and I know that she doesn't do that. However, it would be logical to be angry if your mother really were forcing you to do things against your will. But since she is not doing that, it's irrational to accuse her of it and get angry at her. The fact is, you choose to do everything that you do; that means you alone control you. It's true that you may sometimes have two undesirables to choose from, but you still do the choosing.

B-5. She thinks she can make me do anything she tells me, and I just can't stand that. (bad)
Db-5. True.

Social Worker's Comments

If she does think that, she's mistaken. You prove that every time you ignore what she tells you to do. So, how much sense does it make for you to upset yourself about her mistakes? By getting upset, you are acting as if her mistake is an objective fact. Why not calmly accept the fact that your mother is *only* a fallible human being? Then you'd see that she is just as entitled as you are to make mistakes.

> B-6. I can't take it anymore, always having to jump when she says jump. (bad)
> Db-6. I really felt like this.

Social Worker's Comments

You probably did feel as if your thoughts were true; but the objective reality is, they are false. You have not been jumping. Therefore, your feeling was inappropriate for what you have been doing. Has your mother ever told you to jump? Of course not. Rational thinking always starts with the objective reality. If your mother doesn't tell you to jump, it's irrational to accuse her of doing it.

> B-7. I'll show her I have a mind of my own. (good)
> Db-7. That's what I wanted to do.

Social Worker's Comments

I don't think that you need to show that to your mother; she's already well aware of it. But even if you were to do everything your mother asks you to do, that would not mean that you don't have a mind of your own. It would just mean that you do what your mother asks you to do. But you still would have chosen to do it with your own mind.

> B-8. I'll just leave. That'll show her. (good)
> Db-8. All it will do is give her more reason to fuss when I get back.

Social Worker's Comments

Your Db-8 response is the most rational thought you've had so far in this RSA. I agree with it completely.

> B-9. She's such a witch and she deserves to suffer. (good)
> Db-9. That's what I honestly believe.

Social Worker's Comments

Merely believing an idea doesn't turn it into a fact. Something is a fact when it can be objectively demonstrated. Objectively, witches don't exist. So your mother can't be a witch. Calling her one is just as irrational as accusing her of upsetting you, when in reality you upset yourself.

Author's Note

At first, Cathy objected to the social worker's insistence that she call people, "people;" dogs, "dogs;" and objects, "objects." As many people do at first, Cathy thought the social worker was just playing a silly word game.

To get Cathy past that irrational hang-up, the social worker asked: "Do you ever call your mother an angel?"

"Of course not," Cathy answered, "she's no angel!"

"Is she really a nonexistent witch?"

"Well, not really."

"Then," the social worker asked, "which one of us plays silly word games? What do you really think is sillier? To call people what you know for sure they really are not, or to call them what you know for sure they really are? If it really didn't make a difference to you what you call your mother, you'd call her an angel about as often as you call her a witch. The one label is just as silly and inappropriate as the other. So, if you really want to stop playing silly word games, just call your mother a fallible human being. We both know she's that."

Cathy answered, "It still seems kind of silly, but I see what you mean."

"Just try thinking about your mother without any word games for one week and see if you still feel as angry at her as you have been feeling," replied the social worker.

"Okay, I'll try anything once."

    B-10. When I'm gone, I'll be able to have peace of mind. (good)
    Db-10. That's not true. I'll probably worry and feel guilty just like I did last time.

Social Worker's Comments

That's a very good insight. Running away doesn't help you get the permanent peace of mind you want. You have to create your peace of mind with rational thinking. You can do it at home, at school, or wherever you happen to be.

Author's Note

Cathy decided it was probably in her best interest to accept the social worker's suggested debates and reject hers. She also agreed to stop the word game for a week. At the next class she reported: "Wow, I feel like a different person. It really worked!! I never knew I controlled myself before. I always thought my mom did it to me. It's really great to know that you can choose and feel the way you want."

Rational Self-Analysis is an effective, safe, emotional self-help technique. You are now ready to try doing your own RSA. It really can help you to help yourself to happiness.

For additional recommended readings, see *You and Your Emotions* (Maultsby, Rational Self-Help, Inc. P. O. Box 8178, Lexington, Kentucky 40503), a cartoon book illustrating the basic principles of rational emotional self-help techniques; and *Help Yourself to Happiness* (Maultsby, Marlborough/Herman, Boston, 1975), describing how to stop unwanted emotions safely, quickly, and privately. Suitable for anyone interested in a comprehensive yet practical discussion of rational, emotional, self-help theory and techniques.

Romantic Love vs. Rational Love

Warren A. Shibles
Charles Zastrow

One of the human being's greatest desires is to achieve a really fine, long-lasting love relationship. This experience is perhaps equalled by no other, yet few people are able to achieve or maintain it. Rather, most people have serious, unattended problems that specifically involve love. For instance, they may not be able to love anyone, do not know if they are in love, are not able to sustain a love relationship, or fall in love with someone who does not love them. Mediocrity and failure in matters of love are more the rule than the exception. It is one of the most critical issues of any age.

One of the main reasons for failure in matters of love is that most people, including psychiatrists, pyschologists, philosophers, and other professionals and scholars, have been confused about emotions including the love emotion. Recent work, however, has contributed to a greater understanding of emotions.[1] To increase our chances of achieving a great love relationship, we must understand how emotions work and must clarify the concept of love. This chapter gives a conceptual framework for understanding love, a framework

---

This article was especially written for this book.

[1] See Chapter 1 in this text, "The ABCs of Better Emotional Self-Control, and Warren Shibles, *Emotion: The Method of Philosophical Therapy* (Whitewater, Wis.: The Language Press, 1974), see especially "An Analysis of Love," pp. 343-429. A bibliography on love is included.

that has significantly changed people's ability to love. The senior author of this chapter has taught this approach in university graduate and undergraduate seminars on emotion, and specifically in a seminar on love. The emphasis is on specifying the kind of thought and necessary conditions for making love possible. Much of what we usually believe about love and emotion will be objected to. As will be demonstrated, this approach is also very useful in counseling people who have love relationship problems.

Many people say, "You can't define love. It is just an abstract thing. You have it or you don't." This view is not only false but harmful. If we do not define love and reduce it to concrete, everyday acts, thoughts, and feelings, we will not know how to love. You cannot love well if you are not clear about what love is. You may say "I love you," but yet may not be able to develop a satisfying love relationship.

One of the greatest abuses is when a person says "I love you" to gain a personal advantage, or says it and then mistreats the other person. It is important to know what is experienced and meant when someone says "I love you." One way to avoid confusion and abuse is to ask, "What do you really mean when you say you love me?"

Also, if we do not define love we will not be able to answer questions such as, "How do I know if I am really in love or not?" or "Do I love this person more than that one?" If love is just an unintelligible, indefinable abstraction, we would not be able to answer these questions, and so it is harmful to regard love as a mystical abstraction.

"Love" can and should be reduced to concrete and specific things. It involves specific actions, thoughts, and feelings. By love we may mean someone's touch, a feeling, concern for another, politeness, consideration, a warm tone of voice, and such. Although love may mean a great many different things, this is no reason to say that we cannot find out what they are. In fact, one of the greatest problems is that we mistake the wrong things or just a few things as being love. One of the most common popular mistakes is to regard love as being only a feeling.

What, then, is an adequate and useful definition of love? Love, like other emotions, involves certain thoughts that cause a certain feeling and action. Here, "feeling" is used to mean bodily sensation. Love is not just a physical feeling. If it were, we could be in love without being in love with anyone or anything. One may then ask. "Who are you in love with?" and receive the reply, "I don't know. I just have the feeling." That makes little sense. We would not understand such a reply.

If love were just a feeling, we could take something to affect our physical self, such as a drug or a pill to rid us of the feeling; for example "Have a martini. It will make you feel differently." But we would still be in love after the martini. That is because love involves not only a feeling, but also thought (beliefs, attitudes, self-talk).

Love is an emotion, and similar to other emotions, according to Chapter 1, it occurs according to the following formula:

1. An event — You meet or become acquainted with another person.
2. Self-talk — "This person is attractive, charming, cares about me, has the same interests as I do, is the kind of person I would like to spend the rest of my life with."
3. Emotion or gut response — Feeling of being in love.

This definition leads to a number of significant consequences that should revise our thinking and action.

In the first place, love is no longer opposed to reason or thought. There is a cognitive or judgmental part of love; it involves and includes thought. Love is not just irrational and feeling. But, most important, by saying that love is thought that causes feeling, we can now see that we can change our love by changing our thought. This is in opposition to the very popular view that we cannot change our emotions. We very definitely can change them, even radically, and, furthermore, we can produce or induce love by having the right thoughts.

Because love is often viewed as being only a feeling, it is erroneously believed to be something that happens to us passively. It is viewed as being out of our control. Emotions used to be called "passions" (from the Latin word *passio* meaning "being acted upon," or passive). Thus, people often say, "I couldn't help myself," or "I did it out of passion." This falsely presupposes that emotions are only feelings and just happen to us and that we have no control over them and that we did nothing to cause them. To illustrate, the following situation shows where mistakes are made.

While attending a convention in a distant city, a married woman meets an attractive man and has an affair with him. She justifies this by saying that it was "situational"; that is, she claims she was only following her passions that arose in this particular situation. This justification is based on the current popular notion that it is permissible to ignore obligations to others in favor of one's own happiness of the moment. But the situation does not justify her actions. She put herself into this situation and could do so again and again. It is not the situation that caused her to do it. She could have been in control and done otherwise. It is one's self-talk about the situation that primarily causes the feeling and actions, not the situation itself.

Suppose she says, "I didn't know what was happening. I couldn't help myself." This won't do either. It has been seen that love and other emotions are not passive, but involve thought. By changing the thought we can change the emotion. She either wanted to have the affair or self-talked herself into being an active participant. She could not claim "I couldn't help myself because feelings are not something one can control or prevent."

Her assessments or thoughts could have been some of the following:

> My husband cheats, too.
>
> This is just happening. I can't do anything about it.
>
> This man is handsome. I'm not going to think about anything.
>
> It's a bore to be restricted. I want to be warm and intimate with this man.
>
> What will be will be.
>
> My husband isn't such a great lover, maybe this will be better.
>
> It will be exciting to have a lover and feel desirable again.
>
> It may improve my marriage.

Such thoughts cause her feelings and allow them. She purposely tries to find reasons to justify the affair or to avoid thinking about the consequences. She, in effect, lets her thoughts about her feelings overtake her. That is an active not a passive act. She says to herself, "I won't think. I'll just let it happen." This thought makes it happen. She cannot then claim, "My passions overcame me," or "I just couldn't help it."

In summary, it is often not acceptable merely to claim, "I did it out of passion," or "I couldn't help myself," or "It was situational." It would be more accurate to say, "I did it out of ignorance," or "I did it because of sexual needs."

One is also misled into thinking that love is only a feeling because of the common expression, "I fell in love." It seems that when someone "falls in love," it is just a feeling that is overpowering. It is considered a passive "feeling." However, this is not the case. Although there is a strong feeling, we "fall in love" because of our prior assessments, thoughts, and needs. "Falling in love" does involve thought. The principle may be illustrated by this simplified case:

A woman is impressed with football players. She decides she would like to date one. She also likes tall men with dark hair. Music is also very important to her. If she then meets a six-foot-tall football player with dark hair who likes music, she is apt to become attracted to him. This feeling is based on prior as well as present thoughts and assessments.

Thus, self-talk (personal attitudes, beliefs, present assessments) largely determine when we will fall in love and with whom. The sources of our self-talk are numerous, including: parental influences from earlier years regarding desirable attributes of a spouse; peer influences regarding who is rated highly as a date; goals that we want to achieve in life; our particular life-style and interests, our socioeconomic values, religious, and political affiliations; our sexual needs; and our sense of personal identity and personal security.

ROMANTIC LOVE

Romantic love is very much like "falling in love." The feeling involved is strong, but the reasons or thought that cause the feelings are weak. Romantic love is often brought about by great unsatisfied desires and frustration. Some main causes are great loneliness, extreme sexual frustration, inability to cope with loneliness, excessive desire for security or protection against society, parental and personal problems. Romantic love will be seen to be largely based on excessive needs and confused thinking, rather than on reason and understanding.

Webster's Dictionary defines "romance" as: To exaggerate or invent detail or incident, something that lacks basis in fact. "Romantic" is: impractical in conception or plan (visionary); marked by the imaginative or emotional appeal of the heroic, adventurous, remote, mysterious, or idealized.

Romance, as in the legend of Tristan and Isolde, in Romeo and Juliet, or Don Quixote, involves need, desire, and obstacles. The more forbidden the love, the stronger it becomes. The more social customs are threatened, the higher the wall is to climb. The more the self-sacrifice, and the greater the physical and psychological distance between lovers, the greater the "passion." Romantic love is a paradox, a combination of opposites. The greater the frustration, the greater the love.

Both courtly and chivalric love involve chaste love. The lover seldom or never sees his love except at a distance. A knight battles secretly for a woman who doesn't know of his feelings and who is already married. If she ever does meet him, it may involve only a kiss or a quick embrace. To obtain such love fully is to lose the romanticism involved. Thus, romantic love requires distance. The loved one is being idealized and used as a symbol of all of one's hopes. Romantic love, to be romantic, must never "touch down."

Romantic love can be diagrammed according to the following:

1. An event—Meeting/becoming acquainted with a person who has some (a few) of the overt characteristics you idealize in a lover.
2. Self-talk—"This person is attractive, charming; has absolutely all the attributes I desire in a lover/mate."
3. Emotion—Feeling of being swept off your feet, romantically in love.

In romance, one goes from absolute lack or nothingness to all that can be imagined, yet without achieving anything but the experience of love itself. It is ideal. In romantic love, if the goal is achieved, the love is lost. This is its madness. It must defeat itself to exist at all, violate moral codes and customs, use clever schemes to defeat intelligence (as in the "I did it out of passion" example), or involve clever deception. It is "infatuation," which is defined by Webster as: To make foolish; to inspire with a foolish or extravagant love or admiration. The lover is in ecstacy.

Romantic love is also often confused with sexual feelings. We erroneously tend to think that because we have strong sexual feelings for another, we therefore love them in every other way. However, sexual attraction alone is notoriously insufficient as a basis upon which to establish a lasting or adequate love relationship. Sex is merely one of our needs and interests. We also need to enjoy talking with the other person and must be able to communicate openly with him or her so as to solve problems as they arise. The confusion of love with sexual desire is one of the most common mistakes made in matters of love—thus, the need for a more clear and adequate analysis and definition of love.

Romantic love is a mixture of temporary feelings and make-believe. It is the defense mechanism by means of which reality is distorted and idealized in order to, as if by magic, make life suit all of one's hopes and desires. The lover sees the loved person as an item of overwhelming importance. He says, "You are the moon, the stars, and everything to me." However, romantic love requires that we never love the real person, only the person we imagine. The main thing about romantic love is that it is often pleasant but tends not to last very long, and it frequently involves frustration, depression, and jealousy. The romantic feeling soon goes when the lover sees what the loved one is really like.

RATIONAL LOVE

Certain thoughts and actions are required for a fulfilling, gratifying, and lasting love relationship. Rational love can be diagrammed according to the following:

1. Event—While being clear about your own needs, identity, goals, and desires, you become well-acquainted with a person who fulfills to a fair extent the essential characteristics you desire in a lover/mate.
2. Self-talk—"I admire this person's strengths, am aware and accepting of his/her shortcomings, and this person has many of the characteristics I seek in a lover/mate.
3. Emotion: Rational love.

To expand, the following thoughts and actions create the feeling of rational love:

1. Your self-talk about the other person is self-enhancing, realistic, and rational. Your feelings are not based on fantasy, pity, or on excessive needs or desires. Thus, the philosopher, Seneca, wrote, "Only a wise man knows how to love."

2. You know the other person well.

3. You are clear about your own needs and desires. We often do not know ourselves well enough, so we say one thing yet find that we act in a much different way.

4. One of the most essential requirements is that you are able to communicate honestly and openly so that you can constantly enhance the relationship, solve problems as they come up, and enjoy talking with one another. The relationship is likely to be as good as the openness and honesty of the communication. The ability to love depends on one's ability to think clearly and communicate.

5. Because love is thought that causes feeling, it is you who create love. It is, then, quite possible and frequently desirable to work positively to control feelings of love. It is theoretically possible to love anyone by making changes in your self-talk, which guides feelings. Love is something you do, not something that just happens to you. Thus, the situation does not arise where the spouse says, "I can't help it, my feelings have changed — I no longer love you." We do not just "happen" to change. The change, if there is one, is caused by our own thinking. If we do not work aggressively to create and improve the love relationship, it will deteriorate due to neglect. The stress is on loving rather than on being loved. Love involves a number of very specific things, such as communicating openly and warmly, being kind, knowing what pleases the other person, erotic satisfaction, and so on. Love involves knowing of, learning of, learning how, and doing these specific things. Shakespeare wrote, "They do not love that do not show their love." It is not enough merely to say now and again, "I love you." It is one's actions that count.

6. It is necessary that we know how emotions work so that we can develop gratifying love relationships and avoid abusing/hurting either ourselves or our partner. Whenever we have a problem involving love, we need honestly and extensively to analyze the self-talk underlying the problem. Through such an analysis, it is almost always possible to develop one or more strategies for resolving/improving the situation. By challenging and changing our self-talk, we can change our emotions, actions, perceptions, and mental images.

The following counseling illustrations show how romantic love problems can be analyzed and constructive approaches formulated to develop more rational relationships.

Identity through sex. A somewhat depressed freshman college girl felt guilty and unhappy about "being used by men." She indicated that she had had a series of "one-night stands" but always felt guilty and depressed afterward. Using the rational behavior technique described in Chapter I, her guilt was analyzed as stemming from such self-talk as "I am promiscuous" "I am letting men who don't love me use my body" "I am giving myself to men whom I don't love" and "I'm a bad girl—a whore." Her feelings of depression were closely connected and stemmed from additional self-talk, "No one really cares about me as a person, only my body" "I am leading the kind of life I really don't want to lead" and "I give everything I have to these guys, and they don't even call to ask me for a date." When asked to analyze her self-talk carefully prior to intercourse, the following was given, "At times I really feel like it, and enjoy/need sex" "Sex is the one way I can get a guy interested in me." After these problems were explored more fully, the counselor mentioned that there were several alternative approaches to resolve this set of problems. The choice of which strategy to use had to be largely hers, as she was in the best position to know which would be most suitable to her values, to her current life-style, and to her goals in life. Among the approaches discussed were:

1. Choose not to have sex until marriage.
2. Choose not to have sex until she is assured that the other person, whom she loves, is in love with her. Also, in response to a question she raised, it was pointed out that until such a person could be found, her sexual tensions could be relieved through masturbation.
3. Choose to continue her present series of "one-night stands" with men she is attracted to. If this approach was chosen, it was pointed out that through challenges to her self-talk she could probably change her degrading ideas about being a "whore" and being promiscuous, which would relieve some of her feelings of guilt and depression.

The second strategy was chosen, and four additional sessions dealt with helping her to clarify her goals in life and to establish an improved sense of self-concept and identity. Three months later, on a routine follow-up evaluation form, she noted that she now was clearer about her life goals, was happier and dating someone she had recently met in a history class.

Don Juan wife. After four and a half years of marriage, a husband discovered that his wife had had affairs with several other men, and they were

[2]These illustrations are partial case summaries taken from the counseling experiences of Charles Zastrow.

wondering whether to continue the marriage. The husband was angry and-possessive with his wife, having such self-talk as, "She has cheated on me" "She is disgracing me" "She is threatening the future of our marriage, and also my current way of living." On the other hand, he still had strong feelings of affection toward her and wanted to continue the marriage on the condition that she would promise not to have another extramarital affair.[3]

The wife felt some guilt about hurting and deceiving her husband, and stated that she was still "in love" with him. However, she stated that she could not abide by the condition of having to discontinue extramarital affairs. Her self-talk about her desire to have extramarital affairs was, "I not only love my husband, but also other men" "I need to have sex with more than one man to provide variety and meaning to my life" "I do not believe people were born to be monogamous." This set of self-talk prompted the counselor to probe further, to examine her self-talk regarding what she found enjoyable about extramarital sex. Her self-talk revealed, "I enjoy the feeling of being able to seduce someone who I am attracted to" "The people I seduce then feel somewhat obligated to me" and "The conquest of someone who is very attractive is three-quarters of the thrill."

Several approaches to resolve this situation were possible, including a divorce or continuing the marriage with the husband attempting psychologically to become accommodated to his wife's extramarital affairs. A third strategy was, however, chosen. Through counseling, the wife discovered that what she was primarily seeking from extramarital affairs was not sex per se, but the thrill of a conquest and making others feel obligated to her. With this insight, she came to realize that the "thrill of a conquest" was less important than maintaining her marriage. In addition, her "need for a conquest" was partially met by taking a part-time job as a commercial artist. She also realized that her desire to make people feel obligated to her was inconsistent with her ideas about not exploiting others, and also inconsistent with her self-concept and her life goals. Therefore, she switched to attempting to form more equalitarian, constructive relationships with others.

This couple was also referred to a professional sexual counseling center in the area to explore ways to make their sex life more exciting. (Clearly her feelings of love and sex were determined by her assessments about others and about sex itself.)

Jealous husband. A couple was contemplating divorce. They both expressed feelings of affection for each other, but stated that they were having frequent violent arguments. Both were college graduates. He was an electrical engineer and she had obtained a job about a year before as a store manager of

[3]For a further analysis, see Shibles, *Emotion*, pp. 422–427.

a chain discount store. Her job entailed some evening work and attending occasional meetings in other cities. The couple had been married for three years, with intense and frequent arguments developing about a year ago. The husband objected to his wife's attending meetings in other cities and working in the evening. When asked about his reasons, he stated (his self-talk), "A wife's place is at home in the evening" "You never know what might happen in a strange city" "We've all heard stories about drinking and orgies at conferences." (The wife denied any interest in being unfaithful, but the husband did not appear to accept this fully.) It gradually became clear that the husband was possessive. Another area of frequent arguments centered around the husband's objecting to his wife talking at length with men at parties they attended. The husband also objected to his wife's clothes that accentuated her physical attractiveness.

Again, several solutions were available. These were explored, with the husband choosing to explore his need to be possessive. The self-talk underlying his possessiveness was: "I want to provide for my wife financially" "A man is only a man when he supports his family" "A wife's place is in the home" "A wife who talks with other men is flirting" "When my wife is away from home, she may be seduced by others" "A man should be the boss in his family."

With counseling, it became clear to him that his possessive approach would probably end up in a divorce, and he then sought to counter his possessive feelings and strove to achieve an equalitarian relationship based on mutual trust and understanding. Some of his challenges to his possessive self-talk were: "My wife has as much right to a career as I" "With our two sources of income, we will be able to travel and enjoy many things that we otherwise could not" "I talk to many women and don't flirt, I have no right to accuse my wife of flirting when she talks to men" "An equalitarian relationship will result in a happier, more satisfying marriage for both of us."

As these cases demonstrate, through an analysis of our problems involving love, particularly by honestly examining our self-talk underlying any painful/undesirable emotions, we have the potential within ourselves to work toward achieving a truly gratifying, long-lasting love relationship. Emotions can be induced and changed. It is we who create and sustain the emotion of love.

How to Handle Being Depressed

Charles Zastrow

INTRODUCTION

Everyone, at times, feels at a "low tide" or mildly depressed. Feelings of depression come from a number of sources: a broken romance, low self-esteem, feelings of inferiority, the death of someone we know, failure to attain something one has expended considerable effort in trying to achieve, loss of financial resources, being seriously handicapped following an accident, being informed that one has a terminal illness, and many, many more. The depth of a depression varies widely, ranging on a continuum from mild to severe. Mild depressions occur much more frequently than moderate or severe depressions. Fortunately, several effective techniques have been developed for relieving mild depressions, and these will be discussed in this chapter.

There are a variety of symptoms that are elicited by a depression. A depression is usually indicated when one or more of the following reaction patterns is present:[1]

1. Depressive mood: dejection, despair, suicidal ideas, loss of interest in people and in usual activities.

[1]Quoted from James P. Page, *Psychopathology* (Chicago: Aldine, Atherton, 1971), p. 239.

2. Anxious self-blame: high anxiety level, self-castigation.
3. Retardation: slowing of action, thought, and speech.
4. Impaired functioning: loss of energy and drive, difficulty in making decision, inability to get started, to concentrate, and to work.
5. Somatic symptoms: lack of appetite, weight loss, disinterest in sexual activity, gastrointestinal symptoms.

Each of these symptoms may vary in intensity from mild to severe.

In rare cases there is also a manic phase, where the disturbed person fluctuates in periodic manic-depressive mood swings. In mild disorders the manic stage is difficult to distinguish from a normal state of elation, display of confidence, and high activity. With severe or delirious mania there is a complete loss of control, with the person being disoriented, wildly excited, incoherent, and even violent. Hallucinations and delusions are often present, and sedation or physical restraint is sometimes necessary to avoid exhaustion and to prevent the person from injuring him- or herself or others. Some authorities see the manic stage as an effort by the individual to counteract and avoid the pain of depression.

CAUSES

Although there are a number of theories on the causes of depression, the precise determinants are as yet unknown. In addition, several types of classification systems have been developed, but these are based on clinical syndromes (that is, patterns of symptoms) rather than underlying determinants. Examples of labels based on varying symptom patterns are manic-depressive psychosis, retarded depression, agitated depression, delirious mania, normal depression, neurotic depression, acute depression, and depressive stupor. Such labels, however, do not identify separate casual factors, nor do they identify separate emotional disorders.

There are several pyschological determinants of depression that have been identified. Depressions are sometimes a reaction to a loss (death of a loved one, broken romance, loss of financial resources). Sometimes a depressed person's behavior can be understood partly as a cry for love or help (a display of helplessness and a direct appeal for affection, security, or assistance in obtaining the lost object). Other depressions can be seen as anger turned inward (rage or hostility turned back upon the self when the person feels it cannot be expressed against the outward source of frustration). At times some depressed people use their depression as a way to control others; their mood elicits attention, is an excuse to avoid responsibilities, and plays on the humanitarian value to help those in need. In others, depression involves a heavy guilt component, expressed as feelings of having made a serious error and the feeling one deserves to be punished.

There are also physiological factors involved in depression. Studies have shown there is a genetic predisposition to depression; that is, there is a tendency for depression to run in families.[2] The relative importance of hereditary versus environmental factors in contributing to a depression has been a controversy for many decades. Research has also been conducted on biochemical factors, for example, varying hormone levels, basal metabolism rates, the functioning of the nervous system, and dietary determinants. Certain biological and maturational stages are also known to correlate with depression, for example, menstruation, the first few weeks following the birth of a child, menopause, and male climacteric.

Although the symptoms of depression have been fairly well identified, the psychological and physiological determinants are not precisely known. In spite of this lack of knowledge regarding causal determinants, there are a number of general guidelines that if followed have a high probability of relieving a mild depression. (Fortunately, human problems can at times be resolved without fully knowing the causes, for example, tranquilizers can be used to relieve high levels of anxiety without knowing the specific causal determinants.)

GUIDELINES FOR RESOLVING MILD DEPRESSION

Guideline 1. One of the most successful ways of relieving a depression is getting involved in some meaningful activity. When one becomes involved in activity that is meaningful, it provides satisfaction and enjoyment (which counter feelings of depression), and structures and fills time, thereby taking one's mind off what one is depressed about. If a person already is aware of things he or she enjoys doing (for example, a hobby, going to the movies, traveling, dancing, playing tennis) then usually the most difficult thing for that depressed person to do is to take the first few steps to get involved. In rarer cases a person may not be aware of any activities that he or she finds meaningful. Such people tend to be more deeply depressed, and for a longer period of time. Finding meaningful activities to get involved in is still the key to relieving the depression, and such people should be strongly encouraged to try various activities on a trial-and-error basis — sooner or later they will find something meaningful. *Doing* something is much, much more useful than allowing the depressed person to *think* about what he or she may or may not

[2]Robert White, *The Abnormal Personality,* 4th ed. (New York: Ronald Press, 1973).

like to do. The author remembers occasionally becoming depressed as an undergraduate student. The depressed feelings occurred on those days when upon waking he knew he had nothing planned for that day. With nothing to do, he would lie in bed thinking about what he might do. As he thought, he became more depressed, and his motivation to do something thereby lessened. A downward spiral was being created. As he thought, he became more depressed, which lowered his energy level, which kept him thinking since he did not have the desire to do anything else.

Guideline 2.   Everyone should develop an "escape valve" list of things they enjoy doing: taking a walk, golf, visiting friends, going to a movie, shopping, whatever. By using such a list, a person can quickly derail any initial feelings of depression. The author solved his mild feelings of depression in this way. One day he simply analyzed what was happening with this downward spiral and developed such a list. In the future when he awoke with nothing to do, he would dress and quickly get involved in an activity. The most difficult step usually proved to be making the effort to get out of bed.

Guideline 3.   Rational therapy correctly points out that generally we make ourselves depressed, not outside events that happen to us.[3] Rational therapy presents an extremely useful formula for analyzing and countering feelings of depression. Skill with this formula can be used to control any feelings of depression that one has. The formula is:

1. An event that occurs.
2. Self-talk, our thoughts about that event.
3. Emotion or gut response caused primarily by the self-talk.
4. Challenges to the self-talk, geared to changing the thoughts we have about an event, which will thereby change the emotion. Challenges to self-talk is the therapy segment of this formula.

An example will illustrate the formula:

1. Event: A man informs a woman their engagement is off.
2. Self-talk: The woman tells herself:
   a. He has ruined my plans for the future, and for future happiness.
   b. He is the only person I ever loved and will ever love, and now he is gone.
   c. How could he do this to me, after all I've done for him?
3. The emotional response, primarily on such self-talk, is depression. On the other hand, if her self-talk was "Thank God, I'm not ready to marry

[3]Albert Ellis, "Rational-Emotive Therapy," in *Current Psychotherapies,* ed. Raymond Corsini (Itasca, Ill.: F. E. Peacock, 1973).

yet, and the more I see of this guy, the less I like him," she would not be depressed but relieved. Or, if her self-talk was, "That louse, I don't love him, but I spent a fortune on putting him through college and I was hoping he would earn the money for us in the future," then the emotional response might well be anger.

4. Challenges to the self-talk. Following is one possible self-challenge to each of the statements in the self-talk section above:

  a. My plans for the future have been changed, but Jane and I will take a trip and I'll play the future "by ear" for awhile.

  b. There are a couple of guys I'm interested in dating, and with several million eligible bachelors in the world, there certainly are others I'd be interested in forming a relationship with.

  c. As he indicated to me when he broke our engagement, he does not feel he is ready to get married or settle down as yet. It probably is better finding this out now than after we're married. Perhaps I'm not really ready to get married myself.

Effective use of this formula requires considerable honesty, practice, ability to analyze one's self-talk, and some creativity in arriving at realistic self-challenges. But the payoff is well worth the effort, for a person will then be potentially able to control any feelings of being depressed.

Guideline 4.   Medication can provide relief from depression and certain related symptoms. The drugs include antidepressant drugs (such as imipramine and lithium) and medication for insomnia. If a mild depression lasts for a few weeks, or if the depression moderately drains one's emotional resources, a physician should be consulted.

Guideline 5.   In counseling someone who is depressed, show empathy but do not give sympathy. Empathy is the capacity to convey that you are aware and can to some extent feel what the other person is saying. Sympathy is also a sharing of feelings but has the connotation of offering pity. If sympathy is given to a depressed person, that person will continue to pour out his or her feelings over and over to you. Empathy is problem-solving oriented; sympathy tends to be problem prolonging. Giving sympathy to the depressed person usually leads that person to dwell on his or her emotions without taking action to improve the situation. By giving sympathy, the depressed person will become emotional, the emotions will then keep his or her thinking focused on the depressed story, and thereby motivate him or her to tell you the story over and over again. Repeating the story simply serves to reopen old wounds and prolongs the depression. (By listening to the sad story over and over, you also are apt to find that you will become somewhat depressed yourself.)

In counseling someone who is depressed, listen to the story one or twice to understand the depth and nature of the depression, but then focus on what the person should be doing about the situation, saying something like: "I can see you are depressed and I can understand the reasons why. Going over the reasons again will not be helpful. What we need to talk about is what constructive actions you now should take."

Guideline 6.   Seek professional help (from a social service agency or a physician) when the depression lasts more than a few weeks or when the intensity of the depression is in the moderate/severe range. The prognosis for relief of symptoms is good. About 80 percent of severe attacks of depression terminate well within nine months.[4] In addition, modern drugs can usually bring symptoms under control in a week or two. However, for severe depressions, since recurrence of attacks is common, the main objectives of treatment are generally to decrease the severity of symptoms, to shorten the duration of attacks, and to reduce the likelihood of a recurrence.

Treatment for severe depressions varies, depending on the nature of the symptoms and upon other problems with which the depression may be associated. Medication, for example, is available for women undergoing menopause. If the depression is associated with a drinking problem, treatment would focus on the drinking problem (referral to Alcoholics Anonymous, antabuse, counseling), as well as on the depression.

Antidepressant drugs generally work well on severely depressed people; they create a sense of euphoria and relaxation for the stress that is felt. Psychotherapy is at times not too useful because the severely depressed are frequently unresponsive. Hospitalizing those who are suicidal may be necessary. Those experiencing severe mania also may need to be hospitalized to prevent exhaustion or to prevent them from harming themselves or others. Hospitalization is less often and less quickly resorted to than in the past; care on an outpatient basis (if the person is not a threat to him- or herself or to others) is as effective and more economical. The decision to hospitalize someone is based on the nature and severity of the depression, the kinds of treatment needed, the risk of suicide, and the capacity of the family to cope with the depressed person. Physicians and social service professionals are in the best position to recommend the needed type of treatment.

Everyone has feelings of depression. If the depression is mild, many of the feelings can be handled by the individual without professional counseling. The prognosis, even for severe depressions, is good. Even though depression is widespread and the causes are not precisely known, effective techniques are available to relieve or resolve this common emotional disorder.

[4]Page, *Psychopathology,* p. 255.

How to Cope with a Sense of Failure

Merlin J. Manley

A sense of failure can be a deep-seated, all-consuming feeling. It is one's whole being, behavior, and the way he or she interacts with others. This "failure filter," or screen through which we interpret things, becomes built into our thought processes. An individual's behavior is determined not so much by rational or objective criteria, but by looking at the world through his or her "failure filter." Needless to say, this can cause one to engage in irrational and often inappropriate behavior. All of us have filters as an integral part of our perceptual and decision-making processes; this is quite natural. These filters decode signals coming to us and can be used to our advantage, such as a "self-confidence filter," or they can be harmful, as with a "failure filter."

Failure orientations have a variety of symptoms. Some of the more common include excessive worry, anxiety, fatigue, boredom, loneliness, and/or general feelings of misery. Extreme feelings of failure can even produce emotional depression. Frequently, people try to cope with these symptoms by rationalization (a popular defense mechanism), which involves the individual's making excuses for existing shortcomings. Boredom, for example, could be a symptom that might cause one to rationalize and say to him- or herself, "People really bore me. They're so uninteresting. Why should I bother with them?

This article was especially written for this book.

I'm better off without them. That way I can do whatever I want." People who fail often rely on emotion to dictate their behavior. Logic and reason frequently take a "back seat."

If one analyzes this line of thinking, it becomes apparent that the individual really felt that he or she was a failure at gaining the acceptance of people. To compensate for this perceived nonacceptance, he or she begins to tell him- or herself that people are boring and he or she is better off without them. Uninvolvement, then, can be interpreted as the person's choice and not the result of others' rejection. It is easier for him or her to accept this line of thinking. He or she uses rationalization as a way of coping with the pain of uninvolvement.

Uninvolvement, often the product of failure orientation, is bound to be psychologically painful. The need for involvement has been built into the human central nervous system. If this need is not met, dissonance is certain to emerge. Besides rationalization, there are other means that individuals use in minimizing the discomfort of not being involved. Some turn to alcohol, some to other drugs as an answer. Excessive use of alcohol and other drugs is an inappropriate response for a number of reasons, not the least of which is that these commodities may neutralize the symptom to the degree that it makes the uninvolvement or failure identification tolerable. Consequently, the symptom has been treated, but the root cause remains to continue to impair the functioning of the individual. In other words, he or she still has a sense of failure.

A sense of failure is determined by (1) how one perceives others seeing him or her and (2) how one thinks he or she should be. To the degree that one's perceptions are accurate, he or she can function as a responsible (both to him- or herself and others) person. However, if he or she has internalized too many crippling filters through which he or she forms perceptions, this is certain to have a disabling effect.

People with failure identities are characterized by a very narrow perceptual field, or sense of awareness. This limits the feedback that they permit themselves to receive. Everyone needs feedback from others to develop and mature psychologically. This permits the formulation of a value system, a self-concept, and a behavioral repertoire. Feedback can be classified in one of two categories: how others feel about us personally and how they feel about our behavior. In interpreting feedback it is important to continue to distinguish between these two. Because individuals are so concerned with being accepted personally, they often consider any feedback (whether directed toward their person or their actions) as applying to them personally. This presents a problem when they are the recipients of unfavorable feedback regarding their actions. Instead of interpreting it as such, they assume that it is directed toward their person. Frequently, only negative or failure feedback is considered. Any type of success feedback is simply disregarded. This can cause one to become defensive and spend most of his or her psychic energy defending him- or herself and actions. There is not much energy left for positive pursuits.

The second determinant of failure involves one's expectations and the standards by which one measures oneself. Frequently, the person has unrealistically high or even perfectionist expectations. This is bound to produce a high level of self-criticism, a feeling of guilt or shame, and a sense of failure. A common fallacy regarding these expectations can be explained through the following diagram:

(C)	(B) (D)	(A)
Low		High
Success	any trait or endeavor	Success

Any trait or endeavor can be described as falling on a continuum from low success to high success. This might include such things as popularity, religious fervor, success with a tennis game, or anything else that is important to the individual. It is very natural to continue to assess how much success one is having. The failure-oriented person tends to evaluate him- or herself by the following method:

To evaluate him- or herself, a person must set up some comparison. Evaluation is not possible unless a comparison can be made. The first step is to identify a person or a group of people who exemplify success within the person's area of concern. These are the individuals who are observably successful and consequently are easily identifiable. Diagrammatically, these people would fall at Point A on the continuum. Next, the person compares him- or herself with these individuals and decides he or she is not that proficient. Because failure-identity people tend to generalize or categorically classify themselves as a success or failure (I am either good or bad, high or low), the person concludes, therefore, that he or she has a low proficiency (Point C). This conclusion results in a great deal of pain and misery, but worst of all, it continues to reinforce his or her general feelings of inadequacy. Unless the person is a super performer, with this kind of comparison design, he or she will continue to perceive his or her achievements as being minimal. The more he or she evaluates, the more the cycle continues to intensify attitudes of nonaccomplishment.

Realistically, a different comparison should be made. The person needs to identify someone or some group at Point B that characterizes more average accomplishments. This should be the comparison group. If the person would use this as a "measuring stick," he or she might well find that he or she is indeed better than that group and should more accurately be placed at Point D. This should produce less self-criticism, greater feelings of accomplishment, and more of a success orientation. This is essential if the person is to break out of the "failure" mold.

A sense of failure becomes a further problem since it limits the amount of risk-taking behavior in which we are willing to engage. If we feel that we are failures, we will feel threatened by any new behavior patterns that we perceive as risky. Accordingly, we will be very reluctant to try any such behaviors. This means that we will continue to operate as we have in the past, thereby creating somewhat of a "rut." To the degree that we follow this practice, we are precluded from growing psychologically or expanding our behavioral responses. We are stultifying ourselves from greater use of our potential and becoming a more complete individual. We learn and grow by our experiences. If we limit ourselves to only the "tried and true" modes of behavior, we are putting disabling constraints on ourselves and seriously limiting our growth potential.

To this point, a foundation and basis for the development of a sense of failure have been laid out. Understanding various causes of and reasons for the problem is only a part of resolving it. Appropriate action needs to follow. What, specifically, can one do about overcoming the feelings of failure?

The first phase of problem resolution involves a sincere resolve to do something about it. Unless we genuinely feel this ourselves (instead of doing it because others have told us we should do it), we will not be willing to expend the necessary effort needed to bring about this change. Unless we are really committed, we will make only a token effort, lose interest and quit, and probably blame the advice givers for not knowing what they were talking about. A second aspect of this first phase is concern with the notion that feelings of failure can be used as a "crutch." Failure has one advantage; it reduces what others expect of us and what we expect of ourselves. "You can't fall out of bed if you sleep on the floor." If the individual uses failure orientation as a means of meeting some of his or her own needs (such as a need for sympathy or a need for others to expect only minimal effort), there is little motivation for him or her to modify behavior. *No person can overcome failure unless a sincere commitment is felt.*

Assuming the necessary commitment is present, one can delineate a step-wise approach that will help cope with, and essentially overcome, a sense of failure. This approach is a modified version of a program presented by Robert Carkhuff in his book, *How to Help Yourself*.[1] It begins with a character called Jim.

Jim is a young man with a deep and abiding sense of failure. This feeling is pervasive in that it has an adverse effect on almost anything he does; his job, his recreation, his relations with his family, and his friends. He has become increasingly introverted, alone, and guilt-ridden because he sees himself regressing further and further into his "failure role." This regression has occurred to the extent that the "self-fulfilling prophecy" has come into play. Others expect him to project the failure image, and this expectation motivates him to do just that.

His relationship with his family has become particularly strained due to the fact that his parents only recently discovered that Jim had turned to drugs in an attempt to cope. He has an older brother and sister who live their lives with a great deal of confidence and zest. They are unable to understand, much less accept, what they would describe as Jim's childish, somewhat bizarre behavior. As is typical of people like Jim, he perceives their nonunderstanding as rejection. This causes him to uninvolve himself even more, and his failure cycle continues to intensify itself.

Let us work step-by-step with Jim as we proceed through our plan of coping with failure. We will assume that Jim is seriously interested in overcoming these feelings of inadequacy and that he is willing to commit the necessary energy toward this goal. He needs to recognize that the road will be "long and hard" because his failure orientation has been the result of intense and long-term conditioning. This habitual way of perceiving his world will need to be modified. Breaking old habits and forming new ones is a difficult task; therefore. Jim must feel a great deal of dissatisfaction with his present functioning and thereby be sufficiently motivated to change.

Analyze the failure orientation.   Jim needs to analyze his feelings of failure in an attempt to identify the various areas or aspects of his life to which they apply. An attempt should be made to delineate these areas as specifically as possible. However, the approach will accommodate some broadness at this point. As Jim reviews his own situation, he might generate the following list of failures:

    a. parents
    b. brother and sister
    c. job
    d. friends
    e. self

[1]Robert Carkhuff, *How To Help Yourself* (Amherst, Mass.: Human Resource Development Press, Inc., 1974), pp. 9-132.

We must keep in mind that this list involves Jim's perceptions. He may, for example, do very well on his job, but if he feels a sense of failure in relationship to his work, then that is reality for him, and he deals with it accordingly. As Earl Kelley once said, "Reality is what one perceives it to be." Keep in mind that Jim is perceiving his world through his "failure filter."

The primary purpose of this step is to get Jim to begin to look at his life and himself in somewhat of an analytical way. Analysis is a necessary behavior in any problem-solving process.

Establish a goal or objective.   Because feelings of failure tend to permeate every aspect of such a person's life, he cannot deal with the entire problem all at once. In step 1 Jim subdivided his feelings of failure as best he could. Next, Jim will need to take one facet of his failure orientation (items *a* through *e* in step 1) and deal with that.

It is advisable at this point to select the area where one feels he has the greatest likelihood of success. We are looking for some kind of success experience, since nothing succeeds like success. So we build in the greatest probability of success by selecting the easiest area to work on first. After this area has been dealt with, the next easiest would be considered and so on. This is not a "cop out"; it is simply a plan to maximize the chances of success. Unless the individual can attain some feelings of success, the plan is doomed. Also it must be recognized that an individual like Jim is probably going to approach the plan with failure expectations. So immediate success is essential if we expect him to stick with his plan.

After surveying his list, Jim decides that item *d*, friends, might be the easiest for him to work through. He felt that he would have major problems within the parent, brother and sister, and job areas because there were roles or expectations of certain behavior patterns that were expected of him. On the job, for example, his coworkers expected him to behave in a certain way and had, therefore, assigned him a role. It is difficult to change these role expectations because not only must one break out of the assigned role but also develop a new role. Jim had some acquaintances but no close friends; therefore, role expectations within this area would not be as well defined. With regard to item *e*, self, he felt that if he could attain success feelings within the other areas, the self area, to a degree, would take care of itself.

Operationalize the objective.   No objective is attainable unless it is operationalized. This means defining it by subdividing the objective into observable and measurable components, breaking it down into all of the operations or behaviors necessary to attain the objective. To complete this step it might be advisable to subdivide by categorizing the behaviors necessary to complete the objective, that is, listening, speaking, responding, doing, and other behaviors. Or one might list all of the specific behaviors required to achieve the objective.

After the objective has been completely subdivided, the various subdivisions should be either (1) ranked in terms of complexity (from the most difficult to accomplish to the easiest), or (2) listed in some kind of chronological order. Obviously, within the ranked-by-complexity approach, we are again concerned with accomplishing the easiest steps first so as to guarantee initial success with the plan.

Jim's objective is to overcome a sense of failure in dealing with his friends. Stated positively, he is concerned with improving his interacting with friends. As he operationalizes this objective, he might do the following:

> Develop a close, trusting relationship with some selected friends.
> Become a better conversationalist.
> Develop a better sense of humor.
> Take the initiative in meeting people and forming friendships.
> Not only be able to maintain friendships but also build these relationships.
> Be able to talk before a group of people.

These are all specific behavioral components of Jim's major objective. It is essential at this step that he zero in on as wide a variety of behaviors as he can generate from his objective. This will be somewhat difficult because failure-oriented people tend to be vague in terms of identifying their specific behaviors. However, to the degree that vagueness is evident, the chances of success are minimized. So the greater the degree of specificity, the greater the chances of the plan's succeeding.

The next step for Jim is to rank these from most to least difficult for him to achieve. Here is his ranked order:

1. Develop a close, trusting relationship with some select friends.
2. Be able to talk before a group of people.
3. Develop a better sense of humor.
4. Become a better conversationalist.
5. Not only be able to maintain friendships but also build these relationships.
6. Take the initiative in meeting people and forming friendships.

Sequential consideration of objective components.   This step involves considering item 6 in the above order. (This would be the item selected by Jim as the easiest to accomplish.) It is necessary for him to view this item as an objective and operationalize it, much like the process that was used in step 3, but applied at a more specific level. What more precise behavior might Jim enumerate so that he can become more proficient at meeting people and forming friendships? He needs to generate an all-inclusive list of behaviors, the attainment of which will bring about the accomplishment of item 6.

Jim's list might include:

1. Meet one new person each month. (If the other person initiates the meeting, that does not count.)
2. Carry on at least a five-minute conversation with that person. (Less than five minutes does not count.)
3. During the conversation the following must take place:
   a. Remember the name and at least five pertinent facts about his new friend.
   b. Share at least three things about himself.
4. Complete a 5 x 8 card on each new acquaintance. This card should include:
   a. The person's name.
   b. As much information about the individual as Jim can remember, but at least five pertinent facts. (This card is simply for remembering and review purposes.)
5. Join or enroll in at least three new groups or organizations during the next year. (Becoming an active member in organizations to which he already belongs would also count.)

Again, these steps need to be ordered, either chronologically or in terms of difficulty. If possible, the step with the greatest likelihood of success should be the first one undertaken. It is necessary to continue to *maximize the chances of success*. In addition, all of the above steps should be small enough to be attainable by Jim. If the chances of success with any step are minimal, then that step should be further broken down. For example, item 4a might be considered difficult for Jim. He may feel that he has acquired insufficient skills in meeting people for the first time. If this were the case, then the item should be further broken down into subareas. They would focus on specific, measurable, behavioral skills within the area of meeting people for the first time. Perhaps Jim would need to go to the public library and check out some books on how to meet people. He might acquire new techniques and practice them in front of a mirror to perfect them. All of these subareas would need to be completed prior to the entry into the behaviors called for.

People with failure identities are often unaware of the various methods and procedures that they could use in coping with this feeling. Public libraries, which are available to practically everyone, are a resource that is often overlooked. It, therefore, behooves everyone to become familiar with the library that is available and the proper procedures to utilize these resources. Even though some libraries are small and carry only a limited number of books and other reading material, many libraries are tied into an interlibrary loan network that permits them to borrow from larger and more complete libraries. One can find a great deal of assistance through libraries but must take the initiative in using these facilities.

After Jim has completed item 6 of step 3, he then embarks on item 5. This is subdivided into subareas, the same as item 6. The process repeats itself with one exception. While Jim is attaining the behaviors in item 5, he is also continuing the behavior called for in item 6. As these behaviors are continued and repeated, they gradually become a part of Jim's everyday pattern of behavior. As Jim proceeds through his plan, he continues to practice previously learned behaviors so that these become a part of his person, his way of behaving. It is very important that the plan not be interpreted as a program made up of six separate and independent steps. The steps are very much interrelated, and the plan will only be effective to the degree that it is implemented as a whole.

Using this operationalizing and repeating process, Jim progressively works his way through the subareas of step 3, item 6, then item 5, then item 4, and so on. After completing all of step 3, Jim should then select another of the subareas of step 1. Steps 2, 3 and 4 should then be repeated for this general area of concern, at the same time continuing to repeat the previous behaviors. If this procedure is followed, the plan gradually becomes part of the individual's way of life and accordingly will lead to a greater success orientation toward others.

It may be practical to include a time limit on the completion of each step and substep of the plan. (You will notice that some time limits were established as Jim developed his behaviors to be used in attaining item 6.) This often avoids protracting the plan so that its completion is never achieved.

There are other considerations regarding the plan. Because we are dealing with a sense of failure, it is crucial that a success monitoring system be built in. In dealing with people who have a failure orientation, any method of changing this outlook that does not incorporate success experiences will be found wanting. These people need to begin to view themselves as somewhat successful, at least as far as their plan is concerned. Two things will provide this feeling of success or accomplishment. One, as previously mentioned, involves structuring the plan with small steps that are attainable. Any step that is unattainable needs to be subdivided so that the subdivision consists of small, specific, attainable steps.

The other factor that will bring about a sense of succeeding is an effective reward system. Upon the completion of each step, Jim should build in some reward for himself. This may be something as simple as adding $5 to his savings account for each successful completion. Or it might be more interesting for him to decide upon something he really wants—a trail bike, car, trip, or perhaps some new clothes. The cost of the particular item should then be divided by all of the steps and substeps of his entire plan. The quotient might be the amount of the reward that he would pay himself as he completes each step of his plan. This would permit him, upon the completion of the entire plan, to reward himself with this long-awaited item.

Naturally, the flip side of the reward system is the nonreward or punishment approach. If one is going to use rewards effectively, then punishment must also be utilized. This means that for every step that is not completed within the conditions set forth in the plan (here time limits can be used very effectively), a specific amount of money (the punishment amount should be the same as the reward amount) needs to be subtracted from the savings account or the nest egg that one might be building for the trip, the car, or whatever. All of this may sound a bit "mickey mouse," but the plan is doomed to failure if the reward and punishment system is not judiciously adhered to.

A down-the-road or long-term value of the reward-punishment arrangement is that the individual will begin to perceive him- or herself as succeeding at some things, even if they are only small substeps of a larger plan. A sense of failure can only be overcome by patience and perserverance in small success steps. It is a long-term process that needs to be conceptualized as a series of many, many small steps. And each of these steps needs to be success oriented.

The plan that is suggested here as a means of overcoming feelings of failure is demanding in terms of time and energy. It is not simple. There is no easy approach. Feelings of failure are formed over an individual's entire lifetime; therefore, replacing them with positive feelings is bound to be difficult.

If we follow a plan toward improvement, it seems that we are courageously saying two things. We are acknowledging that we are willing to be responsible and accountable for our own improvement. If the plan is set up properly, and it does not work, we have only ourselves to blame. This frightens many failure-oriented people because they depend heavily on being able to blame others for their shortcomings. They continue to delude themselves with this face-saving gimmick. Unfortunately, it does nothing for them growth-wise. Second, we are admitting that the psychological pain that we are suffering as a result of our failure in life is greater than the perceived and actual pain that we will experience as we work our way through the plan. An integral part of human nature is the avoidance of pain, either physical or psychological. Motivation to behave in a certain way or engage in a set of behaviors is determined by our perceiving less pain if we perform the behavior than if we did not. The alcoholic will not "dry out" until he or she is convinced that the misery of continuing with the problem is greater than the pain of the "drying out" process and a future life of sobriety. Until such a decision is reached, rehabilitation cannot occur.

A plan such as this can help us to help ourselves with a variety of life's problems. It is a matter of deciding on a workable strategy of plan and committing ourselves to it. Winners have plans; losers do not. As Carkhuff so aptly put it, "There is an infinite variety of losing strategies and only one winning strategy."[2] Analysis, commitment, and perserverance are necessary ingredients of a winning strategy.

Today is the first day of the rest of your life, a life that finds people constantly changing and modifying their behavior. It is a matter of choice whether you are going to adopt a winning strategy as you change, or whether you will stumble from one losing strategy to another. It is really up to you.

SELECTED REFERENCES

CARKHUFF, R., *The Art of Problem Solving*. Amherst, Mass.: Human Resource Development Press, 1973.

_____, *How to Help Yourself*. Amherst, Mass.: Human Resource Development Press, 1974.

COMBS A., D. AVILA, AND W. PURKEY, *Helping Relationships: Basic Concepts for the Helping Professions*. Boston: Allyn & Bacon, Inc., 1971.

GLASSER, W., *Identity Society*. New York: Harper and Row, 1972.

_____, *Schools Without Failure*. New York: Harper and Row, 1969.

GREENWALD, J., *Be The Person You Were Meant To Be*. New York: Dell, 1973.

HOLT, J., *How Children Fail*. New York: Dell, 1964.

LAIR, J., *I Ain't Much Baby But I'm All I've Got*. Greenwich, Conn.: Fawcett, 1972.

POWELL, J., *Why Am I Afraid To Tell You Who I Am*. Niles: Argus, 1969.

[2]Carkhuff, *How To Help Yourself*, p. 1.

Your spirit's life, my brother, is encompassed by loneliness, and were it not for that loneliness and solitude, you would not be you, nor would I be I. Were it not for this loneliness and solitude, I would come to believe on hearing your voice, that it was my voice speaking; or seeing your face, that it was myself looking into a mirror. [1]

How to Cope with Loneliness

Wanda L. Bincer

The experience of loneliness is common to all of us. However, we have different ways of viewing it and dealing with it. Most of us are afraid of loneliness and try to escape it in many different ways. Seldom are we aware what potential inner riches we can make available to ourselves through the pain of loneliness. Most of us also rarely accept the fact that human existence is, of necessity, filled with loneliness, as inevitable a part of life as death itself. Therefore, the more familiar and accepting we can be of our deep sense of existential aloneness, which is an essential part of living, the better we can benefit and grow through it.

Basically, loneliness is a condition where we have only ourselves to rely on for any strength or sustenance. It is a time when we may be totally alone or, although we are with others, we may feel alienated from them and unable to share our unique experiences with any other human being at that particular moment.

Of course, it is important to remember that throughout our life we all need contact with other people. We need to have a sense of belonging, we need feedback from others, recognition, and a sense that there are others who care

This article was especially written for this book.
[1]Kahlil Gibran, *The Voice of the Master* (New York: Citadel, 1958), p. 43.

about us, understand us, and that we matter to them. Without that our existence may become totally empty and without any meaning. We also know from experiences of people isolated for long periods of time without any contact from the outside world, as in prisoner or concentration of labor camps, that usually people are unable to survive and hold onto their sanity under those circumstances.

Solitude may be a very pleasant and peaceful enjoyment of life when there is no urgent need for contact with another human being. We all have moments of pleasure alone—be it with nature, or music, or books, or a favorite activity, when we are perfectly content or even ecstatically happy to have the time alone. Those are special moments of grace when we feel at one with the universe and are glad to be alive.

Times of loneliness, by contrast, are usually sad times, experienced at tragic moments in our lives, accompanied by despair over the loss of somebody through death, illness, or abandonment. These are times when we feel totally separate and alienated from the rest of the world, alone with our pain and suffering, perhaps ill and unloved and unlovable. We may lose our faith in ourselves and feel unworthy or inadequate and unimportant. It is important to recognize that those moments can be very valuable and also can be turned into moments of grace and value that will ultimately make us stronger, worthier, more compassionate, and more mature human beings.

The kind of loneliness we will discuss here is the loneliness that people feel when they experience the need for deep human intimacy, but it is not available. The experience is usually very painful and devastating and may grow to dangerous proportions. One can be overcome by a paralyzing sense of hopelessness and a feeling of inability to change the situation, which tempts one to give into despair and give up.

At the time of your life when you experience deep loneliness, it is extremely important, first to admit that it is a very painful condition and that you cannot go on feeling this way indefinitely or you are going to be plunged into absolute and total despair. In other words, you have to do something that will eventually change your situation or the way you feel about it. It is useless at that point just to sit and wait and hope that this will blow over or that someone will rescue you or that you can ignore it and escape your feelings. So the first step is to face up to it. Admit it—you feel lonely and desolate. At the time of appraising the degree of your loneliness, it is important to decide whether you have the strength to deal with this state on your own or whether you need some outside help at the beginning.

Anything that is available to you that will make the task easier is certainly worth exploring. Most communities have helping people available through many agencies, such as counseling agencies, mental health clinics, psychiatrists, psychologists, social workers, ministers, and others, and the appropriate person may be found by checking with your family doctor, friends, or your local church.

When you define and admit your feelings and express them, whether just to yourself or somebody else, you have taken the first step. At least you are not pretending that things are otherwise or ignoring your feelings, but you are facing the truth. The first step in learning to cope then is to admit the reality. This will be more useful than many would suspect, for now you know what you have to deal with. The next step is to decide to examine carefully your strengths and to recognize the enormous power you have in your will to survive and overcome difficulties. You can remember times when life dealt you blows that you somehow managed to survive and go on living, and you need to rekindle your faith that you can do so again. By the way, it is important to be fair about this with yourself and not to say, "This does not apply to me." Undoubtedly, you can think of examples when you felt at the end of your rope as a child or as an adult but managed to go on.

The next task would be honestly to face up to your weaknesses and liabilities. View it as a chance to get to know yourself without critical condemnation but with compassion. None of us are perfect human beings, and to expect ourselves to be perfect is a losing battle. If you admit to yourself, fairly and honestly, your weaknesses and accept them, you may be able to change some things and learn to live with some that you cannot change. The crucial quality to bear in mind is to focus on being charitable to yourself and not destructive. This ironically is a very difficult process for most of us, but it can be learned.

The next point is recognizing your basic attitude toward yourself. Is it loving and accepting, or is it hateful and destructive, where you cannot win whatever you do? Obviously, if you struggle and learn to be compassionate and understanding of your true self, you also will be able to be more tolerant and loving toward other human beings. Strangely, whatever faults we have are easier to change once we freely and honestly acknowledge them than if we fight against them or pretend that they are not there.

You may discover that your basic attitude toward yourself is hateful and critical and that you hardly find a reason to be pleased with yourself. This should lead you to question yourself and try to identify at what point in your life you began to view yourself in this manner—you may discover and be able to identify an important person in your childhood who always scolded and criticized you and found little worthy of praise. Most likely, this was a parent who could have loved you deeply but had no time to give you positive strokes or felt that praising children resulted in spoiling them.

What is important and relevant to your task today in conquering loneliness is to make a decision that there is no need for you to perpetuate this parental attitude. This decision requires a commitment on your part to work on changing yourself and allowing yourself to be more generous in praise and encouragement and less impulsive with criticism and contempt of yourself.

It may be a hard process for some and you may need constant daily reminders—for instance, you may start by looking for some action or thought or behavior each day that genuinely merits praise and then reward yourself in some fashion for it. Hopefully, as time goes on, you can find more and more things each day that you like about yourself.

Conversely, you have to learn to watch yourself carefully before you jump to criticize yourself. It would help to ask questions such as:

1. Do I really deserve this criticism?
2. Will the criticism be helpful, that is, constructive and enable me to do better in the future?
3. Will it be destructive and paralyze me with the feeling of failure?
4. Would I judge somebody else as harshly as I judge myself?

The task of examining your attitude toward your own self and other people will pay its own dividends. If you are still lonely, at least you are caring and supporting of yourself in your predicament, and this loving feeling will automatically encompass other people you come in contact with. The quality of recognition of the human fallibility and tolerance is easily sensed by others who will respond in kind. Warmth and acceptance is almost always rewarded by the same response from others, and so the loneliness becomes less acute and the aloneness decreases.

Once you are able to define your pain and isolation, take the responsibility for your predicament and make a conscious decision to change your situation, you may be ready to take other steps. Perhaps you could now focus on what activities and experiences you normally enjoy the most. It is important at this point to indulge yourself and treat yourself to some pleasures, whatever they may be. It could be anything from a warm luxurious bath, a walk in the country, listening to good music, reading a good book, or finding something enjoyable to make. Sometimes a new and different activity never attempted before may bring unexpected rewards. I am mostly talking about learning new ways of nurturing oneself and being good to oneself. This sounds like a very simple thing to do, and it is, but it is not always easy to learn and often involves making changes in the way you live.

Now would be a good time to look at your relationships with others and recognize your needs for contact with other human beings. Obviously, you also need to discover your own unique preferences for the kind of people whose company you enjoy the most and with whom you can share something in common. It helps if you know what you are seeking from others and can ascertain whether they are able and willing to respond to you. So often loneliness may become even more painful among people who may be insensitive to your needs and who cannot hear what you are really saying.

As Max Ehrmann says:

> Go placidly amid the noise and haste, and remember what peace there may be in silence. As far as possible, without surrender be on good terms with all persons. Speak your truth quietly and clearly; and listen to others, even the dull and ignorant. They too have their story. Avoid loud and aggressive persons, they are vexatious to the spirit.[2]

Every community has organizations where people meet together or work together or learn something new together. Most of the time, appreciation of oneself and others is sufficient to establish meaningful relationships. Sincerity, openness, and compassion help, as well as some ability to empathize with other people and the realization that when all is said and done we all share similar feelings, needs, and self-doubts.

Today many communities have ongoing therapeutic groups who help deal with specific problems. If you are in the process of divorce and feel your whole life is falling apart, it may be helpful to join a group of people in a similar situation. The focus on such a group would be to share experiences and feelings, offer each other much needed support, and focus on practical steps that can be taken to help you deal with the situation. Deep friendships often form in groups like these that not only help people overcome the immediate crisis but also often develop into lasting relationships. The painful experiences are made more bearable by the knowledge that it is not totally unique, and often much can be learned from other people in similar situations. Similarly, there may be groups for widows or widowers, alcoholics, singles, parents, and so on.

For women who today are beginning to recognize the need to enrich their lives, there are many consciousness-raising groups throughout the country. Information about these may be obtained through the nearest National Organization of Women, and these may be appropriate for women interested in the women's movement as well as women who simply are seeking companionship of other women. Fortunately, there are also men's groups available, although less numerous at this time.

We are all bombarded by a great deal of messages about how we should lead our lives and what roles we should play. Our lives are stressful and demanding, and therefore it is imperative that we treat ourselves with care and compassion. The idea of being in touch with the state of our emotional resources and the need to replenish them regularly is somewhat foreign to the way most of us have been brought up. Somehow, we all know a lot more about the need to consider other people's feelings than our own. We are a great deal more knowledgeable about the kind of food we ought to eat and

[2]Max Ehrmann, *Desiderata* (Boston: Crescendo, 1927).

the vitamins we need to include in our diets than what is essential to our emotional well-being.

Most emotional difficulties, at different times in our lives, result in the experience of loneliness and alienation. So often this is caused by an inadequate knowledge of ourselves and an inability to recognize our true needs, wants, and abilities. Yet there is tremendous fear and resistance in many of us to correct this lack of information and to assume responsibility for our lives. We find it easier to blame external circumstances or other people for our misfortunes, rather than to admit the need for assuming more control over the way we live. As Martin Buber says:

Man is afraid of things that cannot harm him, and he knows it, and he craves things that cannot be of help to him, and he knows it, but in truth the one thing man is afraid of is within himself, and the one thing he craves is within himself.[3]

Generally, our fear of the unknown is so overwhelming that we often are willing to remain in an unhappy but familiar situation rather than consider making changes. The same holds true for our inner life. Frequently, we avoid learning more about our emotions and refuse to face up to changes in ourselves. Instead, we keep busy and seek to escape any further growth that may be painful.

Therefore, if you are lonely, you owe it to yourself to take steps to increase your contact with other human beings. You can do this in many ways, whether taking a new class in your community, joining a discussion group, volunteering for a community project, or finding a new job. You can look for the availability of an appropriate group to join or contact the local mental health clinic or church. You can remember to initiate conversations with strangers at a public library or museum, at a PTA meeting of the local school, or at a YMCA exercise class. You need to allow yourself to feel interested in others as well as feeling worthwhile yourself.

So far we have discussed looking for new people you may learn to enjoy in different places. Now let's discuss the relationships with people you already know. Many of us may feel extremely lonely although we are not alone. We may have husbands, wives, children, parents, neighbors, coworkers, and others, but our relationships with them are not good or enriching, and we experience loneliness. It is important to examine what role we ourselves play in these relationships and what changes we could make.

Presumably you would prefer for these relationships to be more loving and intimate, but perhaps you have given up and are not making it possible for

---

[3]Martin Buber, *The Tales of Rabbi Nachman*, translated from the German by Maurice Friedman (New York: Horizon Press, 1956), p. 37.

these relationships to flow freely. You may, for instance, never express your own feelings and share very little of yourself. You may never express your needs or desires or your resentments and disappointments. This would naturally create a distance and reserve that is not helpful in providing a climate where closeness and warmth grow and nourish you.

In my experience as a psychotherapist, it never ceases to amaze me how many people who come to me as "patients," underestimate their own importance and view themselves with a degree of intolerance and criticism that their worst enemies could never muster. Of course, if we find ourselves so undesirable and inadequate, we also assume others must view us the same way, and therefore, we must be careful not to show anybody our real selves. So much of our contacts with others are cautious and hypocritical, and we hide our shortcomings and pain from each other for fear of being judged. True intimacy between human beings is, on the other hand, a relationship where people are real with each other and have the courage to risk being hurt and come out from behind their facades.

I have learned for myself that the times I feel closest to people and least lonely are when I share my inner true feelings with them, no matter how painful or embarrassing that may be. However, I do not do this indiscriminately, since there are always people who are cruel and judgmental.

I have also found that those who seek my help as a therapist make the biggest strides toward their own growth and maturity when they can be open about themselves and take risks with other people. Their feelings of isolation from others dissipate and are replaced by a sense of belonging and acceptance.

Obviously, none of us can avoid loneliness altogether, any more than we can avoid suffering or self-doubt. We are all separate individuals, each with somewhat different experiences, some of which we cannot share. We have to be able to accept loneliness and sorrow as an unavoidable part of life. We also need to learn from it, grow through it, and go on with our lives, without being totally defeated by it.

To quote from the sermons of Ecclesiastes:

> For everything there is a season, and a time for every matter under heaven: A time to be born, and a time to die; a time to plant, and a time to pluck up what is planted; a time to kill, and a time to heal; a time to break down, and a time to build up; a time to weep, and a time to laugh; a time to mourn, and a time to dance; a time to cast away stones, and a time to gather stones together; a time to embrace, and a time to refrain from embracing; a time to seek, and a time to lose; a time to keep, and a time to cast away; . . .

There is a time in our lives when we need to accept loneliness and suffering. Therefore, let us remember to recognize the value of loneliness and receive it openly and with dignity. Instead of fearing it and making futile attempts to avoid it, we have at those times an opportunity to discover new resources in ourselves and to deepen our awareness and sensitivity. Each one of us is individually responsible for our own life. In learning how to cope with loneliness, you have a chance to enhance your capacity to live life more fully. Your courage to live through sorrow will make your joy greater.[4]

[4]For further reading, see Clark Moustakas's classic works, *Loneliness* (Englewood Cliffs, N.J.: Prentice-Hall, Inc., 1961) and *Loneliness and Love* (Englewood Cliffs, N.J.: Prentice-Hall., 1972).

How to Adjust to the Death of a Parent, Close Relative, or Friend

Jane K. Burgess

The thought of death comes as a threat to most people. Thus, it is not surprising that the question of how to adjust to the death of a parent or a friend was paramount in the survey[1] of college students about personal problems with which they need help. Students also have revealed to me a variety of fears about death. They fear the process of dying, the pain, the isolation, and even the grief that their death may cause others. For example, Jill[2] told me,

> I think I will always be afraid of death because it is something unknown. No matter how much we talk about dying, I still am afraid. I fear leaving the people I love, not being physically and mentally close to them anymore. I fear the hurt that my death would cause to those who love me, and it almost makes me cry thinking about it now. Leaving the people I love and care about and not knowing what being dead is like are my main fears.

This article was especially written for this book.

[1]The survey made at the University of Wisconsin — Whitewater to determine the most crucial problems facing your people, for purposes of this text.

[2]In the process of teaching a course, The Social Psychology of Death and Dying, I have discussed with many students their fears about death and dying. They have expressed three basic fears: 1) fear of the process of dying; 2) fear of what happens after death, and 3) fear of losing a loved one and the pain of grief.

While Jill is fearful of her own death and dying, many people fear not knowing how to cope with the death of others as much as they fear death itself. Another response, typical of students who have talked to me about their experience with death, came from Wayne.

I wasn't really sure how to deal with it. This was the first time, and I hadn't thought about it at all. Death was something that wasn't yet a part of my personal life. When death did appear, I knew I had to work it out inside myself. I wish I could have been prepared to accept death and to be able to handle it when it came.

There is little question in my mind that most people are not prepared to accept death. It might be argued that the answer is formal education. Simply take a course in death education; a course designed to give a student an opportunity to accept the fact of death for him- or herself— "I am going to die." Then he or she would be able to understand his or her own emotions and thus be ready to help others adjust to the idea of death.

However, few people are prepared to accept the fact of death through formal death education. Further, although there are many ways to confront death, there is yet no research to tell us which is the best way to a "healthy" response to death. It seems to me that these obstacles can be best overcome through intensive exploratory work from which, hopefully, confidence in the usefulness of "programs on how to cope with death" will ensue. The exploratory work I would like to discuss leans heavily on the insights of my students who have had to confront the problem of death.[3]

EMPATHY

Believing that possessing empathy is a prerequisite for giving solace to those who grieve, I asked students who have experienced the death of a loved person to share their feelings about ways to cope with and adjust to death. Their response was overwhelming, their willingness to try to help others through bereavement is beautiful, and I am grateful to them for their contributions.

I did not understand death or appreciate living until after I had lost my mother and worked through my grief. Now, I feel I can understand and empathize with others who lose someone they love.

This poignant expression from Mary underscores an obvious assumption— that those who are best in the position to help others cope with death are those who have already experienced the loss of a loved person.

I have been able, through my own training and research, through my own experience with death (when my husband died leaving me with two children),

---

[3]In preparation for this article, I asked students in four sociology classes to write an essay on "How I coped with the death of someone dear to me." Fifty-two students responded.

and through these personal documents, to discern some basic needs that people must fulfill in coming to terms with death: 1) the need for self-identity, 2) the need for realism about death, 3) the need for expression of emotion, 4) the needs of others, and 5) the need for belief. However, although we may attempt to establish guides for adjusting to death, we must recognize that there are no generalizations for how one can best get over the end of a close relationship. Everyone's problem is somewhat unique and is compounded by such factors as age, emotional maturity, the kind and intensity of the relationship that existed between the person who died and the bereaved. Nevertheless, it is hoped that through sharing the experiences of other young people as they have gone through the adjustment to the death of a loved one, you may gain the help to adjust to death in your own experience.

Bill recognized that there are no easy solutions to grief:

> I had thought when you asked for this paper on how to cope with death that it would be easy to get things down and possibly offer some answers to other people's problems and questions, but what helped me was a combination of small things, and no one answer ever came.

This, then, should be a point that those involved with death must realize; there is *no one answer.*

THE NEED FOR SELF-IDENTITY

Many of my students stressed the need for knowing one's own feelings and beliefs about one's self — self-identity. Apparently, through experiences with death, the person becomes more introspective, begins to concern him- or herself with significant questions about self-identity. Donna, for example, advises:

> When death strikes a friend of 23 (my own age), you really start to identify with that person. All I could think of was that people who are young are not supposed to die. People who are young laugh, talk, joke, love, marry, and have lovely children. But suddenly the reality of death does become very personal, even though you know that you are not ready emotionally to accept it. After the initial shock of the terrible revelation that someone has died suddenly and without warning wears away, you begin to try to put death in perspective. However, the accepting of death by those left behind to grieve is very difficult. I could not understand why a God or a Universal Force would deprive a young man of life. It seemed to me such a waste of a son, a friend, a strong man, so vital.
>
> I think if there is any chord that death especially strikes in me, it would be the need to develop a strong self-identity. If I ever have to face death myself over a prolonged period of time, a strong self-identity would greatly help me to understand the reason for my dying. A little philosophy of my life has been — you come into this world alone to make your own way and you go out of this world alone to meet your Maker. No one

else may be delegated to perform either of these tasks in your place. Therefore, you had better be prepared psychologically to exist alone. You had better know yourself and your ability to cope at all the levels of living and dying. The first step, then, in accepting the death of another is the acceptance of the inevitability of your own death.

Debra wrote a poem to tell of how she found herself through the death of her mother.

> *If only I could have said goodbye.*
> *If only I could have hugged her.*
> *She would have known I was there and always would be.*
> *The coldness and the vacant stare consumed me into the world of dense wilderness.*
> *The path out is so hard to find.*
> *The leaves wind around my head as if to strangle the life out of me.*
> *I shall escape,*
> *And when I do, I'll be one step closer to finding myself.*
> *Thank you for being.*

For advice to someone who is grieving, Debra says:

All I can say is that an experience like losing a parent can help a person in finding himself. Much crying should be done to release some of the anxiety. Try to be with people that mean something to you. Knowing others loved me filled some of my emptiness. This gives you a sense of security and brings you closer to others you love. Remember that life continues no matter what, and you have to accept it and grow with it. This was just another step I made, and became closer to knowing my real self.

Implicit in the above expressions of the need for identifying one's own feelings about life and death is the thought that adversity is not necessarily negative in its effect on those who grieve. Adversity can serve to prepare us, give us strength to carry on, to overcome future hurdles. A strong sense of "who I am" is closely related to another need that must be fulfilled to deal with the loss of a loved one, the need for a realistic appraisal of the inevitability of death for us all.

THE NEED FOR REALISM

Most of my students in some way or another speak of the importance of a realistic acceptance of death — to understand that death is inevitable and, at the same time, life goes on. Yet, there is no question that these same students acknowledged that there are many emotions that must be dealt with before a realistic acceptance comes about. Two young students who have had to deal with death more than once have obviously reflected deeply on their painful experiences, and they illustrate how it is possible to come to terms with fear of death by being open with oneself and others and by perceiving that life should be lived from moment to moment.

When Lew's mother died, he already knew that death can come at any time and to any one, and that there is nothing one can do about it. He had previously experienced the death of his father and older brother. He says that:

Coping with death is not really coping with death, but coping with what faces you afterward. I wasn't fearful of death itself. I was fearful because I was unsure of what would happen after both my parents died. Once I realized that if you do all you can to keep on living, life will go on, differently, with more effort many times, but still it goes on. You can't ever bring the people you have lost back, so you just have to look ahead and live for your future.

Sherry shares a wide range of emotions that she experienced as she worked through her bereavement:

No matter what others say and do during this time of sorrow, there isn't much anyone can do for you. The feelings that envelop you are totally personal. What others say to help you cope with the situation are only suggestions, only you can find the way to face reality. It is a very private and personal feeling that we all face at some time in our lives. You have to dig into your inner self and define it to yourself before you can totally understand and accept what has happened; you must face up to this reality.

At the age of 14, I had my first memorable experience with this thing known as death. It had taken the life of my 14-year-old boyfriend. It came as a total shock to me. Only two hours before I had walked home from school with him, and now I would never see him again. I cried and cried, really not even knowing why I cried. More for my own selfish reasons, I guess. What was I going to do without him? To this day I still don't know the answer.

My feelings were of hatred toward something I didn't know. It seemed cruel and unjust to take the life of this person, who hadn't even started to fully live his life. Why was God punishing me, taking away one of the things that I loved? After this experience I didn't know whether to believe in God or not. Why would God who loves me want to hurt me, or was it for punishment for something I had done wrong?

What seemed to help me most through that tremendously painful time was just talking about this person, about all the good things he had done, about how others felt about him. When people avoid the issue of death, it only makes it worse. It is best to get the issue out in the open, examine what has happened and rationalize the situation. Don't be afraid to talk about someone who has died in the presence of those who loved this person. It hurts more not knowing what others think about the deceased than having people coming right out and revealing their feelings. Death can be more painful to those who survive it and have to deal with it than to the person who died.

In the last few years, I have lost several other close friends, but as I grow older death becomes easier for me to accept. I realize now that other people really aren't insincere and now I listen openly to their suggestions on how to cope. Because people are afraid of the unknown, we fear death, and when death strikes someone close to use we realize how very near death is to all of us at all times. It is from this fear that we are so upset at the loss of a close companion or parent. You miss them, it hurts at first, maybe even for a long time. But there are so many other things to be thankful for. Just to be alive, to be able to remember the beautiful things that your dead friend had brought into being for you is worth more than all the materialistic things in this world.

The life of man is such a complex matter. Birth is the entrance and death the exit, and living is just the pathway between the two. Men and poets over the ages have tried to express their feelings about death. James M. Barrie said, "God made memories so we could have roses in December." This could be a very consoling thought to someone who has mixed feelings about what death is. To me the most beautiful and most helpful thing was this quote by Rossitor Worthingon Raymond, "Life is eternal; and love is immortal; and death is only a horizon; and a horizon is nothing save the limit of our sight."

It was after reading what I have written and really thinking about what I said that I really felt I understood what death is about and what it means to me. From my experiences with death I have learned to value every friendship highly and really cherish each loving relationship with parents and friends. I have learned that to really love someone is to realize that at anytime you may lose him, whether by means of death or otherwise. I have learned to live each day to its utmost, to value each moment with another person because they may not be with you in an hour or a day from now. This is a very important lesson everyone must learn.

There are many emotions that one experiences during a period of grief; fear of the unknown, hatred, resentment, self-pity. Sherry felt that God was very unjust to take the life of her young friend. She tells us she cried for selfish reasons — self-pity took hold until she came to a realistic acceptance of death. Many of my students admonished against too much self-pity. Rick, for example, felt that when his father died, his own life had ended. His advice now is:

Go back through your feelings of emptiness, helplessness, loneliness, bitterness. These are not what anyone who loved you would want you to feel. Actually these are selfish feelings and pity for only yourself, not for the one who has died. They are "I feel" rather than "he feels." His problems have ended, his hurts and pain that he may have had before death are gone. So here is the first step in adjusting to the death of a parent. Forget how you feel, become involved and active in life around you and your emptiness will soon be taken over by feelings of usefulness. Don't waste your energy on self-pity. It is an impossible state of mind to be in for it inhibits any useful accomplishments. Don't feel resentment and bitterness about a death of someone you loved. Thrive, instead, on the opportunities and happiness you have had knowing and loving that person. And, remember, life goes on — time does heal like a miracle, but, while miracles sometimes occur, one has to work very hard for them.

It is clear from the above that many emotions are involved with the working out of a realistic acceptance of death. It is important that these emotions be recognized and expressed.

THE NEED FOR EXPRESSION OF EMOTIONS

In the throes of grief, one feels that he or she has very little control over his or her feelings; feelings of anger, guilt, self-pity. Even more important is the mistaken position that one *should not* have these feelings. This is a problem that only compounds the suffering of the bereaved. It should be recognized that these feelings cannot be simply willed away. They are an inevitable consequence of past experiences and the person's own way of looking at what is important or of value to him or her.

Many of my students were able to release their emotions and, coupled with reflective thinking, were able to go on living in a healthy manner. Cheryl illustrates this process as she relates her painful reactions to the death of her grandmother:

When my father first told me the news of my grandmother's death, my first reaction was shock. Then after it settled in my mind for a few seconds, the tears began. These never seemed to stop. After a few hours of shutting myself up in my room, crying, I began to wonder what it actually was that I was crying about. At first I was angry with grandmother for dying on me. I wondered why she hadn't had enough will to live through a heart attack. I wondered if she died because she didn't love or care about us anymore. Maybe she was just tired of living. Silly thoughts, but every one of them crossed my mind at some time or another.

I thought about fate, and it really seemed that my grandmother had not made the choice to die. Something else had to be involved. So I began to direct my anger at that something. In my mind, it was God. I hated God for taking away someone so close to me. Why couldn't it have been someone else? This is kind of ridiculous too, because it does happen to all the "someone elses" in the world, all the time. After I had confronted her death, and used up my anger, I knew I had to try and accept it. "It's real, it happened, it's not just a dream," I told myself over and over. I went through the funeral, still almost in a dream, but in a way I had already, inside, accepted that she was gone forever. And forever is hard to imagine.

During the first few weeks after grandmother died, it seemed like she had just gone away for awhile and would be back soon. I didn't really miss her until I found myself thinking of what I was going to tell her when I called her up; or, when going to her house where my folks now live, catching myself almost calling out to her. Then I began to feel the loneliness and the emptiness. I thought of the times I didn't call her because I said I didn't have time or of the times when I was younger and I would get mad when she would "bother" me with an extra blanket on a warm night, not realizing it was only because she cared. I wish I could have taken back some of the things I said in anger that I didn't really mean. I love her more now than ever, but all I have left are memories. (It was a comfort to me, Dr. Burgess, to hear you say in class that it is not humanly possible always to be loving even to those we love most.)

After my anger was spent, I was able to experience a happy acceptance of grandmother's death. Having been brought up to believe in God, I had been taught that existence after death is much greater than the time spent on earth. This made it easier to accept. Thinking that my grandmother would have none of the pain or hurt that had troubled her in the past years, I was almost happy for her.

The point that should be stressed here is *not* that the bereaved should emulate Cheryl's specific reactions and solution. It is the *general* message that is important: 1) feelings of hate, doubt, guilt, self-pity, and so on are real, 2) allow these feelings to be expressed, and 3) let them *"rest"* in peace* as you begin to live life anew.

THE NEEDS OF OTHERS

It is extremely important to realize that *you* are valuable to others, just as you found those who have died were valuable to you. To realize this is to realize a fundamental human need — the feeling of one's worth. If you see that you *are* valuable to others, you will then see the reason why life *is* worth living. Mary relates the significance of this basic need:

It was impossible to describe my thoughts and feelings when I first learned of my mother's death. It was surprise, disbelief, anguish. If I would have let myself, I could have cried for hours. I still could. It was the *knowledge that my father and my brothers and sisters needed me that helped me pull myself together* (underlining author). We needed each other and we relied on each other for our strength. This tragedy has brought our family closer together than it has ever been before and I believe our ties will always be stronger because of it. It was our love for each other and for a very special woman that has kept us all going.

My research on 30 families that have suffered the loss of a wife/mother reiterates the significance of Mary's message. With few exceptions, the fathers in my study reported that a new sense of rapport, cooperation, and closeness between them and their children developed out of the knowledge that they were needed each by the other in a way never before experienced. Recognition that others need us is indeed an essential element in a "return to normalcy."

THE NEED FOR BELIEF

Another fundamental human need is to believe that the inevitable fact of death is not senseless; that both life and death have meaning beyond the mundane; that there *is* some purpose to it all. Whether the belief is founded on supernatural or secular dictums is not important. What is important is that the person finds solace in some way that is meaningful to him or her. The way that many of my students found helpful was a belief in God.

For example, Sandy believes that having faith in God and warmth and love of friends are the two most important variables in coping with the death of someone close. She says:

As I am a Christian raised in the Lutheran faith, the thought of my grandmother's death was a little easier to bear when I thought of her in heaven with her creator. I also knew that she had lived a Christian life and was truly a strong believer in God. Believing as I did in God and knowing my grandmother truly believed in God were two of the most comforting thoughts when I had to face her death. Comfort also came from friends, both mine and my grandmother's. My grandmother had some devoted friends she had known for years. These friends offered to help in any way that they could, giving both moral support and physical help. I was really overwhelmed by their kindness and willingness to do anything they could for us. The death of a loved one is a cruel, heartbreaking experience for anyone to have to go through. But in my case, my religion, family, and good friends gave me the comfort I needed in my time of sorrow.

Many of my students wrote that their first reaction to the death of someone they loved was to wonder why God was punishing them by taking away one of the things they loved so much. Liz, for example, questioned God:

God, who is so just and fair, all righteous and knowing, had purposely taken my boyfriend away from me. After this experience I didn't know whether to believe in God or not. Why would God who loves me want to hurt me, or was it for punishment for something I had done wrong? I went to church for many Sundays, and one day asked the minister to explain death to me. I found great comfort in his explanation that death is not a final thing, but that it is a continuation of life on a grander scale. It was God who chose this person to be with him at his side as his disciple for Eternity. It was because this person was so good and pure that God felt it was time to take him into his arms and make him one with God. We should not fear death because God is watching over us and he would not do anything to harm us. We are his children.

Joan adds that:

If you can try to picture heaven and your loved person really being in it (as I'm sure most of us will as we all seem to idealize them), this can help soften the blow. Just think how they don't have to worry about petty human problems such as the world condition, sickness, financial worries. Try to do something constructive; pray for their soul, go out of your way to be kinder to those more directly (or also) affected by the loved person's death, such as the deceased friend's children. They probably feel even worse than you do and you all will profit from a closer relationship. Belief in God will give you strength to overcome your problem.

A fitting close to the discussion of the need for faith is a letter that was written to give comfort to a young lady who had lost her mother:

There once was a time when I wondered how I could ever be happy again after I had lost my mother . . . The face I looked for, the hands I reached for, and the smile I longed for had disappeared from my sight and proximity. And now I am happy although I still look, reach, and long. For I am more complete and I can live and love more fully having experienced and overcome my grief. And when I feel the love I can give and receive, I thank God for this wonderful gift.

SUMMARY AND CONCLUSIONS

As I review what has been said by my students about how to adjust to and cope with the death of a loved person, I find certain trends of thought, a consensus in their advice: Anyone who experiences the death of a person he or she loved goes through a variety of reactions and feelings. This is normal. First, there is the sense of shock, disbelief, and denial, followed by anger at being left without the loved person, feelings of self-pity, resentment, hatred toward anyone or anything that may have been implicated in the death, guilt, and fear that you are being punished through the death of the one you loved.

A return to normalcy, a recovery from grief, requires that you recognize these reactions and feelings and work through them. Several ways to help accomplish this have been suggested:

1. You must learn to accept the inevitability of death, yours and others.
2. Crying is a good release from the tension that is a part of grieving.
3. Being with others who love you and need you at the time of bereavement and talking to them gives you a sense of security and brings you closer to others you love.
4. It is possible to come to terms with fear of death by being open with yourself and with others and by perceiving that life should be lived from moment to moment. Value every moment with another person because they may not be with you in an hour or a day from now.
5. Don't dwell on how unhappy you feel. Become involved and active in life around you. Don't waste your energy on self-pity.
6. Having a faith in God helps you to accept the inevitability of death. It is comforting to leave what happens after death in God's hands.
7. In most cases, it is impossible to cope with grief alone. Find someone to talk to, seek help from the clergy, from friends and family, and, if necessary, turn to a professional counselor.

Everyone needs to be prepared to accept death. Yet with the taboos and restrictions placed on discussion of death and dying in our society, few of us are given the opportunity to come to terms with the fact of death. Whether or not we can accept the reality of death depends upon our attitudes, including fears, doubts, and anxieties that have developed through our knowledge and experiences. Parents are our primary source of learning during the time our basic attitudes are being formed. But few parents know how or what to tell their children about death, probably because they have not been able to come to grips with the fact of death for themselves. It is very difficult to develop a realistic view of death when we are filled with the prevailing superstitions, myths, and ignorance about the end of life. Death generally is associated with concepts such as darkness, pain, separation, sadness, and fear of the unknown. When we are children, we have many confused thoughts about death. As we become older, our anxiety about death is likely to increase. And on the day that we must face the reality of our own impending death or the death of a loved one, we face it largely alone and unprepared.

It is rewarding to hear college students express a recognition of their need for death education. I am certain that the students who have so willingly portrayed their experiences with death have contributed greatly toward helping others in their preparation for and acceptance of the reality of death. I *am* going to die. You *are* going to die.

BIBLIOGRAPHY ON DEATH AND DYING

Books:

BECKMAN, GUNNEL, *Admission to the Feast* (A 19-year-old girl, dying of leukemia, writes a long letter to a friend in an attempt to stabilize her crumbling world). New York: Holt, Rinehart and Winston, 1972.

GREEN, BETTY R., and DONALD P. IRISH, eds., *Death Education: Preparation for Living.* Cambridge, Mass.: Schenkman Pub. Co., 1971.

GROLLMAN, EARL A., ed., *Explaining Death to Children.* Boston: Beacon Press, 1967.

KASTENBAUM, ROBERT, AND RUTH AISENBERG, *The Psychology of Death.* New York: Springer Pub. Co., 1972.

KUBLER-ROSS, ELISABETH, *On Death and Dying.* New York: The Macmillan Co., Inc., 1969.

————, *Death: The Final Stage of Growth.* Englewood Cliffs, N.J.: Prentice-Hall, Inc., 1975.

LESHAN, EDA, *What Makes Me Feel This Way.* New York: The Macmillan Co., 1972.

LEWIS, OSCAR, *A Death in the Sanchez Family.* New York: Random House, 1969.

SCHNEIDMAN, EDWIN, *Death and the College Student.* (A collection of brief essays on death and suicide). New York: Behavioral Publications, 1972.

ULANOV, BARRY, *Death: A Book of Preparation and Consolation.* New York: Sheed and Ward, 1959.

VERNON, GLENN M., *Sociology of Death: An Analysis of Death-Related Behavior.* New York: Ronald Press, 1970.

WEISMAN AVERY D., *On Dying and Denying: A Psychiatric Study of Terminality.* New York: Behavioral Publications, 1972.

ZIM, HERBERT S., AND SONIA BLEEKER, *Life and Death.* New York: William Morrow and Co., 1970.

Articles:

BLANK, J.P., "To Be Young and Know That Death Is Near: L. Helton's Esteogenic Sarcoman," *Reader's Digest,* 100:78-84 (January 1972).

COOPER, R.M., J.G. SOBOSAN, AND J.A. PHIPPS, "Facing Death," *Christian Century,* 90:225-32, February 21, 1973.

"Death With Dignity: The Debate Goes On," *Science News,* 102:118 August 19, 1972.

FORBES, C.A., "Death: No More Taboos," *Christianity Today,* 16:31-2, May 26, 1972.

GALLAGHER, T., AND T. MORRIS, "Can Death Ever Be Merciful: Pros and Cons," *Good Housekeeping,* 174:90 (January 1972).

HOFFMAN, J.W., "When A Loved One Is Dying," *Today's Health,* 50:40-3 (February, 1972).

JURY, MARK, "The Nobility in Gramp's Decision to Die" (photo essay), *Today's Health* (January 1975), p. 18.

ROSS, E.K., "Facing Up to Death," *Today's Education,* 61:30-2 (January 1972).

"Thanatology 1: College Courses." *Time* 101:36 (January 8, 1973).

Health is not equivalent to happiness, surfeit, or success.
It is foremost a matter of being wholly one with whatever
circumstances we find ourselves in. Even our death is a
healthy event if we fully embrace the fact of our dying.
. . .The issue is awareness, of living in the present.
Whatever our present existence consists of, if we are at
one with it, we are healthy. (Latner, p. 64)

Dying
as the Last Stage of Growth

Mwalimu Imara

My life at this moment seems to be one long line of growth experiences. At one place, one way of living became something I could no longer envision myself as being a part of, something that put me out of phase with what I felt myself to be. I died to those situations and went through the agony and rebirth in a new city, a new country, a new job, and a new trade. When being a printer no longer felt right to me, the old nagging call to the ministry became stronger, I pulled up from my job, my business connections, my expensive tastes, and went to college for seven years to learn about the life-style of ministry. At thirty-one I was giving up the safety and comfort of a life as a successful businessman for the god-knows-what of the world of the religious professional. I remember eleven years earlier having left the relatively liberal atmosphere of Montreal for the racially restrictive climate of the United States. I wanted to leave my hometown for some strange place, why, I don't know. I did know that home had become too much of something that was not for me. So, in fear and trembling, I left Canada for the brimstone and hellfire of New York.

This article is reprinted from Elisabeth Kubler-Ross, *Death: The Final Stage of Growth*, a Spectrum Book (Englewood Cliffs, N.J.: Prentice-Hall, Inc., 1975). Reprint permission has gratefully been received from the copyright holder, Mwalimu Imara.

Take a look at your life. What were those moments of chosen separation and pain when you were about the business of your own growth, when all the hounds of heaven could not have stayed you from those acts of your becoming. We may seek new professions or new locations or simply begin to experience ourselves as new in a therapeutic situation—whatever the situation, our experience of our own growth is really filled with anxiety and fraught with a sense of danger, as it is with excitement and fulfillment, as it is with pain as well as joy. Human life, my life and your life, have potential for this growth experience from the first moment at birth until our last breath at death.

We may be healthy persons with few major conflicts and splits in our sense of self, but our being spiritually-physically sound humans does not eliminate the inevitable crises and fears that accompany growth and change. When we abandon the old familiar patterns of life, whether voluntarily or involuntarily, we always have a sense of risk-taking. When the new situation involves changes which may have grave consequences for our future well-being, the level of anxiety is bound to be great. Abandoning old ways and breaking old patterns is like dying, at least dying to old ways of life for an unknown new life of meaning and relationships. But living without change is not living at all, not growing at all. Dying is a precondition for living. Growth is a precondition for living. To limit the process is to exist as compressed beings.

In all of our growth situations except one, we can look forward to new vistas, new goals, new projects, and new enriching relationships. When we look forward to that time of dreaded news when our own death becomes imminent reality, we draw back in fear and rejection. That is the one journey, the one labor few of us look forward to. Fear of that final separation, death, is natural. The thought of sleep without dreams, timelessness without concern and conversation with others is the most difficult thing we humans face.

Where there is love there is the anxiety about loss of life, and love it is that makes the loss of life in the psychical sense a dreaded thing, because death appears as the end of love, which is life. (Haroutunian, p. 89)

We abhor and reject the moment when we will confront the nearness of our death. But the dying stage of our life can be experienced as the most profound growth event of our total life's experience. The shock, the pain and the anxiety are great, but if we are fortunate enough to have time to live and experience our own process, our arrival at a plateau of creative acceptance will be worth it.

Death is not a shock to our systems when we read about it in a book or discuss it philosophically in an armchair. The feelings of powerlessness and isolation come from our whole being and not our intellectual fantasies. The problem of death, in general, does not reach us in the core of our being. Only when it is "my" imminent death or the imminent death of someone I love do I feel the pangs of "life-hunger." The soul in torment is a person tortured from attachment to life, a torture which surges through our whole being, chilling us to our heart one minute and breaking us out in a flushing sweat the next. This is our frantic struggle to clutch at life while slipping over the brink to death. This is the self in battle with the nonself. The concrete possibility of our own imminent death is so great a shock that our first response must be denial. Thomas Bell, the author of *In The Midst of Life,* an autobiographical account of his own struggle with his own terminal situation, wrote:

Now and then the whole thing becomes unreal. Out of the middle of the night's darkness, or bringing me to a sudden, chilling halt during the day, the thought comes: This can't be happening to me. Not to me. *Me* with a malignant tumor? *Me* with only a few months to live? Nonsense. And I stare up at the darkness, or out at the sunlit street, and try to encompass it, to feel it. But it stays unreal. Perhaps the difficulty is my half-conscious presumption that such things happen, should happen, only to other people. . . . People who are strangers, who really don't mind, who . . . are born solely to fill such quotas. Whereas I am me. Not a stranger. Not other people. Me!

I can see how you might have some difficulty in reading about his experience or seeing a person you know and love go through a similar experience, and still consider this pain and anguish to be the beginning of a potential growth experience. But it is just that. The pain is great because the loss is great. Death separates us from all that we hold dear, including our very selves. It is the ultimate of separations. And unlike other growth situations, we have little choice as to whether or not the separation will occur. However, what is in our control is the quality of the separation experience — making it "life" affirming or life-denying.

When the things we value most in life are destroyed, we can respond in several ways. We can live a life of depressed feelings and in extreme circumstances, give up investing in life entirely by developing a life of psychotic separation. This is the ultimate or extreme despair. The second alternative is to conceal the negative of our existence from consciousness. This is always an attempt at concealment because the defense is seldom effective for very long especially in situations of extreme stress like those involving our own death or the death of a significant other. The third alternative, I call religious. It is investing ourselves in creative and appreciative relationships with others. Becoming open to other people and remaining open to them is more easily said than done in time of crisis. It is especially difficult if we have not been in the practice of relating that way with others. In those moments when we experience the pain of our own dying and the dying of others, we are not likely to reach out to give or receive comfort or support unless our lives have been previously open to others in situations of joy, sorrow, anger and hate. This third response, our reaching out to others, is the step leading to a growth experience for the terminally ill person.

Our struggle for growth as we approach death is "the struggle . . . for meaning and significance of our person." Being, existing at this time of crisis *"is to mean something to someone else."* As we mature as adults, the threat of losing relationships with other significant persons in our lives is greater than the fear of losing our own life. We are animals who think of ourselves through our transactions with other persons. We are basically social being fellowpersons. And we cannot break our bonds with one another without becoming of no value. Since our highest values focus on ourselves in relation to others, death means termination of transaction with others or a "failure in communion." (Haroutunian, p. 83)

A CASE STUDY

Several years ago when I was a student chaplain, there was an old lady who taught me what growth during the final stages of life really meant. We were seated in the interviewing room with Miss Martin. It was our regular Wednesday morning Death and Dying seminar conducted by Dr. Elisabeth Kubler-Ross. Miss Martin was one of our patients, who was willing to attend the seminar and talk to us about what her experience as a terminal patient was like. Miss Martin, Dr. Ross, and I sat facing one another, our chairs and the patient's wheelchair forming an intimate triangle in the small room. The students and staff were sitting in the observation room beyond the glass partition.

Miss Martin looked serene and soft in her blue nightgown. Her quiet voice, so different in tone from its loud stridency of months past, raised thoughtfully the regrets and pains of her past and her present to share with us and the students beyond the partition. We listened to the hardships and loneliness facing a single woman making her own way in the man's domain of business during the 1930s. We listened to her recount and recall the steps by which she became so alienated from her brother and sister, that even now when cancer was consuming her intestines, they would not travel a few hundred miles to visit her on her deathbed. Quietly she continued to speak.

Her voice trailed to a stop. Her head tilted a little to one side and her eyes seemed to focus on some vision, some thought far into the deep recesses of her being. Then she looked up at the glass screen separating her from the crowd in the other room and she said with a quiet firmness:

I have lived more in the past three months than I have during my whole life. . . . I wish I knew forty years ago what I know now about living. I have friends. Thank you.

We cried. All of us. Nurses, social workers, ministers, physicians, all crying for that miracle that was Miss Martin. Here, before us was a woman, an old woman, who had lived a long life with few friends and close relationships of any kind. Here was a woman with tremendous will and presence who could still frighten people who crossed her. She had grown bitter in her ruthless encounter with the world of her experience, taking but unable to give or receive from anyone, that is, until she met us. The miracle of Miss Martin was the transformation from a life-style of hardness to the open softness of the beautiful old woman before us at the seminar. The growth of Miss Martin was no sudden conversion. It was a long, almost daily battle lasting several months. Many of the staff bore the psychic scars to prove it.

You should have met that sweet old lady several months before the seminar. She became one of my hospital "Parishioners" as the result of an urgent request for a chaplain from the charge day nurse of her unit. I stopped by the nursing station on my way to the patient's room to see if there was anything I should know. The charge nurse on the unit, usually a kind, considerate person, was not in any such mood that day as she gave me the scoop on Miss Martin, the unit's number one problem. It was the first time that I had heard any patient referred to with such colorful, yet unprintable, epithets. From my encounter later that day, I would have to agree with all the epithets.

I was told that the patient, Miss Martin, was recovering from rather extensive abdominal surgery for cancer, and the more she healed, the more demanding, abusive, foul-mouthed, and cantankerous she became. The chaplain's office was called in as a last ditch effort to sweeten her up a little for the staff's sake until she was well enough to be sent to a nursing home.

Reluctantly, I went to meet Miss Martin. She was everything the nurse had promised, in triplicate. She was, indeed, a very graceless old lady. My first visit dislodged an unending stream of complaints about her treatment, the nursing service, her pain, ministers, religion, her doctor—everyone and everything that came to her mind. But, somehow, I had the feeling that she was afraid to stop talking—afraid somehow, she might go crazy. Her voice was angry and violent, but her eyes read panic. As I stood up from the chair, I told her that *we*, Dr. Ross and I, would be coming back to see her the next day. And we did. She became one of the many very special people with terminal illness in University of Chicago Hospital to be befriended by us. In four weeks she was actually smiling at us and other people, some of whom were complete strangers. She had begun to grow, at age sixty-eight. With terminal cancer, she was becoming a new person.

During that month, Miss Martin unfolded the power and pain of her sixty-eight frustrating years. She had struggled to become a success in business and she had succeeded, but she belonged to no one. She had no friends. Her only surviving family were a brother and sister, who lived in cities not too distant from Chicago, but who would not visit her. And no wonder. She had built up very little credit in the bank of affection with them or anyone else, for that matter. She lived a long life of isolation, possessed by her work, but giving herself to no one. We, the staff, became her family, her friends. And she began to change. She began to smile. She began to appreciate more and complain less. She actually became a joy to visit. In those few months with us she built a new life. She wrestled with her new identity as an old woman, dying alone, without anyone to care. She struggled through her grief's anger at losing all that she had in her barren world, which was now becoming enriched by others. Her angry attacks on the staff were less bitter and destructive in tone. We watched as the sixty-eight-year-old caterpillar became a graceful butterfly. She accepted the fact that she could not erase decades of living and magically bring about a warm relationship with her brother and sister, where no basis had been laid in their history and little potential existed in their unrelenting, rigid personalities. She could not have them, but she could have us. As she accepted her illness, she became more able to accept the human contact that was still available to her.

Thus, she could say in a seminar a month before her death, "I have lived more in the past three months than I have during my whole life. I wish I knew forty years ago what I know now. . . . I have friends. Thank you." She was *at one* with the people in her present existence, possibly for the first itme in many decades, if, indeed, ever.

Miss Martin died a larger person, a person whose life was enlarged as she risked moving through the five stages of her grief process with us. And she died as she grew. Her horizons expanded to include Dr. Ross, myself, several nurses and many students from any number of disciplines who were related to the Death and Dying seminar. It was the irony of her last days that her life became richer as it approached termination. It was so and is so with many of our patients and parishioners as we help them find their way through life's last stage. I call this process, this drive toward "self-expansion," growth, our most basic human response to life.

The most important area of expansion for Miss Martin was her being allowed and willing to participate in something beyond herself—the lives of other people. This is the one level of human growth where we are totally dependent on one another. "On the physical level, we have only to maintain what we already clearly are." On this level "we do not start even with potentialities. We start with nothing. To be is to mean something to someone else. *This existence we cannot directly create for ourselves: it can only be given to us by another.*" It is a blessing.

In a group therapy session I was recently coleading, a young woman, who knew that I was a minister, asked me for a blessing. I took the request seriously since it came after my asking her if there was anything further she wanted from me. I was stunned to silence for a few minutes. I am not accustomed to being asked for blessings even in church. Then the human meaning of blessing came to me out of its historical religious meaning. The feeling of "blessedness" comes out of the experience of *being accepted.* The Christian concept of God's grace is an experienced acceptance that was unearned and unearnable. Paul Tillich describes the experience of being blessed in this way:

It happens or it does not happen. And certainly it does *not* happen if we try to force it upon ourselves, just as it shall not happen so long as we think, in our self-complacency, that we have no need of it. Grace strikes us when we are in great pain and restlessness. It strikes us when we walk through the dark valley of a meaningless and empty life. It strikes us when we feel that our separation is deeper than usual, because we have violated another life, a life which we love, or from which we were estranged. It strikes us when our disgust for our own being, our indifference, our weakness, our hostility, our lack of direction and composure have become intolerable to us. It strikes us when, year after year, the longed-for perfection of life does not appear, when the old compulsions reign within us as they have for decades, when despair destroys all joy and courage. Sometimes at that moment a wave of light breaks into our darkness, and it is as though a voice were saying: "You are accepted. *You are accepted,* accepted by that which is greater than you, and the name of which you do not know. Do not ask for the name now; perhaps later you will do much. Do not seek for anything. *Simply accept the fact that you are accepted!*" If that happens to us, we experience grace. After such an experience we may not be better than before, and we may not believe more than before. But everything is transformed. In that moment, grace conquers sin, and reconciliation bridges the gulf of estrangement. And nothing is demanded of this experience, no religious or moral or intellectual presupposition, nothing but *acceptance.*

Going through the five stages of the terminal person's grief is a process moving toward a blessing, "acceptance." But we are able to journey fully through the process only when we feel the "acceptance" of another person. Our "acceptance" of our own being, that is, our sensing that we are significant as a person, depends on *knowing* that we are accepted by someone or something larger than our individual self. It is at this juncture that those who minister to the needs of the dying may become physicians to the soul. It is the dying who can teach others the importance of "grace" in our lives. Acceptance is the beginning of growth.

RELIGION AND GROWTH

Miss Martin's transformation was religious. Now, you and I may differ over what we understand religious to be, so let me first tell you how I approach religion. Religion deals with belief and ritual systems, and so do the family, industry, government, banks, the military, and all institutional interests in society. Each institutionalized interest serves a basic social and personal need. The religious issue deals with our personal need for commitment to something in which we can center our lives, something which enables us to recognize and act upon what we know is good, something which allows us to expand to our full potential as persons.

We human beings are capable of a wide range of experiences and behaviors. We can be savage and cruel on one occasion and loving and saintly on another. We can experience extreme horror at one time and be moved to ecstasy at another. We can, as Miss Martin, be rejecting and defensive at one life juncture, only to be transformed into an open, lovable person at a later time. Our capacity for "radical transformation" is one of our four most characteristic features. But the religious issue is: What in our life can keep us from the distinctive transformations and enable us to experience the greatest good our life can achieve? Religion has to do with our commitment to whatever enables us to do that. Miss Martin's "commitment" enabled her to experience her most creative potential during the last months of her life. I will come back to Miss Martin's commitment shortly. So the issue for religion is: what commitment helps us live creative lives and lessen our destructive potential?

Another characteristic we have which is basic to religious commitment is our capacity for "original experience" or personal awareness. Much of our lives, too much, is lived as "conventional experience." We force ourselves into the molds fashioned for us by our families, our employers, our friends and our public images until we experience ourselves as no self at all, but as the empty caricature of someone else's image. We lose touch with what and with who we really are. We lose touch with the freshness and vitality coming from that "original" awareness of ourselves, our own needs, our own choices. Losing this capacity we live lives of self-destruction, sometimes resulting in the destruction of those other lives we touch. Our inner conflicts, our chronic guilts, our boredoms and lassitudes, and our acute loneliness begin with our denial of our own awareness, our own "original," creative experiencing. Is there a religious commitment which will enable us to transform our borrowed identities into authentic selves? What can we commit our lives to that will help us become more authentic as persons? That is the religious issue for all, whether or not we are terminal.

Each religious faith attempts to supply a formula for the commitment which will enable us to creatively grow and transform our lives, but I have found that the actual content of a person's faith is irrelevant to whether or not they move creatively. *How* we interact with one another and *how* we experience ourselves are more important for dying persons than the content of their religious myths or their articulated philosophy of life.

Miss Martin was an agnostic. She neither believed nor disbelieved in a divine agency. The question of God was irrelevant to her way of looking at the world. As her world became more loving, as she became less destructive and more open to her own experience and the experience of others, the concept of God still remained irrelevant. There was no last minute dramatic pietistic conversion.

Dying patients are at a stage of new transformation in their lives. They may, like Miss Martin, experience their only options as fighting in panic, backs against the wall, or giving up in despair. But even at the moment of being diagnosed as having a terminal illness, we are still human, with those possibilities for radical growth in terms of our experiencing life. But there is a cost to participation in our own radical change for the better. The price is that we become committed persons. Not committed in the sense that we become committed to a religious dogma or ritual. The commitment is an act or series of actions and is our opening up to the experiencing of who we really are in this new situation in life, not what our conventional coding of that experience tells us we feel. Miss Martin made such a commitment. After finding out that she was terminal, she still pretended to be that same rich old lady who could shout and rage to achieve satisfaction. Prior to her illness she had lived a life out of touch with her actual situation. She had built a stereotype for herself back in the early days of her business carreer when she did have to struggle to succeed. But when her situation changed, she continued to live according to the same old script. She had to become successful in business, but like so many of us, she became trapped in a role and gave up her capacity for original experience.

Her becoming more in touch with what was happening to her in the hospital was not something that just happened out of the blue. She had to increasingly commit herself to experiencing herself as she was, in the present, as she was in her new situation as a person approaching death. Although she had at her disposal the opportunity to work through the barriers to do her own experiencing, she did not have to do so, but took the risk and experimented with engaging with her present feelings, meanings, dreams, fantasies and perceptions. She became *committed* to the cherishing of herself as a person, valuing herself as a body knowing joy, sorrow, love, hate, confusion, clarity, being alone and being with. This commitment to experiencing our identity is basic to every transformation of our lives. If we are neurotic, living life-styles of self-destruction, our first order of business in therapy is to get in touch with our actual present experience of ourselves in our present situation. Transformation of our lives for the good begins as we commit ourselves to the experiencing of our own identity, a commitment to answering the question: Who am I? Now. Here. This is the first level of religious commitment.

Miss Martin, in order to realize her full potential in this period of new transformation, had to make another commitment. She had not only to commit herself to awareness of her own original experiencing, but she had to communicate, to share that experience with others and in turn appreciate and understand the original experiences of others in her life. She increasingly committed herself to dialogue, to conversation of mutual exchange with others. She was heard and allowed herself to be heard, to be understood and understand.

We seldom think of conversation as commitment, but it is. I find that expressing what I really feel and telling another person what is actually important to me at the moment is difficult. It requires a "commitment" on my part to do so, and I sense that this is true for most of us. It is equally difficult to listen. We are usually so full of our own thoughts and responses that we seldom really listen close enough to one another to grasp the real flavor of what the other person is attempting to convey. Creative communication in depth is what allows us to experience a sense of belonging to others. It is the force that limits the destructive potential in our lives and what promotes the growth aspects. Life is a struggle. Coping with a lifetime of change is a struggle, but through a lifetime of change we will experience ourselves as full persons only to the degree that we allow ourselves that commitment to others which keeps us in creative dialogue. It is the way we mature. One measure of maturity is the degree to which we extend our interests and concerns beyond our immediate desire for personal comfort, and I am not suggesting that maturity is wearing a hair shirt. Human maturity, person maturity and religious maturity to me, all mean the same thing—can be measured by the degree to which we are able to commit ourselves to this form of human interchange. At every stage of our life, but most especially during the terminal stage, this question is the most crucial: Can I be open to expressing my original self and experiencing others doing the same thing?

This is my answer to the second problem of religion (after the problem of identity), that is, the religious problem of: What should I be committed to? What is my purpose in life? What will enable me to maximize the good? What will keep me from boredom, loneliness, inner conflict, and chronic guilt feelings? Most of our religious belief systems give us a prescription telling us to trust in God or to love one another. Creative dialogue is my way of saying similar things. Many people can express their lives in this form of dialogue and experience its benefits without calling it anything, or having a traditional designation for it. Miss Martin didn't call it anything. But after two months of practice she knew from her experience what loving and receiving love was. To be transformed, dying patients must be committed to 1) achieving a sense of their own identity through experiencing their own ongoing awareness or "original experience" and 2) committing themselves to a mutual dialogue about that experience with significant other people.

There is a third level of religious commitment which is essential to us in times of personal transformation, like that of the dying patient. At this level our prime consideration is the operational blueprint or life script we refer to in order to determine our next steps in life and to make sense of the last few. Each of us has our own special way of looking at the world and putting that experience together in some sort of coherent fashion, which helps us make sense out of what we did, are doing and plan to do. Some call this our philosophy of life, others call it our theology. Call it what you will. The name is not important. What it is is the characteristic way we go about getting what we want and how we explain that to ourselves and others. Religious commitment, the commitment to transform our lives in creative ways, regardless of our situation, requires us to have some coherent sense of the world we act in, why we do some things we do, and why other people act in the way that they do. This understanding need not be articulated in any systematic way or even be entirely conscious, but it must express itself as a dominant integrating pattern in our life. Our understanding, conscious or not, must make sense of our behavior and the behavior of others. Without some sort of blueprint which makes our activities and the acts of others somewhat predictable, without a sense that we are moving in a direction that will give us more of what we want and need, and without a sense that our life has a plan or a direction, we experience our lives as fragmented and aimless.

Is it so strange to think of a dying patient as having a direction, as having a life plan? Moving and living our days with a sense of coherence is the dividend that the terminally ill patient receives for moving through the five stages. The stage of acceptance, the final stage in the transcendence of the patient, is the time when the person's life becomes recentered and more self-reliant and self-sufficient. This is quite often a very difficult reality to face for close friends and family of the patient. An accepting person is a person who lives life with a more or less unified sense of themselves. People living committed directional lives give others the impression that they have a sense of surefootedness about their lives, a stable center, a core.

This comes from the third level for religious commitment, and answers the religious problem: In what way will I live my life? The answer may not be recited in any current poetry of a standard religious faith, and it doesn't matter if it is. What is important is whether we actually behave and experience our lives in the centered manner. When Miss Martin said, "I have lived more in the past three months than I have during my whole life," she was speaking from a centered sense of herself. She spoke from a center which gave her waning life a perspective and understanding she had not experienced before. She had grown. She had transcended one life-style for another which was more authentic to her actual situation. Her life, my life, your life — in common have a wide range of possibilities of being human, our seemingly endless capacity for creative change, transcendence. We are created for transcendence as birds are for flight and fish for swimming.

Living to the fullest, to capacity, to transcendence, demands that we live lives of awareness, mutual self-communication and direction. Said in another way, religious commitment has to do with the issues of self-identity, commitment of ourselves to others and receiving their commitment to us, and a coherent, directional style of living. Our answers to three questions sum up our religious commitment. Who am I? To what do I commit myself? How do I go about living my commitment?

The answers I have given to these three questions come out of my own life experience, my reflection and reading the reported experiences of others. Verification comes from my observations of how people undergoing the most important transcendent experience of their lives, living with the imminent reality of death, respond to themselves, their situations and to others in those situations. There are patterns and the patterns bear out the above assertions.

Working with patients going through their grief process for several years, I have noticed that not everyone completes the process. Some people got stuck at one stage (see the chart of the Five Stages—Figure 1) and seemed to remain there until death. Some people were stuck at one place and then began to move toward resolution after a period of time. Other people seemed to move through the five stages relatively smoothly with very little intervention or support on the part of the staff.

I designed and executed a research project, hoping to gain an understanding of the religious dynamics behind the denial process and the terminally ill patient's resistance to moving through to acceptance. The most important finding for me from the study was that there was empirical support for all that we have been discussing up to now. It demonstrated that people who deny less and are more able to move through the five stages after they discover that they have a terminal illness are those people who 1) are willing to converse in depth with significant others about what their present experience is like, 2) meet others on equal terms, that is, are able to enter into real dialogue with others where both can share what is "real" with the other, and 3) accept the good with the bad. They have a framework within which the tragic and happy events of their present and past life take on meaning and give their life a sense of direction and fulfillment.

The study showed, among other things, that the process of dying is a process of recommitment to life, coming out of a new situation. The three indicators of this recommitment process are very much like the three attributes of the mature personality described in the writings of Gordon Allport.

The dying patient's willingness to converse in depth about his or her present awareness of memories, dreams and hopes while remaining fully cognizant of the present realities of the illness is what Allport calls "self-objectification." Allport describes self-objectivity as "the ability to objectify oneself, to be reflective and insightful about one's own life. The individual with insight sees

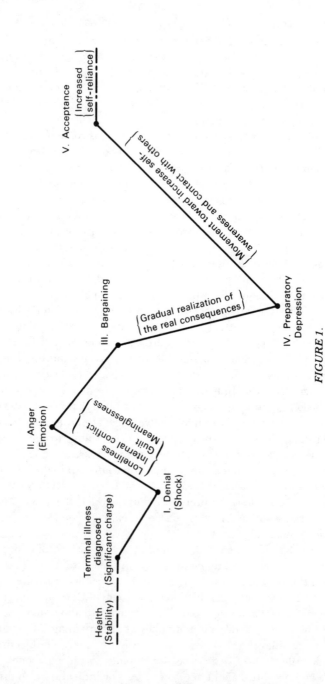

FIGURE 1.

himself as others see him, at certain moments glimpses himself in a kind of cosmic perspective." This "includes the ability to relate feeling tone of the present experience to that of past experience" provided the past doesn't overshadow the quality of the process of the present experience. Allport sees present awareness of one's self as a major attribute of maturity. And this coincides with what we experience in the behavior of terminally ill people who move toward resolution of their grief.

The dying patient's willingness to enter into peer type relationships with other people instead of remaining in self-pitying relationships compares with what Allport refers to as "ego-extension," which he describes as "the capacity to take an interest in more than one's body and one's material possessions." Really communicating with another person is an effort for most of us during the best times of our lives. It is always a struggle. It seems that those who have practiced this kind of openness are more readily able to do it when the crisis of terminal illness arrives.

The patient's ability to fit his or her present situation into some meaningful life pattern is what Allport describes as a "unifying philosophy of life . . . which may or may not be religious, but in any event, has to be a frame of meaning and of responsibility into which life's major activities fit." It need not be "articulated in words, nor entirely complete. But without direction and coherence, supplied by some dominant, integrative pattern, life seems fragmented and aimless."

These three attributes or commitments, call them what you will, comprise the central religious issues of our lives. Identity, commitment, and direction are the basic channels of personal human meaning, regardless of what cultural ideologies we may use to explain them. And I consider them to be the religious sub-strata of human life. Allport says that "these three attributes of maturity are not selected in an arbitrary manner. They are chosen because they represent the three primary avenues of development that are open to any human being in the course of his growth; the avenue of widening interests (the expanding self), the avenue of detachment and insight (self-objectification), and the avenue of integration (self-unification). I doubt that any scientifically supported criteria of maturity would differ substantially from these three." (The Individual and His Religion, p. 60 ff).

Like Miss Martin, we are all transcendent creatures with extremely wide potential. We can plunge from peaks of glorious joy to depths of despairing anguish. From towering rage we can flow to caressing gentleness. Miss Martin's destructive anger became calm appreciation. When we feel "accepted" in our grieving, our denial riskily moves toward acceptance and resolution. We humans are, above all, capable of experiencing great transcendence. In dealing with significant change situations in our lives, we go through a process very much like that of the dying patient, as illustrated in the diagram of the five stages.

Learning how to live life as a dying person is not unlike the relearning necessary after a divorce or a separation from an important person. Leaving a job or receiving an important award or recognition may begin us along the same path of transcendence walked by all of us if we have the opportunity to experience our last days of life. Religious conversion, opening ourselves to radical new life directions, will also take us along the road of the five steps. Isaiah, chapter 6, of the Old Testament is a reporting of the prophet's experiencing of those same five steps, beginning with shocked denial, moving through the emotions of awe and guilt, the redemptive bargaining, the working depression as he faces the reality of the true cost of his new commitment, to the final acceptance of his prophetic task. Paul, the Apostle, has his Road to Damascus experience and the conversion experience of Jesus is described in the Gospel of Luke, beginning with his baptism and continuing through his temptation on the mountain (Luke 3:21ff).

The "five stages" are the way of optimum growth and creative living. The three modes of human commitment and human development are our guides along the journey. We *can* live life fully until we die.

BIBLIOGRAPHY

ALLPORT, GORDON, *The Individual and His Religion*. New York: The Macmillian Co., 1950.

———, *Personality and Social Encounter*. Boston: Beacon Press, 1964.

ANGYAL, ANDRAS, *Neurosis and Treatment: A Holistic Theory*. New York: Viking Press, 1973.

BELL, THOMAS, *In the Midst of LIfe*. New York: Atheneum, 1961.

HAROUTUNIAN, JOSEPH, "Life and Death Among Fellowmen," *The Modern Vision of Death*, ed. Nathan A. Scott, Jr.

KUBLER-ROSS, ELISABETH, *On Death and Dying*. New York: The Macmillan Co., 1969.

LATNER, JOEL, *The Gestalt Therapy Book*. New York: Julian Press, 1973.

THURMAN, HOWARD, *Disciplines of the Spirit*. New York: Harper & Row, 1963.

PART TWO
SEXUAL PROBLEMS

Making Your Sex Life More Rewarding

Lloyd G. Sinclair
Richard L. Timmers
Jane Rea James

This chapter is written for couples such as those who have confided to the authors, "We're bored with our sex life" or "Lately I'm turned off to sex" or "My sex drive isn't what it used to be." It discusses four ideas designed to inject new life into sexual intimacy. If you follow the suggestions outlined in this chapter, chances are your sex life is going to benefit. And you don't have to be all that bored—remember, you don't have to be sick to get better.

We seem to be in constant quest for new techniques that will deliver us to greater orgasmic heights. The media, especially the pornographers, scream at us to try this and experience that—to reach ecstatic climax. Years of experience as professional sex therapists have convinced the authors that although new techniques may generate temporary highs, they are just that—temporary. If you want a temporary high, buy a glossy magazine. If you want more lasting change, take a new look at your sexuality.

There are really only four things you need to do, and they are easy to understand. The hard part, albeit the fun part, is incorporating them into your life. If that seems too troublesome, perhaps you had better stop complaining about being bored.

This article was especially written for this book.

SLOW DOWN

Slow down. Most of us are in such a hurry to do everything — including sex — that "quickies" become our entire repertoire. A steady diet of quick sex rapidly becomes routine; routine breeds boredom; boredom defeats sexual response. Soon we decide it's too much bother. Intimate physical interaction is something to savor, to relax with, and to enjoy leisurely. When we remember that getting there is at least half the fun, we're on the right track.

Remember your younger years, before you were having intercourse? You would pet and stroke and fondle for hours — or at least you would have liked to, given the opportunity. For many of us, those were some of the best sexual experiences we ever had. Why? Not because we were sexually sophisticated — quite the opposite — but because we did *one thing* right. We savored every precious second, extended every minute. But when we became adults, we added intercourse and subtracted petting and stroking. We hurried. We wanted to get to the "real thing."

So step 1, and we said it was simple, is slow down. Instead of taking 20 minutes, take two hours. To do this, you had better forget the idea that time for sex needs to occur "spontaneously." Although there are days when sex does occur spontaneously, that works mainly for people with lots of time. Most of us, however, need to plan intimacy time with a partner. We schedule much less important things than sex. If we wait for sex time to occur magically, it never will. Everything else invariably fills the space.

KNOW THYSELF — AND THY PARTNER

Next, we need some information. There are two ways we can go about this: 1) hunt and poke until we stumble onto the right combinations of touch, or 2) know our own responses so that we can tell our partner what is most pleasing. Most of us rely on the hunt and poke method. If it has worked for you, you are lucky. But most of us can benefit from a more direct approach.

Knowing about ourselves and our partners involves gathering information. It is useful to know, for instance, that a woman's clitoris is an exquisitely sensitive organ. Caressing a lubricated clitoris is likely to be exciting for a woman; caressing a dry clitoris is likely to be irritating. When sexual stimulation does not cause the clitoris to become lubricated naturally, vaginal lubrication, lotion, or saliva may be helpful.

It is useful to know that nipple stimulation can be as pleasant for men as it is for women.

It is useful to know that introducing artificial lubrication into a dry vagina may make penetration easier, but it does not cause important physical responses to occur in a woman. These responses include the movement of the cervix up and out of the way to make room for the penis.

It is useful to know that penile erection is a waxing and waning process, similar to the waxing and waning process of vaginal lubrication. Men should not expect to have one continuous erection throughout an extended sexual experience, any more than women should expect to lubricate continuously.

Where do you get such information, since your parents didn't tell you and your teacher wasn't allowed to? There are many good books on the subject — but not the sex technique manuals. If you don't want to buy the original, get a good synopsis of the studies on sexual behavior by William Masters and Virginia Johnson.[1]

Besides this important general information, we also need personal information. What do we, as individuals, especially like? What has erotic value? What kind of touch is best? What turns us off?

The single best way to answer these questions is to explore ourselves — in other words, self-pleasuring, or masturbation. We know by now that masturbation does not cause acne, insanity, or even hair on our palms. But most of us still view it as rather shameful, a neccessary evil, a poor substitute for the "real thing." But nobody is suggesting that you replace partner interaction with masturbation. We all prefer the warm intimacy of an interested and interesting partner. But we have more to give and receive when we assume responsibility for our attitudes, needs, and feelings; not in a selfish way, but in a self-concerned, self-representing way.

So, don't expect your partner to know all about you if you don't know all about yourself, especially if your partner is of the other sex. How on earth does a man know what it feels like to have a vagina? Men, just like women, don't know everything there is to know about sex. They need to learn. How could anybody — intuitively, instinctively — know about their partner's sexual likes and dislikes? Because sexual response is a natural physiological process combining head and body, it depends mostly on learned behaviors. It is the learned behaviors that make the difference between an adequate sexual interaction and a great one.

Therefore, step 2 involves becoming informed — generally through written material and specifically through self-exploration — about sex. This is not so difficult, but very important.

TALK ABOUT IT

Now that we have decided to take two hours for sex, and we have become informed, where do we go from here?

---

[1]For instance, there is an excellent paperback on the subject; see Ruth and Edward Brecher, *An Analysis of Human Sexual Response* (New York: Signet Book, New American Library, 1966).

,e are going to relate to another person, we need to convey the informa-
.. Although nonverbal communication is what most of us use when it
c mes to sex, it tends to work well only in novels. If we are really going to
share this self-knowledge, we need the specificity possible only through verbal
communication.

Most of us are very bad at verbal communication. We can tell our partner
exactly where we want our back scratched, but we can't seem to find the
words when we want a specific sexual touch. Why? Partly because we believe,
mistakenly, that if he or she really loves me, he or she should know. We have
already discussed why this romantic notion does not work in real life. The
other part is that we are uncomfortable talking straightforwardly about sex,
particularly when it comes to asking for something from our partner. We feel
selfish, or we fear our partner will feel put down.

To be a full and equal participant in a sexual interaction, we need to have
respect and concern for our partner's needs, but also respect and concern for
our own. Sex is not meant to be something you do *to* someone or *for* someone;
rather, it is something two persons do *with* one another. Our needs and
desires are equally as important as those of our partner.

How do we learn to verbalize this knowledge? We can learn to use "I
language"[2] — a simple, straightforward, and honest method of communicating. It begins with "I" — taking responsibility for ourselves — and is
followed by a feeling. "I appreciate your tender ways." "I'm upset because
you're late." "I would like to go to that new movie tonight." "I would like you
to touch me here, like this."

This very simple method of communicating encourages several things. We
take responsibility for our feelings. Other people do not *make* us feel anger —
we respond with anger in certain situations. The statement "You make me so
angry" is not really honest and is likely to be met with a defensive reaction.
We must own our feelings.

"I language" promotes self-knowledge. If we are going to identify our feelings, we need to be in touch with them first. If we only use "you language," we
never stop long enough to know what we feel. "I language" encourages honesty and clarity. "Do *you* want to make love?" This statement leaves our partner
having to second guess — does he (or she) want to make love, does she (or he)
think I want to . . .? A much clearer message would be: "I would like to make
love now, and I'm wondering if you want to."

---

[2]"I language" is a communication technique suggested by many helping professionals. For a
more thorough treatment, see Thomas Gordon, *Parent Effectiveness Training,* (New York: Peter
H. Wyden, Inc., 1970).

Remember, feelings don't have to be rational. That's not the point. We interact in an intimate relationship much more through feelings than through thoughts. For us, feelings are facts, and nobody can take them away from us. Getting in touch with feelings takes some practice at first. Don't be discouraged if you can't identify your emotions right away. After some time and some practice, you can know what you feel most of the time.

The purpose of "I language" is not to demand agreement but rather to promote accurate communication and understanding. Only with accurate understanding can we ever really know if we agree or disagree. Try it. You'll be amazed at how it cleans up communication, and you'll probably learn a lot about yourself and your partner.

FORGET THE GOAL

All our lives we are encouraged to set goals for ourselves, so it should be no surprise that we set sexual goals too. We spend a good deal of our time thinking about intercourse and orgasm. We call the touching before intercourse *foreplay,* as if it were a preliminary to the main event, a means to an end. Following this attitude, foreplay becomes merely a repetition of familiar behaviors we use to get us to the "real thing." This pattern becomes "a kiss on the lips, a touch on the breasts, and a dive for the genitals."

What is wrong with that? For many couples, sexual interaction follows such a rigid pattern that: 1) it denies the value of foreplay and focuses only on intercourse and orgasm; 2) if something goes wrong on the way through the pattern (the phone rings, the erection is no longer there), the entire experience feels like a failure; 3) we start to avoid caressing, holding, and hugging unless we are ready to proceed to intercourse; 4) the repetition of familiar behaviors becomes boring, taking its toll in sexual interest; 5) the energy and attention taken by observing our performance (to be certain we are following the correct steps to reach the goal) often leaves us feeling disappointed and frustrated; and 6) even if the goals are reached each time, we have sacrificed maximizing the joy and pleasure of the journey. We cannot observe ourselves, evaluate our sexual performance, and absorb sexual feelings at the same time.

We can replace this step-by-step, goal-oriented approach with something better. Begin by thinking about touching, holding, kissing, and caressing as *sexplay,* not foreplay. These behaviors have value in themselves, not only as preliminaries to the "real thing." Each couple can develop, through self-knowledge and accurate understanding, their own group of valued behaviors.

These include intercourse and orgasm, but they also include backrubs, genital caress, holding hands, showering together, and so on. One behavior is not more valuable than another, and one does not need to precede another. Certainly, experiencing a backrub is different from experiencing an orgasm, but ordering or ranking their value only limits you. Couples who order or rank say, "We never touch anymore unless it's going to lead to intercourse. We miss that."

When all the behaviors have value, sexual experience does not lead necessarily to any particular goal. You are free to respond to your desires at the moment—unconstrained by what is *supposed* to happen. If all you do after an exhausting day is get and give a backrub, what is wrong with that?

Try these things. Slow down, become informed about yourself and your partner, talk about it, and get out of the goal orientation. You will be a more relaxed, responsible, and satisfied sexual being.

Overcoming Difficulty with Erection

Lloyd G. Sinclair

This chapter discusses what many people refer to as "impotence," a term the author abhors. "Impotence" implies a general lack of power or weakness in masculinity. Erectile difficulty, on the other hand, is a specific problem defined as "difficulty in attaining or maintaining a penile erection when one is desired."

Unlike women, men have the unenviable task of having to demonstrate — with an erect penis — genuine sexual arousal before intercourse can take place. You can't fake it, you can't will it, and you can't command it. But you don't have to be victimized by it either. No matter what pornographic and men's magazines try to con you into believing, no one can achieve an erection any time, any place, any number of times.

This chapter is designed to help you, the male, to get the "most" from your natural sexuality and — if you have some problems achieving an erection — to overcome those problems. Even if you have never had an erectile problem, you probably will some day. Virtually every man does — it's natural, but it doesn't have to make you feel like a failure.

This article was especially written for this book.

REASONS FOR ERECTILE DIFFICULTY

Here are some very common reasons for erectile difficulty:

Fatigue. No matter how willing your spirit is, when you are tired, your body has an insidious way of shutting down, even when you don't want it to. Age, unfortunately, accentuates that problem. You might not be able to do today what you could do without problems five years ago. So, if you are having erectile problems, look back at what you have been doing. Perhaps you need to be better rested. Try going home at midnight rather than three in the morning.

Depression. If you have had "one of those days" — your boss hollered continually, your car wouldn't start, your term paper was lost in the union, your ex-wife demanded more support money — it really caps it off when you get into bed and nothing happens. But, again, it's a natural thing. It isn't fun and you don't have to like it, but don't worry about it. If you worry, you'll get even more depressed and that will start the cycle over.

Alcohol. Alcohol is a very two-faced drug. It increases your desire but decreases your ability. If you had a few martinis, followed them with wine, and then had a couple of nightcaps, don't be surprised when your penis refuses to respond. Age, again, also rears its ugly head in regard to alcohol. At 18 you may be able to drink all night and still have no difficulties. But are you still 18?

Food and drugs. Try not to gorge yourself next time and see if it helps. And drugs can also interfere with erections, although if you are totally spaced out, you may not care.

Just remember that penile erection is a very normal part of your body's functioning — and like every other body function, it is going to work a lot better if you are rested, sober, mentally "up," and in good health.

NECESSARY COMPONENTS FOR ERECTION

Erection is a natural mind and body process that always occurs when three components are present:

1. Adequate stimulation; defined by every man individually. Some men find an erotic photograph sufficient stimulation for erection; others need direct genital stimulation.
2. Receptivity to sexual stimulation. Receptivity depends upon many environmental and psychological factors, including relaxation and freedom from fear and anxiety.
3. The body. Physical problems sometimes interfere with the body's natural ability to respond with erection. Physical response results from adequate

blood flow, a healthy hormone balance, and a properly functioning nervous system.

Erectile difficulty can be, although is not in most cases, the result of a physical problem. You can easily check your body's response. If you can achieve an erection at any time — awakening from sleep, through masturbation, by viewing an erotic film — you body has the capability to achieve an erection. Your difficulty with erection is, therefore, in the first two components above. But if you have experienced no erection for months, you should have a complete physical examination. We are concerned here with men whose bodies function adequately to experience erection at some times, but whose minds often interfere when erection is desired.

FACTS ABOUT ERECTION

The most important thing to realize about your erection is that it is renewable. Most men, in an extended sexual encounter, have several erections. During part of the sex play, a man might become quite aroused. Later, as he concentrates on pleasuring his partner, he may forget about himself and the erection will subside. Then it will come back.

That is normal — it is no problem at all. But if you panic when it happens, then it becomes a problem. You worry about it, you think about it, you forget about sex altogether as you concentrate on regaining that erection — and nothing, but nothing happens.

Of course, nothing happens. There is no "turn on" in thinking about a nonerect penis. Forget it and start thinking about the sexy situation you are in. In other words, relax and enjoy yourself so that you can respond to the sexual stimulation being in bed with someone you care for brings about.

AVOIDING UNREALISTIC EXPECTATIONS

At the risk of repetition, age influences erections — but not badly. Older men tend to be better lovers; they make up in technique what they lose in not being 18. However, young men, who may not have the know-how, do have the stamina. Older men have stamina too, but some of it is based in the brain.

You will probably be able to sustain an erection when you're 92 years old — you may even be able to sustain one when you're 96 — but your physical capabilities slow down as a normal response to aging. A man in his fifties, sixties, or eighties will still have erections, but they might not occur with the same frequency, speed, and intensity as they did when he was a teen-ager (for which many men, in remembering those days, may say, "Thank heavens for that!"). He may need direct genital touch by his partner even though 15 years before the mere thought was sufficient. His erection might not be as firm as it was or as he remembers it, when he was younger but generally it will still be firm enough.

Aging is a process that occurs very slowly, and often the changes in sexual response are barely noticeable from one decade to another. Don't let it bother you. If a man reports loss of erection as an overnight occurrence, the problem is not aging. In fact, the *problem* is almost never aging. What you lose in physical stamina, you gain in increased understanding, acceptance, and willingness to be concerned about your partner. Those qualities make you a better lover.

Remember that your sexual system is like other body systems. It functions best when you exercise it. So if you want to experience erections when you're 96, keep your body in tone by having regular erections now. However, you may be having trouble doing that even though you don't overdrink or overeat, take drugs, feel depressed or feel old. You may actually have a problem and that is no fun at all. But, assuming your doctor says you are physically okay, the problem can be solved.

THE SIX STAGES

The remainder of this chapter is a step-by-step process for overcoming difficulties with erection. It has been used throughout the country and has proved helpful to countless men. It will work for you. It might not work tonight; there is no timetable involved. Some couples resolve their difficulties in a few weeks, other take longer—but it does work. So, move at your own pace. If you are having erectile difficulties, you are having an embarrassing time. But even if it takes a few weeks, the result is worth it.

Although the steps outlined refer to a male-female relationship where both partners are working together, some imagination can easily alter the process to apply to a same-sex relationship or to one where the partner is unaware of the erectile difficulty. The optimal situation for positive change is always two informed persons who are in a warm and encouraging relationship. Each partner must be committed to reversing the erectile difficulty. The man will personally enjoy sexual interactions more with erectile confidence; so will his partner.

Take extra care to be honest and open with your partner. Above all, understand that the six stages that follow are "ideal." You are going to make mistakes along the way, but talk it over with your partner. If she is in bed with you in the first place, chances are that she cares enough about you to be patient—and the end result will be worthwhile for both of you.

Stage I—Getting comfortable

The first thing to do is to make the environment as helpful as possible. Find a place that is private and free from interruption. Find a time when both you and your partner are awake, relaxed, and not bothered by nonsexual thoughts (if today is the day your company went out of business, try tomorrow).

Feel good about the setting. Usually, it helps if both partners are nude. But if that turns either you or your partner off, wear anything you want to, but in this beginning stage, feel comfortable.

Since this *is* the first stage, forget about erection. The purpose of this first session is comfort; erection is not the goal. Begin by touching and caressing your partner all over her body, but skip her breasts and genitals. Ask her not to reciprocate now, but just to enjoy your caresses. The purpose here is for you to enjoy her body; her turn comes next. Try to do that for 20 minutes or longer—try to do it longer. After you have touched her for a long time, reverse roles. Have her touch you, except your genitals and nipples. She is going to enjoy exploring your body.[1]

The main thing is not to make attempts at intercourse or orgasm at this step. Make that understood with your partner from the beginning. Then you won't worry.

When you have finished touching, talk about it. What was pleasurable, neutral, unpleasant? What was new? How could the next encounter be more comfortable and pleasing? What feelings did you have when you were receiving touch without reciprocating? Talking about it is really important. Don't forget to do it. After you've done this once, do it again at least twice. You want to be very relaxed and comfortable, and that takes a little while.

Stage 2—Exploring feelings

When Stage I has been completed, and you both wish to proceed, the same interaction takes place—except now genital caresses can be included. Both partners are encouraged to supplement the whole-body touching with the introduction of genital exploration. But the largest amount of time should continue to be involved with nongenital touch.

The purpose of Stage 2 is exploration, relaxation, and comfort—not arousal. Remember that comfort and relaxation are prerequisites to arousal.

[1]William Masters and Virginia Johnson developed this invaluable concept.

If arousal occurs—lubrication in the woman, erection in the man—the partner should modify the caresses away from sexual stimulation. This stage also should be repeated three times or more, followed by discussion.

Stage 3—Heightening the experience

Stage 3 expands upon Stages 1 and 2. Here, the imagination and ingenuity of both of you are called upon to increase the sensual pleasure of the experience. Nongenital and genital caresses continue; exploring what is pleasant to the person who is touching by caressing at separate times.

You can add to the experience by sharing new ideas and behaviors. Try slowly applying a massage lotion or oil (preferably a nonalcohol, edible one with a pleasant scent) to each other's bodies. Take your time; let the lotion or oil absorb luxuriously. You may want to let your minds take you on an erotic trip by thinking of exciting fantasies. Fantasies are individual thoughts meant to be enjoyed; there is no such thing as a "bad" thought in this situation.

Be imaginative in when and where you experience Stage 3. Many people find morning times to be particularly enjoyable, by placing the sexual encounter before daily tasks. If either of you is bored with the bedroom, which may be where physical intimacy is usually experienced, you may wish to try showering together or caressing each other in another room of the house. You may want to introduce oral sex to the experience. If this is new, talk about it. Most people find mouth-genital contact pleasant when they feel clean and comfortable. If you or your partner doesn't, forget it.

If erection occurs during this stage, it is meant to be enjoyed. Many couples are tempted to rush into intercourse as soon as there is an erection. Don't make this mistake. Arousal does not *need* to be present and should not, in Stage 3, result in intercourse or orgasm. Erections come and go; they are not precious. If the man experiences erection, there is always the potential for many more.

Stage 3 encourages both of you to experience leisurely the joy of erotic sensations without demands placed upon either of you. Continue to discover the wide range of pleasurable sexual experiences without the need for an erect penis. That will become useful later. Intercourse is pleasurable, but so are hugging, holding, kissing, caressing, fondling, and stroking. Getting in touch with these possibilities adds variety to sexual expression and, perhaps more importantly, de-emphasizes the demand for erection. Now is the time to stop defining your sexual experiences in "success" and "failure" terms. If the interaction is pleasurable, you're on the way.

Stage III should be experienced several times, always followed by talking it over with your partner.

Stage 4—Waxing and waning

Stages 1 through 3 provided both of you with an increased knowledge of each other's sensual preferences. Stage 4 sharpens this new knowledge by encouraging specific communication about sensations that are most erotically pleasurable. You can expand what you have learned in the first three stages; continue to take lots of time. Communicate—verbally or by demonstrating touch nonverbally—particularly pleasant strokes, rhythms, and pressures.

Now the woman should practice stimulating the man to erection, then consciously letting it dissipate, and then restimulating. (The use of lotion or oil may be especially helpful here.) This exercise should be repeated several times in each encounter; it will help you to realize that erection is indeed a waxing and waning phenomenon and that the waning is not to be feared.

Either or both of you may want to enjoy orgasm at this stage; this is appropriate, but it should take place without intercourse. At this point, you should begin to understand that sexual pleasure is not solely intercourse.

Stage 5—Beginning intercourse

Each stage 5 experience should begin by briefly rerunning the four stages practiced previously. When the man has an erection and the woman has adequate natural lubrication, she can insert the penis into the vagina. The easiest position for most couples at this stage is female astride: the man is lying face-up and the woman places most of her weight on her knees and lower legs and straddles him, and inserts the penis. If the erection subsides, she can raise her body and restimulate the penis with her hands. If the female astride position is uncomfortable for either of you, experiment with a more comfortable one. In any case, the woman should guide the penis into the vagina. Delay having an orgasm as long as possible to fully enjoy your sexual experiences. And remember that you can have intercourse with a partial erection (you have probably noticed that you can have an orgasm that way too). So you do not need to be at your peak erectile strength to be in the vagina. Many men do not get great erections until they are in the vagina.

Repeat Stage 5 until erectile confidence is achieved.

Stage 6—Forever

Stage 6 is meant to last a lifetime. It consists of mutual exploration and discovery of the wide range of sexual experiences you are capable of sharing. When erection sometimes does not occur when desired, both of you recognize that this is normal. The man does not need to experience erection for sex to be enjoyable. If erection does not occur during several sexual encounters, a brief review of Stages 1 through 5 can refresh the reflex and restore the erection.

There is a small percentage of men for whom this process does not yield desirable results. These persons should seek the services of a qualified sex therapist. A professional organization that certifies competent sex therapists is the American Association of Sex Educators and Counselors, 5010 Wisconsin Avenue, N.W., Suite 304, Washington, D.C. 20016. This organization provides, upon request, the names of certified sex therapists.

For Men:

Controlling Premature Ejaculation

Richard L. Timmers

If you ejaculate quickly after becoming sexually aroused, congratulate yourself for having a strong physical sexual response. If you are an "average" man who grew up in the American culture, strength and speed were qualities that everyone encouraged you to cultivate. Very often those qualities were equated with maleness and became goals and expectations for you to reach for. Very few messages came through for you to relax, to slow down, to feel, and to enjoy.

Most early sexual experiences as boys and men re-enforced speedy performance. Very often we masturbated quickly because we felt we might be interrupted. Being masculine meant we should not enjoy slowly touching all of our body, exploring good feelings. When we began to share our sexuality by relating to other persons, speedy sexual response indicated, we thought, our sexual strength and vigor. Some of us even bragged about how quickly we ejaculated. We continued to be concerned about "being caught," or discovered by parents or others, as we began early sexual relationships in automobiles or living rooms. Some men worried that their erection would decrease or disappear, and, therefore, went from erection to penetration to

The sketches in this chapter were drawn by Robert Gustafson.
This article was especially written for this book.

thrusting to orgasm to assure themselves that they would be able to "perform" (a really negative word regarding the expression of our sexuality).

Much of man's "maleness" has been assigned to his erect penis. In reality, he needs only to feel confident that he never has to do anything with his erection except enjoy pleasurable feelings. During extended sex play, the penis of most men softens then hardens, softens then hardens. Begin to relax and enjoy those pleasurable feelings. If you do not have a firm erection when you wish to enter the vagina, it simply means that your head and body need more stimulation. You will naturally re-erect. These anxieties with the concern about what we are doing and how well we are doing it encourage rapid ejaculation, setting a pattern so that even when time and privacy are maximized, a man still ejaculates before he wants to.

Basically, a man learns how to ejaculate quickly and easily gets in a pattern. But the pattern can be broken. He can unlearn rapid ejaculation and learn ways of delaying ejaculation so that he may enjoy being at a high level of sexual arousal for a longer period of time prior to going on to orgasm and ejaculation.

Premature ejaculation is best defined by the man and the feedback of his partner or partners. Quite simply stated, a man is a premature ejaculator if he experiences orgasm before he and his partner want him to. For one man that may mean he has an orgasm before he touches himself or his partner, for another it may mean genital contact for 10 minutes or longer.

Once a man labels himself as a premature ejaculator, his anxiety starts a series of astounding behaviors based on stories he has heard and read. He feels that he has no control over his ejaculation, so first he makes sure that he and/or his partner do not stimulate his genitals too much or he will have even less control (or so he thinks), thus denying himself and his partner pleasure. His anxiety grows, which compounds the problem. Now he begins to think nonsexual thoughts so as not to be too "turned on" (more denial of pleasure); or he counts backward from 100, trying to make it down to 94. He only proves to himself that he can count backward while breathing heavily — for awhile. He might rub some "over-the-counter" cream or ointment on the head of his penis to desensitize that area. Although the cream usually does not delay ejaculation, it might desensitize his partner. As another resort he might put three or four condoms on his penis, succeeding only in increased stock dividends for the company that makes them. He might try to divert his attention by pinching his arm or leg. If he continues to feel anxious about his prematurity, the behavior continues and he may begin to experience erectile difficulties.

WHY DELAY

There are varying estimates concerning the amount of time a man is able to maintain thrusting, while his penis is in a woman's vagina, before ejaculation. The most often mentioned statistic indicates that about 75 percent of men ejaculate from in a few seconds to more than two minutes. Many men, in addition to enjoying a high level of sexual arousal for a longer period of time, also enjoy the physical and emotional sensations of being inside the vagina for a longer period of time before orgasm and ejaculation. It is also true that many women enjoy enveloping a penis for longer period of time.

Make a decision about whether or not you wish to last longer *for you*. It makes more sense to last longer because you want to rather than because someone else wants you to. Try on the thought that you would like to learn to last longer for you, first, and second for someone else's pleasure. Explore, understand, and meet your own needs before you make efforts to explore, understand, and meet someone else's needs. Until you are knowledgeable about and comfortable with expressing your own needs to yourself, you will find more difficulty in sharing an intimate experience with another person. Thus, you assume an attitude of self-representation, not selfishness, and encourage a similar self-representation on the part of your partner. You may then optimize the learning that takes place between the two of you.

HOW TO LEARN TO DELAY BY YOURSELF

First of all, you *can* learn to delay ejaculation. Give yourself permission to unlearn some behaviors and to learn new ones. Start by telling yourself that you would like to learn more about your own sexual response, alone, by yourself—without interruption and/or concern for meeting others' needs for the moment. Put aside all the old messages about not touching your own body. Stop thinking that self-pleasuring is a substitute for being sexual with others. It can be, but so can eating or reading become substitutes for relationships with others. Begin to consider self-pleasuring as an adjunct to sharing your sexuality with others, as well as a behavior one does with oneself simply because it feels good.[1]

[1] Richard L. Timmers, *Self Pleasuring for Men* (Madison, Wis.: Midwest Sexual Counseling Center, 1975).

Begin to explore your body all over, not just your penis and testicles. Take time for yourself. Slow down your touch and your movements. Move your hands circularly and touch with varying degrees of firmness—stroke lightly, caress, squeeze. As your penis and scrotal sack begin to engorge with blood and become firmer, put some body oil or lotion on them and notice the similar feeling to the well-lubricated vaginal barrel, or touch yourself in a shower and use slippery soap on your genitals for the same sensation. Begin to recognize your point of no return, that special feeling you get when you are at peak arousal, are about to have an orgasm, and know that nothing—nothing—will stop you from having an orgasm.

Now become aware of the three to eight-second time interval that comes just before your point of no return. Stop all stimulation when you sense yourself in the time period before your point of no return. Let part or all of your erection decrease. Retouch your body and bring yourself to that period before your point of no return again. Use this stop/start technique[2] three times before going on to orgasm. You have already delayed orgasm.

Begin to be more assertive with the stimulation of your penis, stroke hard and then vary the pressure. Usually when men are in high arousal states for longer periods of time, they notice a few drops of crystal clear fluid oozing from the penis. This fluid, which neutralizes your urethra to make a better environment for the eventual delivery of sperm, is from the Cowper's Glands. It often contains some sperm. As you stroke your penis, *concentrate on the feelings in your genitals.* Men who cannot delay orgasm usually try to distract themselves from genital feelings to suppress good feelings. Now think only about the feelings in your genitals. As you reach that time period *before* your point of no return, stop, let part of your erection decrease, and begin again to stimulate yourself. Practice this at least three times before orgasm. Then practice the whole technique three to six times over a week or two to reenforce your comfort and success with it.

Now you are ready to learn two squeeze techniques for delaying ejaculation that were developed and expanded by Masters and Johnson.[3] Figure 1 shows how your partner would apply the frenulum squeeze. You will need to practice this squeeze on yourself. It is somewhat awkward to do on yourself, but it is possible. Use the squeeze on yourself right after having an erection so that you will be comfortable with the proper placement of your fingers and with the fact that you can really squeeze your penis hard when you do it this way.

After learning the technique, begin self-pleasuring until you are in the time period *before* your point of no return and then apply the squeeze tech-

---

[2]James H. Seman, "Premature Ejaculation: A New Approach," *Southern Medical Journal* (April 1956).

[3]William Masters and Virginia Johnson, *Human Sexual Inadequacy* (Boston: Little, Brown and Company, 1970).

Figure 1.   Frenulum squeeze technique

nique on yourself. You may need to use both hands to apply sufficient pressure.

Squeeze hard for 10 to 20 seconds, then release. This will cause you to lose your feeling of urgency to ejaculate, you may also lose 20 to 30 percent of your erection. After 15 to 30 seconds, restimulate yourself to erection and use the squeeze again to decrease your need to ejaculate. Do this at least three times before going on to orgasm and ejaculation. After practicing this procedure for at least a week (and at least three times during the week), you will want to learn the bulbar squeeze.

The bulbar squeeze is based on the same principle as the frenulum squeeze, but it is applied to the ventral bulb at the base and underside of your penis, just above the scrotal sack (see Figure 2). Teach yourself the bulbar squeeze in the same way in which you taught yourself the frenulum squeeze. Use oils or lotions on your penis while stimulating yourself to duplicate the feeling of the vaginal barrel.

As a result of using the squeeze techniques, you will experience an extended period of direct genital stimulation before ejaculation. You will have begun to break your pattern of rapid ejaculation. Remember to concentrate on genital feelings while practicing the squeeze techniques on yourself.

HOW TO LEARN TO DELAY WITH A PARTNER

You will need to discuss with your partner her desire to have you last longer and her willingness to participate in helping you to do so. Assuring yourselves that premature ejaculation is a reversible behavior pattern gives you and your

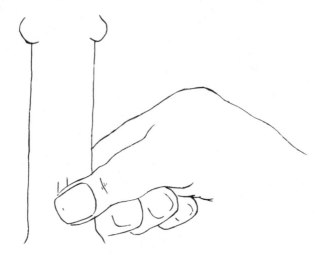

Figure 2.   Bulbar squeeze technique

partner an enormous amount of confidence and support and will help to reduce your mutual anxiety levels. You have already experienced success in learning to delay your ejaculation by yourself and have learned several techniques that you will be explaining to your partner.

With intercourse *prohibited* (to remove any anxieties about having to perform; *do not* cheat on this prohibition), you and your partner are to proceed with a nongenital touching experience and then a genital touching experience. On three separate occasions the two of you should set aside at least an hour's time and have a nongenital touching experience. Your partner lies on the floor or bed, nude and you begin to touch her body all over, except her breasts and vaginal area. You touch her in varied ways, circularly, with soft pressure and hard pressure, squeeze and caress. You touch her to discover what she feels like *to you.* She tells you only if your touch hurts, is irritable, or tickles. You concentrate on what *you* are feeling while you are touching her. Do this for at least a half an hour before you change off and she touches you in the same nondemand way, excluding your nipples and genital area. Repeat this experience until you are both comfortable. You may wish to use nonalcohol-based edible oils or lotions while doing the touching.

Once you are both comfortable with the series of nongenital touching experiences, do the same thing, this time adding the genitals to your touching. If she becomes aroused, move away from that area and return to it in a few moments. If you become aroused while she is touching you, she should move away from that area and return to it in a few moments. You should repeat this genital touching experience at least three times and until you are both comfortable with the experience.[4]

If either of you is highly aroused after a touching experience, it is possible for you to separate and bring yourselves to orgasm in private, bring yourselves to orgasm while in each other's presence, or bring each other to orgasm manually. Do not have penis/vagina contact at this time. The experiences will encourage you both to explore and touch each other, first to find out what feels good for yourself and then to interpret that to your partner. You will both discover that your penis can be touched, that it feels good, and that you do not ejaculate.

Once you are comfortable with the genital touching experiences, practice the squeeze techniques. Your partner sits up in bed or on the floor. You lie on your back facing her. Position your body between her legs. Place your feet on the outside of her thighs (see Figure 3). She caresses your genitals to encourage an erection. You simply lie back and relax as she does so. You will need to show her how to do the frenulum squeeze[5] after you have an erection so that she may practice the technique. You may also have to demonstrate to her that squeezing hard on your penis in this way, when you are erect, does not hurt you. After she knows the squeeze technique, you tell her just before your point of "no return." If you have your hands resting on her legs to steady

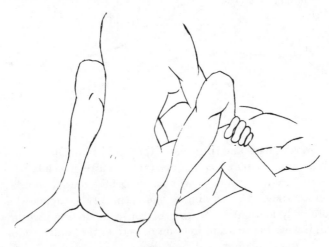

Figure 3.

[4]This is a summary of a technique described by William Masters and Virginia Johnson at a symposium (July 16-17, 1973) at the Reproductive Biology Research Foundation, St. Louis, at which the author was present.

[5]Masters and Johnson, *Human Sexual Inadequacy*, pp. 92-115.

her or to maintain body contact, you may squeeze her leg to tell her you are almost there . . . or you may simply shout "now." She then applies the frenulum squeeze. She squeezes hard for 10 to 20 seconds, then releases the pressure. She may have to use two hands. After 15 to 30 seconds she stimulates you to erection and uses the squeeze technique again. By using the frenulum squeeze it is possible for you both to have 15 to 20 minutes of continuous sex play without ejaculation. To make sure that your partner understands the squeeze technique, you may wish to refer again to Figure 1. When you have comfortably accomplished this procedure, teach your partner the bulbar squeeze (show her Figure 2).[6] Demonstrate it for her. When she is familiar with the technique, she assumes the position shown in Figure 4.

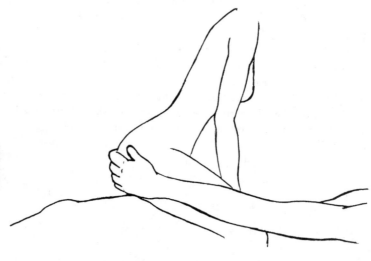

Figure 4.

You lie on your back and she squats over you to stimulate you to erection. She needs also to be aroused so that her vaginal barrel is well lubricated. She leans forward to envelop your penis by moving back onto it with her vaginal barrel. Concentrate on the feeling of your penis in the vagina while she remains absolutely motionless. Neither of you is to do any thrusting at this time. This is what Masters and Johnson refer to as the "quiet vagina." If you feel the urge to ejaculate, signal your partner. She raises her body slightly, reaches down, and applies the bulbar squeeze. She pauses for 30 seconds, restimulates you, and envelops the penis again. You need to practice this three or four times during each session. Once you can control your ejaculation

[6]Ibid., pp. 92-115.
[7]Ibid., pp. 106-108.

in this manner, you may ask your partner to begin slow circular and in-and-out movements sufficient for you to maintain your erection and for her to explore her vaginal feelings. Practice the squeeze at least three times. Then if you both wish, proceed to orgasm and/or practice a few stop/start techniques prior to going on to orgasm and ejaculation.

After this stage is comfortably mastered, you may try slow thrusting, using the squeeze until you wish to have an orgasm. By being able to last 15 to 20 minutes longer in this position, you slowly, with practice, gain more time and more control without the squeeze. As control increases, you may try having your partner lie on top of you, a position that gives her the most possible freedom for experimentation and offers the best ejaculatory control for you. Couples are usually unaware that the man above position is the most difficult one in which to gain ejaculatory control since the man is building muscle tension in his body in addition to sexual and genital muscle tension.

Continue the squeeze technique at least once a week for six months or whenever sexual tensions are higher for you. It usually takes about six months before complete ejaculatory control is accomplished.

Of major importance in learning to delay orgasm is a reduction of anxiety regarding what you are doing and how well you are doing it. Self-knowledge about your own body and the need for nondemand pleasuring experiences are vital components in restructuring your attitudes about sharing your sexuality with another person. Communication with a partner that represents *your* feelings, attitudes, and needs will encourage a similar self-representation from your partner — thus enhancing your total sexual relationship.

For Women:
Reaching Orgasm

Jane Rea James

Without emotional closeness, sex can seem mechanical. Without orgasm sex can become physically and emotionally frustrating. Any woman who achieves orgasm by any means at all is orgasmic, even though her wish may be to reach orgasm in intercourse. Orgasmic behavior includes orgasm in sleep, orgasm through fantasies, or orgasm with one's self (masturbation). With few exceptions, all women are capable of orgasm. Those few have physical disabilities that prevent orgasm.

This chapter is specifically directed to the woman who wants to become orgasmic, more so than she is at present. It contains a detailed program to help each woman experience and enjoy orgasm, by starting with responsibility for her own orgasmic response.

SEXUAL ANATOMY

We learn about the reproductive parts of our bodies in school, but not the sexual aspects. To accept responsibility for our bodies, we need to know our

This article was especially written for this book.

sexual anatomy, where the parts are and what they do.[1] Two very important areas in the female are the clitoris and the pubococcygeus muscle.

The clitoris has no purpose other than for physical excitement. It is full of nerve endings and is very sensitive. There is no lubrication around the clitoris. Anytime that area is touched, make sure that it is wet or, because it is so sensitive, it may hurt. Use some sort of oil or lotion, or the natural lubrication from your moist vagina. Each woman's clitoris is different in size from that of any other woman, just as each woman's valva (vagina) looks different from any other one. It is not the way it looks (big, small, fat, thin) that is important, but how well it serves its purpose — physical excitement.

The pubococcygeus (P.C.) muscle is located two finger-joints deep inside the vaginal opening. With arousal, this muscle draws tight, helping the woman to feel more sensations inside her vagina. A woman can learn to exercise this muscle to improve her control over it.

POSSIBLE PHYSICAL PROBLEMS

Check very carefully the clitoris, clitoral hood, and the P.C. muscle for any physical problems that may inhibit orgasm.

Clitoral adhesions. Some women, because they are totally unaware of their clitoral area or because they do not realize the importance of keeping the area clean, have allowed the clitoral hood to become stuck to the clitoris. Using a mirror if necessary, check yourself by pulling back the fold of skin at the top of the inner lips to uncover your clitoris (see Figure 1). It should look like the smooth top of your little finger. If the skin does not move off the clitoris, the hood is stuck to it. Some physicians believe that this makes it more difficult for a woman to feel clitoral stimulation, because the hood cannot move freely over the clitoris. Others give it no great significance. Check the clitoral area anyway. If you find strong adhesions, consider having them surgically freed.[2] Remember, you clitoris has no other physiological function except for sexual pleasure and excitation. Although some women have orgasms through fantasy alone, it helps greatly to have one's body in the best possible physical shape.

---

[1]For further detailed information on sexual anatomy, see Fred Belliveau and Lin Richter, *Understanding Human Sexual Inadequacy* (New York: Bantam Books, 1970), Chapter 5.

[2]Helen Singer Kaplan. *The New Sex Therapy* (New York: Brunner/Mazel, 1974), p. 72.

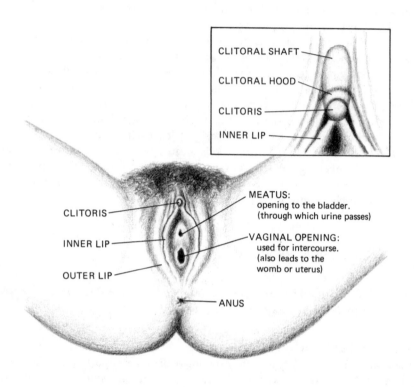

Figure 1.

Poor P.C. muscle tone.[3] You can check your own P.C. muscle by inserting one or two lubricated fingers into the vaginal opening and squeezing with the muscle. If you don't feel any pressure around your fingers, then you need exercise. Another way to check the muscle is to spread your knees widely apart when you are urinating and try to stop the flow. If you can do so, you are using your P.C. muscle. Each contraction exercises the P.C. muscle.

P.C. muscle exercises.   Inserting a tampax during the exercise may help you feel the muscle as it tightens around the tube. Hold one hand on your stomach to make sure you are not contracting the stomach muscles. In con-

[3]Dr. Arnold Kegel worked with women exhibiting poor PC muscle tone. His exercises form the nucleus of the following suggestions. For further information, see Lonnie Barback, *For Yourself: The Fulfillment of Female Sexuality* (New York: Doubleday & Co., Inc., 1975), pp. 53–56.

tracting the P.C. muscle, you also are contracting your buttocks and the anus.

1. Tighten your muscle slowly. When you are squeezing as hard as you can, hold it for a count of three, then give a final short squeeze.
2. Relax the muscle, count to three, then relax it again.
3. It is important to squeeze the P.C. muscle as hard as you can, and then to relax it.
4. Begin with 10 contractions in a row six times per day. Have one session before getting out of bed in the morning, four during the day, and one after going to bed. The sessions should be done either lying flat or standing.

You should be doing a total of 300 contractions a day in approximately two to four weeks. The exercises should be continued steadily for six to eight weeks (longer for women with especially weak P.C. muscles). Once in tone, the exercises may be discontinued except for a once-a-week practice session. You will want to use the muscle often during self-stimulation as well as when you are with a partner, for both your own and your partner's pleasure. Doing some squeezes before you begin any sexual activity increases your feelings in your vagina.

WHAT IS ORGASM?

Clinically, orgasm is the very pleasurable feeling caused by the release of entrapped blood and the relaxing of tense muscles.[4] Orgasm is felt in both the P.C. muscle and the clitoris. There is no such thing as just a vaginal or a clitoral orgasm. If the woman is stimulating just the clitoral area, she may feel as though only the clitoris is reacting — tingling, feeling hot, feeling full. If the woman is being touched or touching herself around the vaginal opening at orgasm, she may be most aware of the grasping action of the P.C. muscle inside the opening.

When a woman is really excited, she may become aware of a tightening of muscles throughout her body, and then a sense of relaxation and peace. That could be what is called a low-level orgasm. All she feels is the difference between being very excited and then feeling very good. With practice, that kind of orgasm becomes stronger. The more stimulation a woman receives, the more sexual tension she has throughout her body, and the more likely she is to have an orgasm.

---

[4]William Masters and Virginia Johnson, *Human Sexual Response* (Boston: Little, Brown and Company, 1966), p. 6.

THE CHOICE

A woman can have her first orgasm with her partner or alone. It is more difficult to be orgasmic with a partner the first time, for some of the following reasons:

1. The one person who will most quickly respond to your requests for certain strokes or touches is you. It is easier for you first to explore your own body for pleasurable sensations than to complicate the situation by adding another person.

2. Whatever your responses will be to your own actions, fantasies, or sounds, since you will be alone, only you yourself will be witness to them.

3. Until we first know our own bodies by self-exploration and examination, we cannot expect our partners magically to discover the answers to arousing us.

THE PROGRAM

Practice your P.C. muscle exercises. *Relax.* The most important message of this entire program is not to push yourself, but to give yourself time to get used to and enjoy pleasuring yourself. You should be completely comfortable with each step before going on to the next one. You can *choose* to learn about your body and to experience your own orgasm.

Step 1. A shower or bath first is helpful, and complete privacy is essential in creating a mood in which you can relax. You may want to shower in the dark first, to begin learning about how your body feels as you touch it, rather than going through the usual quick bathing routine. Try using a body lotion after bathing, and as you rub it on, touch carefully and slowly all parts of your body. Again, using a hand mirror to examine your genitals closely, identify the various areas from Figure 1.

Step 2. You may wish to use reading material to arouse yourself prior to and/or while you are self-pleasuring. It may help to keep your mind off negative messages about touching your body, and may suggest fantasies that may be exciting for you. *Fanny Hill,*[5] *The Pearl,*[6] and *My Secret Garden*[7] are ex-

---

[5] John Cleland, *Fanny Hill* (New York: G.P. Putnam's Sons, 1963).
[6] *The Pearl* (New York: Grove Press, 1968).
[7] Nancy Friday, *My Secret Garden* (New York: Pocket Books, 1974).

amples of literature that have been helpful to some women. Give yourself permission and time to get used to and enjoy pleasuring yourself. Allow yourself time to become familiar with touching your genitals. At the beginning you may or may not find your touch sexually arousing—either reaction is fine.

Step 3.   As you caress yourself, you may want to use a body lotion or oil. Be sure whatever you choose has no alcohol in it, alcohol will sting on the genital area.

Step 4.   Through touching, locate the sensitive and pleasurable areas of your vagina and breasts. Explore your nipples, your clitoral shaft and hood, inner and outer lips, and your vaginal opening and perineum (the area around and between your vagina and anus). Experiment with varied pressures and differing motions. Stimulation of the breast and nipples by oneself usually feels good. Some women enjoy light gentle strokes, some like firmer caresses around the nipples, and some like tugging motions. Every woman has some sensation in her breasts, but not all women are aware of it.

Step 5.   Remember, the clitoris, unlike the vaginal opening and inner area, has no natural lubrication even when you are aroused. Do not touch the head of your clitoris directly if it causes discomfort. There are many nerve endings throughout the clitoral head and, for some women, direct rubbing may be too extreme a sensation. Try rubbing around the head of the clitoris, through the hood, and around the inner lips. Allow your feelings to build slowly at a comfortable pace for you.

Step 6.   Consciously contract your P.C. muscle and buttocks slowly during stimulation. You may wish to move from light to heavy pressure and more intense stroking, or circular rubbing. Some women use one or two fingers (others use the pressure of both hands) to stimulate the clitoris, vaginal opening, or inner lips. As you are caressing the clitoral area, continue contracting your P.C. muscle and buttocks, holding the tension for at least three or four seconds or more if it is pleasurable. By consciously tightening and relaxing this muscle, you increase your level of arousal. Once you have started to become aroused, stimulating the muscle with your fingers or a vibrator is usually extremely pleasurable. In some cases, if the simulation is continued long enough and if you use different pressures on the muscle, you can bring on your first orgasm.

Step 7.   Continue each experience as long as the sensation is pleasurable or until you become tired. Your first orgasm may take three seconds of stimulation or as long as 45 minutes to an hour, so don't become too easily discouraged. Allow for daily 45-minute sessions. *Relax*. Don't concentrate on a goal, enjoy the pleasurable feelings you can give to and get from yourself. Remember, it is impossible to will an orgasm, orgasm is a natural body function and will happen—if you let it.

ORGASM WITH ONE'S PARTNER

For many of us, orgasm does not occur because we give up too soon. We can easily ask someone to scratch a specific area on our back and give very detailed directions, but we have a hard time asking that same person to touch or stimulate us sexually in a particular way. Learning to share your orgasms with your partner means just that—*learning*. Once you are easily orgasmic with yourself, you have to practice telling your partner what you need from him. Share the information that you are already orgasmic. It may be hard for you to say to him, but you will be surprised how relieved he may be to find out that he does not have to make you orgasmic. Realize that communication takes patience on both your parts as you both learn to talk in detail about what you want sexually.

Step 1.   Take time to look carefully at each other's genitals. Show your partner where your clitoris is and tell him what areas of your vagina feel especially good when touched. Let him tell and show you how he likes to be touched.

Step 2.   Have your partner turn away from you on the bed and, if necessary, have him put a pillow over his head so he can't hear or see you. With him present but not watching, bring yourself to orgasm. Realize that this behavior is *very* new to you and it may take a long time (perhaps an hour) to reach orgasm the first few sessions. Have him do the same thing with you present.

Step 3.   Once you both have experienced orgasms in each other's presence, but not in each other's view, self-stimulate to orgasm in each other's sight. Remember, you are learning to be more relaxed and open with your own and your partner's behaviors. When you are both able to be orgasmic in each other's presence, you are then ready to begin bridging over to orgasms with intercourse.

Step 4.   Find an intercourse position that is comfortable for the two of you to maintain for a prolonged period of time — a position where the penis is inserted in the vagina but neither of you need to move. You might want to try the woman-on-top position as one of the easiest ways (see Figure 11-2). Once your partner has an erection *and* you are excited enough to be lubricating, insert his penis into your vaginal opening. Grip with your P.C. muscle (which should be very strong by now) and then by touching your clitoris, bring yourself to orgasm while enveloping him. He is not to move.

Take as much time as you need to explore these new sensations while his penis is inside you. If he loses his erection, don't worry; simply restimulate his genitals until the erection returns. Also, if you are not able to have an orgasm the first few times, again don't worry. Your body has to get used to the sensation of something inside the vaginal barrel. You will be able, given time and patience, to experience orgasm in this position. Allow yourself the time; enjoy what feeling you *do* get, and eventually orgasm will occur. You can still share orgasms in the other ways already described in this chapter while experimenting with this new behavior. *Don't* get stuck on only one way of being orgasmic; that can become very boring!

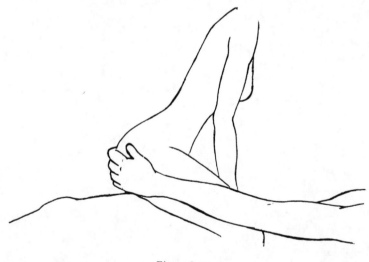

Figure 2.

Step 5.   You can now start telling your partner to begin his thrusting just as you bring yourself to orgasm. Slowly his thrusting may replace your stimulating yourself, and you may need less direct clitoral stimulation.

Remember the statement at the beginning of this chapter — an orgasm is an orgasm, and *how* it occurs is less important than the fact that you make sure it *does* occur in some way. Sharing orgasms does not mean that it can *only* be done through intercourse. Be gentle with yourself. If you just concentrate on enjoying and increasing your pleasurable sexual feelings, orgasm will happen. It may not happen today or tomorrow, but it will happen in the near future.

Protecting Yourself
from Unwanted Parenthood

Sol Gordon
Roger Conant

GOOD REASONS FOR KNOWING HOW TO PREVENT PREGNANCY

Lying in bed one morning, Candy feels like she's just swallowed a frog. She thinks, "Wow, it's been six weeks since I had my period. But I *can't* be pregnant! I only had sex with Tom a couple of times and for just a few minutes! It can't be *that* easy to get pregnant!"

Add Candy to the more than 600,000 teen-agers who become pregnant each year. The next few months will probably read like a soap opera — heartaches, embarrassment, maybe a forced marriage, dropping out of school or the hassle of an abortion, and a whole new set of responsibilities that neither Candy nor Tom is ready for.

It is too bad that so many young people have to go through all of this when pregnancy can be easily and safely prevented. Whatever *you* do, can you accept the idea that it is wrong to bring an unwanted child into the world? Many children grow up emotionally disturbed, roughly treated, and poorly cared

This article is reprinted from an educational comic book entitled *Protect Yourself From Becoming an Unwanted Parent.* Reprint permission gratefully has been received from the authors and Ed-U Press, 760 Ostrom Ave., Syracuse, N.Y. The illustrations for this 1973 copyright educational comic book have been deleted.

for because their parents, whether they know it or not, are angry at them for being born. Sometimes a baby who starts out unwanted does later become wanted, but many times that doesn't happen. If a girl has one baby and finishes school, things may work out. But an unwed mother who doesn't finish high school and has more babies may find herself on welfare, and the children don't have much of a life to look forward to.

HAVE SEX OR NOT?

If you have sex before you're ready for it, you may have a confused, unhappy experience, which could harm your future sex life. If your partner doesn't care about you, or if you don't care about your partner, sex with that person is really a drag. If you use sex as a way of trying to "prove" that you are manly or womanly, then you are an exploiter, not a lover. An exploiter is a person who uses another person. The exploiter usually screws himself or herself up at the same time that he or she is not caring about someone else.

Of course, we know that many young people will have sex, no matter what any adults think they should or should not do. If you do decide to be sexually active, at least learn to protect yourself from unwanted pregnancy (as well as unwanted venereal disease).

A person who feels unsure about him- or herself may try to talk others into having sex—for his or her own selfish reasons. Such people don't consider the other person's needs.

People who brag about their sex experiences are usually lying, and they don't enjoy sex much at all. If they enjoyed what they were doing, they would keep it private (once in a while they might talk it over with a close friend). People who are always "on the make" may not know it, but they don't like the opposite sex. And they really don't like themselves much either.

WHY KIDS SHOULDN'T HAVE KIDS

The mortality rate for babies born of mothers under 18 years of age is high.

The younger the mother, the greater the health risks—for her and her baby. The risks include prematurity, low birth weight, and difficult labor, as well as serious illness in mother and child.

Teen-age mothers try suicide more often than do people in other groups.

Half of teen marriages end in divorce.

Unwed fathers, many of whom experience great guilt, suffer emotionally and often financially.

If you enjoy your own growing-up years, you are more likely to enjoy your own children later and have a good relationship with them. Parenthood should be a satisfying experience, not a burden.

PREGNANCY AND CONTRACEPTION

An amazing number of men and women—old, young, married, unmarried, childless, or parents—do not know or understand the basic, simple facts regarding pregnancy and contraception. For instance: after a girl has her first menstrual period (usually somewhere between the ages of 11 and 15), she is able to become pregnant. Almost from the time a boy has his first erection (between the ages of 11 and 15 usually) and ejaculates, he is able to father a child.

There is no 100 percent safe time when a girl can have intercourse without risking pregnancy. But, in general, if a girl's periods are regular, she probably won't get pregnant if she has sex during her period or two or three days before or after it. However, it doesn't take much to throw off her regularity—even simple tension can (and does) do it. She can get pregnant the first time she has sexual intercourse, and whether or not she experiences any sexual feelings during intercourse.

Sometime between one menstrual period and the next, a tiny egg is released from one of the ovaries.[1] It passes through one of the Fallopian tubes into the uterus (womb). If a woman has intercourse within two or three days before or after the egg is released, some of the man's sperm cells can meet inside the egg, fertilizing it. The fertilized egg then travels the rest of the way down the tube and attaches itself to the lining of the uterus—and pregnancy begins. If the egg is not fertilized, it falls apart in the Fallopian tube.

Methods to prevent pregnancy and still have sex are known as contraception (or birth control). The best contraception works in one of these ways:

The sperm can be blocked from reaching the egg cell if the male correctly wears a condom on his penis during intercourse, or if the female has been properly fitted by a doctor with a diaphragm.

Contraceptive creams, foams, and jellies destroy the sperm cells before they can reach the egg.

The Pill stops the egg from developing; no egg is released into the Fallopian tube where a sperm cell can fertilize it.

Many scientists think that the IUD (intrauterine device) placed inside the uterus prevents the fertilized egg from attaching itself to the wall of the

---

[1]The egg is released about 14 days before the next period is due, if the periods are regular. If a girl's periods are not regular, the egg may be released at a different time of the month. Some girls may release more than one egg during a month.

uterus. The experts are not sure about this, but they do know that the device works very well in preventing pregnancy.

Douching (washing out the vagina) after intercourse—no matter with what—does not prevent pregnancy. The male sperm cells do not take long to get from the vagina to the Fallopian tubes. Douching before intercourse does not prevent pregnancy either.

Feminine hygiene sprays and suppositories—such as Norforms, Pristeen, Feminique—are mainly deodorants, not contraceptives. (And since the vagina cleans itself naturally, they are not necessary for cleanliness.) Anything that is not sold as a contraceptive (such as Saran Wrap, Coca-Cola, balloons) *is not a birth control device.* Some people are good at telling others how to avoid pregnancy. Believe them, and, if you are having sex, you risk becoming a parent.

Following are some of the ways, with varying degrees of security, to prevent pregnancy:

Although not generally recommended, *withdrawal* and *rhythm* "sometimes" work and are better than nothing. However, withdrawal cannot be trusted. Even if the male can control himself and stop himself from ejaculating inside the female, some of the sperm cells can leak out before ejaculation and can fertilize the egg. Even if he releases his sperm outside the vagina, it is still possible for her to become pregnant. If sperm get into the moisture around the vagina, they can swim on up to join the egg.

The rhythm method is based on the idea that a woman can have sex except around that time when, supposedly, the egg is released. This method is not very good because very few women are so regular in their periods that they can always figure out for sure when the egg will be released.

The Pill. In general, if a girl has been menstruating for at least a year, the Pill is one possible method to prevent pregnancy. The doctor will help her to decide which type of pregnancy prevention is best. For medical reasons, some girls should not use the Pill.

There are different types of contraceptive pills and one kind of pill might affect your body differently than another. That is why you should not use someone else's pills. The doctor will know which pill is right for you and he or she will go over the instructions with you. A girl can get contraceptive pills from her own doctor, a Planned Parenthood Center, or a family planning clinic.

Taking one or two pills a month is no help. They must be used as directed. If you forget to take a pill, you should call your doctor.

Diaphragms. The diaphragm comes in different sizes and must be fitted by a doctor who will explain how to use it. It is a rubber cup that fits inside the vagina and covers the cervix (opening to the uterus), blocking the sperm from getting through. It must be used with a jelly or cream; the doctor can tell you which kind to buy. They[2] can be bought without a prescription in drugstores. If the jelly or cream you are using irritates your skin, try another brand. If it still bothers you, call your doctor.

The diaphragm must be inserted before intercourse. The jelly or cream is best inserted not more than half an hour before. This can be done with a special applicator if the diaphragm has already been inserted. Cream and jelly lose their effectiveness about one hour after insertion.

If you do not have intercourse within half an hour after the cream or jelly has been inserted, or if you have sex again after that time, you must apply it again. The diaphragm must be left inside the vagina for at least six hours after intercourse.

The diaphragm does not hurt. If it is properly inserted, you cannot feel it when it is inside. And neither can your partner. It does not lessen sexual pleasure.

The IUD (intrauterine device). "Loop," "coil," "shield" are the names of some kinds of IUDs. A doctor places this small device (usually made of soft plastic) inside the uterus; the doctor can also easily remove it at any time.

Menstrual periods may be heavier, last longer, and be closer together for the first few months (and sometimes longer) after a woman starts to use the IUD. It does not lessen sexual pleasure, and it cannot be felt once it is inserted.

Many young people find it difficult to get the Pill, a diaphragm or IUD (and some people simply don't want to use them). In that case, the male may use a *condom* and the female may use *foam.* When used together, chances of pregnancy are much less than if only one is used.

Condoms (also known as rubbers, safes, and by other names) can be bought without a prescription in drugstores. Some Planned Parenthood Centers, health departments, and street clinics supply them. If you are embarrassed about asking for contraceptives, go to a drugstore where you are not known. You might even want to wait to be served by a clerk of your own sex. Most clerks are used to people who feel uncomfortable about this and will know how to serve you.

When buying condoms, ask for a brand name, such as Trojan, Ramses, or Sheik. They are sold in a pack of 3, 6, or 12 (lubricated or regular).

Condoms are not only useful in preventing pregnancy, but they are also very effective in blocking venereal disease (VD) germs from passing from one partner to another—although not 100 percent of the time. The man protects

---

[2]Refering to creams and jellies; a diaphragm cannot be bought without a prescription.

himself from catching VD (such as syphilis and gonorrhea) from his partner and he protects his partner from catching it from him. (You cannot always tell if you have VD, and you can hardly ever tell if someone else has it. Males usually can tell if they have VD, but females usually cannot.)

Some men claim they experience no sexual feeling when using a condom. But that is not true. If the woman is not using a contraceptive, she should insist that her partner use a condom. Even if she is using a contraceptive, the male should use a condom for protection against VD, unless they are both very sure of each other.

To use a condom: *Before intercourse,* pull the condom over the head of the erect penis. Leave a ½" space at the end. (Some condoms already come prepared with this space.) Slowly unroll the condom until the entire penis has been covered. *After intercourse,* slowly withdraw the penis, holding the end of the condom with one hand to prevent its sliding off.

Delfen and Emko are two names of contraceptive foams. Foam does not last long. If you do not have intercourse within a half hour after you have put it into the vagina, you must apply it again. Use one shot of foam before each act of intercourse. Apply foam by pushing the applicator down against the nozzle of the can until the applicator is filled with foam. Then insert the applicator into the vagina (as you would a tampon) and push the plunger, which squeezes the foam out and into the vagina.

Prefilled applicators, good for one application, are available for your purse. One kind is Conceptrol. Emko Prefil has an applicator that may be prefilled and stored up to seven days.

PREGNANT?

If you do miss a period and fear that you may be pregnant, go to your doctor for a pregnancy test. If you are pregnant, the pregnancy test will show up positive 14 days after the first expected day of your last missed period or 42 days after the first day of your last actual period. The longer you wait, the more upset you will feel. The longer you wait, the less choice you may have about what to do.

If you find that you are pregnant, you might want the help of trained counselors at places such as Planned Parenthood, Birthright, and family planning clinics. If you need financial help, they may be able to send you to a place where you can get it. Once you have decided what to do about your pregnancy, they will be able to tell you where to go. For instance, if you decide that you want to have the baby, they might refer you to an agency or special school program that works with pregnant girls of your age.

If you have intercourse without good protection, go to your doctor or a family planning clinic within 48 hours after intercourse. You may be able to get a "morning after pill" that will prevent pregnancy. Caution — many doctors are reluctant to use this pill because no one is yet sure how safe it is.

HEALTH AND INFORMATION SERVICES

If you are sexually active, you should be alert for VD. If you think you might have it, tell your doctor or go to a local health department clinic. Don't let embarrassment get in the way of your cure. If VD is not treated, it can cripple mind and body and can sometimes cause sudden death. But if the disease is found early, the cure is usually quick, easy, and complete. In almost all states, minors can be seen and treated without their parents' knowledge or consent.

It is very important for young women to see a doctor at least once a year for a Pap smear (a test for cancer of the cervix), a breast exam, and a blood pressure count. A girl with high blood pressure, for example, should not use the Pill.

It is difficult in many areas for young people to get the information and services they need on matters of sex and pregnancy. The best place to try first is Planned Parenthood or a hospital or health department family planning clinic. If they can't serve you, they will tell you who can. Other places to contact are a hotline, crisis center, street clinic, or free clinic. For college students, university health centers give contraception and pregnancy advice.

Coming Out of the Closet:

Discovering One's Homosexual Identity

Steven E. Webster

Until recent years Western religion, science, and psychology have regarded homosexuality as sinful, perverse, aberrant, and indicative of mental illness. Over the last 20 to 30 years new information has been coming to light; people have begun talking about a once-forbidden subject, and ideas and beliefs have been changing dramatically. To be sure, there are still many persons and institutions who regard homosexuality as sinful or abhorrent and mental health professionals who maintain that homosexuality is maladaptive or sick, but there are clear signs that the mental health professions are changing. On December 15, 1973, the American Psychiatric Association declared that homosexuality per se does not constitute a mental illness. On January 24, 1975, the American Psychological Association followed the psychiatrists lead and adopted the following resolution:

Homosexuality per se implies no impairment in judgment, stability, reliability, or general social or vocational capabilities.

Further, the American Psychological Association urges all mental health professionals to take the lead in removing the stigma of mental illness that has long been associated with homosexual orientations.[1]

This article was especially written for this book.
[1] American Psychological Association, press release, January 24, 1975.

It is being discovered that homosexuality is not an affliction of a few miserable "perverts," but that a substantial percentage of persons are homosexual by preference and that a larger group, although primarily heterosexual in orientation, have experienced homosexual feelings or have been sexually involved with persons of the same sex.[2] The realization is dawning that if we are fully to understand human beings, their affections, their loves, and their sex drives, we must begin to treat homosexuality with the same interest, caring, and openness with which we have begun (so recently) to treat heterosexuality.

Still, because of the strong disapproval of homosexuality that remains in American society, individuals who become aware of homosexual feelings and/or tendencies or who have a homosexual experience are likely also to experience great emotional stress. Such an individual probably will be afraid to talk about these feelings and may repress them, or he or she might seek out a friend or counselor whom he or she believes to be open, supportive, informed, and nonjudgmental.

The object of this chapter is twofold. First, it should aid interested and caring individuals in thinking through the problems of counseling persons who are discovering homosexual feelings or tendencies. Second, it should help the reader who is struggling with some of these feelings or tendencies within him- or herself. Based upon the writer's own counseling experience, this chapter will attempt to provide some insight into the sorts of pressures a person dealing with homosexual feelings may experience and then discuss some of the key questions that may arise for persons dealing with their own homosexuality. As the sensitive reader thinks through these questions, it is hoped that he or she will be prepared to be helpful to persons in real life situations, or become more secure with a growing self-knowledge of him- or herself.

"COMING OUT"—A CRISIS OF IDENTITY

Gay people[3] describe the process of recognizing and coming to accept their homosexuality as "coming out of the closet" or simply "coming out." "Coming out" is one of the very meaningful and joyous words of the Gay Liberation Movement. Repressing (hiding in the closet) a substantial and important part

[2]Alfred Kinsey, et al., *Sexual Behavior in the Human Male* (Philadelphia: Saunders, 1948), p. 650. According to Kinsey, 13% of adult American males have been predominantly homosexual and 25% have had more than incidental homosexual experiences for at least three years between ages 16 and 55.

[3]"Gay" is the self-identifying word of the homosexual minority and has been popularized by the Gay Liberation Movement. It has been defined as "having substantial freedom from guilt, remorse, or shame about one's homosexuality."

of oneself, such as one's sexuality, can be a painful and debilitating experience, but coming out means the ability to say, "Yes, I have homosexual feelings. This is really part of me, something I can accept and feel good about."

Although coming out may be a joyous experience of self-understanding and acceptance, it can also be incredibly difficult for persons raised in our culture. It is a threatening experience to discover one's homosexual feelings because of what "being a homosexual" means in our society. Since sexuality is a very important and central facet of human personality, sexuality and sexual orientation are closely connected to one's sense of who one is.

"Who am I?" The person who is biologically male in American culture has been taught and in varying degress still is taught to answer, "I am a boy (and little boys don't cry). I am a man (and I know how to handle women). I am a husband (and I am a good provider)." The person who is biologically female has learned to answer, "I am a girl (and I like playing house). I am a young lady (I am reserved, soft, and nice). I am a wife (and my place is in the home)." There are, of course, many other roles in our culture and the male-female roles now show signs of some change, but these serve as an example of what has been called "the norm."

When a person discovers that he or she does not fit the role that is or has been expected, an identity crisis may arise. "I'm not the sort of person I thought I was/I'm supposed to be/my parents wanted me to be/my friends think I am!" When one begins to bring one's homosexual feelings out of the closet, one is confronted with society's expectations of who homosexuals are. Homosexuals are considered abnormal, deviant, perverse. People think of homosexual men as either dangerous and threatening (child-molestors, security risks, corrupters of young men) or ridiculous (faggots, sissies, fairies, queers). Likewise, homosexual women have been depicted in threatening ways as men-haters and, on one nationally broadcast television program, as murderesses. On the other hand, love between women is ridiculed. For instance, it is erroneously though that one lesbian in every couple must act as a surrogate male — dressing like a man, acting "butch," and using an artificial penis.[4] Thus, lesbianism is thought to be a second-rate substitute for the real thing, which, of course, is heterosexuality. Accordingly, one supposed cure for lesbianism, many men think, is quite simple: all a lesbian needs is to have intercourse with a *real* man.

Positive images of who homosexuals are have been in short supply. For black persons in this country to come to a positive understanding of who they

[4]Such a picture of lesbian sexuality presented in such widely read books as *Everything You Wanted to Know About Sex* by David Reuben is simply unsupported by research and as a generalization is quite false.

are, it has been essential that the black movement find positive images of black persons with whom to identify. Likewise, as the Gay Liberation Movement makes progress, there are more examples of gay persons who are happy, creative, successful, fulfilled, respected and so on. It is beginning (but only beginning) to become possible for the gay people of the 1970s to speak of "gay pride." And as gay pride grows in our society, it will become easier for people to come out.

"WHOM CAN I TALK TO?"

When a person discovers that he or she has homosexual tendencies and feels the need to discuss these feelings with another, he or she will look for a friend or counselor who appears to be open, supportive, nonjudgmental, and well informed. Persons who display these qualities in other areas will likely gain the confidence of one wishing to discuss homosexual feelings.

Persons who have displayed openness and knowledge about sexual issues in general, or who have specifically indicated interest, sympathy, and knowledge about the issues of homosexuality and gay liberation also may be judged "safe" counselors by one struggling with homosexual feelings. Especially in a society where unkind jokes, unsympathetic attitudes, and negative stereotypes concerning homosexuality are common, persons who openly disassociate themselves from such attitudes may soon find that they have gained the confidence of one who is struggling to come out.

"AM I REALLY HOMOSEXUAL?"

This is one of the first questions a trusted friend or counselor may receive from one concerned about homosexual feelings and tendencies. The assumption underlying this question is that individuals must be either exclusively heterosexual or exclusively homosexual. As it turns out, many studies of human sexuality indicate that sexual orientation is seldom so clearly defined in individuals. Alfred Kinsey made use of a seven-point scale in his study of sexual orientation. This scale represented a continuum between exclusive heterosexuality and exclusive homosexuality.

Rather than trying to decide the question, "Am I homosexual or heterosexual?", one should struggle with the questions, "What do I feel toward persons of my own sex?" "What are my fantasies about sexual and loving relationships with persons of my sex or the other sex?" Through this sort of questioning over a period of time, persons may come to recognize aspects of their sexuality that are heterosexual, homosexual, or bisexual, and may eventually identify their sexual *preference* as predominantly heterosexual, homosexual, or bisexual.

"AM I THE ONLY ONE WHO FEELS THIS WAY?"

Nearly all gay persons have experienced a sense of aloneness as they come to realize their feelings. The silence and ignorance of our culture in the area of homosexuality offers no models, information, or support to one who has feelings of love and/or sexual attraction to persons of the same sex. Homosexual feelings seem strange, freakish, or abnormal because it seems that no one else ever feels these things.

One of the truly liberating experiences in the life of one who is coming out is the discovery of some other real, flesh-and-blood persons who "feel the same things I do and have gone through what I have!" The counselor or friend of a person coming out should be acquainted with homosexual or bisexual persons who can provide this sort of supportive affirming contact. By all means, one should introduce an individual coming out to persons who are comfortable with their homosexuality and who display gay pride.

A related concern is the need to dispel a feeling that "I'm not like *those* people." Meeting gay persons face-to-face tends to dispel rather quickly simplistic and generally negative stereotypes that are part of our cultural myths about homosexuality. Discovering what other gay persons are really like is essential to develop a sense of comfort about one's own homosexuality.

"WHAT DO HOMOSEXUALS DO IN BED?"

Sexual attraction, loving relationships, and sexual performance are very different things. Because factual information about sex is available for those who seek it, this chapter will deal generally with the feelings underlying this question. Homosexual sex is not strange, unusual, or foreign. It involves the same experiences of general warmth, contact comfort, and cuddling, as well as the same physiological processes of arousal and orgasm. In discussing homosexual sex, the counselor should be informationally prepared but should also take care to convey a positive attitude toward sexual acts as acts that are normal, beautiful, and human.

"ISN'T HOMOSEXUALITY A SIN?"

Many persons have been taught that most if not all sexual acts and thoughts are sinful. From time to time homosexuality has been singled out as particularly sinful. For the counselor or friend who is not theologically inclined, it is well to be prepared to refer an individual with such a concern to a religious text or religious person who holds a positive view toward homosexuality. There are persons, books, and essays with positive attitudes toward homosexuality in nearly every branch of Judeo-Christian religion. The bibliography at the end of this chapter will offer some resources.

"WON'T I LOSE ALL MY FRIENDS?"

The blunt answer to this question is, "No, you'll find out who your real friends are." Although this answer is for the most part true, it may not be helpful. Many persons coming out find heterosexual friends of both sexes drawn closer to them as they share their inmost feelings, fears, and joys. Others experience painful cooling or rejection of friendship. The task of the counselor or friend is to support and aid the person coming out in relating to old friends and in making new friends.

One's friendships are frequently quite central to one's self-identity. Most people want friends who respect, love and care for them. Making friends is a skill that some persons may need to learn. The counselor who lacks knowledge and ability in teaching social skills to one who has difficulty making friends should seek outside resources.

"SHOULD I TELL MY PARENTS?"[5]

Despite the desirability of openness and honesty with one's parents, a son or daughter should not in every case tell a parent of his or her homosexuality. Parents who are very old, ill, or infirm should probably not be told. Parents who are distant, hostile, and unlikely ever to become close to their son or daughter should not be told of the son's or daughter's homosexuality unless such knowledge might in the long run improve their relationship. Parents should never be told so that an angry son or daughter can retaliate or hurt the parents.

Parents should be told of a son's or daughter's homosexuality if there is any chance that they will discover this in a hurtful way from a source other than the son or daughter. They should be told if in the long run it will draw the family closer, even if initially it results in conflict. A son or daughter should

[5]George Weinberg's *Society and the Healthy Homosexual* (see bibliography) has a particularly helpful chapter on this subject. Also, there is a best-selling novel that deals with this subject from the point of view of a mother who discovers that her son is homosexual—*Consenting Adult* by Laura Hobson.

tell the parents of his or her homosexuality if the possible gain of self-esteem and personal freedom outweighs temporary conflict or pain in the family relationships. The individual coming out will need to weigh carefully his or her particular situation. There may be a need for a specialist in family counseling who also possesses knowledge and skill in the area of counseling homosexuals.

"SHOULD I TELL MY SPOUSE?"

There are many persons who come out after they have married a person of the other sex. The counselor or friend of such an individual will have to guard against moralizing or pushing for a particular solution. Many of the same issues involved in telling parents and friends apply here. Solutions range from a decision to honor a monogamous commitment to the spouse to a decision to separate or divorce. In between these two extremes are couples who have worked out open and honest ways of continuing their marriage while one or both spouses have occasional outside "affairs" or relationships, and others who decide to lead a "double life," not admitting to the spouse that he or she is having outside affairs or relationships.

The married person coming out should be encouraged to consider all alternatives acceptable to him- or herself and to arrive at a solution that takes into account the happiness and welfare of him- or herself and the spouse. Frequently the need for referrals in such cases may arise. There is a growing number of professional counselors who have both knowledge and experience in counseling couples in which one or both spouses are homosexual.

A related concern is that of informing one's child of one's homosexual orientation. This situation was sensitively dramatized in a play called *That Certain Summer* on a national television network. The story concerned a young teen-age son who discovers that his divorced father is living happily with a male lover. The story ends on a promising note when it is clear that both the mother and father will cooperate to help the son cope with the feelings that accompany his discovery. The antihomosexual and other prejudices of children are very strongly inculcated and reinforced by their peers in secondary and elementary schools. The calm, rational, and loving support of both parents and other significant adults will be essential for a child to overcome his or her fears and biases.

"CAN I BE CURED?"

"Cure" inplies illness. Although there are still individual psychiatrists and psychologists who maintain that homosexuality is an illness, this is no longer an official position of either the American Psychiatric or Psychological associations. There are psychiatrists and psychologists who claim that they successfully and regularly change homosexuals by eliminating homosexual behavior and/or feelings. No psychiatrist or psychologist has ever clearly proven such a claim to the scientific community, and there is still much open debate. Rather than enter into this debate, this chapter will consider some of the feelings and questions behind this concern.

A desire to change frequently results from dissatisfaction with one's general life situation. Sometimes this is accompanied by a feeling that "the grass is greener on the other side of the fence." "If I were only heterosexual, everything would be okay." "Heterosexuals are happier." "Heterosexual relationships are more fulfilling than homosexual relationships." The counselor or friend who is heterosexual might readily assure the person coming out that life is not so simple and that heterosexual relationships are not so ideal as imagined.

The counselor or friend should attempt to clarify what the underlying issues are. "Why this desire to be heterosexual? How would life be different if you were no longer homosexual?" Again, the counselor should not push the person coming out to a particular decision. The counselor should be prepared with appropriate referrals to *reputable* professionals and agencies who can give more detailed information and provide, on the informed choice of the individual, whatever services or treatment the individual deems appropriate for him- or herself.

In the absence of reliable referrals, here are some suggestions for "shopping around" for reputable therapists. One should avoid therapists with simple answers for the causes of homosexuality. There are no simple answers. Similarly, there are no sure cures. One should probably avoid therapists who surround themselves with an aura of professional omniscience and mystery. Reputable therapists will be frank about their limitations, clear about what they can reasonably expect to accomplish, and how long therapy will take. There should be a clear statement or contract stating the treatment goals before therapy begins and a mutual understanding of what will be considered success.

"CAN I LOVE SOMEONE OF THE SAME SEX?"

Homosexual persons, no less than heterosexual persons, desire friendship, companionship, and close, loving relationships. To many this will mean a relationship to someone special — a lover. In spite of the common stereotype of homosexuals as promiscuous and lonely, there are many homosexual men and women who have developed long-term and permanent love relationships with a person of the same sex.

As with heterosexuals, there may be a need for supportive counseling for persons seeking a partner, training in social skills, counseling for couples in conflict, and support for individuals who have suffered the separation or death of a lover. As society opens up and begins to accept homosexuality, there will be more visible models of successful same-sex relationships.

"HOW DO I MEET OTHER GAY PERSONS?"

To answer this question the counselor or friend must be aware of the resources in his or her own community or locale. Gay people gather socially in their own bars, coffeehouses, gay political groups, and gay service organizations. There are also parties and social events in the gay community, and in some cities there are gay churches.

Gay men meet for more purely sexual purposes in certain well-known (or notorious) public rest rooms (called "T-rooms"), public parks, some bars and "the baths" (turkish baths, saunas, or health clubs that exist specifically to serve as social and sexual meeting places for gay men). Under most circumstances, the social gathering places (gay bars, coffeehouses, organizations, and churches) are legal, comfortable, and sociable places to meet other gay persons. The more specifically sexual settings (all of which are for gay men) may be less legal, less sociable, and, for many, less comfortable.

Frequently, comfortable places to meet other gay people are difficult to find, but they are growing in number and accessibility. If after serious consideration and searching, one cannot find in one's own community a comfortable place to meet with other gay persons, one might seriously consider moving to another community. The bibliography following this chapter cites a directory of gay organizations and services throughout the United States.

CONCLUSION—THE COURAGE TO BE YOURSELF

Too often we think that courage is something that pioneers of a long time ago had or that courage is something that an occasional hero in a book or a newspaper story has. It is not thought of as something that ordinary people have. So while we admire those distant people who have courage, those of us here and now settle for what is variously called "security," "adjustment," "conformity."

In reality, it takes courage just to be yourself, to like yourself, and be happy with yourself. Courage does not mean standing alone. It may mean seeking a trusted counselor or friend who respects and will help discover and support the person you are and can be. It may mean finding or creating a group of others who share in your struggle. Courage does not mean having all the answers to all of the questions. It may mean waiting for the answers to the really big questions.

The counselor or friend of a person who is discovering homosexual feelings and tendencies will need the same courage to be patient, to consider calmly and supportively difficult alternatives, to subordinate personal needs, opinions, and values to the integrity and welfare of the other. The counselor or friend of one coming out will need courage to work through *his or her own* sexual feelings so that personal fears, needs, or inhibitions do not stand in the way of supportiveness toward one who is struggling with homosexual feelings and tendencies.

BIBLIOGRAPHY

It is crucial that not only counselors of homosexual persons but friends and family as well have access to sound and helpful information about homosexuality. In addition to the books listed in this brief bibliography, "A Gay Bibliography" is available from Barbara Gittings, Task Force on Gay Liberation, American Library Association (Social Responsibilities Round Table), Box 2383, Philadelphia, Pa. 19103.

Psychological and Sociological

CHURCHILL, WAINWRIGHT, *Homosexual Behavior Among Males.* New York: Hawthorn, 1967. Also, Spectrum/Prentice-Hall paper ed.

HOBSON, LAURA Z. *Consenting Adult.* Garden City, N.Y.: Doubleday, 1975.

HUMPHREYS, LAUD. *Out of the Closets: The Sociology of Homosexual Liberation.* Englewood Cliffs, N.J.: Spectrum/Prentice-Hall, Inc., paper, 1972.

WEINBERG, GEORGE, *Society and the Healthy Homosexual.* New York: St. Martin's, 1972. Also, Anchor/Doubleday paper ed.

WEINBERG, MARTIN. *Male Homosexuals: Their Problems and Adaptations.* New York: Oxford University Press, 1974.

Lesbianism

MARTIN, DEL, AND PHYLLIS LYON, *Lesbian/Woman.* San Francisco: Glide Publications, 1972. Also, Bantam paper ed.

Religion and Homosexuality

GEARHART, SALLY, and WILLIAM R. JOHNSON, eds., *Loving Women/Loving Men: Gay Liberation and the Church*. San Francisco: Glide Publications, 1974.

OBERHOLZER, W. DWIGHT, ed., *Is Gay Good? Ethics, Theology and Homosexuality*. Philadelphia: Westminster Press, 1971.

PERRY, TROY, AND CHARLES L. LUCAS, *The Lord is My Shepherd and He Knows I'm Gay*. Los Angeles: Nash, 1972. Also, Bantam paper ed.

PITTENGER, W. NORMAN, *Making Sexuality Human*. Philadelphia: Pilgrim/United Church Press, 1970.

A directory of gay organizations and services may be obtained by writing *Gay Yellow Pages*, Box 292, Village Station, New York, N.Y. 10014.

PART THREE
HEALTH PROBLEMS

If You Want to Give Up Cigarettes

The American Cancer Society

This pamphlet seeks to round up helpful suggestions from experimental projects that have been carefully evaluated. No sure techniques are offered, no absolute laws of human behavior provided. There are different kinds of smokers and what helps one may not work with another. Individuals must choose for themselves from what is presented here.

Each man (and woman) makes a personal decision on the important matter of smoking cigarettes. The fact that you are reading this pamphlet indicates that you are properly concerned.

Many millions have given up cigarette smoking. Although for some people it is surprisingly easy to quit, many find it rather difficult. Psychologists estimate that half of all cigarette smokers can stop without too much difficulty once they make up their minds to do so. They feel only minor or temporary discomfort. Others suffer intensely, almost unbearably for days and weeks. Remember that those who have tried to stop a number of times may succeed this time.

Will you really make the effort? We hope so.

This chapter is a reprint of a pamphlet published by the American Cancer Society. Illustrations in the pamphlet have been deleted. Reprint permission has gratefully been received from the American Cancer Society.

ONCE YOU HAVE STOPPED

If you are like most cigarette smokers, you will in two weeks or less say farewell to that hacking, shattering morning cough, good-by to ugly thick phlegm, adios to smoker's headaches and unpleasant, cigarette-induced mouth and stomach complaints.

You will be saving—how much? Well, how much do you smoke up in dollars every week? Could be considerable.

We will no longer burn cigarette holes in clothing, furniture, rugs, or tablecloths. (The National Fire Protection Association says that "smoking and matches" caused a property loss of $80,400,000 in 1965.)

Food will tend to taste better and your sense of smell will return to normal.

Cigarette breath (it can be very offensive) will disappear.

Q Day, cigarette quitting day, might well be renamed K Day—kindness day for both you and your friends.

By quitting cigarettes you are instituting an immediate program of kindness to your lungs, your heart, your stomach, your nose, your throat.

A GARLAND OF FACTS

If you are trying to give up cigarettes, you need strong reasons. These warnings were developed by research in recent years and may help you.

Live a Little More

A longer and healthier life is high on our priorities: giving up cigarette smoking is the most important action that the average smoker can take that will improve the physical quality of his daily life, extend his life expectancy, and increase his chances of avoiding lung cancer, heart disease, emphysema and other illnesses.

The More Cigarettes . . . the More Cancer of the Lung

The regular cigarette smoker runs a risk of death from lung cancer ten times greater than the nonsmoker, men who smoke more than a pack a day have about 20 times the lung cancer rate that nonsmokers have. Unfortunately, only about one in 20 cases is cured. With early diagnosis results are better, but early diagnosis of lung cancer is uncommon.

Six and one/half Years, 78 Months, 2,372 Days

Men aged 25 who have never smoked cigarettes regularly can expect on the average six-and-a-half years more of life than men who smoke one pack or more a day.

Twice as many men who are heavy smokers (two packs a day) will die between 25 and 65 years of age, as those who have never smoked regularly.

Give Your Body a Break

Male smokers (10 or more cigarettes a day) between 45 and 54 have more than three times the death rate from heart attacks than nonsmokers. Between the ages of 40 and 59 strokes kill nearly twice as many men who smoke as nonsmokers.

How to Escape Work

Cigarette smokers between 45 and 64 miss 40 percent more days at work than do nonsmokers.

According to the Public Health Service, if cigarette smokers had the same rates of illness as those who never smoked, some 77 million working days would not be lost annually and there would be one million fewer peptic ulcers.

A Deep Breath

Emphysema, a relatively rare disease a few years ago, is now a major cause of medical disability in this country. Most emphysema is caused by cigarette smoking. The disease is both a crippler and a killer, causing the lungs to lose their elasticity. Eventually the effort to breathe becomes a constant, agonizing struggle.

Keep Nature's Protection

Cigarette smoke paralyzes the cilia, tiny hairs lining the bronchial tubes, that sweep foreign particles out of the lungs. Without this protection, healthy lung tissue can be injured, even destroyed by particles in the smoke.

Best Tip Yet

The evidence suggests that the more tar and nicotine you inhale, the greater your risk. As a result of the hot breath of publicity, cigarettes today have less tar and nicotine than those smoked generally in the fifties and early sixties when research was being done to establish the risks. If your tar and nicotine dosage is lower than it was five years ago, you are probably damaging yourself less. However, the best tip yet is don't smoke cigarettes.

SOME OF THE MILLIONS WHO MAKE IT

(The following brief sketches are based on fact from letters, conversations, reports, but with names and details altered. They have been selected with the intention of helping others to go and do likewise.)

WILLIAM . . . is a psychiatrist who decided soon after the Report of the Advisory Committee to the Surgeon General that he ought to stop cigarettes. What triggered his actual decision? He suspects it was a morning cough, but he is not sure. In any case, he stopped and reports that he watched television for several evenings (which he rarely did), ate rather more often than was his custom, did some strenuous skiing, and was happy that his wife cleared the house at once of all cigarettes and ashtrays. He was uncomfortable for a few days, but not climbing the walls. He hasn't smoked for three years.

JOAN . . . is a writer who reads seriously. After the Surgeon General's Report she stopped smoking cigarettes. Cold turkey. No gum, no candy, no gaining of weight. Some bad temper for a few days but it was not a big or difficult deal.

PETE . . . is a carpenter who smoked two packs a day for 25 years. He was proud, however, that his three sons did not smoke. He wanted to quit but was hooked, he knew it, and he told his boys never to take up the habit. When they believed and obeyed him, he was delighted. He stopped only after an operation in which two-thirds of his stomach was taken out because of an ulcer. He still doesn't discuss the fact that he has given up smoking but he hasn't smoked for a year and he was in the hospital long enough so that when he went back on the job and people began offering him a smoke, he was able to say "no" very calmly.

BILL . . . drives a schoolbus mornings and evenings and has made it a point not to set a bad example to the boys and girls by using cigarettes in their presence. When he delivered fuel oil — as he did the rest of the day — he used to smoke like a chimney. In the evening he smoked with his food, his coffee, his beer. One night he got into an argument about cigarettes and all at once he tossed his package away and said he was through. His friends didn't believe him, but for a week he took a raisin whenever he wanted a cigarette. Boxes of raisins. Three years later he nibbles on raisins occasionally but he never smokes.

JOHN . . . was a brilliantly successful advertising man who smoked two packs of cigarettes a day: when he began to cough, and this happened half a dozen times in a work day, it took him embarrassed moments to get over it. He had thought of stopping cigarettes, even made half-hearted trials—but at last he decided to go for broke. His first step was to keep a careful record of when he smoked each cigarette, and how much he wanted it. Then he selected a future Q Day and told his family and friends what he was doing. He began to cut down, 50 percent each week for four weeks, and he laid in mints and gum. When Q Day arrived he stopped. It was a rough experience and at one time he was in such a serious depression that he frightened his wife. After a visit to his physician, however, he stood by his decision. During the first three months he gained 15 pounds, but he lost all this later, his cough is gone, and he feels a hundred percent better. He hasn't smoked a cigarette for two years.

ARTHUR . . . is a biology teacher who switched from cigarettes—a pack a day with deep inhalation—to a pipe with no inhaling, without too much difficulty. He enjoys handling his pipe, filling it, lighting it . . . and he says that he can now talk to his class about the dangers of cigarette smoking and not feel hypocritical.

BOB . . . had smoked two packs a day for twenty years but he gave up the habit suddenly and completely. He credits TV messages and says that they filtered through to him via his seven-year-old son who began asking why he smoked and why didn't he stop?

Bob has always tried to be honest with his children and so after some thought he replied that he smoked because he was stupid and he didn't stop because he was weak. This was a remarkably uncomfortable admission to make to his boy and to himself. Bob decided that a father who was both stupid and weak would not be much of an influence for his son. So he quit smoking.

JOYCE . . . is a very competent office manager who smoked more than a pack a day for twelve years. When her husband kicked the habit, she tried but did not make it. Her two youngsters, five and seven years old, worried at their mother's smoking. She in turn worried because her boys did not give up their security blankets. Finally her children volunteered to go to bed without their pacifiers if their mother would give up her pacifier: cigarettes. They made a bargain and have kept it, though Joyce reports she backslides occasionally at parties, but never in front of her boys and never more than two or three cigarettes a week.

LINDA . . . reports she really puffed away at cigarettes when she was worried or tense. She was disturbed by stories of the risks of smoking and wished she could stop but continued until (she says) one of the American Cancer Society's announcements gave her just the push she needed. That was three years ago; about the same time her husband lost his job, her four-year-old child broke her arm, her baby had his first nasty cold. Linda wrote the Society that, despite all the tensions, she "came through with a smile and a prayer, but no cigarette."

HAROLD . . . a reporter of considerable distinction—smoked three packs a day: at the typewriter, before and after breakfast, during lunch, in the afternoon and evening. Any tests would have shown him as a habituated smoker, a bad risk for a withdrawal program. However, he stopped, cold turkey, and has not smoked for 10 years. Why? His specialty was science writing and he decided that if the scientists he trusted were right he was a fool to go on smoking. For two weeks he was in considerable discomfort, but with gum and candy he kept going. He says he feels great since he stopped smoking.

YOU CAN KICK THE HABIT

There are twenty-one million ex-cigarette smokers in the United States: about one in five adult men in this country has dropped the habit.

Those who give up cigarettes report a great sense of satisfaction, of tremendous pride in being able to do it. To learn a new way of living, a way without cigarette smoking, is very rewarding to the ego—and to the ego's mate.

AS YOU APPROACH Q-DAY

Many stress willpower as the decisive factor in giving up cigarettes. For them the sense that they can manage their own lives is of great importance. They enjoy challenging themselves and, with an effort of will, they break the cigarette habit.

Thus, some psychologists describe stopping cigarettes as an exercise in self-mastery, one that introduces a new dimension of self-control.

Others, often successful in many aspects of living, find that willpower does not help them in giving up cigarettes. They try to stop, they do not, and they feel guilty over their weakness. This is a mistake, since many smokers fail in their first and second, even their fifth attempts, and then finally succeed. Those whose "will" fails in breaking the habit are not weak but different. Their approach must be less through determination and more through relearning new behavior with patience and perseverance.

Self-suggestion, when one is relaxed, aimed at changing one's feelings and thoughts about cigarettes can be useful.

One health educator remarked recently, "Nothing succeeds like willpower and a little blood in the sputum."

To think of stopping smoking as self-denial is an error: the ex-smoker should not believe that he is giving up an object of value, however dependent he may be on it. If he begins to feel sorry for himself and broods on his sufferings, they may well become more severe and indeed unendurable. He must recognize that he is teaching himself a more positive, more constructive, more rewarding behavior.

TRY CUTTING DOWN

An important first step in the process of giving up cigarettes for many smokers is to set the date for Q-Day, when you are going to stop completely and, as it approaches, to gradually reduce the number of cigarettes you smoke, day by day, or week by week.

A good system is to decide to smoke only once an hour—or to stop smoking between the hours of 9 and 10 o'clock, 11 and 12, 1 and 2, 3 and 4 etc. And then extend non-smoking by half an hour, an hour, two hours.

You may decide to halve the cigarettes you smoke week by week, giving yourself four weeks to Q-Day.

How about smoking half of each cigarette?

In the process of reducing the number of daily cigarettes, try various possibilities; if you have one pocket in which you always carry your pack, put it in another so that you will have to fumble for it. If you always use your right hand to bring your cigarette to your mouth, use the left hand. Is it your custom to rest the cigarette in the right corner of the mouth? Try the left side.

Make it a real effort to get a cigarette:

Wrap your package in several sheets of paper or place it in a tightly covered box. If you leave your change at home you won't be able to use a cigarette machine.

Shift from cigarettes you like to an unpalatable brand.

Before you light up, ask yourself, "Do I really want this cigarette or am I just acting out of empty habit?"

A smoker may find an unlighted cigarette in the mouth is helpful. Others enjoy handling and playing with a cigarette.

Cigarette smoking is a habit that is usually very well learned—learning the habit of not smoking can be difficult. It can help in breaking into your habit chain to make yourself aware of the nature and frequency of your smoking behavior.

KEEP A TRACK RECORD

Many smokers have found that a useful step in understanding their smoking is the keeping of a daily record on a scale like that below.

In your gradual withdrawal you may decide to eliminate those daily cigarettes that you find are rated 1, 2 or 3, i.e., ones you want least.

Or you may wish to give up first the cigarettes you like most. In any case keeping a smoking log will give you information about yourself, make you more aware of what your smoking habits are.

You may find that you are largely a social smoker, that smoking makes you feel closer to others, more welcome at a party, that you seem to have more friends. A cigarette may play a surprisingly large part in your picture of yourself as a mature and successful person.

How do you convince yourself that people like and respect you for more important reasons than for your cigarette? Try not smoking and see.

Plus and Minus

Write down carefully, after some thought, in one column the reasons why you smoke and in another all the reasons why you should give up cigarettes.

As you turn this exercise over in your mind, new material will occur to you for one or the other columns. Thoughtful concentration on your reasons for giving up cigarettes is important in changing your behavior.

FOUR SMOKING STYLES

Dr. Silvan Tomkins distinguishes four general types of smoking behavior. An abbreviated summary of the types follows:

SCORE CARD

Copy this record sheet seven times for seven days. Make a check for each cigarette you smoke, hour by hour, and indicate how much you need it: a mark in the box opposite 1 shows low need, a mark opposite 6 high need; opposite 4, moderate need, etc. Then decide which cigarette you wish to eliminate.

NEED	MORNING HOURS (AM)							AFTERNOON, EVENING HOURS (PM)												
	6	7	8	9	10	11	12	1	2	3	4	5	6	7	8	9	10	11	12	1
1																				
2																				
3																				
4																				
5																				
6																				
7																				

Habitual Smoking

Here the smoker may hardly be aware that he has a cigarette in his mouth. He smokes as if it made him feel good, or feel better, but in fact it does neither. He may once have regarded smoking as an important sign of status. But now smoking is automatic. The habitual smoker who wants to give up must first become aware of when he is smoking. Knowledge of the pattern of his smoking is a first step toward change.

Positive Affect Smoking

Here smoking seems to serve as a stimulant that produces exciting pleasure, or is used as a relaxant, to heighten enjoyment, as at the end of a meal. Here a youngster demonstrates his manhood or his defiance of his parents. This smoker may enjoy most the handling of a cigarette or the sense and sight of smoke curling out of his mouth. If these smokers can be persuaded to make an effort, they may find giving up cigarettes relatively painless.

Negative Affect Smoking

This is sedative smoking, using the habit to reduce feelings of distress, fear, shame, or disgust or any combination of them. This person may not smoke at all when things go well, but under tension, when things go badly, he reaches for a cigarette. These smokers give up often, but when pressure hits them, when there's a challenge, they find it very hard to resist a cigarette. A strong substitute, like nibbling ginger root may be useful.

Addictive Smoking

The smoker is always aware when he is not smoking. The lack of a cigarette builds need, desire, and discomfort at not smoking. With this increasing need is the expectation that a cigarette will reduce discomfort — and the cigarette does give relief — for a moment. Pleasure at smoking is real, just as the buildup of discomfort at not smoking is real, sometimes rapid and intolerable. The enjoyment of the cigarette, however, is very brief, and may be disappointing — but the suffering for lack of even slight relief is considerable.

For this smoker, tapering off doesn't seem to work: the only solution is to quit cold. Once you have been through the discomfort of breaking your psychological addiction, you are unlikely to start smoking again. The experience of giving up has been too uncomfortable — and too memorable for you to risk having to go through it again.

Some such smokers have found it useful to increase during the week before Q-Day the number of cigarettes smoked, to go from two packs to four, to force themselves to smoke so that their bodies will be in actual revolt against the double dose of tar and nicotine.

For information on a Smoker's Self-Testing Kit (four questionnaires, etc., to help one to understand personal reasons for and style of smoking) write to the National Clearinghouse for Smoking and Health, United States Public Health Service, 4040 North Fairfax Drive, Arlington, Va., 22203.

THE WEEK BEFORE Q-DAY

Think over your list of reasons why you should not smoke: the risk of disease, the blurring of the taste of food, the cost, the cough, the bad breath, the mess and smell of morning-after ashtrays.

Concentrate each evening when you are relaxed, just before you fall asleep, on one result of cigarette smoking. Repeat and repeat and repeat that single fact. Drive home another fact the next night and another the next.

Review the facts that you know about the risks of cigarette smoking. Remind yourself that there, but for the grace of God go you; that a man of 25 may indeed, if he continues smoking, lose six and one half years of life, that — if he is a heavy smoker — his chances of dying between 25 and 65 years of age are twice as great as those of the nonsmoker. Would you fly in an airplane if the chances of crash and death were even close to the risks of cigarette smoking.

ACTION: Q-DAY

Let us suppose that you know, now, when and where and how you smoke. You have suggested again and again to your tired mind that smoking is a dangerous business.

"But what will I do the morning of Q-Day when, mind or no mind, I want a cigarette?"

We hope you will prove that you are stronger than your dependence. Here are some tips that may prove useful when you have an impulse to smoke!

For the Mouth

Drink frequent glasses of water.

Nibble fruit, celery, carrots, cookies, eat somewhat self-pleasing food.

Suck candy mints and/or chew gum (sugarless gum will be easier on your teeth).

Chew bits of fresh ginger when you start to reach for a cigarette. (Take this gently, ginger root is aromatic and pervasive — some experience it as burning, others as clean and satisfying.) Bite a clove.

Nicotine Replacement

Lobeline sulphate tablets, available without prescription, are reported to make it easier for some people to stop cigarettes. Authorities disagree, however, as to whether the tablets provide a substitute that will help satisfy the smoker's craving for nicotine.

(Since some individuals — those with stomach ulcers, for instance — should not use these tablets, check with your physician before trying them.)

Be Vigorous: Exercise

Strenous physical activity can be very helpful, particularly in working off the irritation — real anger in some ex-smokers — at not having a cigarette.

Vacation is a good time for some people to stop: try camping, mountain climbing, tennis.

Stretching exercises, calisthenics or long walks can be relaxing.

Go "No Smoking"

For some the cigarette after breakfast coffee, at the end of lunch or dinner, is where smoking is forbidden. Ride in "No Smoking" cars.

A spurt of motion picture or theater-going will pass many hours.

Keep away for two weeks from friends who are heavy smokers.

Use Your Lungs

Deep breaths of fresh air can be wonderfully calming.

Inhalers — that clear sinuses — may help tide you over the first few days.

After Meals

For some the cigarette after breakfast coffee, at the end of lunch or dinner, is most important. Instead of a cigarette try a mouth wash after each meal.

If you have a specific pattern that you follow after dinner you may want to change it: read a book instead of a newspaper, skip familiar television programs, sit in another comfortable chair, try crossword puzzles, do some household task you have been putting off, take your dog out for a walk.

On the other hand, you may prefer to do all the things that are familiar and comfortable for you and to which you are used — except to smoke cigarettes. Take your choice.

Reward Yourself

Be sure that you have your favorite food on Q-Day.

Give yourself all the things that you like best — except cigarettes.

When you have saved a bit of money by not smoking, buy yourself a present: perhaps a record, or a blouse, or necktie, book or trinket. When the impulse to smoke is strong, try a substitute: a drink of water, a piece of gum, a walk around the block, stretching and deep breathing.

These substitutes may only satisfy you temporarily — but they will keep you alert and aware and will soften the strength of your desire to smoke. Equally important are constant reminders to yourself of why you are stopping cigarettes. Remember the reasons that you put down for not smoking? Recall the basic data about disease, disability, and death that are caused by cigarettes.

When you stop smoking, you may be exposed to gentle and not so gentle needling from smokers. What are they really saying to you? Perhaps that they wish they could stop, too.

You may be very uncomfortable but "this too shall pass" relates also to cigarette-less shakes, irritation and temper, the urge to climb walls, depression, anxiety. Time is a great healer.

Unfortunately fear of failure to make it seems to deter men and women from even trying—yet for many, giving up cigarettes while uncomfortable and a strain is by no means agony. After all their terrible expectation, stopping can seem relatively easy.

QUESTIONS & ANSWERS

Do You Believe in "Cold Turkey" Quitting?

Yes, for some, no, for others. If you are a really "addicted" smoker, psychologists favor the sudden, decisive and complete break.

For some, gradual withdrawal is less painful and entirely satisfactory.

Some cigarette smokers shift to pipes and cigars—there is of course some risk of mouth cancer from these but overall mortality among cigar and pipe smokers is only a little higher than among nonsmokers, if the smoke is not inhaled.

What About Going to a Quit Clinic?

If there is a clinic or program in your community, you may find it useful. The American Cancer Society favors such efforts.

Sharing your withdrawal experiences with others and working with them on a common problem can be very helpful. The clinic may make it considerably easier in various ways to stop cigarette smoking.

However, remember, no clinic can provide a sure result. In this matter you must be both patient and physician.

Shall I Make a Big Thing of Q-Day?

Some find it most satisfactory to work on a schedule in which Q-Day, quitting day, is singled out as the important, decisive day in their personal lives—that indeed it is. Others who have known for a long time that cigarettes are bad for them and that sooner or later they will stop, wake up one day and say to themselves, "This is it. No more cigarettes."

What motivates them? An obituary, an anti-smoking commercial on television, a magazine article, a leaflet brought home from school by a child, a worried look from their son, being fed up with a repeated cough. There are many possible stimulants to stopping but almost always beneath the casual-seeming but bold decision are months, often years of serious thought and worry.

What if I Fail to Make It?

Don't be discouraged: many thousands who finally stopped did so only after several attempts.

Some people prefer to stop for just one day at a time. They promise themselves 24 hours of freedom from cigarettes and when the day is over they make a commitment to themselves for one more day. And another. And another. At the end of any 24-hour period they can go back to cigarettes without betraying themselves — but they usually do not.

Is Smoking a Real Addiction?

This depends on your definition of words. In any case smokers obviously can become very strongly dependent on cigarettes.

However, the discomfort that most feel at giving up cigarettes is not like the painful withdrawal symptoms that drug addicts report.

Giving up cigarettes is much closer to the discomfort and the irritation produced by dieting than to the agony of stopping a drug. As so many know, dieting in an effort to lose fifteen or twenty pounds can be a most uncomfortable experience — but when you have done it, you have a fine feeling.

How about Ashtrays?

One school of thought asks, do you leave a bottle of whiskey near an alcoholic? Their recommendation is to get rid of cigarettes, ashtrays, anything that might remind a smoker of his former habit.

Another school of thought takes a different view and even suggests carrying cigarettes to demonstrate to yourself that you can resist temptation. Choose for yourself.

Shall I Tell Others of My Decision?

Some do, some don't. Some find that the wider they spread the news of their decision the easier it is for them to make it stick. Others regard no smoking as their own personal business and keep it almost entirely to themselves. Will you strengthen your decision if your wife and friends know that you have committed yourself to quitting?

Will I Gain Weight?

Many do. Food is a substitute for cigarettes for many people. And your appetite may be fresher and stronger.

During the first few weeks of giving up cigarettes some psychologists recommend pampering yourself: eating well, drinking well, enjoying those things that are pleasant and fulfilling.

Some people, those to whom self-mastery is vital, get rewards out of controlling their wish for fattening food at the same time that they are licking the urge for cigarettes.

Again, it depends upon the person and his approach.

How about Hypnosis?

There is much interest in this technique by some physicians who report success, particularly with hard core smokers. Why not discuss the matter with a physician, if you are interested?

Shall I See My Physician?

YES. However, the problem is yours, not his, and he may not feel that he can be helpful. On the other hand, he may be able to give you sympathetic support and may prescribe medication. He can be helpful, also, in suggesting a diet which will prevent you from gaining too much weight.

Physicians as a profession have been leaders in acting on the risks of cigarette smoking: The Public Health Service estimates that 100,000 physicians (half on the physicians who once were cigarette smokers) have kicked the habit. A California study showed that only 21.3 percent of all physicians in the state were cigarette smokers in 1967.

Why Do So Many People Smoke Cigarettes?

Surely one reason is that the cigarette industry spends about $300,000,000 a year in promoting the habit and in challenging the facts that scientists have produced that point to the dangers of the habit.

Another reason is that something in cigarettes, probably nicotine, is habit-forming: smokers become dependent rather rapidly.

Cigarette smoking is essentially a 20th-century habit, encouraged by wars, by brilliant advertising, and by the development of remarkably efficient automatic machinery that produces those millions of round, firmly packed cigarettes.

It is only within the last 15 years that we have learned, largely through research pioneered by the American Cancer Society, that this personal and socially accepted habit is extremely dangerous. Cigarette smoking is deeply embedded in our life: agriculture, industry, government, the communications media, all have a stake in it. It is still widely accepted, even though proven to be a most certain hazard to health.

Because promotion is important in maintaining the habit's popularity, the Society believes all cigarette advertising in all media should be terminated. We hope that this goal will be achieved voluntarily and that governmental action won't be necessary.

TO SMOKE OR NOT TO SMOKE?

A story is told of two young boys who were determined to challenge and expose a man who was supposed to be wise. They caught a small bird and decided on a formula that they felt could not fail. They would go to the wise man with their hands cupped and say: "Tell us, wise man, is the bird, that one of us holds in his hands, alive or dead?" If he said "dead" they would release the bird. If he said "alive" a squeeze of the hands would prove him wrong. When they confronted him and asked the question, the wise man smiled, and considered, and finally said, "The answer is in your hands."

APPROACHES IN GIVING UP CIGARETTE SMOKING

(If you don't stop immediately and permanently)

1. List the reasons for and against smoking.
2. Select Q-Day—change to a low tar and nicotine cigarette.
3. Chart your smoking habits for at least two weeks: how many cigarettes, when, the most and least important.
4. Repeat each night, at least ten times, one of your reasons for not smoking cigarettes.
5. Eliminate one category of cigarettes: The most or the least desired.
6. Secure a supply of substitutes: mints, gum, an inhaler, ginger root, etc.
7. Quit on Q-Day—try the different substitutes as the wish to smoke recurs—enlist your wife or a friend in a busy series of events: eating well, going to the movies or theater, exercise and many long walks, moderate drinking.
8. If you are depressed, see your physician and discuss your symptoms.
9. Keep reminding yourself, again and again, of the shocking risks in cigarette smoking.

10 Ways to Make Your Diet Work

Jean Mayer

Every nutritionist knows — and every dieter must unhappily agree — that crash diets are no good. They're nutritionally unbalanced, they make you weak, irritable, and dizzy. Worst of all from the dieter's viewpoint, they don't work. After the first thrilling plummet of the scales, the pointer inexorably creeps upward again. Looking back, the disappointed dieter knows that all she has accomplished is one more useless and frustrating cycle in what I call "the rhythm method of girth control."

Yet people keep on crash-dieting in spite of all the medical warnings and their own experience. Young women and teen-age girls, in particular, return again and again to the crash diet, still pursuing the vain vision of instant beauty, since for these people the goal of dieting is rarely better health but greater attractiveness to the opposite sex, something for which they can't bear to wait too long. Few people have the patience for the slow and steady weight loss of sensible dieting. But even that doesn't always work. Why not?

Dieting should work the same way arithmetic works. A pound of fatty tissue is the equivalent in energy of 3,500 calories. Every time you eat 3,500 calories less than you expend—over a period of days—you should use up a pound of fatty tissue. A deficit of 500 calories a day (eating 2,000 calories and using up 2,500, for instance) should lead to a loss of one pound a week, or 52 pounds a year. Double that deficit to 1,000 calories a day, and you can lose 104 pounds a year, surely enough for almost anybody, and certainly enough to convince people that crash dieting isn't even necessary, much less safe.

Yet people keep right on counting calories, cutting them, apparently meeting their daily deficit—and staying the same weight, or practically the same, week after week. There is nothing wrong with the arithmetic or with the laws of the conservation of matter and energy. The problem lies in several specific misunderstandings about dieting. In my judgment, there are 10 basic errors in dieting and 10 ways every dieter can sidestep these traps into which so many well-meaning, determined dieters fall.

1. Beware of nonfattening foods. Because, unfortunately, there's really no such thing, with the possible exception of celery at 7 calories per stalk. Every other food contributes to your calorie balance. Too many people believe that there is one big category of food that is nonfattening, another that is fattening. Such people think a weight-reducing diet consists of a list of foods that are permitted at each meal, and as long as you don't eat the "forbidden" foods, you'll naturally lose weight. Thus, the dieter relieves herself of worrying about arithmetic or the size of her portions so long as she sticks to the first group—for instance, roast beef, yogurt, and orange juice—while scrupulously avoiding group two—bread, potatoes, bananas. This utterly disregards the plain facts: a three-ounce slice of roast beef (barely enough to cover a slice of rye bread decently) contains 260 calories, yogurt 150 calories a cup, and unsweetened orange juice 110 calories a cup, while white bread is a mere 60 calories a slice, and a fairly large baked potato or a banana only 100—not much more than the dieter's standby, the hard-boiled egg. Calories do count. Those three little words should be recited prayerfully morning, noon, and night by everybody who seriously wants to reduce sensibly and successfully.

2. Be prudent about portion size. Few people ever train themselves to look at the difference between a three-ounce hamburger patty and a five-ounce patty. If the calorie chart says 310 calories for a hamburger, that's supposed to be that. Yet the larger hamburger contains about 200 more calories, or a total of 510. Just eating one large-size hamburger a day—but counting it as a small one—will make a difference of nearly two pounds of fat a month. A full eight-ounce glass of orange juice instead of a juice glass changes the figure from 55 calories to 110. This hidden surtax on the larger portion can destroy a calorie budget as completely as an obvious food splurge. The *amount* of

food as well as the *kind* of food does make a caloric difference. So keep your eyes on portion size.

3. Count every calorie. That means *every* calorie. Many people forget to take into account "small snacks," especially if they are nibbled over a long period instead of gobbled down in one handful. A cupful of Brazil nuts, unconsciously devoured while watching a football game, doesn't seem worth thinking about. Yet it represents 900 calories! (Peanuts? 805 calories for a mere two fistfuls.)

4. Cook lean. It's surprising how much the fattening ability of food changes with different methods of preparing it. The so-called fattening potato contains only about 100 calories baked or boiled. With salt and pepper, lemon juice, or Worcestershire sauce, it still contains 100 calories. Add one tablespoon of butter or margarine and you double the count. French-fry the potato or mash it with butter and milk, and you've pushed the total to 250. And if you're addicted to hash brown potatoes, you should know you're absorbing 470 calories per cup.

You can similarly double or triple the calorie content of your 80-calorie egg by frying it in generous amounts of butter or fat, or of your 60-calorie slice of bread by loading it with butter and/or jam. (Incidentally, toasting does nothing to calories; it simply drives out the water and changes the color and texture of the bread.) On the more cheerful side, you can cut the calories in hamburgers or steaks by cooking them in a Teflon pan, which does not require any lubricating fat, or better still, by using a grill that allows appreciable amounts of fat and calories to drip out of the meat.

5. Beware of "wet" calories. Calories in drinks are as easily overlooked as those in the nut dish. There are 320 calories in two small (two-ounce) martinis or manhattans. *One* ounce of after-dinner liqueur costs you 100 calories. And the two beers you drink with the Brazil nuts add another 300 calories to the 900 — in other words, you gained one-third of a pound of fat between lunch and dinner and you never once had a real mouthful of food. It's hardly worth it!

6. Stop leaning on protein. Millions of sensible people have been inadvertently misled into thinking that protein contains few calories, or that protein somehow "burns" fat. Actually, protein contains about 120 calories per ounce, the same as carbohydrates. (Fats are more costly, about 270 calories an ounce.) The idea that protein burns fat started out as a misunderstanding of an old laboratory experiment; it showed, indeed, that if a person ate only pure protein for a meal (and egg white is the only thing in nature that comes close to the definition of pure protein), about 30 percent of

the energy eaten would be dissipated as heat shortly after the meal. The problem is that if the meal contains any fat or carbohydrates — as all meals do — the effect is canceled. It is also widely believed that meat is pure protein, and therefore you can eat steak ad infinitum and emerge as slinky as a cougar. In fact, all meat contains fat. A three-ounce, 310-calorie hamburger contains, on the average, 19 grams of protein (about 80 calories) and 26 grams of fat (about 230 calories). In other words, about three-quarters of the calories in a hamburger come from the fat. Three ounces of sirloin or deboned rib roast contain 20 grams of protein (80 calories) and 20 grams of fat (180 calories). Ham contains even more fat calories in proportion to protein, 260 from the fat.

7. Cut down the easy way — on sugar. Intensive advertising has successfully spread the notion that there's a difference between the "quick energy" of sugar and the presumably harder-to-use-up calories of ordinary carbohydrates, protein, and fat. Sugar contains four calories per gram, just like other carbohydrates. Sugar is absorbed by the body fairly rapidly, but this makes no difference in its contribution to weight gain. The consumption of 100 pounds of sugar per American per year is the equivalent of 192,000 calories, or 55 pounds of body fat, per year, which has to be burned up somehow if it isn't going to be accumulated as extra weight. Sugar is the one food the dieter can easily do without.

8. Clear up the cholesterol confusion. There is a hopeless mix-up about the relationship between calories, fat, and cholesterol. Somehow, millions of people have the idea that any margarine or oil that is high in polyunsaturated fat (or low in cholesterol) is, therefore, low in calories. It is certainly desirable to replace saturated fat with polyunsaturated fat in order to keep down cholesterol. But margarine and butter have almost exactly the same calorie content.

9. Don't worry about water or salt. Attempts to cut down weight by cutting down on salt or water are futile. If you are overweight, it's a good idea to go easy on salt to guard against high blood pressure. And for some people, particularly middle-aged women, decreasing salt may allow a more regular weight loss by preventing temporary water accumulation. But cutting down on salt will not by itself reduce your weight, unless it happens to make food so unappetizing that you simply eat less. As for water, it is the world's one and only calorie-free fluid, and a generous consumption of it is a useful health habit.

10. Balance both sides of your calorie expense account. The final widespread fallacy that stands in the way of successful dieting is the belief that food intake alone determines how fat you are or how much weight you gain or lose. In fact, like your bank balance, your weight depends on how much you

take out as well as how much you put in. It is far more difficult to reduce if the only muscles you ever move are the chewing muscles. As hour's walk at an easy four miles an hour is worth 250 calories if you weigh 150 pounds. This is *half* the calorie expenditure you need to lose one whole pound a week! It is considerably easier and generally far more healthful to lose weight by a combination of calorie reduction and exercise than it is by calorie cutting alone.

How to Adjust to a Mastectomy

Hylda M. Roberts

Remember, first of all, that you are not alone in adjusting to a mastectomy. Many women all around the world, among the famous and the unknown, have been victims of this type of cancer. Each woman has asked herself the same agonized questions you are now asking yourself: "Why did this happen to me?"

When First Lady Betty Ford had a mastectomy because of breast cancer in 1974, there were many articles written on the subject. According to one article, ". . . 90,000 American women will discover this year that they have breast cancer."[1] Another article stated some statistics on breast cancer:

Any woman can develop breast cancer, but some seem more susceptible to it than others. Statistically, the woman in the greatest danger is someone in her mid to late 40s who began menstruating early in life and continued late, who never had children or did not begin having them until she was past 30, who is obese, and whose mother or sister had the disease.[2]

Doctors generally agree that injuries to the breast do not initiate the disease; neither do birth control pills seem to be responsible for the increasing

This article was especially written for this book.
[1]*Newsweek*, October 7, 1974, p. 34.
[2]*Time*, November 4, 1974, pp. 107–10.

incidence of cancer among young women. Breast cancer can, and does, strike women from the 30s through the 80s.

Any abnormality of the breasts, such as a lump; thickening; dimpling; or unusual drainage of the nipples, should be immediately referred to a physician for examination and evaluation. If the physician is suspicious of the condition, he will order a biopsy to determine if there is a malignancy. (This usually requires a one-day hospitalization and the only aftereffect is a small scar.) In a large percentage of cases, there is no malignancy.

If a malignancy is found, a decision is made by the physician as to the management of the problem. The usual treatment for a localized malignancy of the breast would be surgical. This could be in the form of a simple or total mastectomy without removal of the muscles, or a modified radical mastectomy with removal of the breast and the lymph nodes, or a radical mastectomy, which would include the removal of the breast, the muscles, and the lymph nodes, depending on the type of lesion and the decision of the physician. Very occasionally the treatment will be a lumpectomy, which is just the removal of the tumor. If the lymph nodes removed also contain tumor, a decision will then be made as to the need for further chemical or X-ray therapy.

The doctor, of course, will use the method which he considers safest for his patient. Before the operation, he will discuss with the patient the possible choices he will be required to make. Whatever the doctor does will be done with the safety and welfare of his patient uppermost in his mind.

"Did they get it all?" According to Newsweek, "Nine out of 10 can expect to be alive in 1980. . ."[3] These statistics in themselves should give you a sense of reassurance. Also, to have faith in your doctor and a positive attitude as to your complete recovery will also be a great asset to you in your convalescence.

"Why does/does not my doctor prescribe postoperative therapy, such as chemotherapy, x-ray, cobalt?" This is a question you must discuss with your own doctor. Each doctor makes the decision for further treatment according to the extent of the cancer, your personal history and to his or her own judgment as to what is best for each individual patient.

"Will my husband/boyfriend be repulsed by my scar?" *"Will he love me just as much as before?"* One cannot generalize human behavior, but, if your relationship was deep and sincere before your operation, the chances are good that your relationship will be even closer and dearer. A man does not, or certainly should not, fall in love with a woman's breasts, but rather with the woman herself. Admittedly, a mastectomy will be a shock to the man in your life—as it is to you—but discussing the problem with him is the best way to deal with it. Let him know that you need his loving support and reassurance. Be reasonable. If he looks at your scar, don't resent it. You would be upset if he

[3]*Newsweek*, October 7, 1974, p. 34.

did not look at your body at all, or evaded looking at your breasts. He is probably trying to do the right thing, and he has to learn, too. Be patient with him and with yourself. Consider the alternative. You *are* alive—and will appreciate, maybe for the first time, how intensely sweet each day can be. Even the most trivial things have an intense beauty when you realize that you will be privileged to enjoy them for many more years because you found the "lump" in time.

"How will my children react?" You may have to initiate the dialogue between you and your children. You might ask them if they want to see your scar, and then discuss openly and naturally with them anything they might want to ask. You may find them eager to help you in selecting becoming clothes or in giving friendly criticism as to what they do not think becoming to you. Frequently, this experience will draw you even closer to your children, and they will surprise you with the depth of their understanding and desire to help.

"What can I wear; will I have to alter my clothes drastically?" You can wear almost anything you want to, even knits. As to alterations, very seldom is that necessary, if you invest in a good prosthesis (an artificial filling for the missing breast). Prostheses range in price from quite reasonable to quite expensive and can be bought at pharmacies, department stores, specialty shops; and mail order houses such as Sears, Ward's, Penney's. In many cases, your medical insurance policy will cover the cost of the prosthesis. Ask your agent about it. If you do have a question about where or what to buy, or are hesitant or shy about it, call your nearest American Cancer Society. They will put you in touch with someone who will gladly accompany you and help you make the right selection for your comfort, appearance, and finances.

"Can I still swim?" Of course you can! Special suits are designed for your particular problem. Many times suits off the rack are also suitable by just pinning in your prosthesis. As you experiment with your clothes and talk with other women in your position, you will discover many "tricks" to adjust ready-made clothes to your special needs.

"Can I still play golf, tennis or bowl?" Of course you can! One lady was asked, after she had had a double mastectomy, how her golf game was going. Her reply was that "now she played better than ever because there was nothing to get in the way of her golf swing." This is the kind of spirit and adjustment you will find in the majority of women who have had this operation.

"What about using my arm when it so painful?" This too will pass, but it depends largely on you. Do your exercises religiously. Yes, it will hurt—a lot. Nothing important was ever attained easily, and the complete use of your arm and hand is very important for your continued usefulness and happiness. Keep to your regimen of exercise, and gradually the hurt will diminish and the mobility of your arm and hand will increase until it will again function as

well as it ever did. Some women do not have pain or functioning difficulties; this can vary.

"What about the depression I am experiencing?" This is probably one of the hardest obstacles to overcome because you probably will get depressed, especially if you get overtired. Obey your doctor's orders in regard to adequate rest and exercise. The doctor knows your body and what it requires; he or she is most interested that you have a good recovery; and he or she also knows that your body needs the time and opportunity to heal after any type of surgery—the body cannot be "rushed" in this respect. Give yourself "time" to recuperate.

Remember, too, that your "soul" as well as your body has been "hurt." It, too, needs time to heal and to adjust. Talk out your fears to an understanding and trusted friend. Holding in and hiding your fears will not make them disappear, but will make them grow and become even more frightening and depressive. A shared load becomes a lighter load.

"How do I go on?" Keep as busy and involved as your doctor permits and as you feel physically able. Live every day to the fullest. Be cheerful and interested in life and in all that surrounds you. If you need encouragement or help, remember that there are other women who have been through the same experience as you and who are happy and eager to listen to your problems, answer your questions, and share with you their experience. If you don't know of anyone, ask your doctor or call your nearest American Cancer Society office. They will put you in touch with a volunteer who will counsel and help you.

Go on with your life. Return to your home or to your job as soon as you are discharged by your doctor, and "get on with it." Be grateful for each day—every day. Some day you may be able to help another woman over the same rough spots you have experienced.

Adjusting to a Miscarriage

George C. Thosteson

One of the functions of women is the ability to bear a child. Few realize what an intricate process conception is. For example, the sperm and ovum must unite at a specific time, usually a matter of only a few days in the woman's menstrual cycle. Both the sperm and egg must be relatively fresh; that is, an ovum fertilized toward the end of its stay in the Fallopian tube may not be as wholesome as if fertilized earlier. The sperm must be of good quality as well. If not, the product of conception itself may be imperfect.

Once an egg is fertilized, it travels down the tube to be imbedded in the wall of the uterus. The lining has to be properly prepared by appropriate hormone secretions. If these are inadequate, implantation will not occur. If the "take" is good, pregnancy proceeds. This implantation in the uterine wall happens 7 to 10 days after the egg leaves the ovary.

On the uterine wall the placenta develops. This is adherent to the wall by tiny fingerlike projections call villi. It is through these that the blood supply reaches the developing fetus. Imperfections in the villi, the placenta, or the wall of the uterus can mean that the product of conception will not last. Disease of the wall of the uterus and abnormalities in placenta development can be factors in termination of the pregnancy.

This article was especially written for this book.

When the products of conception—the egg, small fetus, and the placenta—are released prematurely, a miscarriage results. This may be complete, meaning everything is cast off, or incomplete, meaning remnants are retained. A woman may not yet realize that she is pregnant and may misinterpret the episode as a menstrual period. There may or may not be enough tissue evident to realize that she has lost a fetus. A miscarriage occurs usually in the first 3 or 4 months of the pregnancy.

If the fetus is more developed, it can be affected by other factors. A viral infection such as German measles is one. Diabetes is another. Defects and malformation in the fetus are still others. A miscarriage thus can be nature's way of terminating an imperfect baby. Analysis of the expelled embryo reveals that it is not alive. Ten to 20 percent of pregnancies result in miscarriage.

We all like to think of ourselves as normal human beings. We can see our skin blemishes and flat feet, but little do we know what is going on deep inside. What is the woman's attitude toward miscarriage? Some get pregnant unexpectedly; others want a baby and cannot conceive. Most are happy to be pregnant and look forward to the birth of the baby. A miscarriage may be a relief for a woman who does not want a baby or who is indifferent toward her pregnancy.

Doctors Corney and Horton[1] of the Psychiatric Clinic of Vanderbilt University state that some degree of psychological distress is not an uncommon sequel to a miscarriage. They say that this may start when the woman is told that a miscarriage is inevitable. For most in their study, the distress lasted only a few days to a week. There may be actual mourning with profound grief. Simon and associates[2] of the Jewish Hospital in St. Louis found that this may be an exacerbation of preexisting psychiatric illness. For some women there was a feeling of depression; for others a disappointment without depression. For the 80 or 90 percent of women happy with being pregnant, a miscarriage can be almost traumatic—a severe disappointment. Not appreciating the complexity of conception, she seeks a reason or cause for the mishap.

Often there can be self-incrimination. Something she has done has caused the loss of her pregnancy. Old wives' tales contribute to her dilemma. There may have been a fall, a car accident; she may have painted the kitchen walls and believes that the exertion or paint fumes caused the miscarriage. A blow on the abdomen or lifting a heavy object may be blamed. The truth of the

[1]R. T. Corney, M. D. and F. T. Horton, Jr., M.D., "Pathological Grief Following Spontaneous Abortion," *American Journal of Psychiatry,* 131 (July 1974), 825–827.

[2]N. M. Simon, M.D., D. Rothman, M.D., J. T. Goff, M.D., and A. G. Senturia, A. B., "Psychological Factors Related to Spontaneous and Therapeutic Abortion," *American Journal of Obstetrics and Gynecology,* 104 (July 1969), 807–808.

matter is that a normal pregnancy cannot be undone and does not terminate by itself prematurely.

In the adjustment to her misfortune, a woman must be made to realize that a miscarriage is not the consequence of her own deeds. She should be told that other factors at work were not conducive to a normal pregnancy nor to a healthy baby. Nature took matters into its own hands and actually has spared the woman the burden or grief of a defective child.

She may wonder if a miscariage will follow with subsequent pregnancies. Fortunately, most miscarriages occur with the second or later pregnancies. Thus, there can be one or more children in the family. It cannot be predicted that the explusion of the fetus will occur again. If the woman has some discernible illness, particularly diabetes, she can expect a recurrence. Some women turn out to be habitual aborters — they have recurring miscarriages — but even with that history, there can be a successful pregnancy. I know of an instance where a woman had 11 miscarriages and then bore a normal child.[3]

Can a miscarriage (technically called an abortion) be prevented? Sometimes. A threatened abortion is heralded by vaginal bleeding. With this symptom, bedrest is important. Intercourse during the first 12 weeks of pregnancy may be a factor in some cases, not only because of the possible trauma to the cervix and uterus but also because the female's orgasm can cause a release of a pituitary hormone that stimulates the uterus to contract. In some instances, the cervix may be "incompetent" so that the growing fetus is not retained. This can be corrected by surgery. Although spotting or vaginal bleeding may be an ominous sign, it does not always mean an impending miscarriage. About 25 percent of pregnant women may spot, and about half of these will abort.

Thus, in the adjustment to a miscarriage, the woman should have adequate counseling by a physician — a rational explanation as to why the pregnancy was interrupted. She should not listen to wild tales of nonprofessionals. The matter of self-incrimination should be dispelled. A miscarriage may be called an act of God because if all factors were in order, the pregnancy would have gone to completion.

What do you do after a miscarriage? Believe that you were spared the grief of an imperfect pregnancy. Then, try again in due time.

---

[3]R. K. Whitely, M.D., obstetrician, personal communication.

When Labeled Mentally Ill

Charles Zastrow

While working at a mental hospital, the author was assigned a case where a 22-year-old male decapitated his 17-year-old girl friend. Why did he do it? Two psychiatrists diagnosed him as being schizophrenic, and a court found him to be "innocent by reason of insanity." He was then committed to a mental hospital. Why did he do it? Labeling him as insane provides an explanation to the general public that he exhibited this strange behavior because he is then thought to be "crazy." But does such a label explain why he killed this girl, rather than killing someone else, or doing something else that is bizarre? Does the label explain what would have prevented him from committing this slaying? Does the label suggest the kind of treatment that will cure him? The answer to all these questions is of course "No."

What is schizophrenia? A common definition is "a psychotic condition usually occurring during or shortly after adolescence and characterized by disorientation, loss of contact with reality, disorganized patterns of thinking and feeling."[1] Let us examine this definition. People who are intoxicated, or stoned on drugs, or who are asleep, or who have not slept for over a day ex-

---

[1]Louis P. Thorpe and Barney Katz, *The Psychology of Abnormal Behavior* (New York: Ronald Press, 1948), p. 849.

perience a loss of contact with reality, and their feelings and thinking patterns become disorganized. Are they schizophrenic? No. What about the severely and profoundly mentally retarded who have a mental age of less than two? They have the above symptoms but are not considered to be schizophrenic. What about people who go into a coma following a serious accident? They also fit the definition above but are not considered schizophrenic. The 22-year-old male who committed the bizarre homicide knew the act was wrong, was aware of what he was doing, was in contact with reality, and told me the reasons for doing what he did. Then why was he labeled schizophrenic?

The truth is that there is no definition of symptoms that separates people who have this "disease" from those who do not. Many authorities in the helping professions are now pointing out that people with emotional problems do not have a mental illness but only emotional problems.[2] Terms such as "schizophrenia," "psychosis," and "mental illness" suggest that those so labeled have a "pathological mind" which is causing them to display strange behavior. The negative effects of such labeling is that the labeled person (and frequently the therapist) believes that the person has a disease for which, unfortunately, there is no "cure." The label gives the labeled person an excuse for not taking responsibility for deviant actions — innocent by reason of insanity. Since there is no known "cure," the person broods about his or her misfortune and idles away the time waiting for someone to discover a cure. The label sidetracks the person from examining the reasons why he or she is displaying strange behavior, from taking responsibility for that behavior, and from making concerted efforts to explore his or her problems in depth, and developing strategies for improving his or her situation.

Thomas Szasz persuasively points out that mental illness is a myth — does not exist.[3] He indicates that the term "mental illness" implies a "disease of the mind." He categorizes all "mental illnesses" into three types of emotional disorders and discusses the inappropriateness of using the term for such human difficulties.

1. Personal disabilities, such as excessive anxiety, depression, fears, and feelings of inadequacy. Such so-called "mental illnesses" may appropriately be considered "mental" (in the sense in which thinking and feeling are considered "mental" activities), but they are not diseases.

2. Antisocial acts, such as bizarre homicides and other social deviations. Homosexuality used to be in this category, but was removed from the American Psychiatric Association's list of mental illnesses in 1974. Such

---

[2] See, for example, Richard B. Stuart, *Trick or Treatment* (Champaign, Ill: Research Press, 1970), and Thomas Szasz, "The Myth of Mental Illness," *American Psychologist*, 15 (1960), 113-118.

[3] Thomas Szasz, *Psychiatric Justice* (New York: The Macmillan Company, 1965).

antisocial acts are in actuality simply social deviations and can be considered neither "mental" nor "diseases."

3. Deterioration of the brain with associated personality changes. This category includes the "mental illnesses" in which personality changes result following brain deterioration from such causes as arteriosclerosis, chronic alcoholism, general paresis, or serious brain damage following an accident. Common symptoms are loss of memory, listlessness, apathy, and deterioration of personal grooming habits. These disorders can appropriately be considered "diseases," but they are diseases of the brain (brain deterioration), which specifies the nature of the problem. The disorders, however, are not a disease of the mind.

Szasz states:

The belief in mental illness as something other than man's trouble in getting along with his fellow man is the proper heir to the belief in demonology and witchcraft. Mental illness exists or is "real" in exactly the same sense in which witches existed or were "real."[4]

There are three steps to becoming labeled "mentally ill": 1) the person displays some strange deviant behavior, 2) the behavior is not tolerated by the family or local community, and 3) the professional labeler, usually a psychiatrist, believes in the medical model and assigns a mental illness label. Scheff and Mechanic provide evidence that whether the family/community will tolerate the deviant behavior and whether the professional labeler believes in the medical model are more crucial in determining whether someone will be assigned a "mentally ill" label than the strange behavior exhibited by the person.[5]

The point that Szasz, Scheff, Stuart, and many other writers are striving to make is that people do have emotional problems, but they do not have a mystical, mental illness. Terms that describe behavior are very useful: for example, depression, anxiety, an obsession, a compulsion, excessive fear, social deviation. Such terms describe personal problems that people have. But the medical terms, such as schizophrenia and psychosis, are not useful because there is no distinguishing symptom that would indicate whether a person has the "illness" or does not have the "illness." In addition, as indicated earlier, such terms sidetrack efforts to explore the labeled person's problems in depth, and then to develop a strategy to improve the situation. Other undesirable consequences of being labeled mentally ill are that the individual may lose some legal rights;[6] may be stigmatized in social interactions as being

[4]Thomas Szasz, "The Myth of Mental Illness" in *Clinical Psychology in Transition,* ed. John R. Braun (Cleveland: Howard Allen), 1961.

[5]Thomas Scheff, *Being Mentally Ill* (Chicago: Aldine, 1966), and David Mechanic, "Some Factors in Identifying and Defining Mental Illness," *Mental Hygiene,* 46, 1962, 66-74.

[6]Thomas Szasz, *Law, Liberty and Psychiatry,* (New York: The Macmillan Company, 1963).

dangerous, unpredictable, untrustworthy, or of "weak" character;[7] and may find it more difficult to secure employment or receive a promotion.[8]

An even more dangerous effect is that the labeled person may come to view him- or herself as being different, as being "mentally ill," and thereby end up playing the role of a "mentally ill" person for a long, long ime. Everyone has a need to evaluate feelings, opinions, and abilities. In the absence of objective, nonsocial means of evaluation, a person will rely on other people to gauge beliefs and feelings. If others define a person as being mentally ill, and react to that person as if he or she were mentally ill, the person may well begin to perceive him- or herself as being insane. Cooley's "looking glass self-concept" crystallizes what is being said here. The "looking glass" says we develop our self-concept (our idea of who we are) in terms of how other people react to us. If someone is labeled mentally ill, other people are apt to react to him or her as if he or she were mentally ill, and that person may well define him- or herself as being different or "crazy," and will begin playing that role.

WHAT TO DO IF LABELED

1. When you have personal or emotional problems it may well be desirable to seek professional counseling. But, be wary if the counselor focuses the attention on medical labels rather than on exploring your problems with you. The main focus of almost all counselors is on exploring problems and helping people to develop strategies to improve their situation.

2. If assigned a medical label, do not view yourself as having some incurable disease. Do not attempt to use the label as an excuse for not taking responsibility for your deviant actions. Do not idly sit back and wait for the medical profession to find a pill to cure your "disease."

3. You should take responsibility for your behavior, and you should attempt, perhaps with the assistance of a counselor, to examine your problems in depth and to develop approaches to meeting the problems that are identified. If you want to improve, it is up to you to make efforts to stop displaying the strange behavior that got you into trouble.

The author a few years ago worked with a group of people labeled as "chronic schizophrenic" at a mental hospital. What was recommended to this group applies to others labeled "mentally ill." At the initial meeting it was explained that the purpose was not to review their past but to help them to improve their present situation and to help them make plans for the future. Various topics, it was explained, would be covered, including how to get out of the institution, how to prepare themselves for returning to their home community, learning an employable skill while at the institution, what to do when

[7]D. L. Phillips, "Rejection: A Possible Consequence of Seeking Help for Mental Disorder," *American Sociological Review*, 28, 1963, 963–973.

[8]Edwin M. Lemert, *Social Pathology* (New York: McGraw-Hill Book Company, 1951).

feeling uncomfortable or depressed or when they have an urge to do something that would get them into trouble again following their release. This focus on improving their current circumstances stimulated their interest, but soon they found it somewhat uncomfortable and anxiety-producing to examine what the future might hold for them. The fact that they were informed they had some responsibility and some control of that future also created anxiety. They reacted to this discomfort by stating that the staff had labeled them mentally ill, that they therefore had some incurable illness, and unfortunately could do nothing about improving their situation.

They were informed that their excuses were "garbage" (stronger terms were actually used), and we spent a few sessions in getting them to understand that "chronic schizophrenia" was a useless label, that what had gotten them locked up was their deviant behavior, and that the only way for them to get out was to stop exhibiting their strange behavior and to convince the staff that they would not be apt to exhibit deviant behavior if released. The next excuse they then tried was that their broken homes or ghetto schools or broken romances or something else in their past had "messed them up," and therefore they could do little about their situation. They were informed that this excuse also was "garbage," that what they wanted out of the future and their motivation to do something about achieving their goals were more important in determining what the future held for them than the past (which they could do nothing about anyway). Finally, after we had worked through a number of excuses, we were able to focus on how they could better handle specific problems (for example, depression); if they desired to be released and to avoid future trouble after release, the need for them to play the "sane game," that is, to stop exhibiting their strange behavior and to present themselves in a socially acceptable manner; their interest in learning a trade or taking educational courses; and what they wanted out of the future and the specific steps they would have to take to achieve their goals. The results of this approach were very encouraging. Instead of idly sitting much of the time brooding about their situation, they became motivated to improve the situation, and most have now been released.

If the reader is not convinced that mental illness is a myth, let us return to the 22-year-old male who was labeled "schizophrenic" for murdering his girl friend. A medical diagnosis should identify the general causes of the medical condition and suggest a treatment approach. In this case the label does not tell us what his problems are, nor does it suggest what type of rehabilitation is needed.

However, after the client described what happened, it was understandable (even though bizarre) why he did what he did and it also identified the specific problems he needed help with. He was a very isolated person who, besides the girl friend, had no close relatives or friends. He came from a broken home, was raised by a series of relatives and in foster homes. Because of frequent moves, he attended a number of different schools and made no lasting friends. At age 20 he met the victim and dated her periodically over a two-year period. She provided the only real meaning that he had in life. He held the traditional vision of marrying her and living happily together thereafter. However, a few months prior to the fatal day, he became very alarmed that he was going to "lose her." She encouraged him to date others, mentioned that she wanted to date others, and suggested that they no longer see as much of each other.

He thought long and hard how he could preserve their relationship. He also had rather intense sexual tensions with no outlet. Putting the two together, he naively thought that if he would be the first to have sexual relations with her, she would forever be tied to him. He therefore tried on several occasions to have coitus, but she always managed to dissuade him. Finally, one afternoon during the summer when he knew they would be alone together, he decided to make an all-out effort, even if it would be necessary to knock her unconscious. He knew it was wrong, but felt it was the one last hope of saving their relationship. Without her, he felt life was not worth living and he felt that if he could not have her, no one else would. (Such feelings are not atypical for isolated individuals involved in intensive romantic relationships.)

He again tried to have sexual relations with her that afternoon, but she continued to dissuade him. Being in a state of passion, he then took a soda bottle and knocked her unconscious. He again attempted to have coitus, but was still unsuccessful for reasons related to her physical structure. In an intense state of passion now, he totally lost control of his emotional passion. (All of us, at times, have done things while angry or in a state of passion that we would not have done in a calmer state.) At this point he felt his whole world was caving in; he realized this act of aggression would make her terminate their relationship. When asked during an interview what he was thinking at this point he stated, "I felt that if I couldn't have her, no one else would either." He sought and found a knife, became further carried away with emotions, and ended up slaying her. He knew it was wrong, and he was aware of what he was doing.

This case description identifies certain factors that help explain why this bizarre murder took place: including this man's loneliness and isolation, his feeling that continuing a romantic relationship with this girl was the only source of meaning in his life, his naive thinking that a forced sexual relationship would make the girl feel tied and attracted to him, having no sexual outlet for his passions, his jealous and possessive desires to go to extreme lengths to prevent this girl from developing a romantic relationship with another male, and his inability (at least during this one afternoon) to control his emotional passions. Such reasons help to explain why the bizarre behavior took place, while the label "schizophrenia" does not. Incidentally, he was seen by a psychiatrist a few months prior to this slaying and was viewed to be "sane."

If the above problems would have been known prior to the murder, the slaying may well have been prevented. What he needed was to find other sources of interest and other meaningful relationships in his life. Joining certain groups or developing hobbies may well have helped. An appropriate sexual outlet for his passions probably would have also been helpful. Better control of his passions and other sources of finding meaning may have prevented him from losing control of his emotions that afternoon. Reducing the intensity of his jealous and possessive feelings, along with developing more mature attitudes toward romance and sexuality, might also have been preventative. These specific problems are also the areas that he needs help with while in a mental hospital, rather than with finding a cure for schizophrenia. In no way does the author feel that this person should be excused for his actions, as implied by the term "innocent by reason of insanity." But he does need help for the specific problems identified.

In summary, when a deviant act occurs, asserting that the behavior was due to a "mental illness" provides no explanation. All such deviant behaviors are understandable when viewed from the actor's perspective.

Drug Facts and Effects

Wayne W. Dunning
Dae H. Chang

INTRODUCTION

America has become a drug-oriented society. We are continuously bombarded by advertisements suggesting the use of drugs that will relieve pain, reduce tension and anxiety, increase alertness, perhaps even help our love life. Most social occasions seem to "call for a drink" (often called "magic drug"), which invariably involves alcohol. Even physicians (who themselves abuse many drugs), subjected to the pressures of drug salespeople and advertisements, may look to a drug prescription to solve medical problems with a minimum of effort. Unfortunately, in many cases this practice is a partial reversion to ancient techniques—cure the symptoms and don't worry about the cause. In a historical context, drugs such as alcohol and marijuana have been used by humans for thousands of years.

A drug is a chemical that interacts with the body chemistry. In general, Americans, young or old, well educated or not, rich or poor, misunderstand the role of a drug as it affects the human body, including the brain, nerves, and other electro-activities. Every drug is harmful when taken in excess. Some

This article was especially written for this book.

drugs, even in normal quantities, can be harmful if taken in certain combinations or by hypersensitive people. Every day, literally millions of Americans abuse drugs, all because of the drugs' effects on the central nervous system. Sometimes the abuse is with the goal of self-medication. Generally, the abuse is due to one or more of the following reasons: 1) peer pressures, 2) the generation gap (this works in both directions), 3) frustration, 4) poverty, 5) parental abuse, 6) rebellion, 7) curiosity, 8) lack of goals, 9) lack of self-confidence, and 10) boredom. These reasons are essentially psychological, not physical in nature, and the abuser is attempting to counteract depression, forget problems, relieve pressures, be stimulated, or experience a sense of euphoria or well-being. Because the causes are psychological, there are no easy medical solutions to the problems of drug abuse. Psychiatry can often help, but the basic requirement needed to overcome a drug abuse habit is self-determination. A basic realization that the drugs are not solving any problems, but may, in fact, be creating or compounding a number of them, is necessary if the habits of abuse are to be overcome.

In this chapter we will look at some of the most typical abused drugs and their effects, both mental and physical. We will attempt to present the best available information on these drugs, but several factors should be kept in mind: 1) There is still a great deal that is not yet known about these drugs, especially the long-term effects of some of them. Just because a drug may not yet be known to be dangerous does not mean it is necessarily safe. There are still uncertainties about aspirin, even though millions of people have taken it for many years. 2) Drugs, especially the abused ones, may differ greatly in dosage, purity, contaminants, and methods of use. These factors can sometimes lead to significantly different results. 3) People are different, and the same dose of the same drug may cause different reactions in different people, and even in the same person at different times and under different conditions. 4) Some people use more than one drug at a time, leading to combinations of effects.

Before looking at the individual drugs, several terms should be defined, although not all authorities agree on these definitions.[1] Drug dependence is a state of psychological or physical dependence, or both, which results from chronic, periodic, or continuous use. Habituation is the psychological desire to repeat the use of a drug because of emotional reasons. Addiction is an actual physical dependence upon a drug; it includes the symptoms such as vomiting and convulsions upon withdrawal or discontinuing the drug use—these unpleasant symptoms lead to the understandable desire to repeat the use of the drug.

[1]The President's Commission on Law Enforcement and Administration of Justice, *Task Force Report: Narcotics and Drug Abuse* (Washington, D.C.: U.S. Government Printing Office, 1967), p. 1

ALCOHOL

Alcohol, the most widely abused drug, has been used in one form or another by humans for at least 5,000 years, and there is no reason to believe that its use will ever stop. Although many millions of people use alcohol more or less frequently without abusing it, there are millions of others for whom it has become a significant problem.

There are many different types of alcohol, all of which are poisonous. Ethyl, or grain alcohol (so called because of its usual source for drinking purposes—fermentation of grain), is much less toxic than any other and is the only one that would ever be drunk. In times of "emergency," many people have tried drinking other kinds. The results have been pretty consistent—they generally died.

Wine and beer can be legally prepared in the home for personal consumption or as gifts, but not for sale. Distillation of alcohol, to increase its strength, is strictly regulated by law. However, because of high taxes, a tremendous amount of illegal fermentation and distillation has been going on for many years—long before prohibition. One sample of this "moonshine" analyzed by the author was 80 percent alcohol, or 160 proof, which is potent indeed.

Medically, alcohol is used as a external disinfectant, as a solvent, and is occasionally prescribed for drinking to serve as a mild sedative. Although many drinkers still believe that alcohol is a stimulant, it is very definitely a depressant to the central nervous system. It seems to be a stimulant because it relaxes tensions and inhibitions. It also slows down mental activity, speech ability, reasoning ability, perceptions, muscle reactions and coordination, memory functioning, and respiration.[2] In sufficient quantities it causes stupor, sleep, coma, and finally death. If this last stage is not reached, the drinker can recover completely, although the process may not be very pleasant—the hangover (or aftereffects, such as headache, thirst, and nausea that follow the use of alcohol) is not much fun. Although people think they have a recipe for quick recovery, none has ever been demonstrated to be effective.

About 90 million Americans drink.[3] Nine million alcoholics are known to Alcoholics Anonymous, but the total number may be four times that.[4] Alcohol addiction involves two factors: 1) Frequent use of large amounts causes the body to adapt and require even larger amounts. This is not the

[2]Joel Fort, *Alcohol: Our Biggest Drug Problem* (New York: McGraw-Hill Book Company, 1973), pp. 22–39.

[3]Ibid., p. vi.

[4]Mimi Ferlemann, "Alcoholism: A Problem to be Reckoned With," *Menninger Perspective*, 6:1 (Spring 1975), 4–9.

same as "building up a tolerance," because, as far as anyone has been able to discover, no one has ever built up a tolerance to alcohol. However, the alcoholic frequently learns to compensate for its effects. 2) The withdrawal illness, or abstinence syndrome, when the alcohol is discontinued can lead to the DTs (delerium tremens) and other unpleasant reactions. Withdrawal from a severe habit of abuse can be dangerous and should not be done without medical supervision.

The physical problems caused by alcohol were thought for many years to be due primarily to nutritional problems. Alcohol is high in calories but lacking in other food value. Because of these "empty calories," alcoholics would tend to be deficient in their diet of essential food elements. Also, alcoholics display a lessened ability to absorb what essential nutrients they do get.[5] In addition, strong drinks can cause definite irritation to body tissues, resulting in ulcers and other problems. It has been shown that alcohol exerts direct toxic effects on the liver and digestive system.[6] Therefore, correction or prevention of nutritional deficiencies will not prevent damage to the body.

The social results of alcohol abuse cannot be overlooked: losses to business from absenteeism; premature death or disability from alcohol directly or from drunk driving (about 50,000 die in road accidents each year, and alcohol is a major factor in up to 70 percent of those deaths); law enforcement, court, and prison costs; and, of course, family problems. The cost of treatment programs for alcoholics is calculated to be at least 20 billion dollars per year.[7]

Alcohol is advertised and is available in many forms with only minimal regulation; usually these regulations deal with age (21 or 18), hours of sale, locations, and taxation. There are laws governing its use by automobile operators. There is a "black market" in alcohol for those who are under age and for those who want to avoid paying the high taxes; the penalties for violation are not heavy.

MARIJUANA

Marijuana (alfalfa, grass, hay, hemp, jive, love weed, Mary Jane, Mary Warner, joints, lid, reefers, roaches, rope, sativa, weed, and so on) is ob-

---

[5]C. S. Lieber, "Alcohol and Malnutrition in the Pathogenesis of Liver Disease," *Journal of the American Medical Association*, 233:10 (1975), 1077–1082.

[6]Ibid.

[7]Fort, *Alcohol*, p. vii.

tained from the flowering tops of the female hemp plant. The plant grows around the world, and in many places is cultivated for its fiber, used for making twine, rope, and clothing. The seeds are used in the manufacture of products similar to linseed oil. The quality of the marijuana depends very much on the location in which the plant is grown, since the active ingredient (tetrahydrocannabinol or THC) is actually a waste product of the plant. Hashish is a purified, high-strength preparation of marijuana.

Marijuana has been described since at least 2737 B.C. as being useful for treating a multitude of disorders.[8] However, there is little, if any, current legitimate medical use. The usual method of use is by smoking, either in cigarettes (reefers) or pipes, or by incorporation in food (marijuana brownies), or by extraction of "marijuana tea." Whether taken by smoking, eating, or drinking, the results are about the same, although smoking generally gives the quickest results. These results are, however, very dependent upon the taker, and his or her mood and personality, and, of course, upon the grade or quality of the marijuana — this varies widely.

The effects are rather complicated, combining both stimulation and depression.[9] It may induce exaltation, joyousness and hilarity, and disconnected ideas, or it may induce quietude or reveries. In the inexperienced, it may induce panic. Or, one state may follow another. There are no lasting physical effects and few reports of serious toxic effects from smoking or ingesting, although two known deaths have been attributed to oral overdoses.[10]

If any tolerance develops, it is very slight. Physical dependence does not develop; marijuana is, therefore, not addicting, but it may be habituating. There are a few physical precautions that should certainly be observed. Some people have tried intravenous injection of marijuana and have clearly demonstrated that this form of usage is hazardous.[11] Also, although the effect on the human fetus is not yet known, it would seem that using the drug during pregnancy is unwise.[12]

It has often been charged that use of marijuana leads to heroin or other stronger drugs. However, there is really no evidence to support this claim. There is also no scientific basis for such a theory.[13] The most reasonable suggestion is that some people who are inclined to use marijuana also would be

[8]C. M. Lieberman and B. W. Lieberman, "Marihuana: A Medical Review," *New England Journal of Medicine,* 284 (1972), 88–91.

[9]The President's Commission, p. 3.

[10]F. A. Ames, "Clinical and Metabolic Study of Acute Intoxication with Cannabis Sativa and Its Role in the Model Psychoses," *Journal of Mental Science,* 104 (1958), 972–999.

[11]R. J. Payne and S. N. Brand, "The Toxicity of Intravenously Used Marijuana," *Journal of the American Medical Association,* 233:4 (1975), 351–354.

[12]S. Hasleton, "Marijuana: A Brief Review," *Australian and New Zealand Journal of Psychiatry,* 6: (1972), 41–45.

[13]The President's Commission, pp. 13–14.

inclined to use other drugs. It also may be that the personal associations one makes through use of marijuana would expose the user to stronger drugs.

With regard to the association of marijuana, crime, and violence, the differences of opinion are absolute and the claims are beyond reconciliation. Neither side can prove their case at this time.[14]

The extent of use is not exactly known, but a 1971 survey indicated that 15 percent of the adult population in the United States had at least tried it, and 5 percent were current users. With regard to college students only, 51 percent had tried it, 41 percent had used it within the past year, and 30 percent within the past month.[15]

The greatest hazard with regard to marijuana is probably that of getting caught, since its use is essentially illegal in this country. The consequences of arrest (there were more than 720,000 marijuana-related arrests in the U.S. in 1974) are greater than any known physical or psychological damage at the present time.

AMPHETAMINES

Slang terms for amphetamines include bennies, black beauties, browns, cartwheels, copilots, coasts to coasts, crystal, dexies, eye openers, footballs, greenies, hearts, L.A. turnabouts, marathons, peaches, pep pills, pinks, roses, speed, truck drivers, wake ups, and whites. Many of these names are derived from the trade name, shape, or color of the commercial products. Amphetamines are synthetic stimulants and are not found in nature. Many years ago they were available on the open market and were used to reduce nasal congestion. They have also been used in controlling overweight, depression, and epilepsy. There are now better medicines for all of these problems. Although there are now only a few rare medical problems for which amphetamines may be justified, they are still dispensed excessively. Before recent production controls, the annual production was 5 to 8 billion average doses; approximately half were believed to have been diverted into black market channels.[16]

Amphetamines are usually taken orally, occasionally sniffed, sometimes injected. They are used to produce excitement, euphoria, and wakefulness. The

[14]Ibid., p. 13.

[15]American Institute of Public Opinion, "Special Drug Study," 1971. Reprinted in U.S. Law Enforcement Assistance Administration, National Criminal Justice Information and Statistics Service, *Sourcebook of Criminal Justice Statistics–1974* (Washington, D.C.: U.S. Government Printing Office, 1975).

[16]G. R. Edison, "Amphetamines: A Dangerous Illusion," *Annals of Internal Medicine,* 74 (1971), 605.

mental effects include irritability, restlessness, anxiety, possible hallucinations, and talkativeness. The ability to perform complex acts will be diminished.[17] For example, abusers have been known to spend many hours trying to repair gadgets that were in perfect working order. Quantity users may experience delusions and become paranoid; oddly enough, they will be aware of this latter effect. The lethargy and depression that appear after the effects wear off tend to induce the user to return to the amphetamine. About a third of a group of heavy users indicated that their memory and ability to concentrate had been impaired by amphetamine use.[18]

Physical effects include tremors, muscle and joint pain, and weight and appetite loss (sometimes leading to malnutrition). Although technically not addicting, amphetamines can be extremely habituating.[19] The long periods of wakefulness as a result of excess use can cause physical deterioration simply from lack of sleep. The human body was never meant to be operated in this fashion.

The phrase "speed kill" is "cute," short enough to fit on a button, and attention attracting. Although the body develops a tolerance to the pleasant effects of amphetamines, it does not develop a tolerance to the toxic effects. Despite this, there are very few documented cases of death directly attributable to amphetamines; one death was due to the swallowing of a great overdose in an attempt to hide the evidence from the police.

Although there is some evidence that amphetamines may lead to violent behavior,[20] there is no direct evidence linking amphetamines to crimes of violence, sex crimes, or accidents.[21] One of the current real dangers with street drugs is that they may contain impurities, some of which may be more dangerous than amphetamines. A few years ago, almost all street drugs were commercial products. However, this has been changing, and a survey of street samples showed that only 60 percent were actually amphetamines.[22] The implied danger here should be quite obvious. The 1971 survey also indicated that 22 percent of college students had used amphetamines at some time.

---

[17]J. C. Kramer, V. S. Fischman, and D. C. Littlefield, "Amphetamine Abuse. Pattern and Effects of High Doses Taken Intravenously," *Journal of the American Medical Association,* 201:5 (1967), 305–309.

[18]Ibid.

[19]J. B. Hart and J. Wallace, "The Adverse Effects of Amphetamines," *Clinical Toxicology,* 8:2 (1975), 179–190.

[20]Everett Ellinwood, Jr., "Assault and Homicide Associated with Amphetamine Abuse," *American Journal of Psychiatry,* 127:9 (1971), 1170–1175.

[21]The President's Commission, p. 30.

[22]Editorial, *Straight Dope Analysis Newsletter,* 1 (1973), 2.

BARBITURATES

Slang terms for barbiturates include barbs, blue birds, blue devils, blue heavens, double trouble, downers, goof balls, rainbows, reds and blues, red birds, seccy, yellow jackets. As with amphetamines, many of these names are derived from the appearance of the commercial products. Barbiturates are synthetic drugs available both in short-acting (4 to 6 hours) and long-acting (8 to 12 hours) variations. They are used medicinally to treat high blood pressure, epilepsy, and insomnia. They are usually taken orally, but are also taken sometimes by injection and in suppositories.

In ordinary doses, barbiturates act primarily on the nervous system. Typical symptoms include drowsiness, reduced coordination, and depressed reflexes. These effects are likely to play a role in traffic fatalities.[23] In combination with alcohol, barbiturates may be especially dangerous, sometimes leading to accidental death.

Overdoses will depress the respiration and circulation, leading eventually to unconsciousness. While unconscious, the user may vomit and inhale the vomitus—this can cause severe lung problems.[24] Sufficient overdoses will cause death, and barbiturates are frequently used for suicide.

The user develops a tolerance to the desired effects rather quickly if the drug is taken repeatedly. However, the lethal dose does not increase significantly, as evidenced by the low survival rate of "accidental" or "suicidal" overdoses. Barbiturates are both habituating and addicting. Withdrawal is more severe than with alcohol—sudden withdrawal can be fatal. As one forensic pathologist told the authors, "Show me someone who goes cold turkey (the sudden and complete halting of drug use) on a bad barbiturate habit, and I'll show you a corpse."

Outside of their illicit use, barbiturates cannot be implicated in criminal acts.[25] The 1971 survey indicated that 15 percent of college students have made use of barbiturates.

HALLUCINOGENS

There are a number of different hallucinogens, but we will be concerned only with the most potent—LSD. Slang terms include acid, chocolate chips,

[23]The President's Commission, p. 35.
[24]M. D. Altschule, "Toxic Effects of Barbiturates on Respiration and Circulation," *Medical Science* (December 1963), p. 83.
[25]The President's Commission, p. 35.

cubes, Big D, domes, flats, microdots, peace, sugar lumps, wedges, window panes, zen, and 25. LSD (lysergic acid diethylamide) is a synthetic material derived from a fungus, ergot, which develops on rye and other plants. Although first produced in 1938, its mind-altering properties were not discovered until 1943, and then quite by accident. It is one of the most potent drugs known, a single ounce sufficing for up to 300,000 doses.

It is taken orally in capsule form, on a sugar cube, licked from the back of a stamp, or swallowed on a tiny pill or "window pane." Labeled a hallucinogen, it may be more of a mind-distorting drug, affecting those parts of the brain that process and decode information. Its effects on users may differ more than with almost any other drug, and a given person may experience differing reactions on different occasions. The effects that can be experienced include the apparent hearing of colors, seeing of sounds, exaggerations of color and sounds, and other distortions and delusions, along with some hallucinations. The experience may be peaceful or may result in panic. There have been psychotic reactions (mental disturbances) that required long-term hospitalization.[26] Some artists believe they are more creative when under the influence of LSD, but none have been able to demonstrate any such improvement to their critics.

Physical effects include hyperactivity, tremors, increases of sweating, temperature, heartbeat, and blood pressure. LSD is not addicting but may be habituating. The body does develop a tolerance upon continued use, but the tolerance drops off rapidly upon withdrawal. Until 1970 at least, there have apparently been no human deaths directly related to LSD.[27] However, there have been indirect deaths, caused by such factors as the user believing he or she could fly or not be hurt by a moving car.

At one time it was widely reported that LSD caused birth defects and/or chromosome damage. There were a number of problems in the research that led to these results.[28,29] Other work seems to show that pure LSD causes no such damage.[30,31] Although there is no reported instance of a malformed child born to a woman who had used pure LSD,[32] there are cases of birth

[26]Ibid., p. 27.

[27]Anonymous, "Hallucinogens and Narcotics Alarm Public," *Chemistry and Engineering News*, 48:47 (1970), 44–45.

[28]R. Taska, "LSD-DMT-STP," *Texas Medicine*, 68:7 (1972), 94–98.

[29]W. W. Nichols, "Genetic Hazards of Drugs of Abuse," in: *Drug Abuse: Proceedings of the International Conference*, ed. C. J. D. Zarafenetis. (Philadelphia: Lea and Febiger, 1972), pp. 93–100.

[30]L. Bender and Siva Sankar, "Chromosome Damage Not Found in Leukocytes of Children Treated with LSD-25," *Science*, 159:3816 (1968), p. 749.

[31]M. J. Corey, J. C. Andrews, M. J. McLeod, J. R. MacLean, and W. E. Wilby, "Chromosome Studies on Patients (In Vivo) and Cells (In Vitro) Treated with Lysergic Acid Diethylamide," *New England Journal of Medicine*, 282 (1970), 939–943.

[32]N. I. Dishotsky, W. D. Loughman, R. E. Mogar, and W. R. Lipscomb, "LSD and Genetic Damage," *Science*, 192:3982 (1971), 431–440.

defects that may have been caused by street LSD combined with the use of other drugs.[33,34] There is slight evidence that LSD may increase the likelihood of babies being female,[35] and some evidence of adverse effects on unborn children of women who take LSD while pregnant.[36,37] Another difficulty in this field of research is that damage may not appear for generations.[38]

Since 1966 there has been a minimum of legitimate medical use and research, largely because of government regulations and red tape. LSD in combination with psychotherapy has proven of some value in the treatment of alcoholics, and LSD has been of some assistance to terminal cancer patients.[39] The 1971 survey indicated that 4 percent of college students had tried LSD.

OPIATES

Here we are primarily interested in morphine (emsel, M, Miss Emma, morph, white stuff) and heroin (dust, H, hairy, horse, noise, skag, skid, smack, TNT). Medically, these are narcotics, or substances that induce sleep, dull the senses, or relieve pain. They also may be used to suppress coughs and diarrhea. For the purposes of legal control, the definition of narcotic includes cocaine (a stimulant), and, in some states, marijuana. In 1971 it was estimated that 2 percent of college students had tried heroin.

Morphine, which constitutes 5 to 15 percent of opium, was first isolated in 1805. At one time it was thought that it could cure opium addiction. When the hypodermic syringe was introduced in 1850, it was thought that intravenous injection of morphine would not cause addiction — the stomach was thought to be a necessary part of the addiction process.

Heroin was first synthesized from morphine in 1874, and it in turn was first

[33]B. Bogdanoff, L. B. Rorke, M. Yanoff, and W. S. Warren, "Brain and Eye Abnormalities. Possible Sequelae to Prenatal Use of Multiple Drugs Including LSD," *American Journal of Diseases of Children*, 123 (1972), 145–148.

[34]T. H. Maugh, III, "LSD and the Drug Culture: New Evidence of Hazard," *Science*, 179 (1973), 1221–1222.

[35]J. M. Aase, N. Laestadius, and D. W. Smith, "Children of Mothers Who Took L.S.D. in Pregnancy," *Lancet*, 2:7663 (1970), 100–101.

[36]C. B. Jacobson and C. M. Berlin, "Possible Reproductive Detriment in LSD Users," *Journal of the American Medical Association*, 222:11 (1972), 1367–1373.

[37]R. J. Titus, "Lysergic Acid Diethylamide: Its Effects on Human Chromosomes and the Human Organism in Utero. A Review of Current Findings," *International Journal of the Addictions*, 7:4 (1972), 701–714.

[38]C. M. Berlin and C. B. Jacobson, "Psychedelic Drugs — A Threat to Reproduction?", *Federation Proceedings; Federation of American Societies for Experimental Biology*, 31:4 (1972), 1326–1330.

[39]Richard Ashley, "The Other Side of LSD," *New York Times* (mag.), October 19, 1975, p. 40.

thought to be a cure for morphine addiction. Due to its high potency, heroin is the narcotic of choice for about 80 percent of the known addicts.

Heroin is sometimes sniffed (snorting), sometimes injected under the skin (skin popping), but most often injected intravenously (mainlining), as this gives the fastest results. Its effects include euphoria, drowsiness, and respiratory depression. It is very often used as a means of trying to escape from an unpleasant reality. The user develops a tolerance to heroin, and it is very definitely addicting. The withdrawal process is very unpleasant, but is very unlikely to result in death. The unpleasant withdrawal symptoms can be relieved at any time by reverting to use of the drug.

Overdoses may cause convulsions and coma, but are not likely to cause death.[40] A number of deaths have been attributed to overdoses of heroin. Although there is no doubt that the persons were heroin users and that they died, there is evidence that these deaths are due to other factors.[41] Possible causes are the quinine adulterant found in much U.S. heroin, or alcohol or barbiturates in combination with heroin. Addicts tend to be very sloppy and dirty in their injection habits, often resulting in infections and even death — these effects are not directly due to heroin.[42] There has also been a high incidence of unusually severe tetanus cases among addicts, at least in New York City.[43]

While under the influence, the addict has little if any inclination to be involved in crime. However, in this country it is rather costly to maintain an opiate habit and avoid the withdrawal symptoms. This generally leads to crimes against property, such as burglary, in an effort to raise money.

The war in Indo-China has been blamed for an increase in opiate addiction. It has indeed been a factor, but so has every war since the American Civil War. In Vietnam, high strength marijuana and heroin could be purhcased at prices well within the soldiers' normal incomes. When these soldiers returned to this country, the situation was, of course, much different.

A variety of programs are available to assist addicts in breaking their habit. However, since the addict's desire for narcotics may persist for six months or more after withdrawal, it is not an easy process, and considerable supervision and control may be needed. Also, one must never overlook the problems that

---

[40]"The 'Heroin Overdose' Mystery and Other Occupational Hazards of Addiction," in *Consumer Reports, Licit and Illicit Drugs*, eds. Edward M. Brecher et al. (Boston: Little, Brown and Co., 1972), pp. 101–114.

[41]Ibid.

[42]T. H. Bewley, O. Ben-Arie, and V. Marks, "Morbidity and Mortality From Heroin Dependence, 3: Relation of Hepatitis to Self-Injection Techniques," *British Medical Journal*, 1, March 23, 1968, 730–732.

[43]Charles Cherubin, "Clinical Severity of Tetanus in Narcotics Addicts in New York City," *Archives of Internal Medicine*, 121 (February 1968), 156–158.

may have led to the addiction in the first place—they may still be present and lead to a return to the drug use.

COCAINE

Cocaine (big bloke, "C," cecil, coke, dream, dust, girl, gold dust, happy dust, joy powder, nose candy, snow, star dust) is obtained from the leaves of the South American coca plant. After the cocaine has been removed, an extract from the leaves is used in making cola drinks. Although legally classified as a narcotic, cocaine is a powerful stimulant and antifatigue agent. Medically it has been used as a local anesthetic, but synthetics have largely taken its place.

In this country, it is generally taken by sniffing, as it is absorbed through the nasal membranes, or it may be injected intravenously. In South America, natives chew the coca leaf. The survey indicates that 7 percent of U.S. college students have tried cocaine.

The mental effects include euphoria, restlessness, and excitement, with a lessened sense of fatigue. Larger doses may result in hallucinations and delusions of persecution. The effects are of relatively short duration and often are followed by a feeling of anxiety or fear. These aftereffects are frequently countered by the user with opiates or barbiturates.

Physical effects include increased pulse rate and blood pressure, insomnia, and loss of appetite. Higher doses lead to agitation, increased body temperature, and convulsions. With overdoses, the breathing and heart functions may be depressed enough to cause death. Habitual sniffers will find that the drug gradually eats away the nasal membranes, sometimes even perforating the septum (the dividing wall in the nose). Injectors face the typical problems of infections, etc.

There is disagreement on whether a user develops a tolerance to cocaine; some say yes[44] and others say no.[45] It is apparently not addicting but quite habituating, and its use may become a major preoccupation in the person's life.

CONCLUSIONS

Moderate use of some of these drugs is nearly harmless, but all of them present hazards when taken in excess. The user, or potential user, should always

[44]David Maurer and Victor Vogel, *Narcotics and Narcotic Addiction*, 4th ed. (Springfield, Ill.: Charles C. Thomas, 1973), p. 150.
[45]The President's Commission, p. 3.

carefully bear in mind that the drugs alter only the nervous system (if undesirable side effects are overlooked) and never alter the reality of the world. Any "escape" is only temporary and may be costly. Ultimately, these drugs really help nothing.

Should a person become habituated or addicted to a drug, there is no medicine or simple way to effect a cure. Self-determination is required. This involves a recognition of the problem (something that most alcoholics certainly refuse) and a desire to overcome the dependence on the drug.

Young people frequently ask: "What harm is there in using one of these drugs? It's my body and it doesn't hurt anyone else." If it, indeed, did not hurt anyone else, we would reply, "By all means go right ahead. We feel that everyone should have the right to go to hell in a manner of his or her own choosing." Unfortunately, abused drugs do hurt other people because in our civilization almost no person is an island. Friends, family, medical and social agencies, innocent victims of drugged drivers, victims of criminal activity to gain money for drugs, are involved. The expenses and problems of drug abuse go far beyond the individual user and abuser. There are some possible solutions that might be considered:

1. Stop the manufacture of these drugs completely. That approach was tried in "The Great American Experiment" (Prohibition) and failed completely. Smuggling and/or illicit manufacturing supplied the demand. These illegal sources are still supplying us with alcohol, marijuana, amphetamines, opiates, and cocaine. The United States subsidized Turkey's opium production, hoping to stop that source of illicit supply. However, the Turkish farmers still supplied smugglers, since they received more money for their crop that way, and other parts of the world also supply opiates to the U.S.

2. In our current society, we may each face daily competition, an attitude of cut-the-other's-throat, family and job pressures, impersonality, alienation, isolation, failures to succeed, jealousy, and other problems. Many of these problems are clearly a result of industrialization and urbanization. Should we advocate a "return to nature," thinking that might reduce these problems?

3. Our schools, churches, civil leaders, and the mass media are not preparing our youth to assume a more responsible role. Parents are equally responsible for their children's drug problems. All could do a better job.

4. American society is, in one sense, a "pleasure seeking" society, with so much being geared to the pursuit of "joy and pleasure." A drug, alcohol, is involved in almost every phase of our social activities. A person drinks because he or she is happy, sad, tired, depressed, angry, because he or she has succeeded or failed. Weddings, funerals, victories, dates, parties, business negotiations, trips, and other "unusual" occasions call for a drink. Perhaps some substitute for drink, such as a tasty low calorie snack, could be found. If so, could it be effective?

6. Every state has laws regulating drugs. The mere labeling of a drug as "illegal" does not stop people from using it, especially with the public awareness of organized crime, and corruption in politics and government in general. Instead of "legal" education, we must look more to "social" education to combat drug problems.

Ultimately, the quality of each person's life depends upon him- or herself. In the words of Tom Lehrer, "Life is like a sewer—what you get out of it depends on what you put into it."

What to Do
When You Discover Your Son or
Daughter Is Experimenting with
Marijuana or Other Drugs

Frank E. Ladwig

Do nothing, that's right—nothing. Sit down, relax, and reflect. Reflect on the television movie you and your family watched about the teen-age drug users interspersed with violence and glamour, but don't forget the commercials lacing the program advertising pain relievers, sleep inducers, cold remedies, and such. Reflect on the chemical intake of your whole family including your pet dog or cat. Additives, emulsifiers, steroids, preservatives all taken daily, without thought or hesitation.

Possibly guilt crosses your mind. "What have *I* done?" "Where have *I* failed?" You might consider your own drug use and maybe a slip into abuse occasionally (alcohol is a drug). Is self-condemnation useful at this point? Probably not, but an excursion into reality may be. If your son or daughter is aware of "being caught," he or she is feeling enough guilt and shame, embarrassment and humiliation for both of you. It may not show, of course, but that does not make it nonexistent. If your discovery is still "unknown," he or she is nevertheless walking a line of guilt and bravado about doing something on a continuum of slightly naughty to illegal. Guilt and fear and grown-upness are all a part of his or her baggage.

This article was especially written for this book.

184

"He (she) is taking drugs." "Maybe a hard-core addict." "A sinister pusher to smaller children." All these thoughts cross your mind. Perhaps you have discovered that his or her experimental batch is something that's been tried only once or twice. Your son or daughter may be engaging in his or her first illicit drug-taking behavior. What else might he or she be into? What about the latest math test or the trouble with French? Has he or she recovered from a latest crush or thinking of a new bicycle? Is your discovery of drug use a brand new facet of your child's life, isolated from everything else, the only missing part? Or has communication decreased somewhat in the growing-up process? Has your interest waned a bit as dependency decreased?

WHAT TO DO

Never despair. Shocks like this can be the beginning of new channels of communication. They can open vistas of rapport and interest from both sides; in short, they can force us as parents to engage our children in dialog. Caution: What you do *is* important. Insinuation, threats, accusations, unloading your emotional shotgun will not be very helpful; this will only serve to force him or her into a position. Your child has been bombarded about drugs, their use, and abuse since birth. He or she has seen it, heard about it, and now tried some—but that's all you know.

Two things are particularly important to keep in mind at this point: 1) he or she probably has more expertise about the drugs he or she is using and their effects than you do, and 2) listen. Ask him or her about the drug use. Don't panic. Muster up your nerves, be calm, and ask about what he or she is doing. You might even try asking why. The chances are good that he or she won't have a very clear answer, although this probably does not mean evasiveness. This is your opportunity to be rational and to listen to your child talk about his or her life. You own level-headedness and acceptance of him or her, not necessarily of the drug use, are the keys to a new understanding. You may want to find out more about other parts of his or her life that you may have misread lately, important aspects that he or she will be glad to know are also important to you. Be calm, relax, and listen.

SOME BACKGROUND

The amount of research in the area of drug use and abuse is overwhelming; the number of clinical and experimental studies on drug effects is staggering. The amount of usefulness in all of these findings is minimal. This is disappointing but true. Many researchers are biased in their positions and consciously or unconsciously bend their outcomes to meet these biases. Much of the information is simply the result of poor research, sample sizes too small or multidrug use among the subjects. There are also the variables of age, sex, frequency, and dosage. What is termed set and setting is also quite important in terms of anyone's drug use. *Set* refers to the mental or psychological state the user is in—happy or sad, reflective, introspective, or simply bored and wanting a new experience. *Setting* refers to the physical location in which the drug is taken, a sterile room, a hospital, a park, a rock concert—all have a definite impact on the drug effect.

Any chemical taken into the body has some effect on tissue and the body's natural chemical balance. Some drugs we know have a much more dramatic effect than others, particularly if they are synthesized into a concentrated form, for example, amphetamines, barbiturates, heroin. Generally, drugs that are organic or used as they are naturally have a less deleterious effect on the body. An example would be marijuana. The way the drug is taken is also important. Drugs taken by injection rather than orally are generally able to upset the individual's body chemistry more drastically.

The age of your child when using drugs on a regular basis is quite important, because significant research on drug effects upon children under age 18 is virtually nonexistent. Therefore, the kinds of possible immediate and long-term effects from drug usage by younger children is definitely something you and he or she should discuss together.[1] Again, listening to what he or she says about usage can give you good clues as to the danger involved, the need for outside help (doctor, social worker, mental health clinic, or such), or if he or she is simply experimenting. The less fuss and to-do you make of the situation probably the better it will be. There are fairly reliable estimates that say the majority of children in school experiment with some drugs at some point in their childhood. Again, listen and learn so that you can put the problem—if indeed there is one—into perspective.

A list follows that is my conception of a variety of drugs with which children might experiment and the order of their damage potential to the user. Remember, some drugs are more damaging for reasons other than the chemical itself; for example, the dirty needles and criminality of heroin, the malnutrition associated with methaphetamines, auto accidents associated with alcohol. Remember also that occasional or experimental use may not cause any actual damage. The following list begins with the most harmful of the drugs to the least damaging. (It is a subjective listing, based on my professional experience; new research findings could alter its order.)

---

[1]For factual information, see Chapter 19.

Glue sniffing—*most damaging*—brain damage, death from suffocation.

Barbiturates (downers)—physical and psychological dependence, withdrawal after regular use should be done only under medical supervision.

Methaqualone (ludes, downs)—same as above.

Methamphetamine (speed)—very high psychological dependence, can cause psychotic reactions.

Alcohol—high psychological and possible physical dependence, heart, liver, and brain damage.

Heroin (junk, smack)—high psychological and physical dependence, multitude of social problems, overdose potential, adulterants.

Cigarettes—psychological and physical dependence, damage to lungs, heart, and other tissue.

LSD-25 (acid)—psychological dependence, disorientation, possible negative psychological reaction.

Marijuana (pot, grass)—some psychological dependence (very little agreement on the fact or degree of physical-psychological damage).

WHERE TO GO NOW

With this beginning understanding about some of the types of drugs and some problems of their use, you as the parent should explore the degree of the problem. To reiterate, if the usage is only experimental probably a low key approach is best, at the same time trying to reopen other channels of communication. Take an interest in his or her own interests, and try to explore some things you can do together.

If, on the other hand, the usage seems to be heavy and you are concerned about his or her health, it may be necessary to consult with a drug program in your area, mental health clinic, private social worker, or psychiatrist. If you have a drug information service available, call them and talk about drug usage in your area. Whenever possible, try to take part in the treatment sequence—go to the clinic as a family or see the doctor or social worker together. If drug usage is heavy and is affecting the child's social relations and schoolwork, then it affects the whole family, and your involvement in treatment or alternatives will be crucial. No matter what the degree of use—he or she is your child and needs your love and acceptance. This can be given regardless of acceptance or rejection of drug-taking (or any other) behavior.

How to Have an Alcoholic Admit a Drinking Problem and Stop Drinking

Ronald J. Barta

On any page of today's newspaper or any popular magazine, on any TV channel or radio station, on billboards and elsewhere, we see and hear advertisements that pleasurably sensationalize the world's most deadly drug—*ethyl alcohol*. The American public has been led to believe that alcohol can provide instant relief and relaxation from a hard day's work by gulping down a couple of dry martinis before dinner, or can give a "high feeling" as a group of young people feel the cool night air at a beach party. Even though most Americans have become overnight ecologists, who filter out smoke pollution or recycle paper, bottles and cans, we still largely repress what Dr. Morris E. Chafetz, former director of the National Institute on Alcohol Abuse and Alcoholism, calls "the most untreated treatable disease" and our nation's third-ranking health problem—the *abuse* of ethyl alcohol in its brews, vintages, and distillations. Therefore, many people are forced to ask the question: "How do I get (someone) to admit that he (she) has a drinking problem, and stop drinking?"

This real question and its terms need clarification of meaning and interpretation; an expression of a feeling tone and behavioral process involved in

This article was especially written for this book.

the alcoholic's denial system and an explanation of the most crucial process of motivation, that is, *who* does it, *when* can it be done, and *how* to do it? It is well to begin by defining our terms clearly. *Alcoholism,* according to Mark Keller and Mairi McCormick, is:

A chronic and usually progressive disease, or a symptom of an underlying psychological or physical disorder, characterized by dependence on alcohol (manifested by *loss of control over drinking*) for relief from psychological or physical distress or for gratification from alcohol intoxication itself, and by a consumption of alcoholic beverages sufficiently great and consistent to cause physical or mental or social or economic disability. Or, a learned (or conditioned) dependence on alcohol, which irresistibly activates resort to alcohol whenever a critical internal or environmental stimulus occurs.[1]

The *physical aspect* is a form of physical dependency manifested by an uncontrolled compulsion to continue to drink, even when others would choose to stop. The *psychological aspect* is an obsession with the emotional need to drink to deaden "pain" or heighten "pleasure," which enables the alcoholic to project and rationalize his or her troubles to other causes rather than his or her drinking or him- or herself, which reinforces the denial (alibi structure) system of the alcoholic. *Alcoholic,* according to Keller and McCormick, is defined as:

One who is unable consistently to choose whether he shall drink or not, and who, if he drinks, is unable consistently to choose whether he shall stop or not. Or, one who exhibits the criteria of *alcoholism.* In popular usage, often equated with *drunkard, excessive drinker,* and *inebriate.*[2]

The key word is "consistently." Most people whose awareness processes are working for them have the decision-making ability to stop or cut down on personal or environmental cues that stimulate problems for the person. Correspondingly, the social drinker knows when to say, "No." Conversely, the alcoholic has an apparent inability to stop or cut down on his or her drinking. According to 1974 statistics,[3] there are 5,500,000 alcoholics in the United States, 4,600,000 men and 900,000 women.

The *alcohol abuser,* or problem drinker, is drinking, usually to excess, to escape from some basic problems in living. There are approximately 10 million alcohol abusers in the United States.[4] When a person, usually unconsciously, disowns his or her drinking behavior and sets up a rationale of behavioral constructs to reinforce that disowning, we call that defensive pro-

[1]Mark Keller and Mairi McCormick, *A Dictionary of Words About Alcohol* (New Brunswick, N.J.: Publications Division, Rutgers Center of Alcohol Studies, 1968), p. 14.

[2]Ibid., p. 12.

[3]Vera Efron, Mark Keller, and Carol Gurioli, *Statistics on Consumption of Alcohol and on Alcoholism* (New Brunswick, N.J.: Publications Division, Rutgers Center of Alcohol Studies, 1974), p. 12.

[4]Keller and McCormick, *Dictionary of Alcohol,* p. 4.

cess "*denial* or *alibi structure.*" Webster's dictionary defines *motivation* as "something (need or drive) that propels action, originating from within the person who acts," or "some inner drive, impulse, intention, etc. that causes a person to do something or act in a certain way."[5] These definitions help to give interpretive meaning to the real question asked—"How to have an alcoholic admit a drinking problem and stop drinking."

Let us now clarify further the feeling tone and behavior of the defensive system known as "denial or the alibi structure" of the alcoholic or alcohol abuser identified in our real question.

The late Dr. E. M. Jellinek, one of the founders of the Yale Center of Alcohol Studies (now the Rutgers Center of Alcohol Studies), presented a study[6] documenting 43 symptoms of drinking behavior and its physical, psychological, and social effects on how the alcoholic or alcohol abuser rationalizes, disowns, and denies drinking behavior from the prealcoholic stage (occasional relief drinking), to early stage (onset of memory lapses or blackouts), to middle stage (loss of control over the choice of taking the first drink and unable to stop drinking on his or her own after drinking starts), to, finally, the chronic stage (obsessive, continuous drinking life-style). Anywhere on this continuum of drinking behavior, the alcoholic or alcohol abuser may be struck by a crisis or behavior that is impossible to explain away, and his or her denial system or alibi structure finally collapses. Now the alcoholic or alcohol abuser may be able to comply and surrender to the undeniable fact that he or she is "powerless over alcohol—that our lives had become unmanageable."[7]

The progression of drinking behavior has finally reached its anxiety-induced desire for change. This desire can also be reinforced and induced at any stage along the continuum of prealcoholism to chronic alcoholism by the process of education of the alcoholic, alcohol abuser, and his or her family, empathetic confrontation of the alcoholic or alcohol abuser by significant others in his or her life experience, and referral to competent people or programs for diagnosis, treatment, and recovery. In most cases, this process of motivation will include any and all of these.[8]

Who is in a better position to motivate the alcoholic or alcohol abuser to make his or her own responsible decision to stop drinking? Logically, the alcoholic or alcohol abuser can best be confronted by those he or she knows

[5]Jean L. McKechnie, ed., *Webster's New Twentieth-Century Dictionary of the English Language* (New York: The World Publishing Co., 1974) p. 1173.

[6]E. M. Jellinek, "Phases of Alcohol Addiction," *Quarterly Journal of Studies On Alcohol*, 13 (1952), 673–684.

[7]*Alcoholics Anonymous*, Alcoholics Anonymous World Services, Inc., New York (1955), p. 59.

[8]"How To Help An Alcoholic Who Insists He Doesn't Need Any Help" (unpublished education material), DePaul Rehabilitation Hospital And Outpatient Clinic, Milwaukee, Wisconsin.

and trusts—family, friends, work associates, and significant others who may be knowledgeable about the illness of alcoholism. The success of the confrontation will depend on these significant others working together to accomplish the goal—intervention for the alcoholic's or alcohol abuser's referral, treatment, and recovery process.

When should the confrontation(s) take place? The old saying about having to reach rock bottom before one can be helped does not necessarily apply to all alcohol abusers and/or alcoholics. Each person has his or her own history and pattern of an alcohol-related life-style. Each person may be confronted by a personal crisis, personal friend(s), or a combination of both that may crack the foundation of the denial system or alibi structure. The result of the confrontation can bring about the gnawing question, "Am I losing control?" Whereupon the alcoholic or alcohol abuser may make his or her own decision to reduce or eliminate his or her own alcohol consumption.

Be that as it may, the timing of the confrontation is most important, that is, the first steps leading to actual confrontation can begin as soon as possible by the family members upon the obvious signs of incipient alcoholism. The timing of the actual confrontation of the alcoholic and/or alcohol abuser will be dealt with later.

How should the family and significant others plan and orchestrate their primary goal of getting the alcoholic to admit and accept a drinking problem and stop drinking? In general, it is necessary for us to accept within ourselves that there is no magic answer or miracle approach to fit every person and guarantee success every time. Before an alcoholic or alcohol abuser will admit and accept the need for treatment, he or she must be confronted and surrounded by the factual reality of his or her own real drinking behavior and its consequences to his or her total person and interpersonal relationships.

Specifically, there are three stages the family and significant others need to experience inter- and intrapersonally before they involve the alcoholic and/or alcohol abuser: education, confrontation, and intervention.

Education. Each person makes decisions based on his or her own knowledge and experience. Making a rational decision about the choice to drink or not to drink, or about how to motivate an alcoholic or alcohol abuser to stop drinking, requires adequate knowledge from competent resources. Hence, each person must learn the nature and effects of alcohol and alcoholism. Competent people such as doctors, psychiatrists, psychologists, social workers, alcoholism counselors, and other helping professionals who are knowledgeable about the diagnosis and treatment of alcoholism are resources to learn from. Most communities have community health centers that offer free an education program for all family members. Other information and referral and/or treatment agencies, such as the local council on alcoholism, general hospitals, social services, churches, and especially Alcoholics Anonymous, are ancillary resources.

The formal and/or informal process by which a person gains knowledge about alcohol and alcoholism should impart that alcoholism is a multifaceted health problem of physical, psychological, emotional, social, and spiritual dimensions. Although its precise causes vary by individual cases, it is generally characterized by progressive dysfunctioning in any one of three major areas: vocational-educational performance, family life, and physical/mental health. As these areas relate to loss of control in the consumption of alcohol, the affected individual and his or her family most frequently turn to community resources for help in breaking the problem's increasingly damaging influence on their lives. If this does not occur, the prognosis of what will probably happen to the alcoholic and the family is not a pleasant prospect — broken families, emotionally disturbed children, increased debt or bankruptcy, suicide or accidental death. If the family and the alcoholic or alcohol abuser do decide to get help, recovery must begin with the decision to stop drinking and stop managing the alcoholic's drinking life, to look honestly at self and do everything necessary to aid recovery, and to achieve some self-acceptance (or serenity) in the new life-style of nonalcoholic diet.

Confrontation. My own experience in helping families set up a confrontive process to motivate the alcoholic or alcohol abuser to face his or her real problem — alcohol abuse and dependence — has indicated four steps to follow:

1. Timing is crucial to the confrontive process for two reasons: first, the significant others (wife, children, brothers, sisters, parents, close friends, work associates) need to be gathered to surround the alcoholic or alcohol abuser with knowledgeable and empathetic concern for him or her, and second, the alcoholic or alcohol abuser should *not* be confronted when he or she is drinking or drunk or "coming off a binge" because his or her reasoning and sensing faculties are not then operating properly.

2. Documenting the drinking pattern and history, drinking behavior and its concomitant effects on interpersonal relationships in the family, job, and community is important. The significant others who document the facts are not present to threaten, cajole, coerce, or bluff the alcoholic or alcohol abuser, but they are present to clarify with feeling tone of empathetic firmness his or her present situation of alcohol abuse or dependency, lack of life-saving alternatives if abuse is continued, and the plan for recovery.

3. Offering hope only becomes apparent when the alcoholic or alcohol abuser complies and surrenders to the fact that he or she has a drinking problem. Hope exists when he or she admits and accepts the fact that he or she is powerless over alcohol and that his or her life has become unmanageable. Hope becomes supportive when he or she discovers that other alcoholics are recovering and living healthy, normal lives. Hope becomes confrontive when he or she experiences and faces each day as it comes and learns to hurdle the barriers to sobriety without drinking, with the aid of antabuse (disulfiram) and aversion therapy. These behavioral therapeutic approaches inhibit the conditioned response of drinking alcoholic beverages when he or she faces the barriers to sobriety.[9]

4. *Persevering* in the confrontive process will eventually penetrate the hard shell of denial, which the alcoholic or alcohol abuser has built around him- or herself. A never-relenting concern for his or her physical, emotional, and social welfare will allow him or her the opportunity to face the reality of the drinking behavior. Help him or her to define the decision, how he or she wants to reach it, when to begin, and when he or she expects to complete the decision-making process. If he or she does not respond right away, it may mean that he or she has not accepted the reality of the condition.

Intervention.   When the alcoholic or alcohol abuser agrees to accept help, he or she is to be guided and referred to the proper resources for treatment. Quick, decisive, and empathetic outreach is necessary to ensure him or her that a proper plan of recovery is being orchestrated. The family members and significant others working in consort will help the drinker ease into the recovery process in a supportive, yet confrontive way by entering any link in the chain of community services for alcoholism. Concomitant with this realization is the learned experience that an alcoholic or alcohol abuser ultimately recovers best in his or her own community setting. Separating a person who drinks from the environment that supplies the tensions, relationships, and other contributing factors is neither realistic nor defensible in treating the illness.

SUGGESTED READING LIST

Al-Anon Faces Alcoholism. New York: Al-Anon Family Group Headquarters, Inc. 1973.

Alcohol and Alcoholism: Problems, Programs & Progress. DHEW Publication No. (HSM) 72-9127. Washington, D.C.: Superintendent of Documents, U.S. Government Printing Office, 1972.

Alcoholics Anonymous. New York: Alcoholics Anonymous World Services, Inc., 1955.

[9]Ruth Fox, M.D., ed., *Alcoholism: Behavioral Research, Therapeutic Approaches* (New York: Springer Publishing Company, Inc., 1967) pp. 186–203, 242–255.

Alcoholics Anonymous Comes Of Age: A Brief History Of A.A. New York: Alcoholics Anonymous World Services, Inc., 1957.

Twelve Steps And Twelve Traditions. New York: Alcoholics Anonymous World Services, Inc., 1952.

BACON, MARGARET, AND MARY BRUSH JONES, *Teen-Age Drinking.* New York: Thomas Y. Crowell, 1968.

BLUM, EVA MARIA, AND RICHARD H. BLUM, *Alcoholism: Modern Psychological Approaches to Treatment.* San Francisco: Jossey-Bass, Inc., 1969.

CAHALAN, DON, *Problem Drinkers.* San Francisco: Jossey-Bass, Inc., 1970.

The Christopher D. Smithers Foundation, Inc., ed., *Understanding Alcoholism.* New York: Charles Scribner's Sons, 1968.

CROSS, JAY N., ed., *Guide To The Community Control of Alcoholism.* New York: The American Public Health Association, 1968.

The Dilemma Of The Alcoholic Marriage. New York: Al-Anon Family Group Headquarters, Inc., 1971.

FOX, RUTH, ed., *Alcoholism: Behavioral Research, Therapeutic Approaches.* New York: Springer Publishing Co., Inc., 1967.

JELLINEK, E.M., *The Disease Concept Of Alcoholism.* New Brunswick, N. J.: Hillhouse Press, 1960.

KELLER, MARK, AND MAIRI MCCORMICK, *A Dictionary Of Words About Alcohol.* Richmond, Va.: The William Byrd Press, Inc., 1968.

KINSEY, BARRY A., *The Female Alcoholic: A Social Psychological Study.* Springfield, Ill.: Charles C. Thomas, Publisher, 1966.

Living With An Alcoholic. New York: Al-Anon Family Group Headquarters, Inc., 1973.

MCCLELLAND, DAVID, et al., *The Drinking Man.* New York: The Free Press, 1972.

MILLER, WILLIAM R., and RICARDO F. MUNOZ, *How To Control Your Drinking.* Englewood Cliffs, N.J.: Prentice-Hall, Inc., 1976.

MULLEN, HUGH, and IRIS SANGIULIANO, *Alcoholism: Group Psychotherapy and Rehabilitation.* Springfield, Ill.: Charles C. Thomas, Publisher, 1966.

PLAUT, THOMAS F.A., *Alcohol Problems: A Report To The Nation By The Cooperative Commission On The Study of Alcoholism.* New York: Oxford University Press, 1967.

STRAUS, ROBERT, *Alcohol and Society.* New York: Insight Communications Co., Inc., 1973.

PART FOUR
INTERPERSONAL
PROBLEMS

*There goes that old feeling again, that dehumanizing,
empty and deep-down inside helpless reaction to an
assault on my dignity . . . a judgment made and acted
upon without reviewing the content of my character . . .
discrimination. This time I'm going to do something
about it, but what? Where do I go and what rights do I
have? Could I be wrong, am I really the victim of
discrimination or am I simply overreacting? A voice from
within, heard by millions of America's people of color
. . . the visible minorities.*

How to Handle Incidents
of Racial Discrimination

Marlene A. Cummings

DISCRIMINATION: REMNANTS FROM THE PAST

On December 1, 1955, Rosa Parks of Montgomery, Alabama, refused to
obey the long-standing Jim Crow ordinance that required blacks in Alabama
and elsewhere to occupy seats in the rear of the bus. Her feet hurt so she
refused to give up her seat to a white and would not move back. Mrs. Parks was
arrested; unknowingly, she had begun what became the famous Montgomery
Bus Boycott. The result of that year-long bus boycott, which kept 17,000
blacks from riding the buses in Montgomery, was a ruling from the U.S.
Supreme Court that laws requiring segregated seating on public conveyances were
unconstitutional. In addition to the legal results of that action, the boycott had
a very important psychological impact upon all people in this country. It proved
that minority citizens need not accept discriminatory laws, but could, in
fact, command equal rights when united behind a common cause.[1]

Racial discrimination in the late 1970s, more than two decades after the
Montgomery Bus Boycott, is stripped of most of its legal power. The passage

This article was especially written for this book.
[1]Harry Ploski and Roscoe C. Brown, *The Negro Almanac* (New York: The Bellwether Co.,
1967), pp. 27–28.

of strong civil rights legislation during the past years has moved the United States into what might be considered a "second reconstruction era." The overseers of the first reconstruction were the military. The overseers of the laws today, aside from the courts, are the Equal Employment Opportunity Commission (EEOC), National Association for the Advancement of Colored People (NAACP), Office of Federal Contract Compliance/Employment Standards Administration, Office for Civil Rights, Department of Health, Education, and Welfare (HEW), various state departments of industry, labor, and human relations/divisions of equal rights, and others, including the most important — we the people.

The laws providing equal rights are now a fact, but they must be understood, guarded, and implemented. The legal separation of people based on color, class, or sex no longer exists, but what does remain are attitudes. If it were not for such things as prejudiced mentalities and discriminatory institutions, we might be able to point with pride to our laws, as Congressman Joseph Rainey of South Carolina did about the justice of the South Carolina constitution during the reconstruction period. He said:

> Our convention, which met in 1868 and in which Negroes were in a large majority . . . adopted a liberal constitution, securing alike equal rights to all citizens, white and black, male and female, as far as possible. Mark you, we did not discriminate, although we had a majority. Our constitution towers up in its majesty with provisions for equal protection of all classes of citizens.[2]

Congressman Rainey had no experience with a previous reconstruction to anticipate the suppression or crippling of the equal rights laws that had been enacted. We do have today a history of what became of such outstanding pieces of legislation as The Freedman's Bureau (1865); Thirteenth Amendment (1865); Civil Rights Bill of 1867; and the Fourteenth Amendment (1866), after the First Reconstruction Act of 1867 was abolished. After the military rule provided by the Reconstruction Act had been lifted in the South, equal rights took a beating from the Ku Klux Klan, politicians who sought government power for personal gain, corrupt northern carpetbaggers and southern scalawags, and these rights seemingly died a violent death. The laws remained on the books and were left to gather dust on the shelves. We remained for too long a period, a country big on laws and small on commitment to them. It has been said in many ways that a person or country ignorant of its history is doomed to repeat it — it is up to us, the most important overseers of our rights, to guard, contest, protest, and challenge any threat to them. It is imperative that we handle incidents of discrimination or we might move into a time very similar to the postreconstruction era.

[2]William Katz, *Eyewitness: The Negro in American History* (New York, Toronto, London: Pitman Publishing Corp., 1967), p. 262.

"Could I be wrong, am I really the victim of discrimination, or am I simply overreacting?" In a society where racial justice and equality have suffered setback after setback and blatant neglect, it is not surprising to find that people who are struggling to attain equal rights question whether they are actually being discriminated against or are simply overreacting. A vital part of handling racial discrimination then becomes the attainment of knowledge about the nature of the problem. Prejudice usually is the prime motivating force behind discrimination. It is important to have a clear understanding of what prejudice and discrimination are. The definition of ethnic prejudice, which serves as a base for this discussion, is the one given by Gordon Allport, a psychologist and researcher noted for his work in social psychology.

Ethnic prejudice is an antipathy based upon a faulty and inflexible generalization. It may be felt or expressed. It may be directed toward a group as a whole, or toward an individual because he or she is a member of that group.[3]

Discrimination as defined by Dr. Allport is the understanding underlying the substance of this discussion.

Discrimination. Here the prejudiced person makes detrimental distinctions of an active sort. He undertakes to exclude all members of the group in question from certain types of employment, from residential housing, political rights, educational opportunities, churches, hospitals, or from some social privileges. Segregation is an institutionalized form of discrimination, enforced legally or by common custom.[4]

To understand prejudice and discrimination is to help the persons questioning their own reactions to an incident gain a greater level of confidence in their judgment. Persons being discriminated against may question the necessity of definitions when they have indeed felt the rejection. However, feelings cannot effectively file complaints. Many employers who intentionally discriminate against people are well aware of the actions that can be used against them and have developed many sophisticated ways to hide their real intent. It takes an alert and equally aware person to assess the situation adequately and later to follow up with a complaint.

The fear of discrimination is a very real threat to minority group members (blacks, Native Americans, Chicanos, Americans of Puerto Rican and Asian

---

[3]Gordon W. Allport, *The Nature of Prejudice* (Garden City, N. Y.: Doubleday Anchor Books, Doubleday and Company, Inc., 1954), p. 10.
[4]Ibid., p. 15.

ancestry, and others) because so much of it has been personally experienced. A recognition of this fear and how it might become so ingrained as to create undue anxiety are important to consider. Anxiety can interfere with a person's perception of a situation and weaken his or her ability to handle discriminatory situations properly. Chronic anxiety tends to put people on the alert and to predispose them to see any stimuli as threatening or menacing.[5] This could represent the indecision over whether an incident is discriminatory or not. An awareness of historical discrimination-related anxiety and a recognition of it in oneself can give an individual a sounder base from which decisions can be made about discriminatory incidents. One of the most frustrating situations for a person assigned to investigate charges of discrimination must surely be the complainant who fails to furnish adequate information because of a basic lack of understanding about the factors described earlier.

"What is there for one to do something about . . . just what is discrimination?" Just knowing the definition of a word is not enough to determine adequately when an act of injustice has occurred; that requires some action. Discrimination appears in many forms; to facilitate ways of dealing with discriminatory incidents, I have grouped them into two categories.

The first type of discrimination is that which is not controlled by law but is discrimination nonetheless, "de facto." This kind of discrimination is the result of habits that have been formed by social attitudes of the past and the kind that must be constantly challenged if there are ever to be meaningful changes. Following is an example.

Scene: department store. Incident: Several people are waiting their turn at a counter. The person next to be served is a black woman; however, the clerk waits on several white customers who arrived later. The black woman finally demands service, after several polite gestures to call the clerk's attention to her. The clerk proceeds to wait on her after stating, "I did not see you." The clerk is very discourteous to the black customer and the lack of courtesy is apparent because the black customer had the opportunity to observe treatment of the other customers. De facto discrimination is most frustrating—there was no law broken, the customer was served. Most people would rather just forget the whole incident, but it is important to challenge the practice even though it will possibly put you through more agony. One of the best ways to deal with this type of discrimination is to report it to the manager of the business. If it is at all possible, it is important to involve the clerk in the discussion. The discussion should include:

[5]Ibid., pp. 146–147.

An inquiry about the store's policy on serving minorities.

What expectations the store has for clerk/customer relations.

An explanation from the clerk concerning the incident. This approach requires an unemotional, assertive approach, which can be difficult when one is feeling upset about a dehumanizing incident. It is important, however, because all customers should be treated fairly.

You may expect a good deal of defensiveness from both the clerk and the manager, but your confrontation will certainly be a learning situation for both of them. Sometimes it may be necessary to write a letter to the manager, especially if the situation is not conducive for you to discuss the situation in person.

Other examples of de facto discrimination include:

Harassment from store detectives.

Failure to accept checks from members of minority groups with a statement, "We don't accept checks here," after it has been observed that the policy has not been applied to white customers.

Minimal service in restaurants.

The same procedure should be followed as for the example given earlier.

Frederick Douglass, noted abolitionist, lecturer, and author said, "Power concedes nothing without a demand—it never did and it never will. Find out just what people will submit to, and you've found out the exact amount of injustice and wrong which will be imposed upon them. This will continue until they resist, either with words, blows or both. The limits of tyrants are prescribed by the endurance of those whom they oppress." Frederick Douglass has been dead since 1895, and we are still resisting injustice.

"What Rights Do I Have?"—"de jure" discrimination.   Many acts of injustice fit into the category of "de jure" discrimination. This means that a law clearly has been broken and that there are measures that can be taken to correct the injustice. Antidiscrimination laws received a great boost by the passage of the Civil Rights Act of 1964. Every member of a visible minority group should be aware of what rights are protected by this act. The Voting Rights Act of 1965 and the Civil Rights Act of 1968, provision for open housing, are other antidiscrimination bills essentially geared to implement the Bill of Rights.

President Lyndon B. Johnson, during a television address in July 1964 to announce the signing of the Civil Rights Act of 1964, stated the purpose of the bill:

Its purpose is not to punish. Its purpose is not to divide but to end divisions which have lasted all too long.

Its purpose is national not regional. Its purpose is to promote a more abiding commitment to freedom, a more constant pursuit of justice and a deeper respect for human dignity.[6]

On the question of how to achieve the goals of the Civil Rights Act, President Johnson added:

We shall achieve these goals because most Americans are law-abiding citizens who want to do what is right. This is why the Civil Rights Act relies first on voluntary compliance, then on the efforts of local communities and states to secure the rights of citizens.

It provides for the national authority to step in only when others cannot or will not do the job.[7]

"What does all this mean?"   One of the greatest obstacles in the way of dealing with incidents of discrimination are the antidiscriminatory laws themselves. There seems to be no end to the acts, bills, and titles. One person, after spending hours trying to acquaint herself with her rights, threw up her arms in desperation, termed them all "title twitties," and said she was back where she started.

The federal law basically says that all citizens have equal rights in all areas by law. Compliance with the laws are left up to local and state governments, with the individual having rights to challenge the decisions of these bodies through the federal government. There are, however, provisions under Title VI of the Civil Rights Act, which guarantees that no person shall be subject to any form of discrimination in any program receiving federal aid. It also empowers federal agencies to take appropriate steps to counteract any such discrimination, particularly by denying federal funds to any state or local agencies that practice discrimination.[8]

Let's take a look at the rights that are protected. There are 11 titles under the Civil Rights Act of 1964 and 3 titles under the Civil Rights Act of 1968. They all basically address themselves to antidiscrimination legislation and can be grouped into four major categories: education, employment, housing, and public accommodations. The voting rights act guarantees all citizens the right to vote. To summarize, it can be said that all people now have equal rights by law and that in many cases these laws will have to be challenged when there is no compliance.

"What is there to do about de jure discrimination?"   It is necessary to have all the background information discussed previously to have a good case for

[6]Harry Ploski and Ernest Kaiser, *The Negro Almanac: The Black Experience in America* (New York: The Bellwether Company, 1971), pp. 147–148.
[7]Ibid.
[8]Ibid., p. 147.

filing complaints or suits and to know that you do have a case. Unfortunately, much of the burden of responsibility for correcting injustices lies with the victim. It is bad enough to be discriminated against; however, to go through further trouble can be worth it. A right given is certainly worth enforcing and keeping.

Antidiscrimination legislation has sought changes in education and attitudes rather than judicial enforcement for implementation of the laws. Conciliation and persuasion are key techniques that agencies use prior to initiating legal investigations and hearings. Taking all this into consideration, the question still remains as to what to do when you have been discriminated against.

1. *Find out who enforces the particular anti-discrimination legislation pertinent to your complaint.* Does the agency you are concerned with have a compliance officer (one who enforces the antidiscrimination legislation? If your particular agency does not have a compliance officer, what agency in your area does? This information may be obtained by contacting your local Equal Opportunity Commission, Human Rights Commission, or Equal Rights Agency, if they are available in your community. Otherwise, information can be obtained about filing general discrimination charges by writing to U.S. Equal Employment Opportunity Commission, Washington, D.C. 20506 or U.S. Commission on Civil Rights, Washington, D.C. 20445. (Agencies equipped to answer inquiries about specific complaints are listed at the end of this chapter.)

2. *Determine how a complaint should be made.* Usually the compliance agency or officer will assist you with this determination. Whether a letter or a complaint form is required will depend upon the nature of the complaint and with whom it is to be filed. A telephone call to the agency in your community that handles antidiscrimination complaints is often all that is necessary to take care of this step.

3. *File your complaint using the method designated by the compliance agency.* Your complaint should specify why you feel you have been discriminated against, giving as much specific information as possible. It is well to assess your case to place it in the proper perspective. It is acceptable to file a complaint where there has been a pattern of discrimination affecting others as well as yourself. Individuals as well as agencies can usually file complaints on behalf of an individual who has been discriminated against. Some types of antidiscrimination legislation require that you file a complaint within 180 days and others give no time limit. You should ask the compliance officer about this stipulation. There is always an advantage in filing a complaint soon after the incident has taken place. The information retained is usually more accurate, and in some places results from your complaint are slow in coming.

4. *Can you expect harassment from the agency discriminating against you?* Establishments or agencies are prohibited from discharging or discriminating against any employee or applicant for employment because a complaint has been made against them. This also holds true in institutions of education where a student may wish to file a complaint.

5. *Other things to do about discrimination.* Inquire at your local bar association about attorneys who specialize in civil rights cases. Hire one and leave most of the work up to the attorney. This route, provided you have the finances, will usually end up in court. If you cannot afford to hire an attorney, contact your local legal aid services. Fees for legal aid services are usually based on the client's ability to pay. If a suit is filed where there is a settlement expected, some lawyers may agree to take your case on consignment. This means they will expect a percentage of what you win in the decision.

Consult your local NAACP. They will usually be able to offer you advice about where to go. They may agree to have one of their attorneys work on your case, depending upon whether the decision can affect large numbers of people or result in amendments to put more "teeth" into existing laws. The effectiveness and types of services that can be rendered by the NAACP depend to a large extent upon the community and the support it receives, because it is a voluntary agency. Also consult your local Urban League. The League's major function in personal discrimination matters is informational. This agency could save you the trouble of writing for information because they are usually well stocked with all the recent information on antidiscrimination laws and compliance agencies.

6. *What can you expect to happen to your complaint when filed through a government compliance agency?* You can expect some compliance with the law or the compliance agency will take the next step, which would involve federal enforcement such as revoking federal funds, delaying new awards of federal funds, and barring the agency from receiving any future funds. The Department of Justice or Attorney General may also file a suit against the agency. In employment complaints, back pay can be obtained, but this usually occurs as a result of a law suit. In these instances, attorney's fees are paid as well as the court cost when the agency has been found in violation of a civil rights law.

GOVERNMENT AGENCIES

Government agencies to be contacted about specific discrimination complaints are:

1. Office of Federal Contract Compliance/Employment Standards Administration, U.S. Department of Labor, Washington, D. C. 20210

   Discrimination in employment (including hiring, upgrading, salaries, fringe benefits, training and other conditions of employment) on the basis of race, color, religion, national origin or sex. Covers all establishments with federal contracts over $10,000 or grants.

2. Office of Civil Rights
   Department of Health, Education and Welfare, Washington, D.C. 20425

   Employment discrimination as above, specifically where federal funds are used to provide employment. Covers all establishments with federal grants, loans, and contracts (except contracts of insurance or guaranty).

3. U.S. Equal Employment Opportunity Commission
   Office of the General Consul
   1800 G. Street N.W., Washington, D.C. 20506

   All employment-related discrimination. Referrals may be given for local agencies.

   State Departments of Industry, Labor, and Human Relations/Equal Rights Division (check directory in your area)

   All discrimination covered by law, housing, education, employment. Referrals may be given for local agencies.

4. Mayor's office
   For all types of discrimination, it is wise to see if there is a local Equal Opportunities Commission or Human Relations Agency.

REVIEW OF THE LEGAL STATUS OF MINORITIES

Employment rights have been covered in this chapter, but a brief review of the legal status of minorities in the areas of voting, housing, public accommodation, and education is important.[9]

Voting

Double standards for minorities are prohibited in all voting procedures. Specifically, the law has abolished literacy, knowledge, and character lists as qualifications for voting.

Housing

There is a federal open housing ordinance; however, many states have not adopted an ordinance. Some states may require a Supreme Court decision on a complaint that has been filed.

[9]Ploski and Kaiser, *The Negro Almanac*, pp. 243-273.

Public accommodations

Discrimination in the use of public accommodations — hotels, motels, restaurants, gasoline stations, and places of amusement — whose operations involve interstate commerce, is prohibited.

Public facilities

Exclusion from and unequal treatment in all public-owned and operated facilities, including parks, stadiums, and swimming pools is prohibited.

Education, public schools

Technical and financial aid is provided to all school districts engaged in the process of desegregation. The Attorney General is empowered to sue for desegregation, provided private citizens are not in a position to do so.

Institutions of higher education and professional schools

Where any federal funding is granted, discrimination for admission is prohibited.

SUMMARY

The United States has traveled a long way on the path toward achieving equal rights for all citizens. The laws have been passed that are necessary for the attainment of these rights. In fact, they have been in existence since the Bill of Rights was passed, but we have needed additional ammunition in the form of acts, titles, and amendments. You, the overseer of your rights, must remember what happened in the past reconstruction era and not allow it to happen again.

Facing Job Discrimination:

What Women Can Do

Leticia M. Smith

WHY IS IT IMPORTANT TO KNOW ABOUT JOB DISCRIMINATION?

There are several reasons why every woman should learn as much as possible about job discrimination. Among these reasons are the increase in participation of women in paid employment, the extensive practice of sex discrimination in employment, and the fact that no one should tolerate treatment as a second-class citizen.

In the 1940s, 25 percent of the work force of the United States was female; in the 1970s, 38 percent of all workers are women. The greatest increase in participation has occurred among older women, followed by the increase among young mothers. On the average, a young woman of 18 today can expect to work for at least 30 years — a large part of a lifetime — and no woman can afford to ignore the direction and quality those years take. The issue is not whether women should work or not; the questions that need to be raised are what types of work they should be able to get, for what benefits they should work, and how they should be able to optimize their work opportunities.

In 1968, 60 percent of the female labor force was comprised of women who were either single, widowed, divorced, separated from their husbands, or

This article was especially written for this book.

married to husbands who earned less than $5,000 a year. Therefore, 60 per-
cent of the female work force was self-supporting or contributing to the essential support of others. Yet, in the same year, the data showed that women as a
group earned only 59 percent of the white male median, and nonwhite
women only 46 percent. Only 14 percent of all full-time women workers
earned over $7,000, compared to 60 percent of all male workers.

These figures are not surprising, considering the fact that women are concentrated in a very small number of jobs. In 1969, the Bureau of the Census
reported that half of all women workers were concentrated in 21 job
categories out of a possible 250; a quarter of that number in just 5 job
categories—elementary school teacher, secretary-stenographer, waitress,
bookkeeper, and private household worker. In comparison, half of the men
were spread across 65 occupational categories.

The limited jobs for women tend to be predominantly female, a fact that
has not changed since 1900. In 1900, half of all women workers were in jobs in
which 70 percent or more of the work force was women. The same is true in
1970.

WHAT IS SEX DISCRIMINATION IN EMPLOYMENT?

In lay usage, sex discrimination in employment means the process by which
gender is used as a basis for making decisions in the employment of an individual or of a group. In legal terms, sex discrimination takes on a more cir-
cumscribed meaning; it refers to illegal discrimination in which the employment practice either has *disparate* impact on one sex compared to the other,
or is one that treats the sexes in a *differential* manner. Whether the employer
intended to discriminate or not is immaterial to determining whether a practice is discriminatory or not. An employment practice is said to have disparate
impact when a rule or standard is applied equally to men and women but
serves to exclude more of one sex, or perpetuate past discrimination on the
basis of sex. Differential treatment is a form of discrimination in which different rules or standards are raised for the employment of men as opposed to
women. It can also mean the use of a single rule or standard applied differently to men as opposed to women. The only justification that an employer
may have for a discriminatory practice is that it is a business necessity (not
convenience) or that the practice is required by the nature of the job.

Sex discrimination occurs in all aspects of employment: announcement of
job openings, job application forms, interviews, hiring, wages, fringe
benefits, conditions of work, seniority provisions, layoffs, dismissals, rehir-
ings. Therefore, a woman who is vigilant about her rights has to be eternally
alert.

WHAT ARE SOME EXAMPLES OF DISCRIMINATORY PRACTICES?

Job announcements.   There are several ways by which employers and unions discriminate in the announcement of job openings. One way is by selective announcement of these openings — by word of mouth or by posting announcements in places infrequently visited by women. A second way is by advertising sex preference. Classified advertisements for the "young, aggressive male" are legion despite the illegal nature of 99 percent of these preferences. A third, and specious, way is by the formulation of requirements that exclude more women than men. Upon challenge, many of these requirements are shown to have little relationship to job performance. Some examples are requirements that the applicant be no shorter than 5 ' 8 " (which disqualifies more women than men), or have five years of a very specific type of administrative experience, which very few women have because of past discriminatory employment practices.

Interview.   There are some behaviors of interviewers who screen and select applicants that set the tone of the interview differently for men and for women. The difference in tone can convey to the applicant a preference for characteristics culturally deemed significant for only one or the other of the sexes. The interviewer may phrase questions in an accusative, uninterested, or discouraging way when the interviewee is a woman. "You are not *really* interested in this job, are you? This job would require extensive traveling by yourself, meeting clients who are all men . . ." Another way is to start out the conversation by addressing the woman familiarly by her first name, without asking her permission. A profusion of comments on the applicant's physical appearance by the interviewer also distracts from the otherwise professional conduct of the interview, and conveys that the interviewer is not going to be too sensitive to the job-related information that might be obtained from the applicant. Young, attractive female applicants, irrespective of their attainment or experience, are particularly vulnerable to this experience.

Aside from the tone of the interview, more direct questions intended to sort out women on the basis of stereotype assumptions are: "Do you have a boyfriend? When are you getting married? What type of contraceptive are you going to use?" Translated, this series of questions communicates: "Well, if you are going to get married, that means that you will either move to follow your husband or have children soon, which means you will drop out of work. You are not going to be a steady, reliable employee. We cannot invest much time and money on you because you will leave us for family reasons." If it is a married woman applying for a job, the interviewer may ask: "How long is your husband going to be in the area? Who takes care of your children?" The assumption behind these questions is that the woman's job is only secondary to her husband's, that it is her primary responsibility to take care of children, and, consequently, the employer should be wary of employing women with children since they frequently take off when the children are sick. Small wonder that these questions are never asked of men.

Application forms.   Most state laws allow an employer to ask any question of an applicant for a job as long as the information obtained is not used in a discriminatory fashion or does not have discriminatory results. However, responses to questions on age, marital status, number and age of children, mode of child care, nature of employment of one's spouse, spouse's income, whether one has relatives employed in the organization have often been used against women. Since more women return to paid employment after the youngest child enters school, or enter the labor market for the first time, there is a growing number of women who are at an age disadvantage in a youth-oriented and work-oriented society. Women who have not followed the same continuous employment pattern as most males' careers are punished for fulfilling cultural expectations of motherhood.

Even when the responses to preemployment forms are not used to discriminate against women, the questions asked may deter women from pursuing jobs in anticipation that employers would not want them because they have small children or because they have at the time of application no reliable means of child care. In effect, women can and have been excluded from employment opportunities by preemployment questions.

Testing.   Tests in employee selection may use one or a combination of the oral, written, or demonstration of performance versions of examinations. Theoretically, results are compared with some predetermined acceptable standard of performance, including comparison of the applicants with each other. Discrimination in the testing procedure can occur in the manner of administration of the tests, in the actual content of the tests, and in the standard of acceptable performance that is used.

There has not been sufficient attention to the effect of the sex of a person administering the test in comparison with the effect of the sex composition of those who take tests together on the performance of women and men in specific types of tasks. As the social sciences become more attuned to and sophisticated in the study of the influence of gender on test performance, it will be more possible to develop strategies to deal with this potential source of employment discrimination.

The content of tests must be significantly related to job performance. Yet employers insist on using tests that have questionable validity. In other words, many tests have not been validated against the performance of incumbents of jobs, have not been validated for a variety of population groups that are potential sources of recruitment, or have not been shown to measure the traits or characteristics they purport to measure. Personality tests, in particular, have generated more controversy than any other class of personnel selection tools. Many industrial psychologists themselves agree that personality tests have a dismal record in predicting job success. As Maier puts it:

> In general, personality tests may be helpful in selection and placement, but they frequently do not survive rigorous validation procedures. Despite the usefulness of current tests for clinical purposes, authorities seriously question their automatic inclusion in batteries for personnel purposes and suggest that well-developed biographic inventories may prove more useful for organizations at present.[1]

Performance tests of physical agility used in police and firefighter examinations are now being reconsidered because of the challenge by minority and women's groups. These groups charge that the use of these tests screens out a disproportionate number of nonwhite minorities and women, because the tests have not been properly validated. To validate agility tests adequately, the sample used must include women and minorities. Another charge is that the tests have not been shown to be truly predictive of one's performance on the job.

Selection standards.   The process of employee selection encompasses all of the procedures mentioned above: the manner and content of job announcements, interview, and testing. In July 1970, the Equal Employment Opportunity Commission issued the "Guidelines on Employee Selection Procedures." These guidelines prohibit any job qualifications or selection standards that disproportionately screen out women, minorities, and other groups protected by Title VII of the Civil Rights Act of 1964, unless 1) the selection standards can be shown to be significantly related to job performance, and 2) no alternate nondiscriminatory standards can be developed to meet requirements shown to be justified by "business necessity." (Courts have interpreted "business necessity" very narrowly, requiring overriding evidence that a discriminatory practice is "essential" to the safe and efficient operation of the business, and for a showing of extreme adverse financial impact in changing the employment practice.) The selection procedures covered by the Guidelines include any paper and pencil performance measure used as a basis for any employment decision, as well as other requirements such as personal

---

[1]Norman R. F. Maier, *Psychology in Industrial Organizations* (Boston: Houghton-Mifflin, 1973), p. 261.

histories, biographical information, background requirements, interviews, application forms, and interviewer rating systems that result in differential rejection of groups.

Two actual case histories will illustrate the use of sex as a selection standard later shown to be unrelated to the requirements of the job.

Margaret Ann Collins vs. Rural Mutual Insurance Co.   Rural Mutual Insurance Company, a small firm of 300 employees, had seven computer operators in its Data Processing Department, where a vacancy occurred. The Personnel Employment Manager, Michael Busold, contacted several recruitment sources, including the Madison Technical College. In the general announcement, there was no indication of sex preference; the only requirement was a junior college education, and the duty on the job was to run a Model 30 computer on the second shift. No other desired qualifications were asked for. John Murray, the Data Processing Manager, personally contacted Werner Schueppel, professor and head of the Data Processing Department at the college, regarding the job opening. Murray implied preference for a male because the plant is located "out in the country," and because the computer operator would be working alone in the building during evening hours. On the basis of the suggested preference, Schueppel posted the opening, with the indication that it was for a male, on one of the college bulletin boards.

Margaret Ann Collins saw the announcement on the bulletin board and, undeterred by the sex preference, applied for the job. Busold, the Personnel Manager, interviewed her and four males. All of the males had a degree in data processing from a technical college and, therefore, met the only announced requirement (aside from being male) for the job. At the time of her application, Collins had a degree in business machine operation and had just completed her first year of college work on data processing. She also had seven years of experience as a key punch operator and a computer operator. Furthermore, she had on-the-job-training as a computer operator. Her competition for the job consisted of two men who had no work experience, and one man who had seven months of experience as a programmer in a state agency, and one man who had 13 months of experience as a computer operator. Only the two men with work experience were referred by the Personnel Manager to the head of the Data Processing Department. The Personnel Manager was aware that Murray preferred a male. One of the two males was hired for the job.

Collins filed a complaint of sex discrimination in hiring with the state Fair Employment Commission. During the hearing, it was found that no woman had ever been hired in the night shift of the data processing department.

Females were assigned to the day shift, males to the night shift. The night shift paid more than the day shift. The Fair Employment Commission found discrimination and ordered Rural Mutual to cease and desist from refusing to hire and from expressing preference for persons of one sex, except where work conditions provide valid reasons for hiring only men or women. The order further instructed that Collins be considered solely on the basis of her qualifications and without regard to her sex for future job vacancies for which she applies.

Marguerite J. Wellner vs. State of Wisconsin, Dept. of Natural Resources. The employer, State of Wisconsin, Department of Natural Resources, is a state agency that operates the Wilson Nursery at Buscobel, Wisconsin. The purpose of the nursery is to grow shrubs, conifers, and hardwood for conservation use. The employment requirements of the nursery vary on a seasonal basis. The staff of full-time personnel who work at the nursery 12 months of the year is augmented regularly by other persons hired to work on a part-time basis. Seasonal employees who work seven months a year are hired through a civil service examination, and they retain their employee status through the entire year. Limited Term Employees (LTE), who work each fall and spring, are hired through an informal process conducted at the Wilson Nursery.

Marguerite Wellner had worked as an LTE with the Wilson Nursery for 14 years. In the fall of 1973, Superintendent Richard Camp of the Wilson Nursery hired 14 LTES: 10 women, who were assigned to the lifting and transplanting crew at $2.25 per hour, and 4 men, who were assigned as interim replacement for seasonal employees at $3 per hour. In selecting persons for seasonal assignment, Camp relied solely upon his own familiarity with the candidates' previous limited term work to determine the ability of each person to do the work. It was his personal view that heavy manual duties made the job one for which no woman could be considered.

Wellner filed a complaint of sex discrimination in pay and in the selection process with the state fair employment agency. It was determined during the hearing that the greatest effort of a person assigned to work as an interim replacement seasonal employee is to lift 100-pound loads. Wellner's work assignments over the 14-year period of her employment at the nursery included heavy manual labor. During the earlier term of part-time employment, she was assigned to pull trees and place them in boxes using moss as a packing material. That work required that she carry a large box of moss weighing 100 pounds along her work area. During the spring of 1973, she worked for two and a half weeks in the Packing Shed. She carried 30- to 100-pound bundles of nursery stock from her work area to a loading station 30 feet away. That fall, she and a full-time male employee were assigned to dig trenches by hand all day for two and a half weeks. The trenches, later used for heeling in shrubs, were between one and one-half feet deep. When Wellner was not working at the Wilson Nursery, she operated a farm. Her work regularly included driving a tractor, operating a thresher, bailing and unloading hay, and shoveling corn. Each winter over the past 14 years she drove a 2-ton truck loaded with Christmas trees, which she loaded and unloaded by herself. Clearly, she was entirely capable of all the duties assigned to the 4 male LTES who were selected to work as interim replacements for seasonal workers. The job as an interim replacement offered definite advantages in comparison to Wellner's assignment. The four men were able to begin work at an earlier date, accrue more time on the job, and be paid 75 cents an hour more over the entire period.

The hearing examiner found no discrimination in wages because there was, in fact, a greater variety of jobs; the hearing examiner found no discrimination in pay differential; however, the selection process that placed the women differently from the men was judged discriminatory. In the words of the hearing examiner, "If reliance upon vague notions of female frailty were not sufficiently discredited, the instant case would well serve that purpose. The evidence clearly shows the complainant (Wellner) quite capable of handling the man's jobs. She was, in fact, repeatedly assigned to perform equivalently difficult tasks in the respondent's employ. The respondent (Wilson Nursery) has been much more diligent in saving her from the rewards of heavy work than in protecting her from its heavy burden." The employer was ordered to cease and desist from discriminating against female applicants and female employees with respect to any term, conditions, or privilege of employment, to pay back wages due Wellner, and to take specified steps to ensure nonretaliation on her.

PROMOTION

The sex-linked barriers to promotion of women on the job include the lack of career ladders that connect predominantly female, low paying jobs and the professional positions within the same organization; the consistent oversight of females by managers in promotion despite demonstrated ability; seniority provisions that require nontransferable departmental or similarly restricted seniority lines; exclusion of women from informal sessions in which job-related information is discussed and decisions made; and veteran's preference points added to test scores in employment. Stereotyped attitudes held by employers and supervisors regarding the importance of women's careers, ability to supervise, ability to make objective/timely decisions in difficult situations, and many others are also strong deterrents to the promotion of women.

The following two cases illustrate discrimination in promotion and how difficulties in promotion can have adverse consequences for job retention.

Louise Stalling vs. Rural Insurance Co. Stalling alleged that she and other female underwriters had been denied promotion opportunities on account of sex, and that she and other female underwriters were receiving less pay than male underwriters doing substantially the same work. She was employed with Rural Insurance for two years, originally hired as a processing clerk, but was promoted to the position of service underwriter after three months of employment. The company established the service underwriter position to expedite policy issues and to create a progressive promotional track to underwriter positions. All service underwriters were females, who were recruited from the all-female clerical line. All the underwriters were male. The salary of underwriters was considerably higher than that of service underwriters.

Stalling applied for the position of a multiple-line underwriter who was leaving the company. Donald Jones, the vice-president of Operations, told her that she was not qualified but was a potential underwriter and should enroll in a course designed by the Insurance Institute of America. A male with a college degree in business, several insurance courses, and three years of experience as agent for another company got the job. Another multiple-line underwriter's job opened up, and Stalling was considered for it. A male with a college degree in marketing, several courses in insurance, and four years as a claims adjuster for an insurance company was hired. A position for a special risk underwriter became available. By this time, Stalling had had considerable experience in auto insurance, two years as a service underwriter, three months of an I.I.A. insurance course, and was 20 credits short of a college degree.

Although Jones interviewed her for the job, he informed her that "certain higher ups" in the company did not want a woman in the position because they believed a woman could not work successfully with field agents. The supervisor of the underwriting sections did not interview Stalling, but merely looked at her personnel file. He interviewed the male who eventually got the position. The man who was hired had a college degree in business, an unspecified number of insurance courses, no I.I.A. course, and had no insurance experience.

Rural Insurance was ordered to cease and desist from discriminating against women in hiring or promotion as underwriters. This case is now under appeal.

Adeline Scherz vs. Briggs & Stratton.   Adeline Scherz became the one female line inspector for Briggs & Stratton only after vigorous intervention of certain union officials. She had been on the job as line inspector for two years when she was bumped from her job during a slack season. She sought to bump into a floating inspector's job in the Sample Department, which was within her salary classification and salary grade. John Frost, vice-president, denied her the job, alleging that she was incapable of performing the job by reason of age, size, and physical disability. However, the job she sought and her present job had identical job descriptions.

Scherz filed a sex discrimination complaint with the state fair employment agency. During her hearing the employer contended that the ability to lift, unassisted, engines weighing up to 175 pounds was a qualification for satisfactory performance of the job. However, no test of weight lifting was specified in the job description and there was no indication that any of the five previous holders of the job, all males, were required to meet such requirements. The present holder of the job, who Scherz tried to bump into according to her rights under the collective bargaining agreement, testified that the average engine he handled was 35 pounds. He did not have to lift the heavier engines and move them from place to place to inspect them. The only occasion he had to move the heavier engines was when several of them have been deposited on the floor as a group and the space was too limited to inspect a single engine without moving it from a group. He simply shoved it aside. There was always an employee from the Sample Department with him who could render assistance. It was also found to be company policy that where an employee reasonably feels that a load or a large engine is beyond his ability to lift safely alone, he must seek the assistance of other employees. In operations where engines of varying sizes were involved, and other employees were not readily available to assist in lifting a heavy engine, a portable hoist was installed.

The employer was found to have engaged in discriminatory employment practices and was ordered to cease and desist from requiring any test of Scherz' ability to do the job of floating inspector that was not directly related to her performance on the job, and that she be permitted to exercise a job preference in her labor grade, classification, and seniority pursuant to the collective bargaining agreement.

Conditions of work.   Conditions of work include such factors as wages, hours or work, fringe benefits (temporary disability benefits, paid leaves of absence, medical and dental insurance), dress requirements, physical loca-

CONDITIONS OF WORK

Conditions of work include such factors as wages, hours of work, fringe benefits (temporary disability benefits, paid leaves of absence, medical and dental insurance), dress requirements, physical location, and facilities on the job. Discrimination against women in conditions of employment takes many forms. A classic one is when women are paid less than men for doing substantially the same work. In some cases, employers make no bones about paying women less than men for the same job. Most frequently, however, the wage differential is disguised by calling jobs in which women are employed by a different name from that in which only men are employed, even when the tasks are quite similar. Another way of discriminating is by assigning the males "additional" tasks, which may take no more than 10 percent of the male employee's time, to differentiate "women's jobs" from "men's jobs."

When women are denied work during night shifts, they are also denied the pay differential between night and day shifts. Denial of overtime work to women obviously also results in financial drawback for them. Practices of employers of excluding part-time workers from fringe benefits and promotional opportunities have also had disparate negative effects on women. Women with working spouses are often routinely excluded from medical and dental insurance coverage under the family plan, while male employees are not even asked about the employment status of their wives.

Differential treatment of pregnancy as a temporary disability in medical disability benefits is a major form of discrimination. The following is one of the many cases of sex discrimination relating to maternity benefits.

Barbara Christenson vs. Wisconsin Telephone Company. Barbara Christenson was employed as a telephone operator by the Wisconsin Telephone Company when she took a leave of absence due to pregnancy. The employer was found to have discriminated against her, as well as other employees temporarily disabled due to pregnancy, in the following respects: 1) requiring her to take a leave of absence for a fixed period of time, 2) not assuring her a return to her former job or to a job of like status in the event that she was able to return to work prior to the expiration of the fixed leave period, 3) not providing payments under the collective bargaining agreement or departmental practice during the first seven days of absence due to pregnancy disability not exceeding 52 weeks, 4) not allowing accrual of seniority during the period of absence due to pregnancy disability, and 5) not granting the telephone concession during the period of absence due to pregnancy disability.

Wisconsin Telephone treated pregnancy differently from other forms of temporary disability. It argued that pregnancy is a "voluntary" condition and is, therefore, distinguishable from other temporary disabilities, and that the cost of treating pregnancy like any other temporary disability would be substantial. However, the company does not restrict the compensation in terms, conditions or privileges of employees with other, nonsex specific disabilities that are in a very real sense as "voluntary" as pregnancy; for example, disabilities caused by plastic surgery to remove disfiguring scars, by self-inflicted wounds, and by unsuccessful suicide attempts.

The examiner who heard the case summed up the decision against the discriminatory practice in this way: "Moreover . . . pregnancy is not always a "voluntary" condition. Even if this were the case, however, it would not change the simple biological fact of life that only women become pregnant, nor would it change the resulting adverse impact on women as a class of an employment policy that isolates disabilities due to pregnancy for less favorable treatment than disabilities due to other causes."

The following case involves a work condition of differential dress requirements for males and females on the same job. The final decision on the case is still pending, and the names involved have been altered here.

Barbara Hall and Etta Bank vs. Turkey Farm Supper Club.   Barbara Hall and Etta Bank were employed as bartenders in the Turkey Farm Supper Club. There were both male and female bartenders with the same job duties employed in the club. During the 15-month period of employment of these two women, the employer required the female bartenders to change uniforms and thus purchase six different sets of outfits. The uniform of male bartenders was substantially the same for that 15-month period, except for one change in the style and color of the jacket. The management selected or approved the precise items—body blouses, body shirts, jackets, hot pants, skirts, and briefs worn by the female bartenders. However, it selected or approved only the jackets worn by male bartenders. Both male and female bartenders paid for their own uniforms, and the total cost was approximately the same for the 15 months in question. The uniforms that female bartenders were required to wear were brief, emphasized leg and breast exposure, and revealed and accentuated female anatomical characteristics in a manner designed to be sexually attractive to male customers. On the other hand, the uniforms of male bartenders covered all parts of their bodies, except their hands, necks, and heads, and were not designed to reveal or accentuate male anatomical characteristics.

In June 1972, Hall and Bank informed one of the managers that they would not wear the new "hunting coat" issued to them because they were too loose (and revealed their breasts when they bent over) and short (and barely covered their underpants as they stood erect with their arms on their sides). They had told the manager that they were prepared to work in their old uniforms, but they were told they could not work unless they wore the new uniforms. When Hall and Bank persisted in their refusals they were fired.

The examiner who heard the case found no evidence that the exposure and display of a female bartender's body was demonstrably more relevant to job performance than the exposure and display of a male bartender's body. The differential treatment was, therefore, unlawful, and the Turkey Farm Supper Club was ordered to cease and desist from exploiting the sexuality of female applicants and employees by requiring them as a condition of employment to wear uniforms that expose and display their bodies in a manner and extent not required as a condition of employment for male applicants and employees performing substantially similar work. The order does not preclude an employer from imposing a requirement that her/his employees wear standard uniforms. Such requirements are often justified by legitimate business reasons. Nor does the decision indicate that an employer must require all of his/her employees to wear precisely the same uniforms regardless of their sex. In fact, because of the traditional differences in the kinds of clothing worn by men and women, such requirements (for example, that all employees must wear dresses) may themselves be unlawful due to their tendency to deny employment opportunities to one sex or the other.

SENIORITY

Seniority provisions affect the opportunities and benefits that women get from their jobs. Certainly, seniority has worked as a source of protection on the job for both men and women. However, in fields where women are new, and where automation and falling profits have required trimming staff, women have experienced setbacks due to their low seniority. Separate seniority provisions by job classification, by department, or by plant (in the case of a multiplant organization) impose severe limitations as to the mobility, as well as to the possibilities of having a job in an economic recession, for low seniority personnel. Ironically, these are the same people who have the least accumulated unemployment compensation and retirement benefits.

The following case shows the impact of restricted seniority provisions in a job where women are concentrated.

Anita Krawczyk vs. Greenfield School District No. 6.   Anita Krawczyk began employment with the school district in 1958 as "matron." At the same time, the district employed "custodians," whose skill, effort, or responsibility did not differ from those of the matrons. The two differences between these jobs were that the custodians worked during the summer and the matrons did not, and that the custodians were paid more than the matrons. The memorandum of agreement between the School Board of Greenfield School

District No. 6 and Local No. 2, affiliated with Milwaukee District Council 48 AFSCME, AFL-CIO, in August 1972 carried a bifurcated seniority roster—that is, one for men and another for women. Seniority was accumulated in two different job classifications depending on the assignment of the individual as a "custodial aide" (formerly matron) or "custodian." Because the position of custodial aide was limited to a part-time basis, and because the pay was so much lower for the custodial aide as opposed to the custodian, no male ever applied for the custodial position. The exception was Ed Zisch, who had a special job classification created for him paid at a higher rate than the custodial aide. For 16 years Krawczyk was compensated at a lesser rate for doing substantially the same work requiring substantially the same skill, effort, and responsibility as her male counterparts. Additionally, she was denied summertime work. When she transferred to a custodian's job, she lost her seniority. When she filed her complaint regarding the loss of seniority, she failed to name the union as a respondent. Nevertheless, the employer was found to have denied equal pay for equal work, and further engaged in sex discrimination by upholding dual lines of seniority progression, which had an adverse effect on women.

WHY SHOULD WOMEN WANT TO DEAL WITH JOB DISCRIMINATION?

In American society, work is a basis of self-esteem as well as of survival. People seek happiness and fulfillment through work, and many fail to find them. It is difficult enough to find a job that is meaningful even when one has choices regarding how one should utilize one's skills and when sex barriers to employment are not strong. It is worse when one is cut off arbitrarily from job opportunities because of one's sex.

If we accept the value that human potential must be fully utilized, I suggest that as women are able to break down sex barriers in all occupations, there would be greater possibilities of rearranging the work world so that it would become more responsive to a fuller array of human talents, interests, and needs. Even if one does not assume any moral or intellectual superiority of women over men, it is an inescapable reality that men and women experience life differently because of social norms. An accelerated speed of integration of women at all segments and levels of the work world would allow women's unique experiences to be a source of humane changes in the norms and structure of work.

A number of psychological and sociological studies have looked into the differences of male and female physiology, mental processes, and interpersonal behavior patterns. Despite the growing statistical sophistication of the social sciences, it is still a futile enterprise to try to allocate precisely which of the differences between the sexes may be attributed to natural endowments and which to the cultural and social influences that shape human lives. A more fruitful approach to the question of the whats, whys, and hows of sex differences is to assume that there is an equal distribution of skill and talent *potential* among men and women, to gather data on similarities and differences, and to use the data as a diagnostic and planning tool regarding ways in which full human potential may be realized.

As indicated earlier, there is an uneven distribution of opportunity and of rewards (money, prestige, power) on the basis of sex. Women individually and collectively must know how they are excluded by the system and how to deal with this exclusion.

WHAT ARE THE MAJOR LAWS THAT PROTECT WOMEN'S EMPLOYMENT RIGHTS?

There are a number of laws that protect women's rights in employment at the federal, state, and local levels of government. Although only the major federal laws will be summarized here, it is important to remember that most states have their own version of these laws. Some municipalities have also passed fair employment ordinances. These laws and ordinances vary as to what entity they cover (for example, terms of the size of establishment, contractual conditions, religious exemptions, or type of business); as to how they proceed in determining the merits of complaints (for example, whether or not the complaint can be anonymous); as to the deadlines for filing the complaint from the date of the incidence of the alleged discrimination; as to the agency that enforces complaints; as to whether one needs a lawyer to have one's complaint processed; and as to the power that the enforcing agency has to give remedy to the complainants and other affected parties and to stop similar future discriminatory activity.

Another reason why women must know about federal, state, and local laws governing equal opportunity in employment is because it is often to their advantage to file a formal complaint or ask for an investigation of an employer through several enforcement agencies. Employers are less likely to ignore a discriminatory practice if several fair employment agencies are investigating them.

The following summarizes the three major federal laws on sex discrimination:

Equal Pay Act of 1963. As an amendment to the Fair Labor Standards Act (FLSA), this law prohibits discrimination on the basis of sex in the payment of wages for equal work on jobs that require equal skill, efforts, and responsibility, and that are performed under similar working conditions. Its provisions apply to "wages" in the sense of remuneration for employment (including overtime) and to employer contributions for most fringe benefits. Employees of small, local retail or service establishments, most farm workers, and employees of seasonal amusement or recreational establishments are not protected by this law.

A number of court cases have overturned long-established practices that provided a lower wage for women than for men. These practices included, for example, paying differential rates set by union contracts.

A complainant's identity is never revealed without that person's consent. Employers cannot fire or discriminate against employees exercising their rights under the laws. The agency that enforces this law is:

Wage and Hour Division
Employment Standards Administration
U.S. Department of Labor
Washington, D.C. 20210

Title VII of the Civil Rights Act of 1964, as amended by the Equal Opportunity Act of 1972. Title VII prohibits discrimination based on sex, as well as on race, color, religion, and national origin by employers of 15 or more employees, public and private employment agencies, labor unions, and labor-management apprenticeship programs. State and local government agencies and public and private educational institutions are newly covered, but religious educational institutions or associations are exempt with respect to the employment of individuals of a particular religion. Employers excluded from coverage are federal and District of Columbia agencies (other than the federal-state employment service system), federally owned corporations, and Indian tribes. Specifically excluded from the definition of "employee" are state and local elected officials and their personal staff and policy-making appointees.

Discrimination based on race, color, sex, religion, or national origin is unlawful in hiring or firing; wages and fringe benefits; classifying, referring, assigning, or promoting employees; extending or assigning use of facilities, training, retraining, or apprenticeships, or any other terms, conditions, or privileges of employment.

The Equal Employment Opportunity Commission (EEOC), which enforces Title VII, has issued "Guidelines on Discrimination Because of Sex." The guidelines bar hiring based on stereotyped characterization of the sexes, classifications, or labeling of "men's jobs" and "women's jobs," or advertising under male or female headings. They specify that the bona fide occupational qualification exemption should be interpreted narrowly, and that state laws that prohibit or limit the employment of women—in certain occupations considered hazardous or in jobs that require lifting or carrying weights in excess of prescribed limits, working during certain hours of the night, or working more than a specified number of hours per day or per week—conflict with and are superseded by Title VII. Accordingly, these "protective" labor laws cannot be used as a reason for refusing to employ women.

Revised guidelines, issued on April 5, 1972, include a provision that, where state laws require minimum wage and overtime pay for women only, an employer not only may not refuse to hire female applicants to avoid this payment but must provide the same benefits for male employees. Similar provisions apply to rest and meal periods and physical facilities; although, if an employer can prove that business necessity precludes providing these benefits to both men and women, the employer need not provide them to members of either sex.

The revised guidelines prohibit excluding from employment an applicant or employee because of pregnancy. They state, among other things, that disabilities caused or contributed to by pregnancy, miscarriage, abortion, childbirth, and recovery, therefore, are, for all job-related purposes, temporary disabilities and should be treated as such under any health or temporary disability insurance or sick leave plan available in connection with employment. Accrual of seniority, reinstatement, and payment under such insurance or plan should, therefore, be applied to disability due to pregnancy or childbirth as to other temporary disabilities.

A number of state fair employment agencies receive complaints for the EEOC; otherwise, complaints may be filed with the EEOC regional office. Further information is available from:

Equal Employment Opportunity Commission
1800 G. Street N.W.
Washington, D.C. 20506

Executive Order 11246, as amended. This order prohibits employment discrimination on the basis of sex, as well as of race, color, religion, or national origin, by federal contractors or subcontractors and contractors who perform work under a federally assisted construction contract exceeding $10,000. Coverage includes all facilities of the contractor, regardless of whether they are involved in the performance of the federal contract. The order does not exempt specific kinds of employment or employees.

Prohibited practices include discrimination in recruitment or recruitment advertising; hiring, upgrading, demotion or transfer; layoff or termination; rates of pay or other compensation; and selection for training, including apprenticeship.

The Office of Federal Contract Compliance (OFCC), which enforces the order, has issued "Sex Discrimination Guidelines." The guidelines state, among other things, that contractors may not advertise under male and female classifications, base seniority lists on sex, deny a person a job because of state "protective" labor laws, make distinctions between married and unmarried persons of one sex only, or penalize women in their terms and conditions of employment because they require the granting of a leave of absence due to childbearing and reinstatement to their original job or to a position of like status and pay, without loss of service credits.

Order No. 4, issued by OFCC on January 30, 1970, required contractors with 50 or more employees and a contract of $50,000 or more to take affirmative action, particularly in setting goals and timetables for the employment of minorities in job categories where they have been underutilized. Revised Order No. 4, requiring goals and timetables for December 4, 1971, effective immediately, gave contractors 120 days (until April 2, 1972) to incorporate the requirements for women into their existing affirmative action plans. Further information may be obtained from:

> Office of Federal Contract Compliance
> Employment Standards Administration
> U.S. Department of Labor
> Washington, D.C. 20210

WHAT CAN WOMEN DO ABOUT SEX DISCRIMINATION IN EMPLOYMENT?

Knowing how discrimination manifests itself is one thing; knowing what to do about it is another. It seems that the only limits to the variety of ways to deal with sex discrimination in employment are the law, moral values, and imagination. The strategies that would be described here are bounded by a respect for the rights of others, by a preference for nonviolence, and by the limitations of space.

Strategies in dealing with job discrimination may be roughly classified into the "preventive" and the "curative" modes. Neither route is easier than the other. Both are accompanied by costs and benefits to the individual woman or group of women involved. In general, both modes of dealing with sex discrimination involve an understanding of what discriminatory practices are, learning the official and unofficial rules of the organization, and asserting one's rights.

The following activities fall in the category I call "preventive strategies":

1. *Learning about the ways employers discriminate against women.* The interpretation of the legal meaning of discrimination is a continuing job for the courts and for lawmaking bodies as well. A brief good introduction to

employment discrimination is *The Rights Of Women* by Susan Deller Ross (American Civil Liberties Union, 1973).

2. *Learning about the laws that protect women in employment.* The Women's Bureau of the Department of Labor has published a pamphlet called *A Working Woman's Guide to Her Job Rights* (Washington, D.C. 20210, 1974), which describes the various laws that cover women on the job in the areas of equal pay, maternity leave, overtime pay, minimum wages, child care, unemployment insurance, social security, pensions, and unions. For an updated source of information as to how fair employment laws are interpreted by the courts and by administrative agencies, the Commerce Clearing House *Employment Practices Guide* is invaluable. This reference is known in lawyers' circles as the "CCH." The CCH is of greatest use when you want to know whether or not a practice has ever been called sex discrimination by the courts or by the EEOC.

3. *Formulating verbal and written responses to anticipated discriminatory questions by employers or supervisors.* Some women learn of what discriminatory questions they may expect to be asked primarily through personal experience; others know of these questions from the experiences of friends, from books, and from the news media. However one learns of discriminatory encounters with employers, it is important to take advantage of the information. As a strategy, this anticipation is particularly important in interviews for hiring and promotion. However, it is significant to note that promotion within the organization does not occur because of the results of a single interview, but is based on the way one deals with the day-to-day aggravations in a male-dominated organization.

When possible, an applicant and prospective interviewee should find out before reporting for the interview who the interviewers are: What is their formal position in the organization, what do they do, what is their background, what activities or causes interest them? Of course, this is not always possible, but sometimes a call to the personnel department receptionist can yield valuable information. Friends within the organization are useful sources of information.

A second step is to list questions that may be asked of you because you are female, and which are not asked of men, as well as questions that are not job related and are asked only because of your sex. Go over your list and write down several ways you may answer them. One way of formulating your answer is to reinterpret the question so that your answer shows the interviewer that you have an understanding of job requirements and that this understanding is not related to your sex. For example, as a response to the question: "How long does your husband expect to stay in his job in town?" you may say, "My husband will stay as long as our mutual job opportunities allow us to stay in the area."

Finally, go over your list of responses and rank them according to how these responses provide adequate information to the interviewer as to your seriousness of purpose, your potentials for the job, and your level of self-respect.

4. *Developing assertiveness through assertive skill-development courses.*[2] Assertiveness is the ability to express feelings and ideas honestly and directly in a confident and self-respecting way. Many women find it difficult to do what is recommended in 3 above because of anxieties about being misconstrued as an aggressive person or because of fear of encouraging hostile, resentful responses from the other person. As a consequence, men, as well as other women, walk all over them. Another consequence of "bottling" the resentment over discriminatory activity is the sudden outbursts of anger over what seem to be trifling matters. Such outbursts are more accurately described as aggressive behavior. In general, aggressiveness refers to inappropriately direct, self-enhancing, hostile, and vengeful expressions of feelings. Women all over the country are now seeking to change their interpersonal relations through assertive skill-development courses which professional as well as lay community groups offer. Women's centers and local chapters of the National Organization of Women (NOW) are good places to ask for information on local assertive skills programs.

5. *Participating in union activity.* Women who are employed have a lot to gain in being active in their unions. Federal and state courts, and EEOC as well, have found many unions guilty of illegal discrimination practices. Among such illegal behaviors are initiating and maintaining discriminatory contracts, discriminatory recruitment practices, and neglect of collective bargaining issues that are of primary concern to women. As active members of unions, women can demand inclusion of nondiscrimination clauses in the employment contract; maternity and parental leave benefits; provision of day care facilities; extension of fringe benefits to part-time workers, many of whom are women; re-examination of job classifications that downgrade "women's" jobs compared to similar "men's" jobs', establishment of career ladders that allow clerical workers to move up the ranks; and an end to sex segregation of jobs.

6. *Learning the rules of the bureaucracy.* Each organization with more than 30 employees may be expected to have some relatively formalized set of personnel rules and operating procedures. A woman on the job needs to take the time to obtain copies of the formal rules of the organization, because these documents are handy in establishing employee allegations of discriminatory policy. Although it may seem like a lot of trivia, a woman who works in a

---

[2]See Chapter 25, "How to Become More Assertive."

bureaucracy must keep written records of her performance and of her interactions with others. It is important to be able to document one's performance, especially when promotions and layoffs come.

7. *Learning the structure of the bureaucracy.* This refers to the process of who does what in the system. Information on the structure of the organization helps to pinpoint responsibility for fair employment practices and who may correct discriminatory practices when they occur.

The curative route in dealing with sex discrimination in employment may take the form of filing a complaint with a federal, state, and/or local administrative agency that enforces fair employment practices laws and administrative rules. Administrative enforcement agencies are part of our legal system; they are created to augment the courts and relieve them of the tremendous burden of dealing with reported cases of discrimination, which increase annually. They have been created with the assumption that victims of employment discrimination are not able to deal on the basis of equality with those responsible for such discrimination. These agencies vary in the speed with which they process cases. The Federal Wage and Hour Division has the best reputation for speed among the federal agents, but the type of discrimination it covers is limited.

Litigation is another alternative. Litigation is generally more expensive than pursuing a complaint of discrimination through an administrative agency. Furthermore, there is no assurance that the court route would be any quicker than the administrative route. Perhaps the primary advantage of litigation, particularly when a case reaches the Supreme Court, is that the decision with respect to the discriminatory activity can have wider impact than an administrative decision.

Pursuing a grievance of discrimination through a union is another possibility. However, unions themselves are notorious for initiating and enforcing discriminatory agreements.[3] Unions have the duty to represent the membership fairly. They cannot bargain away the rights of women. When the union is a party to a discriminatory practice, in a complaint of discrimination, the complainant should name the union as a respondent where allowed by law.

For women who are not represented by a union, protection may be sought under grievance procedures provided for by personnel rules. As stated earlier, it is important that any employee keep published rules of the organization, because employers may be taken to task by pointing to discriminatory use of those rules.

---

[3]For example, see *Papermakers, Local 189* v. *United States,* 416 F.2d 980, 1 FEP cases 875, 71 LRRM 3070 (CA 5, 1969); *Watkins v. Steelmakers, Local 2369 and Continental Can Co.,* 369 F. Supp. 1221, 7 FEP Cases 90 (E.D. La. 1974).

Whether one takes the administrative, litigation, union, or personal grievance route, there are costs that may be incurred. Time, money, and effort obviously have to be expended. However, the costs go beyond these: one could lose a job (if it has not happened before to the complainant or litigant); one could be retaliated against through various forms of harrassment on the job, such as deprivation of duties, the silent treatment, exclusion from information, demotion, constant transfer, transfer to undesirable jobs; one could acquire the reputation of being a troublemaker, and, especially if one lives in a small community, the businessmen's club may effectively disseminate such information and make it virtually impossible for women who have gained such reputations to find other jobs.

However, the costs of doing something should be weighed against the costs of not doing it. When women allow themselves to be subjects of discriminatory practices, they are also deprived of income, positions, and privileges due them. Furthermore, there is no assurance that if one did not do anything about a discriminatory practice that such a practice would magically stop. In fact, what often drives women finally to do something about their rights is because of repeated experiences of discrimination. The other cost of not doing anything is in one's self-concept; the damage done to one's view of oneself by allowing others unjustly to exclude one from due rewards and opportunities is immeasurable.

The rewards of dealing positively with one's experience of discrimination can be immense. One of these rewards is a good feeling about one's worth as a human being who is not pushed around limply and who, in fact, demands that others recognize that value. Other benefits are economic: back pay, a job, a promotion, seniority, better working conditions, award of damages, award of lawyers' fees, interest for the company's use of the money due the discriminated women. When women who are discriminated against are awarded justice, the judgment of the administrative agency, of the court, or of the labor arbitrator can serve to deter the employer from future similar discriminatory activities. Other employers may also take heed.

To maximize returns on investment of time, money, and grief, women must seek to deal with discrimination collectively and to demand changes in the practices and policy that result in discriminatory patterns. The remedies awarded to one woman do not necessarily accrue to other women unless she consciously tries to have a generalized remedy to what other women may experience with the discriminatory employer.

From 1975 to 1980, many of the critical issues in employment discrimination will be decided by the Supreme Court. These decisions could trigger attempts at regressive legislation if the affected groups find adverse outcomes for themselves. On the other hand, the resolution of such painful issues dealing with the treatment of maternity as a temporary disability for purposes of employment benefits, with the questions of what constitutes "business necessity" in a number of individual cases, and with the questions relating to seniority may facilitate the development of policies and procedures that could expedite administrative action regarding complaints of employment discrimination.

The strategies for dealing with sex discrimination in employment are bountiful. Women must recognize that both discrimination and measures to deal with it are realities.

What to Do When He Leaves You

Janet Gregory Vermandel

I once knew a girl who was so much in love with the man she was living with that it took her three months to make up her mind to break it off, despite the most awful evidence that the whole thing was beyond salvage. She told herself that he was the right love, the only love for her; she couldn't walk out on him, couldn't let him go. What she was in love with wasn't the man himself but her dream of perfect happiness with him, give or take a little disappointment she was willing to accept as a necessary part of real life.

Everything had been lovely until the day she learned that he had started an affair with someone he had the honesty (his word) or gall (her word) to tell her he had had his eye on for some time past. Moreover, he wasn't sure which, if either of them, he really wanted.

After she cried for a couple of days, she managed to convince herself that it was only a small thing and shouldn't be blown out of proportion. So she listened to his endearments and reassurances and hung in, even though she knew better. It was the dream, you see, fogging her vision, smothering her brain.

Finally, even though he kept looking at her with spaniel eyes and sighing heavily at the thought of the hurt he was inflicting, he started going out alone for unlikely reasons and coming back to their apartment later and later. In the end, it all happened exactly as she should have known it would. In the meantime, she had wasted three months, and it took a lot more time to pick up the pieces of her life.

WHAT IF IT HAPPENS TO YOU?

The dream has gone bad, you can see the split coming, and how are you going to bear it? It's much better if you can do the getting out, the breaking up. But even if you do, it still hurts. After all, your emotions are tied up in knots. Emotional knots that can't be untangled have to be cut, and you bleed a little in the process. The quicker and cleaner the cut, the less damage you have to survive. If he's the one who does the cutting, you're going to bleed all the more.

No matter how it happens, accept the fact that you're probably going to feel like a basket case for some time, maybe weeks, maybe months, and one of the walking wounded for a while after that. But you don't have to lie down for it like a willing victim.

A FEW THINGS HELP

Realize that no matter how bad the scene, everybody has been there, or is going to make the trip. Man-woman relationships go bad with monotonous regularity. Concentrate on coming out of it intact. Avoid, if you can, the urge to discuss it with him in minute detail. Who is to blame for what no longer matters and those late-night conversational duels never settle anything, only prolong the agony.

If you're still seeing his virtues, take a closer look at what is really there. Make a list of things that are wrong with him. Actually write it out — ways in which your life will be better without him and his foibles — and look it over whenever your mind starts going soggy about him again.

Time heals all wounds, but if you want to heal fast, blank him out. (And tell yourself that time wounds all heels.)

DO NOT BE TEMPTED BACK INTO BED

No matter how liberated you are, this is one time when bed is bad. Sure, you can rationalize it, we all can and probably have, but it doesn't help. For openers, you'll cry at the wrong time. Furthermore, it won't convince him that he should change his mind and stay, if he was the one to leave. Worst of all, it creates the illusion that the problem has gone away, everything is all right again — which it hasn't and isn't, and you'll know that when you wake up in the hard, cold morning light. A few go-rounds like that and you'll find yourself driving along the highway looking at concrete abutments, picking your spot.

You know how it goes in bed, and the better it is, the worse for you. In your highly volatile emotional condition, you're going to give more — not less — the more you love; the more you give, the harder you're hooked. Do you need one more go-round with those hands, that body, the warmth you want so desperately, just to break your heart more?

ACCEPT THE INEVITABILITY OF THE BREAKUP

Until you do, you're going to be paralyzed, running it over and over in your mind, looking for ways to mend something that can't be mended. It matters not whether he leaves in a fit of fury or if he goes smiling, soothing you as he fades from view, half assuring you he'll be back. Either way he won't be, but some men prefer to pay out a little rope to avoid a big scene. It is crueler that way but easier on him, and that's the name of this game. It's a cat-and-mouse game, but that doesn't make you a mouse; it merely means that you — hurt, heartbroken, vulnerable — are reacting like a mouse. Don't play it. Admit that this particular relationship is over. He won't come to his senses, but you will, because you have to, sooner or later. Sooner is better.

BUT YOU'RE SCARED

You'd be dumb not to be scared. Tell yourself one of the great, unadmitted truths: everybody is scared a lot of the time. It's a condition of life once you've left the security of your family. But so what? Everybody doesn't go around talking about being scared, and you don't have to either. What you do have to do is give your mental bootstraps a heave. This is where courage counts, and pays off in proportion. In other less permissive days, resisting temptation was said to strengthen character. Translated to the 1970s, every challenge you meet makes you stronger, more confident that you can meet the next one.

THIS TERRIBLE HURT THAT YOU FEEL—WHAT IS IT?

It helps if you can identify it, take a long look, and know what it is that is devastating you, and know how everybody goes through it in the same way. And what you learn from it you will always know. If you can label things, sometimes you can handle things better, and if you keep in mind that it is a pattern with an end, you may be able to get through its stages with fewer pains.

At first, it's going to be shock. This can't be happening to you. After the initial shock comes pride. You've lost face to yourself, in your world.

Well, you can get past all of that. Get over the shock, figure ways to salvage your pride, and then you're left with the residue, and that's when the real hurt can get to you. Call it loneliness, call it loss, call it heartbreak; by any name it's the toughest of all things to bear—the knowledge that you are not loved. Nothing is more devastating, more totally unbearable.

You've been used to belonging, to being one of a pair, to mattering in the most vital way there is to someone whom you value. Suddenly it's all gone. You stand alone, one. Everywhere you look you see couples, laughing, talking, shopping, walking—all the mundane things you did with him short days ago, and now you walk alone.

It will go away—eventually. You know it isn't going to go away in a day—or even a week—don't you? We're talking about your life, not some passing fancy. Tell yourself it's going to take months, maybe two, maybe more, but that you only have to live one day at a time. And every day it hurts a little less. Concentrate on the surface, what other people can see, and the necessity of that will tide you over the worst days. You'll create your own illusion of being in command of your fate, and find that the illusion creates the reality, given a little time.

HOW TO CREATE THAT ILLUSION

As bad as being the solitary celebrant at the wake is being a gay madcap, looking for parties, jollity, any company at all. Pretending you don't give a damn, when you do give a damn, never rings true. You're bound to come on a little hectic, a little brittle, and bright-eyed onlookers will read you only too clearly. If crying is no good, neither is mad laughter. When you're over the pain, you'll like yourself better for this. Self-respect may not compare with feeling loved, but it's one of the few positive feelings you have left to work with.

Decide to keep your mouth shut, right from day one. Don't bad-mouth him to your friends and family. Sure, they'll rally round with sympathy and join you in damning his name. Is that what you want? Not if you're smart, you don't. For one thing, instant replay only confirms the original verdict, it doesn't change anything. Your sense of injury may batten on pity, but the overall effect is that you become a pitiable object, which is yet another blow to your damaged ego and the worst possible image to show to the world.

No good trying to pretend you don't care; it's better to be quiet about it all. Smile any way you can, short of the tremulous, and get busy.

If it's your apartment, redo it. If you can't afford paint, scrub. If the apartment, house, or whatever was originally yours, he'll be the one to move out. But what if it was his, or something you set up together? Who leaves? Maybe you, but maybe not. Try to make that your choice. And think carefully here. For one thing, flinging yourself out the door is better for your morale than being left. Don't let inertia lick you on this one. When you're down, you're inclined to take the course of least resistance, stick with what you know and have. Well and good, but don't forget, it's going to look very different—and empty—for quite a while.

If you've had the whole scene and can't face memories, move on to a new scene, a new neighborhood, job, city, whatever, You won't feel like it, but at least it forces you out of your hurt little shell. You have to cope, so you get moving. Rotten as the whole of life looks, see this as a chance to try whatever it is you've always wanted to try. It will leave you with a lot less time and energy for mourning a lost cause.

KEEP THE FAITH—ALL MEN ARE NOT ALIKE

If you have any hang-ups about this disaster being a part of the pattern of your life—forget it. One bad affair or three bad affairs running prove nothing. Your head will try to tell you that maybe this is how it's always going to be for you, but don't believe it unless you know that you are purposely courting trouble by picking exactly the same kind of man every time. Otherwise, give yourself the same break you'd give a friend who had a few bad bouts. Admit that luck plays a large role in affairs of the heart. Hang in and stay strong. Think how many times you must have fallen down before you learned to walk. Love is a lot like that. Some men take up a lot of psychic space in your life, which can be scary but rewarding in the end, because they help you find your love.

Most important of all, when you're counting the cost of loving, count the cost of not loving too. Loving is good for your face, your soul, your character, your life. Not loving takes its toll in countless ways, none of which you would choose for yourself.

How to Become More Assertive

Charles Zastrow

Do you handle put-down comments well? Are you reluctant to express your feelings and opinions openly and honestly in a group? Are you frequently timid in interacting with people in authority? Do you react well to criticism? Do you sometimes explode in anger when things go wrong, or are you able to keep your cool? Do you find it difficult to maintain eye contact when talking? If you are uncomfortable with someone smoking near you, do you express your feelings? Are you timid in arranging a date or social event? If you have trouble in any of these situations, there is, fortunately, a useful technique — assertiveness training — that enables people to become more effective in such interpersonal interactions.

Assertiveness problems range from extreme shyness, introversion, withdrawal to inappropriately flying into a rage that results in alienating others. A nonassertive person is often acquiescent, fearful, and afraid of expressing his or her real, spontaneous feelings in a variety of situations. Frequently, resentment and anxiety build up, which may result in general discomfort, feelings of low self-esteem, tension headaches, fatigue, and perhaps a destructive explosion of temper, anger, and aggression. Some peo-

This article was especially written for this book.

ple are overly shy, timid in nearly all interactions. Most of us, however, encounter occasional problems in isolated areas where it would be to our benefit to be more assertive. For example, a bachelor may be quite effective and assertive in his job as store manager, but still be awkward and timid when attempting to arrange a date.

There are three basic styles of interacting with others: nonassertive, aggressive, and assertive. Characteristics of these styles have been summarized by Alberti and Emmons.[1]

In the nonassertive style, you are likely to hesitate, speak softly, look away, avoid the issue, agree regardless of your own feelings, not express opinions, value yourself "below" others, and hurt yourself to avoid any chance of hurting others.

In the *aggressive* style, you typically answer before the other person is through talking, speak loudly and abusively, glare at the other person, speak "past" the issue (accusing, blaming, demeaning), vehemently expound your feelings and opinions, value yourself "above" others, and hurt others to avoid hurting yourself.

In the *assertive* style, you will answer spontaneously, speak with a conversational tone and volume, look at the other person, speak to the issue, openly express your personal feelings and opinions (anger, love, disagreement, sorrow), value yourself equal to others, and hurt neither yourself or others.

Simply stated, assertive behavior is being able to express yourself without hurting or stepping on others.

Assertiveness training is designed to lead a person to realize, feel, and act on the assumption that he or she has the right to be him- or herself and to express his or her feelings freely. Assertive responses generally are not aggressive responses. The distinction between these two types of interactions is important. If, for example, a wife has an overly critical mother-in-law, aggressive responses by the wife would include: ridiculing the mother-in-law, intentionally doing things that she knows will upset the mother-in-law (not visiting, serving the type of food the mother-in-law dislikes, not cleaning the house), urging the husband to tell his mother to "shut up," and getting into loud verbal arguments with the mother-in-law. On the other hand, an effective assertive response would be to counter criticism by saying: "Jane, your criticism of me deeply hurts me. I know you're trying to help me when you give advice, but I feel when you do that you're criticizing me. I know you don't want me to make mistakes, but to grow, I need to make my own errors and learn from them. If you want to help me the most, let me do it myself and be responsible for the consequences. The type of relationship I'd like to have with you is a close, adult relationship, and not a mother-child relationship."

[1]Robert E. Alberti and Michael L. Emmons, *Stand Up, Speak Out, Talk Back!* (New York: Pocket Books, 1975), p. 24.

STEPS IN ASSERTIVENESS TRAINING[2]

1. Examine your interactions. Are there situations that you need to handle more assertively? Do you at times hold opinions and feelings within you for fear of what would happen if you expressed them? Do you occasionally blow your cool and lash out angrily at others? Studying your interactions is facilitated by keeping a diary for a week or longer, recording the situations in which you acted timidly, those in which you were aggressive, and those which you handled assertively.

2. Select those interactions in which it would be to your benefit to be more assertive. They may include situations in which you were overly polite, overly apologetic, timid, and allowed others to take advantage of you, at the same time harboring feelings of resentment, anger, embarrassment, fear of others, or self-criticism for not having the courage to express yourself. Overly aggressive interactions in which you exploded in anger or walked over others also need to be dealt with. For *each* set of nonassertive or aggressive interactions, you can become more assertive, as shown in the next steps.

3. Concentrate on a specific incident in the past. Close your eyes for a few minutes and vividly imagine the details, including what you and the other person said, and how you felt at the time and afterward.

4. Write down and review your responses. Ask yourself the following questions to determine how you presented yourself:

   a. Eye contact—did you look directly at the other person, in a relaxed, steady gaze? Looking down or away suggests a lack of self-confidence. Glaring is an aggressive response.

   b. Gestures—were your gestures appropriate, free flowing, relaxed, and used effectively to emphasize your messages? Awkward stiffness suggests nervousness; other gestures (such as an angry fist) signal an aggressive reaction.

   c. Body posture—did you show the importance of your message by directly facing the other person, by leaning toward that person, by holding your head erect, and by sitting or standing appropriately close?

   d. Facial expression—did your facial expression show a stern, firm pose consistent with an assertive response?

   e. Voice tone and volume—was your response stated in a firm, conversational tone? Shouting may suggest anger. Speaking softly suggests shyness, and a cracking voice suggests nervousness. Tape recording and listening to one's voice is a way to practice increasing or decreasing the volume.

[2]These self-training steps are a modification of assertiveness training programs developed by Robert E. Alberti and Michael L. Emmons, *Your Perfect Right* (San Luis Obispo, Cal.: Impact, 1970), and by Herbert Fensterheim and Jean Baer, *Don't Say Yes When You Want to Say No* (New York: Dell, 1975).

f. Speech fluency—did your speech flow smoothly, clearly, and slowly? Rapid speech or hesitation in speaking suggests nervousness. Tape recording assertive responses that you try out to problem situations is a way to improve fluency.

g. Timing—were your verbal reactions to a problem situation stated at a time closest to the incident that would appropriately permit you and the other person time to review the incident? Generally, spontaneous expressions are the best, but certain situations should be handled at a later time—for example, challenging some of your boss's erroneous statements in private rather than in front of a group he or she is making a presentation to.

h. Message content—for a problem situation, which of your responses were nonassertive or aggressive, and which were assertive? Study the content and consider why you responded in a nonassertive or aggressive style.

5. Observe one or more effective models. Watch the verbal and nonverbal approaches that are assertively used to handle the type of interactions with which you have having problems. Compare the consequences between their approach and yours. If possible, discuss their approach and their feelings about using it.

6. Make a list of various alternative approaches for being more assertive.

7. Close your eyes and visualize yourself using each of the above alternative approaches. For each approach, think through what the full set of interactions would be, along with the consequences. Select an approach, or combination of approaches, that you believe will be most effective for you to use. Through imagery, practice this approach until you feel comfortable that it will work for you.

8. Role play the approach with someone else, perhaps a friend or counselor. If certain segments of your approach appear clumsy, awkward, timid, or aggressive, practice modifications until you become comfortable with the approach. Obtain feedback from the other person as to the strengths and shortcomings of your approach. Compare your interactions to the verbal/nonverbal guidelines for assertive behavior in step 4. It may be useful for the other person to model through role playing one or more assertive strategies, which you would then, by reversing roles, practice using.

9. Repeat steps 7 and 8 until you develop an assertive approach that you believe will work best for you, and that you are comfortable with and believe will work.

10. Use your approach in a real life situation. The previous steps are designed to prepare you for the real event. Expect to be somewhat anxious when first trying to be assertive. If you are still too fearful of attempting to be assertive, repeat steps 5 through 8. For those few individuals who fail to develop the needed confidence to try out being assertive, seeking professional counseling is advised—expressing yourself and effective interactions with others are essential for personal happiness.

11. Reflect on the effectiveness of your effort. Did you "keep your cool?"[3] Considering the nonverbal/verbal guidelines for assertive behavior discussed in step 4, what components of your responses were assertive, aggressive, and nonassertive? What were the consequences of your effort? How did you feel after trying out this new set of interactions? If possible, discuss how you did in regard to these questions with a friend who may have observed the interactions.

12. Expect some success, but not complete personal satisfaction, with your initial efforts. Personal growth and interacting more effectively with others is a continual learning process. Quite appropriately "pat yourself on the back" for the strengths of your approach—you earned it. But also note the areas where you need to improve, and use the above steps for improving your assertive efforts. These steps systematically make sense, but are not to be followed rigidly. Each person has to develop a process that works best for him- or herself.

EXAMPLES OF BEHAVIOR

You are flying with a business associate to Los Angeles for a conference. The associate lights up a pipe; you soon find the smoke irritating and the odor somewhat stifling. What are your choices?

1. Nonassertive response—you attempt to carry on a "cheery" conversation for the three-hour trip without commenting about the smoke.

2. Aggressive response—you increasingly become irritated until exploding, "Either you put out that pipe or I'll put it out for you—the odor is sickening."

3. Assertive response—in a firm, conversational tone, you look directly at the associate and state, "The smoke from your pipe is irritating me. I'd appreciate it if you put it away."

At a party with friends, during small talk conversation, your husband gives you a subtle "put down" by stating, "Wives always talk too much." What do you do?

1. Nonassertive response—you don't say anything, but feel hurt and become quiet.

2. Aggressive response—you glare at him and angrily ask, "John, why are you always criticizing me?"

3. Assertive response—you carry on as usual, waiting until driving home, then calmly look at him and say, "When we were at the party tonight, you said

---

[3]Getting angry at times is a normal human emotion, and it needs to be expressed. However, the anger should be expressed in a constructive, assertive fashion. When expressed in a destructive, lashing-out fashion, you are "blowing your cool."

that wives always talk too much. I felt you were putting me down when you said that. What did you mean by that comment?"

HELPING SOMEONE BECOME MORE ASSERTIVE

Either as a friend or as a counselor, you can be very helpful in assisting another person to become more assertive. The following guidelines are suggested.

1. Together identify the situations/interactions where the person needs to be more assertive. Get information about such interactions from your observations and knowledge about the person, from asking him or her and discussing in depth the interactions where the person feels he or she needs to be more assertive, and from having the person keep a diary of interactions where he or she feels resentment over being nonassertive and those interactions where he or she was overly aggressive.

2. Develop together some strategies for the person to be more assertive. Small assignments with a high probability of successful outcomes should be given first. A great deal of discussion and preparation should take place between the two of you in preparing for the "real event." For a person who is generally shy, introverted, and nonassertive in all interpersonal relationships, it probably will be necessary to explore and explain in great detail the connection between nonassertive behavior and feelings of resentment or low self-esteem. In addition, for very shy people, certain attitudes, such as "don't make waves" or the "meek will inherit heaven," may need to be dealt with prior to developing strategies for the person to be more assertive.

3. Role playing is a very useful technique in preparing for being assertive. The helper first models an assertive strategy by taking the shy person's role. The shy person concurrently role plays the role of the person with whom he or she wants to be more assertive. Then the roles are reversed; the person role plays him- or herself and the helper plays the other role. An example may make this clearer. Using the illustration cited earlier where a wife has problems in interacting with an overly critical mother-in-law, the helper would play the role of the wife first, modeling an assertive strategy. The wife would concurrently play the role of the mother-in-law. Then the roles would be reversed, the wife practicing various assertive strategies, with the helper playing the mother-in-law. The technique is practiced until the wife becomes comfortable with it and develops sufficient self-confidence for the "real event." In addition to the above-mentioned benefits of modeling and practice experience, role playing has the added advantage of reducing the anxiety that the shy person has about attempting to be assertive. For feedback purposes, if possible record the role playing on audio or video tape.

4. Explain the 12 steps described earlier that the person can use on his or her own to handle future problem situations involving assertiveness. If possible, provide reading material on these steps.

Although each person must be able to express him- or herself in his or her own individual style, there are two additional guidelines that will be useful.

1. A good rule is to start sentences with "I feel" rather than making threatening or aggressive statements. Frequently, in our fast-paced society we simply do not take the time to express our real feelings to others, and as a result we end up creating serious misunderstandings, hurt feelings, and verbal fights that take 10 times as long to work through. Take the following example of two busy people, a working mother and her 15-year-old son.

Mother: John, please do the dishes for me tonight.

John: I can't, I'll do them tomorrow.

Mother: (getting angry) You never do anything for me.

John: I said I'll do the dishes tomorrow.

Mother: And you always forget. I asked you to clean your room two weeks ago, and you still haven't done it. (Now angry) I just don't know what I'm going to do with you. Just for that you can't go camping this weekend.

And the argument has ignited. Contrast this to the following approach:

Mother: John, I feel very tired this evening. I had a bad day at work, and I still have to do all the washing and ironing tonight. Could you please help me out by doing the dishes?

John: I'm sorry you had a bad day. I feel I should help you more with the work that has to be done here, but I'm supposed to be at basketball practice in five minutes. I'll be back at 8:30; would it be all right if I did them then?

Mother: Yes, if you don't forget.

John: I won't.

2. The second guideline is not to let guilt control a relationship. Being controlled by guilt in a relationship is extremely discomforting. Usually the best way to counter such a relationship is directly to counter efforts to control through guilt. Control through guilt is particularly common in parent-child relationships.

Here are a few examples of strategies to counter control through guilt: A parent who says, "After all I've done for you, this is what I get" is attempting to control through guilt. An appropriate response would be, "When you say things like that you make me feel very guilty. Are you trying to control me by creating guilt in me?" Or, if a romance is ending and the boy says, "If you leave me, life won't be worth living," an effective counter response is, "I know you're trying to make me feel guilty, to continue our relationship by creating guilt. But do you think a relationship should be sustained by guilt?" Or a girl threatens suicide over an ending affair, an effective counter might be, "Finding meaning in life is really your problem. I feel terribly guilty that I've contributed to your problem. But since I'm so emotionally involved with you, I can't be helpful in counseling you. What I'm going to do is call your mother (or a friend or a counselor) to come over and talk with you."

The structure of the technique in assertive training is relatively simple to comprehend. Considerable skill (common sense and ingenuity), however, is needed to determine what will be an effective assertive strategy when a real life situation arises. The joy and pride obtained from being able fully to express oneself assertively is nearly unequaled.

Effective Communication

Patricia H. Mewaldt

Our behavior as parents, colleagues, friends, as human beings, and how effective that behavior is, depends to a great extent on how we understand any given situation. It is that understanding that determines how we respond to the situation, just as a doctor's understanding of an ailment will indicate the treatment of it. To understand a situation means that we are able to identify its important characteristics, and to be able to do this in our relationships with other human beings is essential, and surprisingly simple.

In any situation, a basic question to ask is "Is there a problem?" Is anyone involved in this situation unhappy? Is anyone giving evidence, verbally or nonverbally, that his or her needs are not being met? Are there any cues or clues that I can read, which tell me that someone is having a problem? Most often the answer to these questions will be no; a great deal of the time human beings manage to be happily engaged in any number of activities. When, for example, a mother is sitting in the living room reading the evening paper while her daughter watches her favorite television program, there is no evidence that either one is having a problem. A few minutes later, however,

This article was especially written for this book. It is based on the principles of Parent Effectiveness Training by Dr. Thomas Gordon.

the mother discovers that a portion of the article she is reading is missing because someone cut a clipping from the newspaper. Or perhaps the daughter turns away from the TV set and says sorrowfully, "I don't think it's fair that boys only date girls that are pretty."

If you were that mother, what you do now depends on how you answer this next question: "Who owns the problem?" A key to answering this question is whether or not you feel accepting toward the situation, and this depends upon whether or not the situation affects *in a concrete and tangible way* your ability to get your needs met. Thus, a clipping from the newspaper you're reading is a situation where you have a problem because you are unable to finish the article you want to read. Because the missing section interferes with your needs in a concrete and tangible way, you don't feel accepting toward the situation. Therefore, you "own" a problem.

When your daughter says, "I don't think it's fair that boys only date girls that are pretty," who owns the problem? Is this situation causing a problem for you? Unless you have an appointment that you have to run off to and talking to your daughter would cause you to miss the appointment, then it is quite unlikely that this situation is a problem for you. Your daughter's sorrowful look, however, as well as her verbal message, give ample clues that this is a problem *for her*. This is a situation where she owns the problem, where her needs aren't being met, and where she feels unhappy. Yet, despite your daughter's sadness, the situation itself *does not* interfere with your needs in a concrete and tangible way. Therefore, you feel accepting toward the situation.

This is a difficult concept to grasp and is often the reason why we fail to be helpful even when we very much want to help. How can you feel *accepting* toward a situation that makes another person sad? This is possible only if you are able to see that other person as a separate person from you. If you can recognize that you are two different people, with different needs, different desires, and different feelings, even though you may be members of the same family or are close friends or colleagues, then it will be possible for you to treat that person as a unique individual whose hurts are not your hurts, whose problems are not yours.

This is not a cold and callous posture. Recognizing, for example, that your brother's problems are not your problems does not mean that you don't love him, or that you don't want to be of help when he has a problem. If you do want to help, however, you will not be successful unless you realize that his problems are his alone — that he owns them.

How can you help when someone has a problem? The first thing is to have a *helpful attitude* toward the person who is experiencing a problem. This attitude will be conveyed if, in your own mind, you don't feel critical of him or her for having a problem; if you feel interested in being of help; and if you feel confident of the person's *own* ability to find a resolution. If you genuinely feel this way, you have succeeded in the all-important first step of being helpful.

Such an attitude inside you is less likely to cause the other person, whether relative or friend, to feel defensive about her or his feelings, and will make the person more likely to talk with you about the problem. If you have trouble feeling accepting of that person when he or she is experiencing a problem, or if you feel uncertain of his or her ability to resolve it, ask yourself to realize that the person, whether child or adult, is a human being who, like all of us, experiences problems, yet at the same time is both resilient and resourceful at handling them.

This attitude is important, but there are ways of being of greater help to someone experiencing a problem, namely by giving him or her the opportunity to talk about it. The person experiencing the problem will feel safe in talking about it *only if* the listener remains interested and noncritical, and does not convey the impression that he or she thinks the individual cannot resolve it alone. This means that the listener should not preach or offer solutions, because neither of these meets the three criteria of a helpful attitude. They just add insult to injury, and the other person will stop talking.

There are four skills you can use to convey a helpful attitude and make it easier for someone to talk about his or her problem. They are called listening skills:

1. Silent listening/silent attending.
2. Door openers.
3. Noncommittal acknowledgement.
4. Active listening.

Silent listening and silent attending mean simply being quiet while conveying with your eyes, face, and body posture that you are interested in what the other person is saying.

Door openers, such as "Would you like to talk about it?" or "Let's discuss it" convey this same message, as do noncommittal acknowledgements, such as "Oh," "I see," or "Mm-hmm." All convey an interest in the other person and a willingness to listen.

Active listening is the best of all the listening skills and takes some practice to master. *Active listening consists of conveying to the sender* (the person with the problem) *your understanding of what he or she has said, especially his or her feelings about it.* For example, your young sister says: "I just hate algebra. I study and study, but I'll never catch on." To "active listen" her, you might say: "It certainly sounds like you're pretty worried about algebra." If your feedback is on target, your sister is likely to respond by continuing to talk about it.

Active listening is a difficult skill to learn because most of us are busy thinking our own thoughts, and we don't focus on the other person's message. We have focused on our own thoughts if we say things such as, "Well, I'm sure you can pass algebra if you work hard enough on it," or "Don't worry, you'll catch on after a while," or "Well, you'd better ask the teacher for some special help." When we focus on our own thoughts, we miss the other person's message and this communicates that we're not interested, that we feel critical of him or her for having a problem and/or don't trust his or her ability to resolve it. This will make the person reluctant to share a problem with you again, and, consequently, your relationship together will not be as close as it might be.

The technique of active listening, which is to feed back to the sender your understanding of what he or she is saying and feeling, is a simple but powerful listening technique. It accomplishes a lot. First, it conveys to the sender that he or she has been understood and that he or she is not so crazy that understanding is impossible. When experiencing a problem, it can be very relieving to someone to know that his or her feelings are understandable. Second, active listening conveys to the sender that he or she is accepted even though he or she is experiencing uncomfortable feelings such as anger, jealousy, confusion, fear. To understand, which is what active listening demonstrates, conveys this kind of acceptance. "You're feeling hurt" conveys acceptance. "You shouldn't feel hurt" does not convey acceptance.

The third benefit of active listening is that it allows the sender to continue talking, which makes it possible for him or her to understand his or her own feelings and the problem in a more thorough way and creates the possibility for a resolution to appear. As we all know, many problems are different than they sound at first. "I don't want to go swimming" can mean anything from hating the way you look in your old bathing suit to fear of drowning to not liking the people at the pool. Buying a new bathing suit won't resolve the fear of drowning or dislike of the people at the pool; nor will swimming lessons overcome dislike of the bathing suit or of the people at the pool; nor will going to another pool resolve the other two problems. Active listening the other person's message will allow an unfolding of the problem, and solutions appropriate to the situation will usually appear.

WHAT DO YOU DO WHEN YOU HAVE A PROBLEM?

This is an entirely different situation. Here your needs are not being met; they are being interfered with and you feel unhappy. The goal here is to get *your* needs met. The trick is to convey to the other person whose behavior is interfering with your needs what it is that is bothering you, but to do so in a way that leaves him or her willing to be of help. Blaming the other person will not help to get your needs met. It will only make the other person defensive, and he or she will be more interested in taking care of his or her bruised feelings than in helping you get your needs met.

What you must do is to send a clear, but nonblameful message about what it is that is bothering you. Since this is a statement about one's self and one's own needs, it is called an I-message. An I-message has three parts: 1) A nonblameful description of the behavior that is giving me a problem, 2) The concrete and tangible effect of that behavior on me, and 3) My feelings about it. For example, "When I find that part of the newspaper has been clipped out (nonblameful description of the behavior), I can't finish the article I'm reading (concrete and tangible effect of that behavior on me), and I feel really frustrated" (my feeling about it).

The person who receives this message clearly realizes what it is that is bothering me, why I'm bothered by it, and how I feel. He or she may even acknowledge my message by active listening me, such as "It's annoying to find part of an article removed," which conveys that he or she has received and understood my message.

Although an I-message is a straightforward, readily understood, and invaluable communication skill, like all new skills it feels awkward at first. If you have been accustomed to sending blameful messages ("You shouldn't have done that") or put-down messages ("That's acting very childish") when someone's behavior has given you a problem, I-messages may at first seem weak and unlikely to work. On the other hand, if your pattern has been to suffer in silence, it may be hard to speak up at all. Whether your messages have in the past been too heavy-handed or virtually nonexistent, the I-message skill can work for you. It can allow you to get your feelings off your chest without putting the other person down or making him or her "wrong." Moreover, it allows the other person to initiate behavior out of consideration for your needs ("Oh, I didn't know you hadn't read the paper yet. I'll get the missing section for you"), and it allows him or her to feel good in doing so!

WHAT DO I DO WHEN THERE'S A CONFLICT BETWEEN MYSELF AND ANOTHER PERSON?

Many times my solution to a particular need of mine will conflict with that of another person's. I'm needing peace and quiet, and my spouse wants to have colleagues over for a planning meeting. Or the family budget is tight, and my daughter wants to take piano lessons.

There are three ways to resolve these and all conflicts. One way is to say: "No, you can't have the meeting here" or "There just isn't enough money for piano lessons." This will meet your needs for peace and quiet or for staying within the budget, but it may cause other more serious problems. The person whose needs are sacrificed is likely to feel resentful, and the price you may end up paying for the "no" is that of damage to the relationship.

Saying "yes" is the second alternative. If you say "yes," the other person will be pleased because his or her needs are met. But the price of this permissiveness is that you will feel resentful of the other person. This resentment may not be large at first, but it too can eat away at the relationship. Relationship damage is a predictable outcome of being either permissive or authoritative.

Happily, there is a third alternative, one that makes it possible for both people to have their needs met in a conflict situation. Unlike a compromise, this skill, called "No-Lose Problem Solving," makes it possible for both people to feel genuinely satisfied at the solution to the problem, and end up feeling close and caring about each other.

There are two basic premises of No-Lose Problem Solving: 1) that all people have the right to have their needs met, and 2) that what is in conflict (except in extreme instances such as famine) between the two parties involved is not their *needs* but their *solutions* to those needs. The distinction between "needs" and "solutions" is all-important. For example: My need is to get to work every day. Taking the family car is one solution, one way to get there. Another example: My need is for peace and quiet. My spouse's need is for a place to meet with colleagues. One solution is for me to wear cotton in my ears so I won't be bothered by the noise. Other possible solutions include their keeping the noise level to a minimum, or meeting in the garage, or that I move into the garage to relax, or that they meet at someone else's house, and so forth.

To any conflict there are numerous solutions. Therefore, it is not necessary to refuse gratification of the other person's need nor of your own. But when his or her solution interferes with your needs and, therefore, is unacceptable to you, it's time to problem solve.

No-Lose Problem Solving consists of six steps:

1. Identifying the needs of each person (defining the problem).
2. Generating a list of possible solutions.
3. Evaluating the solutions.
4. Deciding on a solution.
5. Implementing the solution.
6. Evaluating the solution.

The first step is by far the hardest, especially until No-Lose Problem Solving becomes routine among your family members, friends, and colleagues. During the first step, it is easy to get hung up in the distinction between needs and solutions, but active listening will help you to understand what the other person's needs are, and I-messages as a way to state your own needs will help them to be understandable to the other person. After each person's needs are identified and written down, you have completed Step 1.

Step 2 consists only of generating a list of all possible solutions. It is easy at this point to want to evaluate some of the solutions, but this must be avoided at all costs. The goal of Step 2 is simply to produce a long list; evaluating the solutions as they come up will stifle the creativity needed to accomplish this. Keep the climate free and open to all kinds of solutions.

After you have a list of possible solutions, perhaps 10 or 15, look over the list and throw out all the solutions that are unacceptable to either of you and identify the ones that are acceptable to you both (Step 3). If one doesn't seem quite pleasing to everyone, perhaps two or more solutions can be combined or refined to form an even more satisfying solution.

After you have decided upon a solution that is acceptable to everyone (Step 4), discuss how the solution is to be implemented (Step 5) by identifying *who will do what by when*. It sometimes is useful to write this down on paper and have each person sign it as a contract.

At that point you may plan when you will meet again to evaluate the solution (Step 6), to determine whether it is meeting everyone's needs, and problem solve again if it is not.

WHAT DO I DO IF I DON'T APPROVE OF SOMEONE ELSE'S BEHAVIOR?

There are often times when we don't approve of another person's behavior, yet our I-messages fail to motivate them to change their behavior. Why don't I-messages always work? Often this is because the other may not agree that his or her behavior is interfering with your needs *in any concrete and tangible way*. In other words, he or she doesn't "buy" your I-message. This situation, when another person's behavior does not interfere with your needs in a concrete and tangible way, yet you may have strong feelings about the behavior, is called a *values collision*. Collisions of values are common between parents and children, especially as the children become adolescents and young adults. It often involves values about sexual behavior, choice of friends, clothing, religion, education, plans for the future, hairstyle, eating habits, and so on. In these areas emotions run strong, and parents generally want to be able to influence their children to follow the values they hold important. Children, on the other hand, often think their parents' values are old-fashioned, and they are adamant about being able to make their own decisions about these matters. Thus, the generation gap becomes a reality. Values collisions also occur frequently between adults, and even communities, states, and nations.

This values gap need not occur, however, because there are three ways that values issues can be dealt with effectively. First, you can influence others' values by modeling the values you hold important. If you value honesty, be honest. If you value openness, be open. If you value education, do things that are congruent with that value. Above all, ask yourself if you are living according to the values you profess, and change—either your value or your behaviour—if your values and behavior are not congruent. Congruence between behavior and values is important if you want to be an effective model.

Second, you can influence others' values by acting as a consultant to them. There are, however, some do's and don't's of a good consultant. A good consultant first finds out whether the other person would like his or her consultation. If the answer is yes, he or she then makes sure that all the pertinent facts are known. He or she brings the data and shares it—once. He or she shares the information so that the other person understands it, but then leaves the other person with the responsibility for deciding whether to follow the advice or not. A good consultant, in other words, is neither uninformed nor a nag, otherwise he or she will never be taken as a consultant again.

The third way you can reduce tension over values issues is to modify yourself. By examining the values held by other people, including young and old, you may realize that their values hold some merit, and you may move toward their values or at least toward an understanding of why they hold them as values. Through this form of self-modification, you may be able to close the gap and feel accepting of the other person and his or her values.

CONCLUSION

Each of the four kinds of skills we have looked at takes practice to master, but they all will allow you to handle problems when they occur in ways that are satisfying to the people involved, and will also give you good feelings about yourself. These skills will not, however, mean that there never are conflicts; conflicts are inevitable and predictable occurrences in every human relationship, even between people who love each other. But a commitment to these skills can make it possible to have fewer and less severe conflicts, and more time to spend enjoying your family and friends as people.

Getting Along
When Religious Beliefs Differ

Charles Zastrow

The "how to" suggestions in this area are simple to state, but because of long-standing values, these suggestions are difficult for many to use. The best way for close friends to get along with each other when religious beliefs differ is for each person to do some research about his or her own religion and his or her friend's. Most people who argue about religion are ignorant of their own as well as anyone else's. They believe that their church says X when historically the church has said Y; their memory of a Sunday School lesson 10 years ago is blurry. Personal ignorance is a major reason why people disagree/fight over religion. This includes people who are "active" in the church bazaar or the church council; they usually know little about theology. Most people discover when they study religions (especially Western religions) that there are many more similarities among them than there are differences. Ideally, when discussing religious beliefs, people should have an open mind and share divergent views to gain an increased awareness and appreciation of such beliefs.

Unfortunately, it is difficult in our society to develop an open mind that is geared to appreciation of differences. A closed mind, which is intolerant of religious differences, appears to be more common. Generally, the bulk of

This article was especially written for this book.

society is intolerant of extreme differences in modes of dressing, religious beliefs, political beliefs, ethnic customs, color of skin, and such. Why? First, psychologically, people do not have the motivation to try to understand and gain an awareness of everything that is different—it is simply easier to characterize such differences as "bad," "weird," "useless," and, therefore, not worth the effort to examine. Many people in this society, for example, would probably characterize such religions as Hinduism, Buddhism, Shintoism, and Mohammedanism as being useless and not worthy of study, without having any idea or interest in finding out what their basic beliefs are.

Second is the fear of something unknown or not understood. This fear, combined with ignorance, allows a person to view differences as a threat to his or her sense of security, values, current life-style, whatever. Differing political philosophies are a good example of this. Many people in democratic countries are strongly opposed to such philosophies as socialism, communism and fascism, yet they have never taken the time to assess the merits and shortcomings of these philosophies. In fact, most people do not even know the basic theory underlying these philosophies.

Unfortunately, a third reason for intolerance of differences is to be found within religions themselves. Although national and international offices of religious denominations generally emphasize cooperation and appreciation of religious differences, many local clergy leaders attempt to indoctrinate in their members the belief that their particular religion is the only true religion, that only the members of that faith will be saved. Such a doctrine is undoubtedly a large factor in leading to intolerance of differences—intolerance of other religions and intolerance in other areas. It leads the members to believe that they are right and only they know "the way." Everyone else is wrong. The author was raised in a fundamentalistic religion that even held the belief that it was a sin to pray in the presence of others. Some local clergy leaders tell their members that it is a mistake to discuss their "one true" religion with people who are members of other "false" religions. What are the results of such doctrines? At the family level there are arguments about whether one should be friends with, or date, or marry someone of another faith. At national levels there are wars fought over religious differences, as, for example, between the Protestants and Catholics in Northern Ireland. Religious differences are a significant factor in the conflict between Jews and Arabs in the Middle East. The crusades of the Middle Ages are another example. A number of historians have observed that religious differences have been the cause of more wars than any other factor.

Religion has great value in conveying morals and in giving meaning to living, and it has a social service function in helping to meet the welfare, health, social, and recreational needs of many people. Religion also gives hope to those who look toward an afterlife; it helps to ease current pain and suffering. In addition, diverse religions have deep and rich histories, elaborate and elegant ceremonies, and they generally advocate moral guidelines that are worthy of study, meditation, and appreciation.

With this background, I suggest an open mind and an appreciation of religious differences. Discussion between friends of religious differences is to be encouraged, with the goal being not to change your friends' beliefs, but to become more aware of their religious views and to learn more about your own. Dating and marriage between people of diverse faiths is not to be discouraged; the relationship and feelings toward one another should be recognized as being much more important than any religious differences. In fact, if people are able to communicate openly with each other and to respect such differences, then differing religious beliefs will be an area that has the potential of providing interest, a source of sharing, and personality growth to a relationship. If you cannot tolerate religious differences in your mate, you probably are too rigid to tolerate a lot of other differences which two people bring to a life together.

If a couple with differing beliefs marry and have children, the question may arise as to the faith in which the child should be brought up. In an openly communicating family that is respectful of each other, the answer is to expose the child to both faiths, as well as to others. In addition, let the child decide (when he/she begins to express preferences) which faith (if any) he or she wants to join. The child should be allowed to choose *not* to belong to *either* of his or her parent's faiths; he or she may opt for a third or none at all. Undoubtedly, the child's decision will not be based on philosophical differences in church doctrine, but on such factors as which church his or her friends are attending, or which Sunday school teacher he or she is most attracted to.

The question may also arise, "What should I do if I have an open mind, but my friend doesn't?" If you have an open mind, and in an initial discussion of religion with a friend, it becomes obvious that the other person has a closed mind and is becoming irritated about the discussion (probably because it poses a threat to his or her beliefs), then your best option probably is to change the subject. If the conversation were to continue, the other person would probably become more irritated and threatened, little will be gained, and your relationship may be jeopardized.

"What should I do if I'm intending to marry someone with differing beliefs who has a closed mind?" Several avenues are open to you. You can use the "soft" approach, show interest in that person's religious beliefs and attempt to discuss such differences calmly. Continue to discuss such differences until you sense that either you or the other person is becoming irritated and defensive.

As soon as that happens, change the subject as further discussion will raise emotions and not be beneficial. Discussing such differences in the presence of open-minded clergy also may be helpful. If it becomes obvious that the other person will remain closed minded and intolerant of religious differences, you have two choices: 1) Decide to stop bringing up the subject, let the other person retain his or her beliefs, and continue the relationship. Congruence of religious beliefs is certainly not necessary for a successful relationship or marriage, but respect for the other person is—sometimes you can show respect by simply keeping your mouth shut or by showing constructive interest in the other person. 2) If the differences are very intensely felt (which is rarely apt to happen when one of the persons has an open mind), then carefully examine whether it is in both of your best interests to continue the relationship.

When people of different religious affiliations marry, one of the biggest problems is learning to share religious holidays or traditions. A Jewish mate may feel pressured at Christmas time with all the Christian traditions; an atheist might be offended with Good Friday or Jewish High Holy Day solemnity. Often it is not what you *believe*, but how and when you perform your *rituals*, which affects life-style differences. In marriage relationships, such religious ritual situations are best resolved when there is an appreciation of differing customs, respect for one's spouse, and a give-and-take attitude by both. There is generally no right or wrong way to celebrate a religious holiday or tradition. What counts is what seems most familiar, most right to you. Since most everyone enjoys holidays, it is at times possible for a couple that belongs to different religions to combine the celebration of certain holidays, along with the rituals they enjoy; for example, combining the customs of Hanukkah and Christmas, and of Passover and Easter.

An examination and appreciation of diverse religious beliefs should be encouraged. For those attempting such an examination, these few facts should help to lead to the development of an open-minded view of religion.

1. There may not be a "one true" religion. As indicated earlier, some clergy assert that their doctrine is the "one true" religion. Religion is an act of faith; evidence establishing the rightness of any doctrine is not available. If God exists, it could be argued that everyone (or no one) who lives a moral life, regardless of their particular religion, will be transferred to heaven after death. And even if there is "one true" religion, the probability that your specific religion is the "selected" one is extremely small. There are thousands of religions in the world. Among the largest in terms of members are Judaism, Islam, Christianity, Buddhism, Hinduism, Jainism, Confucianism, and Taoism. And, even in each of these major religions, there are distinct and conflicting segments. Christianity, for example, has such denominations as Roman Catholics, Lutherans, Baptists, Southern Baptists, Mormons,

Jehovah's Witnesses, Quakers, Assemblies of God, Christian Reformed, Christian Science, Congregational, Episcopal, Evangelical, Methodist, Moravian, Nazarene, Presbyterian, Seventh-day Adventists, and many more. And within these denominations are distinct synods and conflicting beliefs.

2. There is no irrefutable proof of the existence of God.[1] Several arguments for the existence of a supernatural being have been developed, but definitive proof is not available. That fact does not mean that one should necessarily become an atheist—one who does not believe in God. If an afterlife exists, it perhaps is less risky to believe in God and lead a moral life than it is to disbelieve and have an unpleasant afterlife. If you are not sure if you do or do not believe, you are known as an agnostic.

3. Many religions assert that their "bible" is the "word of God." Jews have the Old Testament, Protestants have the Old and the New Testaments, Catholics add a few more chapters written by other writers called prophets, and the Mormons have *The Book of Mormon* based on the religious experiences of Joseph Smith in the 19th century. Muslims have the Koran, Buddhism has the Doctrine of the Buddha, Taoism has the Tao-Te-Ching, and Confucianism has the Li Chi. Although each of these "bibles" contains excellent guides and philosophies for leading a moral and ethical life, again there is no irrefutable evidence that any of the writings are the "word of God." Hopefully, the reader will have an open mind when viewing other religions, instead of dogmatically clinging to one's "bible" as the final word, without taking the time to examine other beliefs.

4. Why are there so many different religions? The answer is found in the history of religious development, which we will briefly trace.[2] In the days of early peoples, there were numerous isolated clans, family groupings, and small societies. Without scientific knowledge, many natural events were unexplainable—thunder and rain, lightning, why the sun rose in the east, and why it was sometimes covered by clouds, and so on. Unable to explain such events, primitive people deduced that supernatural beings had control over such phenomena. Names were assigned to these gods. Gradually, people came to believe that it was in their best interests to please the gods, and they attempted to influence them. If, for example, they needed rain, various sacrifices, rituals, and ceremonial rites were attempted. If it did happen to rain, that sacrifice or ritual was usually, by association, incorporated into the religion. Through such trial and error, patterns of worship and sacrifices were either discarded (if unsuccessful) or incorporated (if successful).

---

[1]Terence Penelhum, *Problems of Religious Knowledge* (London: The Macmillan Company, 1971).

[2]Robert Brow, *Religion: Origin and Ideas* (London: Tyndale, 1966).

Most neighboring religions borrowed heavily from one another, especially in the "lives of the prophets" stories. The Egyptian account of Isis and Osiris has many similarities to the Christian writings of Mary and Jesus. The celebration of Christmas among Christians was moved to the winter because of the Roman Saturnalia (the festival of Saturn in ancient Rome beginning on December 17). The story of the flood came from an old Babylonian myth and was incorporated in Israel's teachings following the exile in Babylon. The Christian concept of the dichotomy of body and soul came from the Greek philosophers, not from the Jewish faith.

As diverse religions gradually emerged, certain tribes or societies developed highly elaborate worship patterns and, in the case of most religions, numerous gods. Some religions, partly to reduce the complexity, developed hierarchies of gods, with some gods being accorded more power than others. Some religions developed the idea of one superior or all-controlling god. And, as the religion continued to develop, usually a prophet or a series of prophets, believed to be inspired by God, organized the religious beliefs, expanded on them, and interpreted the beliefs to others in that society. These beliefs were generally excellent guides for a moral and ethical life.

Religion is needed by many; it gives meaning to life. For those with an open mind who are respectful of different beliefs, it is an area of study that leads to personal growth and increased appreciation of the values and beliefs of others.

How to Be More Attractive

Cathy Jensen

For many of us, gone are the days of conformity. Today's "attractive look" is individualistic and personal. Beauty is important for both women and men and is expressed through their personalities. If you want to be more attractive, begin by putting beauty in its proper perspective. First, be honest with yourself. Ask yourself, "What are my best features?" and "What are my faults?" Learn to develop your best features and to compensate for your faults. Second, remember that very few people are born beautiful. Making and keeping yourself attractive takes time, practice, and determination.

Being attractive involves more than just using cosmetics, or wearing the latest hair style or fashion. Beauty begins with basics, such as an adequate program of diet and health, exercise, skin and hair care. Fashion, voice, personal hygiene, and personality are also part of the total attractive picture.

HEALTH AND DIET

Something that all women and men should have in common is good health. Beauty and health go hand in hand. Diet, of course, is the basic factor in

This article was especially written for this book.

health care. A poor diet reflects itself in your overall appearance. A healthy glow is more the result of a well-balanced diet, plenty of exercise, and the correct amount of sleep than the latest beauty aids. Beauty aids enhance or highlight your features; they don't hide them. Exterior beauty is simply a reflection of your inner self.

Whatever diet plan you are presently following, remember that all diets need to be balanced. Any diet should include proteins, carbohydrates, vitamins, fats, and minerals. Each serves a purpose and is important in keeping your body functioning properly. A sudden change in your diet could shock your system. Learning what to eat is just as important as learning how much to eat. Eliminate the extras, not the basics.

When determining your daily calorie intake, keep these facts in mind: your age, height, present or desired weight, body frame, and how active you are. Checking your weight the first thing each morning will help you to keep yourself at a desired goal. Any weight gain or loss can be remedied before it gets to be a real problem. Your family physician is best qualified to answer any questions you may have concerning your diet. You are what you eat, so the better your diet, the better you will look and feel.

EXERCISE

Another important part of good health is exercise. Everyone needs some form of it, because exercise does more than burn up calories. It improves circulation, posture, balance, and coordination, increases flexibility, strengthens muscles, and helps to keep you alert.

When selecting an exercise plan, consider various areas. If you prefer a shape-up plan, such as toe touching or sit-ups, work into each gradually so that you do not strain or fatigue yourself. Breathing correctly is also important, exhaling when bending and inhaling when stretching. Dancing is a good form of exercise. Enroll in a modern dance class, a ballet class, or a tap dance class. Many athletes, for instance, study ballet and modern dancing for coordination and quicker reactions. Consider sports you will be able to do all your life, such as tennis, golf, or swimming. Even judo and karate are forms of exercise. Some types of isometrics and calisthenics are excellent if you are sometimes restricted from a great degree of physical activity. Routine housework and walking can be beneficial, if you stretch and bend or keep moving rapidly whenever possible.

Select a program that is most convenient and comfortable for you, one that fits easily into your daily schedule and has been approved by your family physician. If exercising is to be beneficial, it should be done on a daily basis, rather than exercising strenuously once in a while. Many forms of exercise can and should be continued well into your old age.

HAIR CARE

As with everything else, hair care has its limitations. Before using any product on your hair, consider what is best for your hair type. Most hair products are designed for certain types of hair. Shampoos, for instance, may be for dry, normal, oily, tinted, or lightened hair. Use the one that is best for you. Check also to make sure that the product is pH balanced—indicating a balance of acid and alkaline. If the product does not state the pH level, make the test yourself with Scribb Nitrazine paper, which can be obtained from your local pharmacist. This pH paper is used by dipping the paper into the hair product, and then letting dry for a few minutes. The acidity-alkalinity level of the hair product will turn the paper a certain color. Comparing the color of the pH paper to the color code chart on the container for the Scribb Nitrazine paper will indicate the acidity/alkalinity level. The best reading is between 4.5 to 5.5. Hair products containing too much alkaline can weaken your hair, giving way to more split ends and breakage.

You should wash your hair as often as necessary, but at least once a week. How often you wash it, of course, depends on your hair type and if you use hair sprays or setting lotions. For example, if you have oily hair, you should be washing it every day or every other day. When using sprays or lotions, try to wash your hair at least three times a week. If you are gentle to your hair and you use the correct products, there is no reason why you cannot wash your hair as often as needed. Make sure your hair is well rinsed; if it is not, it will look dull and lifeless.

Before shampooing, brush through your hair to loosen dirt and oils. Bend forward, brushing from the nape of the neck toward the crown of the head. After shampooing always use a comb, never a brush. But when your hair is dry, always use a brush. When combing wet hair, start from the ends of your hair working up toward the top so as not to damage or tear your hair.

Since hair reflects its history, it is important to condition your hair regularly, especially if you use styling combs, blow combs, electric hair setters, or curling irons. These items can burn and dry the ends of your hair. Conditioners will help to prevent breakage, as well as strengthen and promote shine. There are two types of conditioners that should be used—instant and regular. Instant conditioners are designed to be used after every shampoo to remove tangles; regular conditioners are to be used anywhere from once a week to once a month. Regular conditioners should be applied once a month all over your hair, and in between apply the conditioner only to the ends of your hair. Also try to limit the use of combs, hair setters, and curling irons to no more than three times a week.

When choosing a hair style, keep several things in mind. Look at your hair texture—is it thin, medium, coarse, curly, straight? Hair texture helps to determine suitable hair style; the long, straight look won't work if your head is a mess of natural curls! Your face shape is important, too. For instance, if your face is long, you may look better wearing your hair short or in a medium length. Also, think about your age and life-style. Avoid a style that is best suited for a younger or an older person, or one that you cannot take the time to care for appropriately. The same thing can be said for hair color. Some styles and colors suit some people better than others. So before doing anything different to your hair, consider all the factors.

Regardless of hair style, your hair should be shaped or trimmed about every six weeks, because everyone's hair grows unevenly and at a different rate. No one likes to look at a scraggly head of hair, no matter how pretty the color, texture, or length. For men who wear beards, mustaches, or sideburns, it is advisable to have your hair specialist shape and trim them during your visits. It is a good idea to see the same hair specialist each time; he or she will become acquainted with your hair and will be able to spot early warning signs before it is too late. If you cannot find a specialist that you like, contact your nearest barber/beauty college. Give the college a brief history of your hair and any problems you may have. From this information, the college can recommend a specialist who is familiar with your hair type. The college can also analyze your hair or tell you where you can send a strand of it to be analyzed. Having your hair analyzed will tell you the condition of your hair, the best hair products to use, and even the texture of your hair and the style that is best for your hair type. When you are good to your hair, your hair will look and feel healthy.

SKIN CARE

Just as there are different hair types, there are different skin types. Basically, there are four skin types: dry, normal, oily, and a combination. Each should be cared for differently.

Once you have selected the correct products for your skin type, the next step is to make sure that you are cleansing your face correctly. For example, if you have dry skin, you might be able to limit the washing of your face to only twice a day, unless you live in an area of high pollution. Then, of course, you may want to wash your face more often. Avoid using soaps or astringents, as these will dry your face more. Instead, use a dry skin cleanser and a mild skin freshener. If you have oily skin, you should wash your face more frequently, using soaps and astringents. Moisturizers should be used for all skin types, including oily skin. If you have oily skin, you are probably washing it more often and the products you are using are harsher. Frequent washing along with harsh products can overdry your skin.

For really deep-down cleansing, include the use of facials. There are several types to choose from, and basically they all do the same thing—deep cleanse—so the choice is yours. When using facials, keep these three things in mind: 1) always apply to skin that has just been cleansed, 2) do not overuse them, and 3) do not apply to the skin around the eyes.

Select the correct cosmetics, after-shave lotions, or acne treatments. There are several things to keep in mind when choosing these items. If your skin breaks out, do not apply cosmetics or cover-ups until the problem is solved. Be sure to watch for allergic reactions to harsh chemicals in makeup or lotions. Discontinue the use of anything that seems to irritate your skin, and consult your family physician or possibly a dermatologist. Women should choose cosmetics that are sheer and give them a natural glow. Different types of lighting can affect different shades of makeup, so you will probably want to have a selection to choose from. For instance, what you wear for the daytime will most likely be too light for the evening and could give you a washed-out look.

The cosmetics or lotions that are best for you depend on your personal needs. Don't think that just because a product costs more, it will give better results. It is true that more expensive products are of a higher quality, but they may not give you the best results. Cosmetics should be used to highlight and enhance, not to hide and cover up. Remember that a balanced diet, plenty of sleep, and exercise also play an important part in the healthy look of your skin.

FASHION

Of all the areas of beauty, fashion is probably the most flexible. Yet there are things that everyone should consider. Does the style look good on you? Just because the style is "in" or looks good on someone else does not mean that it will look good on you. Check out the colors and designs too. Some colors may be favorites, but they may not look good on you because of your hair or skin color. Your height and weight are important. For example, if you are short and heavy, wearing loud colors and designs will make you look shorter and heavier. Learn to select clothing that will flatter your good points and disguise your bad ones.

The second thing to consider is comfort. Does it fit the way you want it to? If clothing is too tight, it will make the wearer look heavier. The care of the fabric is important, too. Will it wear well and retain its shape after washing?

Learn to rely on your own judgment or an honest friend when selecting clothing. Remember when someone spontaneously compliments you on a certain color or style. Then seriously consider selecting those colors and styles the next time you purchase clothing.

VOICE

Are you aware that *how* you say something is just as important as *what* you say? Does your voice have a smooth soothing sound, or is it harsh, and are your words mumbled? The best way to find out is to tape your voice. If possible, have yourself videotaped to see how you look when speaking. Once you are conscious of your weak areas, you can concentrate on making improvements.

PERSONAL HYGIENE

Without personal hygiene you defeat all other aspects of beauty. Cleanliness is the all-important good habit. Bathe daily. After a shower or bath, the skin is less irritable and should be shaved at this time. Women may also want to douche at certain times—you may wish to see your physician or gynecologist about the frequency of this practice. After bathing use a lightly scented talcum power, unless your physician advises you differently. At bath time you should also care for your nails. They should be cleaned daily and cut and filed weekly. Trim away any rough edges or hangnails.

After bathing include the use of deodorants or dusting powder to stop wetness and odor. Lightly scented body lotions can keep your skin smooth and moist. Finish with a cologne, a perfume, an after-shave lotion, or a moisturizer. Be sure when selecting one of these that they express your personality. Remember that each has a different scent when in its bottle, as well as when worn by you or someone else.

A final touch to personal hygiene is good dental care. Nothing reflects your personality more than a warm smile. Unfortunately, we were not all born with perfect teeth. This is all the more reason why you should take good care of yours. If possible, brush your teeth after every meal, but if you cannot, try to brush at least twice daily followed by a mouthwash. At other times breath sprays and breath deodorants are effective in controlling unpleasant mouth odors. They are available in compact sizes and are easily carried in your handbag or pocket.

PERSONALITY

Almost all of us can see the good or bad qualities in the personalities of others. Yet when it comes to ourselves, we are often the last to recognize faults or to improve them. Some individuals consider themselves practically perfect; others unconsciously never realize that they need to improve. We all have room for improvement. Self-improvement includes improving your bad habits as well as cultivating your good ones.

Expand your outlook by becoming involved in sports, hobbies, or organizations. Keep up-to-date on current events by subscribing to newspapers or magazines. All of these will help you to widen your ideas and interests. Your personality will improve, you will meet new people, and you will also become a better conversationalist.

When you meet new people be sure to show that you enjoy talking to them. Look directly at the person you are speaking with. Don't monopolize the conversation or interrupt others when they are talking. Take into consideration another's feelings before you speak. Before saying anything, consider what effect it will have. Show respect for other opinions, even though they may differ from yours. Learn to be a good listener as well as a good conversationalist.

Once you realize that everyone has room for improvement, including yourself, the next step is a sincere desire to improve. Once you have begun, do not slip back into old habits or give up. Decide on a plan of improvement. Set reasonable goals for yourself; do not set goals too high or expect results overnight. Work on one area at a time to insure that each is given as much time as needed.

Everything you say or do reflects in your overall appearance. You are the only one who can improve yourself. You hold the key to your own success or failure.

PART FIVE
CRISIS SITUATIONS

How to Counsel

Charles Zastrow

Counseling someone with personal problems is neither magical nor mystical. Although training and experience in counseling is beneficial, everyone has the potential of helping another by listening and talking through difficulties. Counseling with a successful outcome can be done by a friend, neighbor, relative, yourself, the local barber, hairdresser, banker, and bartender, as well as by social workers, psychiatrists, psychologists, guidance counselors, and the clergy. This is not to say that everyone will be successful at counseling. Professional people, because of their training and experience, have a higher probability of being successful. But competence and concern, rather than degrees or certificates, are the keys to desirable outcomes.[1]

There are three phases to counseling: 1) building a relationship, 2) exploring problems in depth, and 3) exploring alternative solutions. Successful counseling gradually proceeds from one phase to the next, with some overlapping of these stages. For example, in many cases while exploring problems, the relationship between the counselor and the counselee continues to

This article was especially written for this book.

[1]The focus of this chapter will be on how professional counseling should be done. Since all of us at one time or another counsel others, the closer the counseling (including friend-to-friend counseling) approaches professional counseling, the higher the probability of a successful outcome.

develop; and while exploring alternative solutions, the problems are generally being examined in greater depth.

BUILDING A RELATIONSHIP

1. The counselor should seek to establish a nonthreatening atmosphere where the counselee feels safe to communicate fully his or her troubles while feeling accepted as a person.

2. In initial contacts with the counselee, the counselor needs to "sell" him- or herself, not arrogantly, but as a knowledgeable, understanding person who may be able to help and who wants to try.

3. Be calm, do not express shock or laughter when the counselee begins to open up about his or her problems. Emotional outbursts, even if subtle, will lead the counselee to believe that you are not going to understand his or her difficulties, and he or she will usually stop discussing them.

4. Generally be nonjudgmental, not moralistic. Show respect for the counselee's values and do not try to sell your values. The values that work for you may not be best for someone else in a different situation. For example, if the counselee is premaritally pregnant, do not attempt to force your values toward adoption or abortion, but let the counselee decide on the course of action after a full examination of the problem and an exploration of alternative solutions.

5. View the counselee as an equal. "Rookie" counselors sometimes make the mistake of thinking that because someone is sharing their intimate secrets, the counselor must be very important, and they end up arranging a superior-inferior relationship. If the counselee feels that he or she is being treated as an inferior, he or she will be less motivated to reveal and discuss personal difficulties.

6. Use "shared vocabulary." This does not mean that the counselor should use the same slang words and the same accent as the counselee. If the counselee sees the counselor as artificial in use of slang or accent, it may seriously offend him or her. The counselor should use words that the counselee understands and that are not offensive.

7. The tone of the counselor's voice should convey the message that the counselor empathetically understands and cares about the counselee's feelings.

8. Keep confidential what the counselee has said. People unfortunately have nearly irresistible urges to share "juicy secrets" with someone else. If the counselee discovers that confidentiality has been violated, a working relationship may be quickly destroyed.

9. If you are counseling a relative or a friend, there is a danger that, because you are emotionally involved, you may get upset or into an argument with the other person. If that happens it is almost always best to drop the subject immediately, as tactfully as possible. Perhaps after tempers cool the subject can be brought up again, or perhaps it may be best to refer the counselee to someone else. When counseling a friend or relative, you should be aware that when you find yourself becoming upset, further discussion will not be productive. Many professional counselors refuse to counsel friends or relatives because they are aware that they are emotionally involved. Emotional involvement interferes with the calm, detached perspective that is needed to help clients explore problems and alternative solutions.

EXPLORING PROBLEMS IN DEPTH

1. Many "rookie" counselors make the mistake of suggesting solutions as soon as a problem is identified, without exploring the problem area in depth. For example, an advocate of abortions may advise this solution as soon as a single female reveals that she is pregnant, without taking the time to discover whether this person is strongly opposed to abortions, really wants a baby, or intends to marry soon.

2. In exploring problems in depth, the counselor and counselee need to examine such areas as the extent of the problem, how long the problem has existed, what the causes are, how the counselee feels about the problem, and what physical and mental capacities and strengths the counselee has to cope with the problem, prior to exploring alternative solutions. To illustrate, if a single female is pregnant, the counselor and counselee need to explore the following questions: How does the person feel about being pregnant? Has she seen a doctor? About how long has she been pregnant? Do her parents know? What are their feelings and concerns if they know? Has the girl informed the father? What are his feelings and concerns if he knows? What does she feel is the most urgent situation to deal with first? Answers to such questions will determine the future direction of counseling. The most pressing, immediate problem might be to inform her parents, who may react critically, or it might be to secure medical services.

3. When a problem area is identified, there are usually a number of smaller problems that may occur. Explore all these. For example, how to tell the father, obtaining medical care, obtaining funds for medical expenses, deciding where to live, deciding whether to leave school or work during the pregnancy, deciding whether to keep the child, making plans for what to do after the child is delivered or the pregnancy terminated.

4. In a multiproblem situation, the best way to decide which problem to handle first is to ask the counselee which problem he or she perceives as most pressing. If the problem can be solved, start with exploring that subproblem in depth and developing together a strategy for the solution. Success in solving a subproblem will increase the counselee's confidence in the counselor, and thereby further solidify the relationship.

5. Convey empathy, not sympathy. Empathy is the capacity to show that you are aware of and can to some extent feel what the counselee is saying. Sympathy is also a sharing of feelings, but it has the connotation of offering pity. The difference is subtle, but empathy is problem-solving oriented and sympathy is usually problem-prolonging. Giving sympathy usually causes the counselee to dwell on his or her emotions without taking action to improve the situation. For example, if one gives sympathy to a depressed person, that person will keep telling you his or her sad story over and over, each time having an emotional outpouring supported by your sympathy, without taking any action to improve the situation. Telling the story over and over only reopens old wounds and prolongs the depression.

6. "Trust your guts." The most important tool that a counselor has is him- or herself (his or her feelings and perceptions). A counselor should continually strive to place him- or herself in the client's situation (with the client's values and pressures). To use the earlier example, if the client is 17 years old, single, pregnant, and has parents who are very critical of the situation and who want her to have an abortion, a competent counselor would continually strive to feel what she is feeling and to perceive the world from her perspective, with her goals, difficulties, pressures, and values. It probably never happens that a counselor is 100 percent accurate in placing him- or herself in the counselee's situation, but 70 to 80 percent is usually sufficient to gain an awareness of the counselee's pressures, problems, and perspectives. This information is very useful in assisting the counselor in determining what additional areas need to be explored, what he or she should say, and in figuring out what might be possible solutions. Stated in a somewhat different way, a counselor should ask him- or herself, "What is this person trying to tell me and how can I make it clear that I understand not only intellectually but empathically?"

7. When you believe that the client has touched upon an important area of concern, further communication can be encouraged by:

   a. Nonverbally showing interest.
   b. Pauses. "Rookie" counselors usually become anxious when there is a pause, and they hasten to say something, anything, to have conversation continue. This is usually a mistake, especially when it leads to a change in the topic. A

A pause will also make the counselee anxious, give him or her time to think about the important area of concern, and then usually motivate him or her to continue conversation in that area.

c. Neutral probes; for example, "Could you tell me more about it?" "Why do you feel that way?" "I'm not sure I understand what you have in mind."

d. Summarizing what the client is saying; for example, "During this past hour you made a number of critical comments about your spouse; it sounds like some things about your marriage are making you unhappy."

e. Reflecting feelings; for example, "You seem angry" or "You appear to be depressed about that."

8. **Approach socially unacceptable topics tactfully.** Tact is an essential quality of a competent counselor. Try not to ask a question in such a way that the answer will put the respondent in an embarrassing position. Suppose, for instance, that you are an adult who has a good relationship with a teen-ager and have reason to suspect that person has "hangups" about masturbation. How would you tactfully bring up the subject to discuss? One possible approach is, "When I was your age, I had a number of hangups about masturbating. That was unfortunate. Most teen-agers masturbate, but many have strong feelings of guilt or shame about it. Although masturbation has been stigmatized, it is in reality a natural outlet for sexual feelings and is not harmful. In fact, Masters and Johnson recommend frequent masturbation, either alone or with a partner. If you have some worries about this, perhaps we could talk about them." Informing the youth that you also had hangups about this subject personalizes it and tells the teen-ager that you have experienced some of the concerns he or she is currently facing. Communication and relationship building are fostered.

9. **When pointing out a limitation that a counselee has, mention and compliment him or her on any assets.** When a limitation is being mentioned, the counselee will literally feel that something is being laid bare or taken away. Therefore, compliment him or her in another area to give something back.

10. **Watch for nonverbal cues.** A competent counselor will generally use such cues to identify when a sensitive subject is being touched upon, as the client will generally become anxious and show anxiety by a changing tone of voice, fidgeting, yawning, stiff posture, and a flushed face. Some counselors even claim that they can tell when a client becomes anxious by observing when the pupils of the eyes are dilating.

11. **Be honest.** An untruth always runs the risk of being discovered. If that happens, the counselee's confidence in the counselor will be seriously

damaged, and perhaps the relationship seriously jeopardized. But being honest goes beyond not telling lies. The counselor should always point out those shortcomings that are in the counselee's best interest to give attention to. For example, if someone is being fired from jobs because of poor grooming habits, this needs to be brought to that person's attention. Or if a trainee's relationship skills and personality are not suited for the helping profession, that trainee needs to be "counseled out" in the interest of clients and in the trainee's own best interests.

12. Listen attentively to what the counselee is saying. Try to view his or her words, not from your perspective but from the counselee's. Unfortunately, many people are caught up in their own interests and concerns, and they do not "tune out" those thoughts while the counselee is speaking. This guideline seems very simple, but it is indeed difficult for many to follow.

EXPLORE ALTERNATIVE SOLUTIONS

1. After (or sometimes as part of) a subproblem is explored in depth, the next step is for the counselor and the counselee to consider alternative solutions. The counselor's role is generally to indicate the possible alternatives and then to explore with the counselee their merits, shortcomings, and consequences. For example, with the case of the premaritally pregnant girl, if she decides to continue the pregnancy to full term, possible alternatives for the subproblem of making plans for living arrangements include keeping the child, a possible marriage, seeking public assistance, foster care after delivery, a possible paternity suit, placing the child for adoption, obtaining the assistance of a close relative to help care for the child.

2. The counselee usually has the right to self-determination, that is, to choose the course of action among possible alternatives. The counselor's role is to help the counselee clarify and understand the likely consequences of each available alternative, but generally not to give advice or choose the alternative for the counselee. If the counselor were to select the alternative, there are two possible outcomes: (1) the alternative may prove to be undesirable for the counselee, in which case, the counselee will probably blame the counselor for the advice and the future relationship will be seriously hampered, and (2) the alternative may prove to be desirable for the counselee. This immediate outcome is advantageous, but the danger is that the counselee will then become overly dependent on the counselor, seeking the counselor's advice for nearly every decision in the future and generally being reluctant to make decisions on his or her own. In actual practice, most courses of action have desirable and undesirable consequences. For example, if the unmarried mother is ad-

vised to keep her child, she may receive considerable gratification from being with and raising the child, but at the same time she may blame the counselor for such possible negative consequences as long-term financial hardships and an isolated social life.

3. Counseling is done *with* the counselee, not *to* or *for* the counselee. The counselee should have the responsibility of doing many of the tasks necessary to improve the situation. A good rule to follow is that the counselee should take responsibility for those tasks that he or she has the capacity to carry out, while the counselor should only attempt to do those that are beyond the capacities of the counselee. Doing things *for* counselees, similar to giving advice, runs the risk of creating a dependency relationship. Furthermore, successful accomplishment of tasks by counselees leads to personal growth and better prepares them for taking on future responsibilities.

4. The counselee's right to self-determination should be taken away only if the selected course of action has a high probability of seriously hurting others or the counselee. For example, if it is highly probable that a parent will continue to abuse a child, or if the counselee attempts to take his or her own life, intervention by the counselor is suggested. For most situations, however, the counselor should have the right to select his or her alternative, even when the counselor believes that another alternative is a better course of action. Frequently, the counselee is in a better position to know what is best for him or her, and if the alternative is not the best, the counselee will probably learn from the mistake.

5. The counselor should attempt to form explicit, realistic "contracts" with counselees. When the counselee does select an alternative, the counselee should clearly understand what the goals will be, what tasks need to be carried out, how to do the tasks, and who will carry out each of them. Frequently, it is desirable to write the "contract" for future reference, with a time limit set for the accomplishment of each task. For example, if the unmarried mother decides to keep her child and now needs to make long-range financial plans, this goal should be understood and specific courses of action decided upon—seeking public assistance, seeking support from the alleged father, securing an apartment within her budget, and so on. Furthermore, who will do what task within a set time limit should be specified.

6. If the counselee fails to meet the terms of the "contract," do not punish, but do not accept excuses. Excuses let people off the hook; they provide temporary relief, but they eventually lead to more failure and to a failure identity. Simply ask, "Do you still wish to try to fulfill your commitment?" If the counselee answers affirmatively, another time deadline acceptable to the counselee should be set.

7. Perhaps the biggest single factor in determining whether the counselee's situation will improve is the counselee's motivation to carry out essential tasks. A counselor should seek to motivate apathetic counselees. One of the biggest reality shocks of new trainees entering into the helping professions is that many clients, even after making commitments to improve their situation, do not have the motivation to carry out the steps outlined.

8. One way to increase motivation is to clarify what will be gained by meeting the commitment. When counselees meet commitments, reward them verbally or in other ways. Seldom punish if commitments are not met. Punishment usually increases hostility, without positive lasting changes. Also, punishment only serves as a temporary means of obtaining different behavior; when a person no longer believes that he or she is under surveillance, he or she will usually return to the "deviant" behavior.

9. For a number of tasks where the counselee lacks confidence or experience in carrying out, it is helpful to "role play" the task. For example, if a pregnant single girl wants help in knowing how to tell her boyfriend about the pregnancy, role playing the situation will assist the girl in selecting words and developing a strategy for informing him. The counselor can first play the girl's role and model an approach, with the girl playing the boy's role. Then the roles should be reversed so that the girl gains practice in telling her boyfriend.

Other helpful hints to counseling could be given here, but the basic format is to develop a relationship, explore problems in depth, and then to explore alternative solutions. These guidelines are not to be followed dogmatically; they will probably work 70 to 80 percent of the time. The most important tool that a counselor has is him- or herself (feelings, perceptions, relationship capacities, and interviewing skills).

One final important guideline—the counselor should refer the counselee to someone else, or at least seek a professional counselor to discuss the case with, for any of the following situations: if the counselor feels that he or she is unable to empathize with the counselee; if the counselor feels that the counselee is choosing unethical alternatives (such as seeking an abortion) that conflict with the counselor's basic value system; if the counselor feels that the problem is of such a nature that he or she will not be able to help; and if a working relationship is not established. A competent counselor knows that he or she can work with and help some people but not all, and that it is in the counselee's and the counselor's best interests to refer the person to someone else who can.

Counseling Suicidal Persons

Bernard I. Cesnik
Suzanne K. Nixon

A great number of people at some time in their lives consider suicide as an alternative to living. It is an alternative available to any of us at any time, one guaranteed to remove us from stressful or problematic situations. You do not have to be "crazy" to consider suicide. Nor do you even have to want to die. You may simply not want to remain in your current situation, and no other way out is clear to you.

Suicide is one of this country's major causes of death. In 1974, there were 26,430 certified suicides in the United States. In spite of this number, suicide is generally believed to be grossly underreported. For example, the American Association of Suicidology estimates the actual number of suicides each year as twice the certified number. Additionally, over 200,000 persons attempt suicide and over 800,000 persons make serious suicidal threats each year. It is clearly a problem area affecting many persons.

At some time in your life, especially if you are considering a counseling role, you may be faced with a person who is seriously contemplating suicide. Involvement with a person in suicidal crisis is always anxiety producing and demanding. Attempting to be useful to such a person is frequently frustrating and draining. This chapter will present some primary guidelines for initial

This article was especially written for this book.

counseling of suicidal persons. It does not, by any means, contain all there is to know about the topic, and further reading and instruction is necessary, especially for anyone who will be providing extended treatment to suicidal persons.

PERSONAL CHARACTERISTICS OF THE COUNSELOR

Not everyone is personally equipped to counsel suicidal persons. Professional degrees and training are no guarantee of one's ability to be helpful. For example, if a counselor has a suicidal propensity in his or her own personality, a suicidal person is likely to frighten and overwhelm him or her. Similarly, the hostility that is prevalent in suicidal persons will pose a difficult problem for some counselors and may cause them to retreat at the very moment that the person needs a great amount of support.[1]

As a counselor, a high degree of comfort and security with yourself is fundamental. You must be continually in touch with yourself and able to share yourself appropriately with the suicidal person; providing support to satisfy his or her dependency, yet not getting so involved that you lose perspective. You must be comfortable with the fact that you probably will not have the answers or be able to solve the problems as they are presented to you. You must handle verbal attack, being told that you are not useful and cannot help. You must not become defensive, but must remain open and accept an attack as part of the troubled person's anger and sense of hopelessness.

Of primary importance is your ability to listen attentively, really to hear what the suicidal person is saying. Your acceptance of him or her as a person and your ability to provide a safe, nonjudgmental atmosphere are essential to building trust and encouraging communication. Many suicidal persons have the expectation that others will judge them to be "crazy" or "bad" because of their suicidal thoughts. They are extremely sensitive to the judgment of others and will quickly disengage from a helper if he or she is judging them negatively.

Closely related is the helper's ability to deal directly with the person's suicidal thoughts and plans. This produces problems for many counselors. Your own depression or suicidal potential, the suicide or attempted suicide of family members, and fear and anxiety associated with death can interfere with your ability to listen to someone talk about killing him- or herself. Consequently, your effectiveness will be markedly reduced.

---

[1]Stanley Lesse, "Apparent Remissions in Depressed Suicidal Patients," in *Masked Depression,* ed. Stanley Lesse (New York: Jason Aronson, Inc., 1974), pp. 121-122.

You must be able to present yourself—your attitude and affect—in a calm manner. The inability to do so, in this anxiety-producing atmosphere, is likely to increase the suicidal person's feelings of isolation, hopelessness, and helplessness. This is not to imply that you must feel calm, but rather that you must be keenly aware of your anxiety, fear, anger, and other emotions. You must have them under control and appear calm and in control to the troubled person. Verbalizing such feelings to the person frequently aids in maintaining calmness and control.

EVALUATING SUICIDE RISK

Not everyone thinking or talking about suicide presents the same degree of risk. Not everyone thinking of suicide will attempt it; not all the persons who attempt suicide will do so with the intention of dying. It is, therefore, very important that those who counsel suicidal persons are able to judge the degree of risk involved in each situation. Your judgment of risk will be of primary importance in determining the course and speed of action in your effort to be useful to the suicidal person. Such prediction is difficult and by no means a fully developed area.[2] There are, however, specific areas to investigate and ways to go about investigating.

As in all areas of counseling, your ability to form a solid, positive relationship with the suicidal person is fundamental. Much of your knowledge about a person and his or her problems will come from direct, verbal and nonverbal communication with the person. The correctness and completeness of the information you need will depend upon what the person thinks and feels about you. You must also remember that family members and other significant persons are important sources of information. Involvement with them will give valuable insight into the suicidal person's anger, frustration, and self-esteem.

ASKING THE QUESTIONS—USING THE WORDS

It is difficult for many persons thinking of killing themselves to verbalize such thoughts directly to anyone. They are very personal thoughts and many persons are fearful that sharing them will result in judgments of weakness, craziness, manipulation, and even sinfulness.

---

[2]See Aaron T. Beck, H.L.P. Resnik, Dan J. Lettieri, eds., *The Prediction of Suicide* (Bowie, Md.: The Charles Press, 1974).

Sadly, it is also difficult for suicidal persons, once they have mustered the energy to risk sharing such thoughts, to find anyone willing to listen to them. The general discomfort felt by people receiving direct suicidal communications frequently causes them to evade the topic and even the suicidal person. Comments such as, "Don't be silly" or "You wouldn't do a foolish thing like that" are common responses to the verbalization that "life doesn't seem worthwhile anymore" or "I'm thinking of killing myself." Such responses increase the person's sense of aloneness. They will further isolate him or her and increase the difficulty in trying to share his or her feelings again.

It is not uncommon, therefore, for a suicidal person to talk with a counselor without mentioning suicidal thoughts and intentions directly. You must be keenly aware of this likelihood and be prepared to solicit information about suicide. Many seriously suicidal persons have walked away from counselors without saying they have thoughts of suicide. Many counselors have let seriously suicidal persons walk away without talking about suicide, because they have been too frightened to open up the topic.

Asking directly for information on suicidal thoughts and intentions is often the only way you will receive it. Summarizing the person's reported problems, or reflection on and naming of the upset feelings he or she has presented to you offer a preface for moving directly into the area. Such a summary can be comfortably followed by a question such as "I'm wondering what you've thought about as ways out of all these problems." If the person does not respond with a statement about suicidal thoughts, you can then move more easily to a direct question, such as "I'm wondering if you are thinking at all about suicide?" or "I'm wondering if you ever feel like killing yourself?"

Such questions must be asked calmly and comfortably. The counselor projecting discomfort with the questions, especially the words "suicide" and "killing yourself," can count on the suicidal person's picking up the discomfort. This may thwart an honest response. The suicidal person may well assume that your discomfort will drive you away, just as others may have run away from his or her suicidal communication in the past, and consequently he or she may deny suicidal thought.

Aside from personal anxiety with the topic, counselors are usually uncomfortable with using the words "suicide" and "killing yourself" when talking with suspected suicidal persons for two primary reasons. The first is the fear that, if the troubled person has not been thinking of suicide, using those words will introduce the idea and start the person down the road to suicide. It is extremely rare that the idea of suicide is introduced in such a manner. If it happens at all, it is so infrequent that you must use those words in spite of your fear. Using the words "suicide" and "killing yourself" is essential not only to solicit needed information, but, more importantly, it helps to break the taboo against talking about suicide. If you use the words in a calm, non-judgmental manner, you give the person permission and assurance, enabling him or her to risk sharing suicidal thoughts. You are also saying "I am not afraid of these words or ideas, suicide is not a stigma to me, and we can get beyond the fear of the words together to work at the problem."

The second fear experienced by many counselors in referring directly to suicide is "What will I do if the response is 'Yes, I am thinking of killing myself'?" The rationale seems to be that if one is uncertain about what to do with such information, it is better not to know. The answer to this fear again lies in the probability that direct questioning about suicide gives the person help in sharing such thoughts. Your primary responsibility is to listen and solicit more information as outlined in the following pages. Only after careful listening and information gathering can you meet your second responsibility of formulating and initiating a plan of action.

Those who have not had experience asking direct questions about suicide will frequently use the words "suicide" and "killing yourself" with hesitation apparent in their voices. Since stumbling over these words connotes discomfort with the topic, you should practice asking such questions until they flow relatively smoothly. Your confort level will directly affect the suicidal person's comfort and, consequently, his or her honesty and completeness in responding.

Further, it is important that you use the words "suicide" and "killing yourself" throughout your discussion with the suicidal person. Using the words will help to maintain focus on the subject. Using other words such as "die" or "why do you want to do *it*?" allows the counselor and the suicidal person to skirt the issue and reduces the likelihood of frank, open, and helpful discussion.

SELF-REPORTED RISK

When asked, suicidal people will usually give their own assessment of the likelihood of their attempting or committing suicide. Self-reporting of high likelihood should be attended to closely. Reporting of low risk should be investigated further and not accepted at face value. Direct questions such as "How likely is it that you will try to kill yourself in the near future?" should be asked.

SUICIDE PLAN

Suicide risk ought to be based on the combined patterns of all the areas mentioned so far and to follow. However, the most important information to solicit is whether or not the person has a suicide plan. Any person having a specific, well-conceived suicide plan involving a highly lethal method (which will be discussed later) ought to be considered especially dangerous and alarming.[3]

Direct, specific questioning in a calm, comfortable manner is necessary to obtain needed information about the plan. Again, counselors are frequently reluctant to venture into this area. They fear that asking direct questions may actually assist the person in development of a plan, thus moving him or her closer to suicide. This can be a danger especially if in asking the question you imply that having no plan means that the person is not "serious," and that not being serious indicates that the person is not experiencing severe emotional pain and does not warrant your close attention. Often attempted and successful suicides are not planned at length, especially for those people who experience severe reactive depression. Your discussing their plan with them will not put anything into their heads that they could not figure out for themselves.

A second safeguard against escalating suicide potential by asking about a possible plan is to leave the topic when it seems clear that a plan has not been developed. Inquiry about the plan should move from general questions to increasingly more specific questions. You do not follow the question "Have you thought about how you would kill yourself?" with "Do you think anyone will be around when you take the pills?" Rather, move slowly, a step at a time, and stop when it becomes clear that the plan is not further developed.

There are several important aspects of the person's plan. The first is whether he or she has selected a means to kill him- or herself, and if so, the *lethality of the means* selected. Obviously, different methods have different levels of lethality. High lethality methods include gunshot, jumping from a high place, and hanging. If used, these methods have a high probability of immediate death. There is no time margin between action and death that would make rescue possible. Less lethal methods, such as the ingestion of poison (including an overdose of medication), cutting of wrists, and carbon monoxide poisoning have a time margin allowing rescue. Death does not im-

---

[3]Norman Farberow and Robert E. Litman, "Suicide Prevention," in *Emergency Psychiatric Care*, eds. H.L.P. Resnik and Harvey L. Rubin (Bowie, Md.: The Charles Press, 1975), p. 111.

mediately follow the suicidal action; allowing time during which the suicidal person may change his or her mind and call for help, or may be discovered by someone. This is not to imply that people do not kill themselves by the less lethal methods. Clearly they do. However, many suicide attempts by less lethal methods do not result in death. Conversely, most people do not survive a bullet in the head, a seven-story jump, or hanging (although some do).

Errors about the lethality of proposed methods are often made by both helpers and suicidal people. This is especially true of planned medication overdose. Common aspirin is a case in point. Perhaps its ready availability and wide usage cause it to be unrecognized as a potentially dangerous drug. Remember also that alcohol consumption, accompanying an overdose of medication, significantly increases toxicity level and the resultant likelihood of death. Other factors such as body weight and general physical health also affect the lethality level of poisoning, and a physician, pharmacist, or Poison Control Center should be consulted *when you have any doubt about lethality.*

A final word of caution. The lethality of the planned method of suicide is not related to the severity of emotional pain experienced by the suicidal person. To discredit the pain because of a nonlethal plan is a major mistake that may lead to discounting the person and his or her problems, and could produce tragic results.

A second major factor in the investigation of the suicidal plan is the *availability of the means* selected. Does he or she have ready access to a lethal dosage of medication? Does he or she have a plan for obtaining the means if it is not readily available? How much time will it take for him or her to obtain the means? In essence, you want to find out how difficult it will be for the person to obtain the means. The general rule is, the more readily available the means, the greater the risk.

The third factor in the investigation of the plan is its *specificity of detail.* Has the time and place of suicide been decided? Has he or she written a suicide note or composed one mentally? Has he or she made out a will or given away treasured possessions? Are his or her plans such as to insure that he or she will not be discovered while undertaking the suicidal act? Has he or she started to prepare for death in other ways, such as paying bills or completing unfinished jobs? The more the specific issues and preparations have been decided or carried out, the greater the risk of suicide.

In summary, the more lethal the means, the greater its availability, and the more specific the plan, the greater the risk of suicide. However, remember that the lack of a plan is not, in and of itself, a reason to reduce concern about the seriousness of suicidal thoughts, the possibility of suicide, or a suicide attempt. These factors primarily provide you with information about how much time you have to work toward the prevention of the suicide.

PRIOR SUICIDAL BEHAVIOR

Another major consideration in the evaluation of suicide risk is the individual's history of suicidal behavior. Generally, people who have attempted suicide in the past present a higher suicide risk at any given moment than persons without previous attempts. Similarly, people who have been preoccupied with suicide for extended periods of time, or frequently consider it as a viable alternative, present a higher risk than people who think of suicide only briefly and periodically.

With every suicidal person, you must evaluate the seriousness of past suicidal thought and attempts in the same way you evaluate current risk. You want to know how often the person has considered and/or attempted suicide in the past and what problems he or she was facing in each instance. If he or she attempted suicide, you need to know why death did not result; if no attempt was made, why not? You want to know if he or she seriously intended to kill him- or herself in previous attempts or was something else wanted; how he or she felt immediately after the attempt about not having died; how he or she feels now about not having died; what methods were used or considered previously; what was the lethality of the methods; why were they chosen; what were the specifics of the suicide plan; did he or she actively prepare for the suicide; did he or she communicate the intent to kill him- or herself to anyone; what were the reactions of the important others in his or her life; and how does he or she feel about those reactions now.

A strong suicidal history indicates a more serious current suicide risk. However, people without a strong suicidal history do kill themselves. A history devoid of serious suicidal thought and attempts is not an assurance of current low risk.

SYMPTOMS

Emotional symptoms exhibited by the troubled person are another major consideration in risk evaluation. Depression is the most common emotional state present in suicidal persons. You must always evaluate the symptoms of depression and make a judgment of their presence and severity. Again, direct questioning is necessary. Typical symptoms of moderate to severe depression include loss of appetite; unintentional weight loss or gain over a relatively short period of time; a marked change in sleeping habits usually in the direction of insomnia; loss of interest in physical appearance, daily activities, social events, or hobbies; withdrawal from friends, family, or other normal social involvement; a general feeling of physical and emotional exhaustion; and, very importantly, a feeling of hopelessness about things getting better in the near future and a feeling of helplessness over control of the course of his or her life or the current stressful situation. Counselors of suicidal people must be keenly aware of these symptoms or seek help from experienced psychotherapists in their evaluation. Generally, the more severe the depression, the more symptoms are present, and the higher the risk.

Indications of impulsivity in suicidal persons also merit special concern. Persons with a history of impulsive acts, such as walking off a job or leaving a spouse in times of stress, must be given special consideration. With such persons, there is a special danger of impulsive suicidal actions.

Impulsive behavior is frequently associated with symptoms of severe agitation, such as a high level of tension, anxiety, guilt, rage, hostility, anger, and revenge. When such symptoms are present concurrently with symptoms of depression and a history of impulsivity, a particularly high risk is presented. Unable to tolerate the pressures of his or her feelings, a person in a state of agitated depression will exhibit marked tension, fearfulness about the future, restlessness, and pressure of speech. He or she may express feelings of hopelessness about the future and will feel pressure to act in some way to alleviate the emotional upset. If no other alternatives are obvious, suicide may seem the only mode of relief. Alcoholics, drug addicts, and disturbed homosexuals tend to experience general agitation and to be high suicide risks when depressed.[4]

Symptoms of psychosis warn of another high risk state in people talking of suicide. Psychotic persons are out of contact with the reality that most of us experience at any given time. They may hallucinate voices telling them to kill themselves, be unable to carry on a conversation that makes sense to others, and may demonstrate very poor judgment. Physical appearance may be obviously disheveled or bizarre. Although his or her talk of suicide, and especially the suicide plan, may sound crazy and ineffective, the psychotic person talking of suicide presents a major danger because of the unpredictability of his or her behavior. In most cases, psychotic persons preoccupied with suicide will need hospitalization. They always should be evaluated by experienced psychotherapists prior to any attempt at working with them outside of a hospital.

[4]Ibid., p. 109.

STRESS

Stress must be considered in the evaluation of suicide risk. It refers to the current pressures and problems, *as perceived by the person,* that are precipitating the suicidal thoughts. You must find out what has happened to the person; why he or she is upset at this time; why he or she is considering suicide *now.*

On some occasions, success can be the stress precipitating suicidal thought. Increased job or family responsibilities can cause anticipations of failure and embarrassment. A job promotion, for example, can raise many feelings of inadequacy in the person about his or her ability to meet the responsibilities of the new position.

Suicidal thoughts frequently accompany a significant loss. The most common types of loss include loss of spouse or family member through death, divorce, or separation; loss of a love relationship, especially if the person sees the loss as his or her fault and includes the belief that he or she is not a good enough person to maintain the other's affection; loss of a job, money, prestige, or status; and the loss of health. In suicidal people, these losses produce a major reduction in self-esteem and a consequent sense of little self-worth.

Threatened or anticipated loss can be more stressful for some persons than actual loss. Doubt about his or her ability to achieve a satisfactory life if the spouse proceeds with a threatened divorce, for example, can produce suicidal thoughts that dissipate shortly after the actual event.

You must evaluate the stress or loss from the person's point of view at the time. You may be able to change that point of view, but to understand his or her suicide potential you must understand where he or she is emotionally at the moment.

RESOURCES

An evaluation of the resources available to the suicidal person is necessary. Three basic kinds of resources are included: intrapersonal strengths; family and friendship resources; and general community resources. The general rule is that the fewer the available resources, the greater the risk of suicide.

Evaluation of intrapersonal strengths includes looking at the person's experience in handling similar situations in the past, attempting to draw on the methods of coping that have been used positively, and reinforcing or supporting those applicable to the current situation. Frequently, it is useful to make a distinction with the person at this point between wanting to die and wanting to eliminate the upset feelings and precipitating problems. Many suicidal persons are not ready and do not want to die; rather they do not want to live under the stress or depression they are experiencing. Useful intrapersonal strengths lie in those parts of the person that make life seem worthwhile, those parts of him- or herself or his or her life about which he or she has some positive feelings. These characteristics need to be identified and supported. Finally, as a counselor, you need to explore and assist him or her in developing thoughts of how the current crisis can be alleviated.

In exploring family and friendship resources, you need to keep in mind that most suicidal persons are depressed, and depression distorts one's perception of the world, including beliefs of how other persons feel toward oneself. Suicidal persons may truly believe that no one cares or is interested enough to help them without losing respect. You must find out who the significant other persons are to him or her, what part they each may have in the current crisis, and how available they are to you as a counselor.

Care must be exercised in evaluating the usefulness of these other persons, especially those most involved in the crisis situation. Some family members or others may have a negative effect if brought in to help. They may even purposefully move the suicidal person closer to suicide. This is especially true of spouses who are so angry that they want the suicide to occur. It is advisable for the counselor to talk with these other persons and assess their attitudes and feelings prior to recruiting them as helpers.

Once appropriate family members or friends are found and recruited as helpers, you will have to coach them on how to involve themselves with the suicidal person. Most often they will be apprehensive and unsure of themselves, especially if the suicide risk is high. They will need support and at times direct, explicit instructions. You must also remain readily available and open to contact from them to give further assistance as the situation changes.

In most situations, involvement of other persons ought to be with the knowledge and some degree of consent of the suicidal person. You may, however, be faced with a highly suicidal person who refuses counseling or other treatment and refuses to give permission to contact anyone. On such occasions, preventing the suicide may necessitate contacting significant others in spite of the person's wishes. Such an action may result in a law suit for breach of confidentiality; you must be aware of that possibility and prepared to take that risk.

In exploring general community resources, you should look first for current or recent involvement with other counselors, clergy, or therapists. If the person is currently involved with some other professional, the professional must be informed and recruited to help. If in therapy, the person most often should be referred back to the therapist. Highly suicidal persons should be taken to the therapist, either by you or some other reliable person, and not left on their own to get there.

Knowledge of the agencies, hospitals, mental health professionals, and social services available is very helpful. Knowing about these community resources is not sufficient, however, for most will have waiting lists and red tape to cut through if immediate service is to be available. A mere referral to a welfare department, for example, may involve a long wait and may be so discouraging that it will depress the person further. In making a referral to a community resource, it is recommended that you check whether the resource will deliver the desired service and deliver it rapidly, prior to making the referral. This means that you should personally contact the agency, cut through the red tape, and pave the way for the person.

Finally, it is advisable that you find resources to help you in your work with the person. No counselor should work with suicidal persons without the availability of consultation from other mental health professionals. You will be making critical decisions, and to do so without input from others is a disservice to both yourself and to the person. Otherwise, you are left assuming total responsibility for the case, increasing the chance for fatal mistakes.

INTERVENTION PLANNING

The formulation of an active initial intervention plan should begin during the assessment of suicide risk. To a great extent, the plan should be based on the severity of the suicidal risk and will change as the risk level changes. Clearly, the necessity for action and attentive involvement is greater when the suicide risk is high.

Actually, your intervention starts with the development of a relationship with the suicidal person. Your acceptance of the person, willingness to listen, and ability to talk with him or her about problems and suicidal thoughts and plans is of extreme importance in forming that relationship. With persons who have little else going for them, your relationship with them may be the primary resource available to you in effective intervention.

In high risk situations, involving a readily available means of suicide, the first effort is to remove the means. You must remember, however, that removal of the means may do nothing except buy more time and therefore allow further intervention. Until the weapon or pills or whatever is removed, the person should not be left alone. For example, you ought to accompany the person to get the pills or send someone else while you continue working with him or her.

In situations involving a suicidal person with a gun in hand, special expertise is necessary. Unfortunately, most counselors and police officers are not trained to handle these situations. There is always the potential for homicide in such cases, and extreme care must be exercised. There is no room for heroics, and law enforcement officers should be called for assistance.[5]

Highly suicidal persons with suicide plans containing a means that cannot be taken away, such as jumping from a high place, carbon monoxide poisoning, or drowning must not be left alone during the high risk period. Other helpers may be needed to stay with the person during this time. Hospitalization may be necessary, especially for people who have no others available or willing to assist.

Aside from the need to involve other persons for safety reasons, involvement of others in a supportive role is of extreme importance. As indicated earlier, seriously suicidal persons will usually have a distorted perception of what others think and feel about them. Their depression will contribute to a belief that no one else cares or is interested and willing to help them. The disturbed person's poor self-concept, apathy, and lack of energy will make it additionally difficult for them to approach anyone directly for help. Also, they may be resistive to unloading their problems on friends or family because of sincere feelings of not wanting to bother or worry anyone else. Friends and family may get vague or indirect messages of severe problems and suicidal ideas. They may be reluctant to address these issues directly because of their respect for the personal nature of the problem and a sense of not wanting to push themselves onto the person without being invited to do so. You can make a very significant contribution by helping the suicidal person to share these things with important other people and by assisting and supporting the others in their involvement.

It may be that you will need to enlist others to assume some of the responsibilities of the suicidal person. Finding someone willing and able to care for young children for a couple of days, finding someone who will come into the home and stay with the person, instructing a husband to stay home from work and assume the responsibilities of his suicidal wife, asking an employer temporarily to reduce the responsibilities of a suicidal employee, and finding a friend willing to take the person into his or her home for a few days are examples of how you might provide the suicidal person with the contact of other people and prevent him or her from withdrawing.

The prevention of withdrawal from others through special and specific use of family and friends does several important things. It demonstrates that others do indeed care. It temporarily reduces the person's responsibilities and

[5]For a most comprehensive discussion of this issue, see Bruce L. Danto, *Suicide and Violence,* unpublished manuscript (Dr. Danto resides in Detroit, Michigan).

allows needed rest. It provides supervision and allows less opportunity for a suicidal act or thought about the act. It provides time to solve problems, adjust to losses, and build a renewed sense of hope and self.

The suggestions for counseling a suicidal person so far involve giving the individual needed help without delay, in an environment familiar to him or her. They emphasize the use of other individuals as a means to support the person through the crisis period. Concurrent to this is your therapeutic involvement in clarifying and defining the central problems and actively working with the person to find solutions other than suicide. In doing so, the most critical aspect of your message to the person is that he or she will make it through the crisis. Such a message must be given while showing an understanding of the seriousness of the situation to the person. Central to this message is your belief that the person has been competent and responsible, and will continue to be so. You must keep the person in the active role of dealing with the problem and with you and others responsible for making changes in his or her situation. Rather than helping the person to help him- or herself, you are expecting the person to be him- or herself, while emphasizing the positiveness of using coping behavior and supports during the high stress period.

Counseling suicidal persons is emotionally taxing and difficult. The elements of death and dying, which are normally only tangential to the counseling relationship, are in the foreground and central to the relationship with the person. You must remain calm, exhibit clear thinking, and maintain extensive balance, while knowing that the person may act impulsively and, from his or her point of view, it may take less energy to face death than to face life. You must be secure yourself, for you must put yourself into the situation wholeheartedly. Counseling a seriously suicidal person involves the very difficult art of balancing the weakness felt by the person and his or her need for external support and control with the freedom that is essential for recovery.[6]

It is indeed a difficult balance and is made even more difficult by the intensity of such situations. Within such intensity, it is easy to lose your perspective and objectivity, and such a loss can lead to tragic results. The difficulty requires that any counselor involved with a seriously suicidal person, regardless of training and experience, must seek consultation and assistance from other helping professionals. To do so is not a sign of personal or professional weakness, but rather an indication of strength and competence.

---

[6]Gene W. Brockopp, "Crisis Theory and Suicide Prevention," *Crisis Intervention*, supplement to Vol. 2, No. 2 (1970), 40-41.

SUGGESTED READINGS

CAIN, ALBERT C., *Survivors of Suicide*. Springfield, Ill.: Charles C. Thomas, Publisher, 1973.

DANTO, BRUCE L., *Suicide and Violence*, unpublished manuscript.

FARBEROW, NORMAN L., *Suicide*. Morristown, N.J.: General Learning Corporation, 1974.

LEONARD, CALISTA V., *Understanding and Preventing Suicide*. Springfield, Ill.: Charles C. Thomas, Publisher, 1974.

LESTER, GENE AND DAVID, *Suicide: The Gamble with Death*. Englewood Cliffs, N.J.: Prentice-Hall/Spectrum Books, 1972.

MCGEE, RICHARD K., *Crisis Intervention in the Community*. Baltimore: University Park Press, 1974.

RESNIK, H.L.P., AND H.L. RUBEN, *Emergency Psychiatric Care, The Management of Mental Health Crises*. Bowie, Md.: The Charles Press Publishers, 1975.

How to Avoid Becoming a Rape Victim:

and What to Do If Rape Occurs

Cathryn M. Wagner

Every female in the United States, from adolescent or perhaps younger to adult, has probably had some hair-raising experience that made her, at least momentarily, very conscious of her vulnerability to rape. Perhaps she was followed by a group of men as she walked down a street; perhaps she received some suggestive or threatening phone calls; maybe someone sat too close to her on a bus; or any number of other possibilities. Although most such incidents go no further, not every woman with such an experience has been able to avoid assault. The incidence of rape is shockingly high, with the FBI currently estimating one rape committed every minute in this country, based on the generally accepted view that only one rape in 10 is ever reported. That is about half a million rapes each year.[1] It seems that women are too often rely-

This article was especially written for this book.

AUTHOR'S NOTE: I began my study of self-defense and rape prevention for my own protection, never having any idea that I might be asked to teach self-defense, lecture on rape prevention to high school girls and to educators, or, least of all, to write this article. Television programs, educational films, speakers, workshops, and various magazine articles, books, and pamphlets have all contributed to the development of ideas presented here. Unfortunately, it is impossible to determine exactly where any given thought originated. For any inadvertent omissions, I most genuinely apologize to any one whom I have overlooked.

[1]Catherine McClary, *Freedom from Rape* (Ann Arbor, Mich.: The Women's Crisis Center of Ann Arbor, 1974), p. 1.

ing on luck, companions, timing, or "good samaritanism" to avoid rape—and they aren't working.

If there is anything positive about the large number of rapes in this country, it is the resulting increase in consciousness among women that—yes, it *could* happen to me. This realization is the most important part of rape prevention. Once people recognize that they are in danger and need to protect themselves, they find ways to alter their life patterns and learn self-defense measures. What this chapter will attempt to do is to sharpen your safety awareness by presenting some facts about rapists and their victims, along with some daily life precautions to help you avoid rape situations. Should a confrontation occur, however, a range of alternatives are presented, from which you can select those of use to you and discard those that seem unrealistic. In the event that a rape is committed, there are some guidelines for coping with the aftermath. In this way, hopefully, you can protect, defend, or restore your well-being. Let us first dispel some common myths about rape.

MYTHS ABOUT RAPE

If you think you're safe because . . .	Consider the fact that . . .
You don't flirt and never try to pick up men in the first place.	The National Commission on the Causes and Prevention of Violence reports that only 4.4 percent of rape victims did anything that can be said to have precipitated the attack.[1]
You never allow anyone you don't know to enter your home or car.	Some 48 percent of rapists (almost half) know their victims (this includes neighbors, relatives, fathers of friends).[2]
You don't live in a racially mixed neighborhood.	Most rapes are not interracial. For example, only 3.6 percent are whites raping blacks and only 3.3 percent are blacks raping whites.[3]
You have heard that women subconsciously enjoy rape and, if that is the case, perhaps the experience would not be so terrifying.	Most women enjoy sex; rape is not sex—it is assault. The suffering that raped women endure runs the gamut of physical (internal and external), emotional, social, and psychological, and frequently continues for many years.

[1]Ibid., p. 2.
[2]Menachim Amir, *Patterns in Forcible Rape* (Chicago, Ill.: The University of Chicago Press, 1971), p. 235.
[3]McClary, *Freedom from Rape*, p. 2.

You would never give in, and rape is impossible unless the woman consents.

Violence is involved in 85 percent of rapes.[4] Would you be as adamant with a knife at your throat or a gun at your head — or at that of a friend when you are told to cooperate or else? Consider also that the Denver Anti-Crime Council found that if a woman physically resists, her chances of injury are considerably greater.[5] Also have you ever been frightened into immobility? Some women are when attacked. Consider, too, the possibility of being knocked or drugged unconscious. It happens.

You never stay out late or go to bars.

Although it is true that the greatest number of rapes occur between 8 p.m. and 2 a.m.,[6] you are still not safe at home — about half of rapes occur in or about the home[7] and one third of them involve forced entry.[8]

You have a very good reputation and are respected.

Try telling that to a rapist! Most (82 percent) rape victims have good reputations.[9]

You aren't pretty, or young, or thin, or whatever, and no man looking for a sex partner would choose you.

Most rapists do not rape for sex per se, and all ages, shapes, and sizes get raped. Rapists that were caught, instead, report desires to prove they are men, to take women off their pedestals, to hurt them, and so on. Evidence strongly indicates that rapists are not sex starved; 60 percent of the rapists caught are married and report a normal sex life.[10] In addition, most rapes are planned in advance (90 percent of group, 58 percent of solo, 71 percent overall).[11]

---

[4]Amir, *Patterns*, p. 154.

[5]June Bundy Csida and Joseph Csida, *Rape! How to Avoid It and What to Do About It if You Can't* (Chatsworth, Calif.: Books for Better Living, 1974), p. 81.

[6]Amir, *Patterns*, p. 339.

[7]Ibid., p. 145.

[8]McClary, *Freedom from Rape*, p. 2.

[9]Susan Rennie and Kirsten Grimstad, *The New Woman's Survival Catalogue* (New York: Coward, McCann, and Geoghegan, Inc./Berkley Publishing Corporation, 1973), p. 152.

[10]Andra Medea and Kathleen Thomas, "How Much Do You Really Know About Rapists?" *Ms. Magazine* (July 1974), p. 114.

[11]Amir, *Patterns*, p. 113.

You never speak to strangers.

Some rapists reported anger toward women for snubbing them and decided to "show them" by rape.

You live in a small town, and the chances of a pervert in such a town are slight.

The "perverted old man" stereotype is largely fallacious. Nearly all rapists test out normal when given psychological tests. Only 3 percent of all sex offenders could be considered psychotic.[12] The rest are just "regular guys"—except that they rape women. As for being old, rapists are most commonly 15 to 29 years old.[13]

If you are still convinced that you are not vulnerable, before you put this chapter down for good, talk to just one rape victim or read just one personal account of an actual rape experience. Try to be sensitive to the scars it may reveal, both literally and figuratively, and let her story convince you to protect yourself. Realizing that rape *can happen to you* is the first and largest step you can take toward protection.

PRECAUTIONS

There are hundreds of rape precautions that a woman can and should take in her daily life, many of which you may already be taking. Others you may not have considered and now may be altered to their usefulness. Some things take an effort to initiate, but once they are established as patterns, the protection provided is continual. Taking precautionary measures does not mean that you are paranoid—it means that you are much safer.

In and About Your Home

Remember, almost half the rapes happen in or near the home. If you take only the following precautions, you have done a great deal to insure your safety.

1. When you move into a new place, change all outside door locks to prevent former tenants from entering with old keys. Dead bolt locks that cannot be jimmied should be installed.

2. Install a chain lock secured by long screws to allow you to check identification before admitting people, and use it. These locks are not impenetrable, but breaking them takes time and makes lots of noise, probably enough to discourage would-be intruders, or at least to allow you to get to the phone.

[12]Medea and Thomas, "How Much Do You Really Know," p. 113.
[13]Amir, *Patterns*, p. 113.

3. If you have double doors, be sure to lock both of them. Otherwise, when you open the inside door in response to a caller, you have removed your only barrier.

4. Install a lock on any window that can be reached from the ground. There are also devices that limit how far windows can be opened, and decorative (but effective) bars. Put a broomstick or pole in the tracks of sliding doors so that they cannot be opened.

5. Have brightly lighted entrances and hallways, and beware of places where attackers might hide, such as between buildings or parked cars, under stairways, and such.

6. If you live in a high crime area, consider an electronic burglar system of some sort.

7. Do not list your full name on the door or mailbox; use only your first initial and last name. If you live alone, you may want to list nonexistent housemates too.

8. Don't leave house keys with your car keys in parking lots; intruders sometimes conspire with lot keepers and duplicate keys while you are parked. Likewise, don't leave your address on your key chain.

9. A noisy dog can be a good defense, although some get too friendly with strangers to be of assistance.

10. Keep shades and curtains drawn at night, as a potential assailant is more likely to enter when you seem to be alone.

11. Never let a stranger into your home. If someone comes to your door because of an apparent emergency, offer to make the necessary call while he waits outside. If you are expecting a serviceperson, ask for identification before admitting anyone. If you are suspicious, have the person wait behind your locked door while you call the company involved, or the police.

12. When alone and answering the door, consider yelling, "I'll get it" to an imaginary companion. If you actually do have a companion, don't be overly secure. There is not much a spouse or anyone can do if the person you opened the door to puts a knife to your throat.

13. When you leave the house, even if it is just to work in the yard, lock the doors. It is a good idea to leave a radio on, along with a light or two at night. (There are mechanical devices that turn lights on and off if you go on an extended trip.)

14. Close the garage door when you are leaving home, so that the gaping door does not signal your absence to all passersby. An open door also suggests you will be returning, and a potential rapist may seize this opportunity to hide and await your return.

15. Do not hide a key anywhere. Given enough time, they are easily found. Instead, give your spare key to a trusted friend.

16. If you do keep anything hidden (keys, valuables, money), do not talk about it with anyone except trusted friends, and never in the company of strangers.

17. When returning home, have your key ready before you get to the door. If something seems amiss at your home, don't go in. Go somewhere else (neighbors, phone booth) and call the police.

18. If you ever hear noises or sense movement that makes you suspect an intruder in your home, don't look for them or indicate your knowledge. Calmly get out through a door or window and get help. (Turning on lights in the dark signals them to hide. Then they can jump out and "surprise" you.)

19. If you hear someone in your room when sleeping, stay "asleep" so as not to threaten the intruder. Hopefully, he is after money, not you, and you will avoid an encounter. If you startle him, he is likely to be dangerous.

In Elevators

1. Elevators can be halted by the push of a button, and they can provide a soundproof, uninterruptable site for attack. Beware.

2. Do not enter an elevator with a stranger. Be especially cautious if the person has just come up from the garage or basement. In an office building, wait a few moments until more people will be getting into the elevator with you.

3. Don't get into an elevator that is going to the basement when you are going up.

4. If a man enters an elevator you are riding in alone, and you are in any way uneasy, pretend you almost missed your floor, and get off. Take the stairs or wait for another elevator.

5. If you did not react in time and *are* riding with a man you distrust, stand by the control panel and push the button for the nearest floor. Note the location of the alarm button in case you need to set it off. If bothered, push as many buttons as you can so that the elevator will stop at each floor. Hopefully, someone will be waiting at some of them, and you will have help.

On the Telephone

The helpful, essential telephone can provide a vehicle for harrassment and annoyance, and it can be a tool for discovering easy victims. If you receive an obscene or threatening call, show no fear and provide no satisfaction whatsoever to the caller.

1. Do not list your telephone under your full name; use only your first initial and last name.

2. Avoid giving information to strangers over the telephone. If you are alone or babysitting, do not reveal it to the caller. If the caller asks if your husband is home, don't get confused and say "I'm not married" or "No, he isn't." Instead, say he is busy and will call back later if a number is left.

3. If a man says he may have dialed incorrectly and asks your number, don't tell him. Instead, ask what number he is calling.

4. If suspicious calls are repeated, keep records of when they were received and what was said or done so that you can file a report with the police should you desire. You can also get your number changed and keep the new number unlisted.

5. Possible reactions to the prank caller include blasting into the phone with a whistle, or jiggling the button and saying "Operator, this is the call you've been waiting for." You can also try saying things like "Bill, it's for you," but this has limited value. The best thing to do is to provide no reinforcement at all — just hang up.

On the Streets

Probably the best way to prevent an encounter with an attacker on the street is to act very confident and purposeful. If you look meek and fearful, you appear an easy victim. There are other things that give additional protection.

1. Wear clothing that allows you to move fast if you need to. Platform shoes, clogs, and some sandals can make running fast almost impossible.

2. Heavy chains and necklaces are easily grabbed and can be used to choke you into submission or worse.

3. Try to avoid establishing obvious patterns in your life. Remember, most rapes are planned in advance. If your actions are easily anticipated, you are a likely candidate. If you must walk the streets at night regularly, you might consider dressing "like a man" to help deter would-be attackers.

4. You may want to wear a whistle around your wrist or carry some loud noise-maker to make a commotion if bothered, but have it handy (not in your purse).

5. Do not walk through a group of men. Cross the street or go around them.

6. Don't stop to "window shop," especially at night. Look deliberate about your travel, as if you are expected some place immediately.

7. Avoid using public rest rooms alone or at night.

8. Plan your route, taking the most well-lighted, populated path possible. Be aware of spots along the way that you could run to in need.

9. Avoid parking lots, dark, empty parks, and other areas in your community where assailants might be likely. Especially avoid walking along bushes, alley entrances, garages, and other places that you could be pulled or pushed into. Walking down the middle of empty streets is sometimes advisable.

10. Be alert. Listen and watch for people. Look around and behind you when you have suspicions so that you can anticipate problems.

11. If a motorist asks for directions, stay away from the car as you answer, and move away promptly thereafter.

12. If you are followed by a car, turn the wrong way up a one-way street (if possible) or just turn around in your tracks (a car can't) and go to a busy place for help. Don't lead the follower to your own home.

13. If you are followed by someone on foot, try to head off an encounter before contact occurs. Either run (but only if there is a lighted, busy place that you can make it to) or employ a defense technique (e.g., taking a short pointed object from your purse) before you are restricted by the follower.

In Your Car

Awareness is the imperative. If you are alert to the fact that attacks can and do happen, you will think of all sorts of safeguards. It is the unsuspecting woman, who unthinkingly climbs into her car in a dark parking lot, who may well find she has a "guest" in the back seat.

1. Before you enter your car, always check to see that no one is inside.
2. Lock all car doors when you get out to insure that it will remain empty. Do not keep spare keys hidden anywhere. Give them to a trusted friend.
3. Don't park your car in unlighted or deserted areas. Have your keys ready as you return.
4. Don't leave house, trunk, or other keys with car keys when having your car serviced.
5. Keep your car in good repair and full of gas so that you will not be made vulnerable by a breakdown.
6. If your car does break down, open the hood, get back in the car, and lock the doors. Do not get out or roll down windows if someone stops. Ask them to make a call for you and give them a slip of paper with the necessary information on it through a small opening. If you leave your car and walk along the road, you have no protection. If you go to a nearby residence, you may have to contend with dogs and the people inside, who may not be trustworthy or who may not trust you.
7. If you pass a disabled car and wish to help, don't get out of your car. Drive to the nearest phone and call the police or sheriff's department. They can offer more assistance than you can, and without the risks.
8. Avoid deserted routes. Take a well-traveled route to your destination, which, hopefully, is well policed. Be aware of places to go to along the way if a problem arises.
9. Keep doors locked and windows up almost all the way when driving in a city where you must stop frequently; people have often been attacked when an assailant got in at a stop. If it is too hot and a window must be open, open the one nearest you so that you can roll it up quickly if someone approaches.
10. Never pick up strangers — period.
11. To avoid being followed, tucking your hair up into a man's hat is effective. You can also create a "traveling companion" when traveling alone by using an inflatable dummy, a large teddy bear in a coat and hat, or balloons and newspaper wads stuffed into clothing.
12. If you are followed, try noting the car and driver descriptions and drive to a police station, all-night gas station, or other lighted, busy area. Do not lead the followers to your home, and don't speed up; that will only increase the dangers. Other possibilities include blasting your horn continually until you get aid or driving without lights at night in hopes that the police will stop you.

13. If a car follows you into your driveway, stay in the car with the doors locked and the windows up. Sound your horn repeatedly and await help.

When Dating

No one likes to think that the person she is dating is a threat to her well-being, but remember that about half of rapists know their victims and over half of rapes are planned in advance. You can tell yourself that it can't happen to you — until it does.

1. Know your date well before you plan to spend time alone with him. Trust your instincts. If you have any suspicions about the person — *don't go* at all.
2. Know specifically where you are going, and tell someone. Then if something happens, you can be located. Avoid going to deserted areas where you will have no help if your date tries to rape you.
3. If the date involves a group, be certain of its components. Many a victim of group rape (90 percent are planned) have gone to "parties" to find that they are the only female there.
4. If you are already with someone and then begin to distrust him, get away from him. Go home with a girlfriend, get out at a stoplight, or call someone for help. Don't worry about hurting his feelings. (He's obviously not concerned about yours!) If you must, tell him you are sick.
5. Don't under any circumstances, take a "pickup." Many men regard this as an open invitation for sex. If resistance is encountered, they tell themselves "she's just playing hard to get."

When Hitchhiking

Hitchhiking is designated as *the* most dangerous position a woman can put herself in to risk rape by nearly every available resource on rape and/or self-defense. When you get into the car of a stranger, you have removed all barriers between you and the driver. You cannot now avoid a confrontation if he initiates one, and you usually cannot run either. You have narrowed your methods of protecting yourself to direct encounter tactics (verbal and physical) — or none at all. Generally speaking, this is not good enough. Nonetheless, no one is naive enough to believe that knowing the vulnerability of a hitchhiker will wipe out this mode of travel. For women who insist that they must or will hitch, the best they can do is attempt to control the conditions of their hitches.

1. The first rule on hitchhiking is — *don't!* But if you do . . .
2. Whenever possible, avoid hitchhiking by yourself or at night.
3. Take well-traveled routes and keep your window open, so that in case of attack you can be heard if you yell. A good whistle or other noisemaker might also be carried.

4. Consider dressing very "unsexy," as men have said that they evaluate their passengers by what they are wearing.

5. Try to hitch only with female drivers, but if you must ride with a male, never accept a ride with more than one or with a driver who made a big fuss about stopping (U-turn, slammed on brakes).

6. Before you get into a car, check the back seat to see if anyone is there, and look for any beer or liquor bottles. Check the man over as well. Be sure he is fully dressed, and try to assess his intentions. Trust your evaluation; don't ride if you are suspicious.

7. Ask the driver where he is going before he asks you. Then you need not reveal your destination, and he cannot say he is going where you are, even if he isn't. If you distrust him when he answers, you can say that you aren't headed there—thanks anyway.

8. Be certain there is a working door handle on the inside of the door where you would be riding. Don't get into the back seat of a two-door car.

9. Don't take a ride that will drop you off in a deserted area. Instead, turn it down and wait for one that goes through to another town so you won't be forced to take the first ride that comes along.

10. Anytime you refuse a ride, stay clear of the driver and any passengers, and move away quickly.

11. Probably the safest way to hitch is to pick your ride rather than to have a driver pick you. This is possible at restaurants, service stations, and sometimes parking lots. Talk with people and find out where they are going. Then ask if they would mind a rider.

12. If you accept a ride, watch the driver so that you can anticipate any problems and prepare yourself to handle them. Carry any packages or your purse on the left side and keep your right hand on the door handle. Then you can strike with the left and open the door at the same time. A lighted cigarette can be an effective weapon also.

13. If possible, know the route to your destination so that if the driver makes a wrong turn you will know it immediately.

14. If you ever must jump out of a moving car, be sure that no other cars are coming that might run you over. Protect your head and keep your body curved so that you will roll, rather than scrape, over the ground. Keep your arms in close to your body to decrease the chances of injury.

In Other Tight Spots

There are numerous other situations where precautions are indicated, from work events to babysitting. Many of the precautions are similar, and if you have begun to develop some safety consciousness, you can undoubtedly think of many mistakes you have made in the past, as well as countless ways to change your present personal behavior patterns to safer ones.

Let's assume that you have been unable to avoid or prevent an encounter with a potential rapist. What exactly will you do now? Don't shrug the question off with an "I'll think of something" or "I won't know until it happens." If you don't examine your abilities, your values, and the possibilities, there is a good chance you won't do anything. Put yourself in a hypothetical situation and plan a *definite* course of action. Are you able to? What, specifically, will you do if you are riding in a city bus and a man sits too close and starts stroking your leg? What, specifically, will you do if you go to sleep alone and wake up with a strange man in your bed? What, specifically, will you do if you open your closet door and are grabbed by a man?

Generally speaking, either you will defend yourself actively or you will use a passive method of protection. By "active" I mean physically resisting and fighting, whether with weapons or with nothing but your own body. Passive techniques involve either doing nothing at all and hoping, as a result, no violence will take place, or seeming to do nothing until such time as you can catch the attacker off guard. The many decisions involved are yours to make. If you are a pacifist who could never strike someone with intent to injure, you may select passive techniques; others may choose to perfect some combat techniques, and so on. It is important that whatever method you prefer is suited to you, that is, it involves things that you personally could and would, in fact, use. (No matter how effectively you practiced kicking to break someone's leg, if you would never *do* it, it is of no use to you.) You then need physically and mentally to review your plan until your responses to threat become automatic. In an actual encounter situation, you usually will not have much time to review.

Active Defenses

In any active battle, the woman needs to realize that it is not enough to cause pain. Hurt leads to anger and that may have serious and dangerous repercussions. She needs to *injure* the attacker so that she can get away. If a woman tries to kick a man in the groin, he will be furious and vengeful, but if she hits the target, he will be incapacitated.

The Use of Weapons

Whether or not to use weapons for defense is a very controversial topic; the results of their use have been both good and very bad. The main objection for attempting to use a weapon is that it could be used against you. Thus, instead of being raped by men, some women are also raped by umbrellas, beaten or cut with objects they grabbed for self-defense, maimed or scarred for life, or, ultimately, found dead. Although there is no assurance that brutality would not have occurred without the presence of the weapons, common sense and women's past experiences indicate that when someone strikes out they are likely to get reciprocal action, or worse. Thus, if a woman wants to use weapons, she must not fail.

Some weapons are more risky than others and some may have legal consequences besides the physical risks involved. Check the laws in your locality. Should you decide that you are competent with your chosen arsenal, be sure that the weapons are available immediately. Mace, a hatpin, or a knife in your purse is useless to you if you are grabbed. You must know exactly how to use what you choose as well, for you will rarely have time to fidget or make a second try if you miss your mark. Go for vulnerable areas and be direct and forceful—your life could depend on it. If you feel weapons are for you or might be in some situations, consider the following items. If not, you are not left defenseless, for many possibilities remain.

1. Firearms and knives have apparent use, but check the laws in your state. Deodorant, perfume, hairspray, or other aerosol spray, plastic lemons filled with juice—spray or squirt into the eyes of an assailant.

2. Umbrella—poke hard with the pointed end. Don't swing it. It is easily blocked, and even if you struck someone it would only hurt, not injure.

3. Corkscrew, ice pick, pencil, pen, nail file, lighted cigarette or cigarette lighter in car, hatpin, rattail comb—strike with the object aiming for the eyes, neck, or ears.

4. Keys—put keys between the fingers of a fist with the pointed ends sticking out. Strike the assailant's face with your fist.

5. Book—jab eyes or ears with a corner. It is not effective just to hit with the flat part of the book and would probably just cause anger, not injury.

6. Fireplace poker, baseball bat, rolling pin, vase, lamp, brick, or other heavy objects—crash into the head or hard onto the foot to impede movement.

Actually, almost any situation you find yourself in could afford some weapons if you are alert to them. Some people strongly recommend that when threatened, you should "grab an equalizer," but others heartily discourage it—so you decide. One thing, however, on which there is almost across-the-board agreement—if you are threatened by someone with a weapon, do not resist.

Yell, Don't Scream

Many people respond to fear with sound. This, too, is a controversial matter. Some who are concerned with self-defense for women recommend screaming to attract attention (and thereby, hopefully, assistance) and to frighten the assailant. Many say it is useless and will probably result in a few slugs to shut you up.

If noise is your automatic response, consider changing it from a scream to a yell. Screaming indicates helplessness and fear; thus, the perfect victim. Yelling can instill self-confidence or, if well done, can make the assailant think twice. It still carries with it the possible benefit of attracting help. (Yelling "help" or "rape," however, tends to make people pull down their shades out of fear. "Fire" is more likely to bring a helpful response.) If you feel that noise is a good idea or you just can't squelch it, at least convert it to an aggressive, commanding sound, not a helpless wail.

Use Your Body

Your body has tremendous potential for active defense, and, unlike weapons, it cannot be taken away from you. Some techniques are complex and require years of training, but some are easily learned. Basically, you want to utilize your readiness against an attacker's vulnerability. Most attackers choose and expect passive victims. Generally, they are not afraid of the women they choose and tend to be greatly surprised by return aggression. This gives a prepared female an advantage.

To fight with her body, a woman needs to use her hard, strong areas against the soft, weak areas of her assailant. Vulnerable parts to strike include the eyes, ears, Adam's apple, and groin. The elbows and knees are easily broken if forced any way other than the way they are made to bend. Your head, knees, and elbows make strong, hard striking surfaces and the palms and sides of your hands and the balls and sides of your feet can be useful for striking and kicking. Good technique can vastly increase your effectiveness, so try to find a place to receive at least some basic training. The martial arts do well to prepare people for personal defense, but they are complex and require years of dedicated training. If you are not ready to devote that amount of time and effort, you can still learn some simple defenses. For example, if you have no training and a man grabs you, you would very likely reach for his hand or arm and probably fail to break the hold. Instead, grab onto a finger (especially the little finger) and jerk it back—hard. Or just ignore the hold entirely and strike at his face or groin. If a man on a bus puts his hand on your breast, pulling at his hand will only make things more arousing; poking him in the eyes, clapping the palms of your hands over his ears, slamming him in the groin, or striking the Adam's apple with the side of your hand will probably achieve the desired results.

Timing and certainty are the keys to success with active defenses. You must not be blocked and cannot ease up during your attack. If you do, you have lost the advantage of an unsuspecting male, and you have begun a battle, rather than, in one quick act, prevented one (by winning). It is a single elimination tournament—either you win or he does.

Passive Defenses

The passive approaches provide tremendous flexibility and a wide range of alternative defenses for women, which many never think of when discussing "self-defense." They more commonly think only of meeting physical assault with physical assault. This is unfortunate because it is assumed that men as a group tend to be stronger in terms of sheer muscular strength than women and that a man will almost invariably choose a seemingly meek or weak woman as a victim. (This can serve as a reminder to appear very self-confident and strong. Whether you are or not, that air about you can ward off potential rapists.) In a match of strength, then, the odds do not favor the woman over the rapist. Perhaps she ought to consider, instead, a match of wits.

The idea of passive defense is that, if no battle is begun because the woman puts forth no initial resistance to an attacker, the man will put up no defenses and will, in fact, lower any that he did have. A woman then can use her judgment as to exactly when and how to counterattack, or not to do so at all in hopes of being the least harmed this way.

Many resources suggest fainting as a viable defense, which makes a lot of sense. For one thing, if a man puts a weapon to your back to force you to go somewhere (car, bushes, or whatever) he cannot accomplish that if you "pass out." Second, a struggle is arousing and satisfies the needs to overpower, to prove "manhood," and to "take her off her pedestal," which men state as motivations for raping women. About 125 pounds of dead weight to deal with is far less satisfying. Third, he may fear that he has caused a heart attack or some other ailment he never intended or expected, and may just run away. If he doesn't, you always have the option, of course, of "coming to." Last, he certainly won't fear you in your unconscious state, so the chances of his beating you (into submission?) are considerably lessened, and, certainly, he will not be prepared to defend himself against you should you decide it is time to strike. In this state of vulnerability, his groin, eyes, and all sensitive areas will likely be at your disposal.

Another possibility is to "come to" and pretend to respond to the man as if he is a husband or lover, or not to faint at all and just act as a willing sex partner from the start. You again remove his defense barriers and probably impede beating and general bodily harm, and can now deal effectively with rape. You can gently stroke the man's face, and put your thumbs through his eyes. You can kiss him tenderly, and bite off his lip. You can fondle his testicles and then squeeze them — hard. Or you can stimulate him orally, and bite his testicles off. You will win. It's not pretty. It just works. You have to decide if you could live with such actions, which could result in shock and perhaps death. If not, you might choose to be raped and be glad not to suffer additional abuses (if indeed you don't) or you could choose other methods of defense. (If you decide to cooperate during the rape to its conclusion, you might consider inviting the rapist back. Women have successfully done this, enabling police to catch the man on returning.)

Some techniques merely involve stalling for time in hopes that another solution will present itself. One possibility is to suggest that the two of you would be much more comfortable, or that you could respond much better, elsewhere (motel, your apartment). Telling the man you would like him to meet your friends is another possibility, which may allow you an escape if he agrees. Imagine getting out of your car to enter a store late at night and being seized by a man. If you acted all excited, hugged and kissed him, and said "I never thought I would be so lucky! I'll be right out after I go buy some wine for us," chances are that he would be excited, too, and would wait for you as you went in. Once in, of course, you could get help. Mission accomplished.

Other passive approaches work by repulsing the man. These include defecating, urinating, picking your nose, belching, or vomiting on him,[16] having a feigned epileptic seizure, acting just plain weird (screwing up your face, grunting, shaping your hands into tense, clawlike forms, or whatever), pretending to be a lesbian if another female is around (on a bus, hitchhiking, with a friend), pretending you are mentally retarded, or virtually anything that works. It doesn't matter if it makes any sense at all. Telling the man you have V.D., cancer of the uterus, or herpes syndrome (a virus that causes blisters) might deter him. Some men have been turned off by being told that the woman was pregnant and they would kill the baby if they raped her. Undoubtedly, you can think of numerous other such devices that have potential for defense if you are able to keep your head and make use of them.

If you are confronted with a gang rape situation, struggling will surely be ineffective, but some of the passive techniques might work. Usually, a group has a leader of sorts, who ordinarily will "go first." If you can convince him that you would be more responsive alone, or that you really are extremely attracted to him, or even care for him and would like to see him regularly, you

---

[14]Storaska Frederic, *How to Say No to a Rapist and Survive* (New York: Random House, Inc., 1975).

may succeed in isolating him from the group. Then you can try to deal with the rape in a one-to-one situation. Repulsing the group with your behavior is another possibility to consider, especially if you anticipate the attack and exhibit your "condition" before the group has committed itself to attacking you (when they are following you but before anyone touches you).

YES, BUT WHAT IF . . .

None of the precautions or defenses holds any guarantees. None of them insures you against rape. It can still occur, and it can still happen to you. These measures will reduce the likelihood, but there will still be rape. Unfortunately, the horrors of rape do not end when the rapist leaves. Not only do the victims have to deal with having their bodies and their lives violated during the assault, but they face a whole set of needs and problems afterwards, too.

Physically

Whether you wish to report the rape to police or not (and most authorities recommend doing so), you will need medical attention. You need to be treated for internal injuries and possible infection, as well as for other bodily harms that may have resulted if force was used against you. The doctor will check on evidence of intercourse, last period, and contraceptive use. Unfortunately, insensitive treatment is frequently reported by rape victims, so you may want to call a rape crisis center (located now in many cities) for assistance, or you may want a friend to accompany you to the hospital or doctor's office. Another medical concern is venereal disease, for which most doctors give a preventative penicillin shot, but which must be checked again in six weeks. If the possibility of a pregnancy exists, a "morning after pill" (DES) taken within 48 hours of the rape is a possible prevention method, but it has side effects including nausea and depression, as well as some other serious health consequences that the rape victim and her doctor should discuss. Menstrual extraction 10 days after a missed period and abortion are other possibilities. Accurate pregnancy tests can be made after six weeks.

Legally

Legally, your alternatives are not to report the rape, to report the rape and not prosecute, or to report the rape and prosecute. If you wish to report and prosecute the rapist, call the police immediately. You can ask them to come to your home, meet you at the doctor's office or hospital, or you can go directly to the police station. Do not wash or change clothes, or you will destroy necessary evidence. Be sure that the doctor notes all signs of struggle and rape, including semen, bruises, cuts, blood, any hairs, and any skin or blood of the rapist under your nails if you scratched him. Likewise, as soon as you can, you should write down all the details you can remember about the experience, including the time, place, the rapist's build, skin color, hair color, or marks. Make mention of any marks you think you may have left on him, any conversation between you and the rapist, and his specific actions. Note especially any distinguishing clothing. These details will help you to avoid confusion later when you are asked probing questions and pumped for details.

If your decision is to prosecute, you should be prepared for what that process may include. Procedures vary somewhat from place to place, but generally, you will face the specific questions of police officers,[17] the questioning of doctors and others during the medical check, and tests to yield actual evidence of rape. There may also be photographs taken for evidence. Later, you will be questioned by the district attorney's office (often repeatedly), and have a preliminary hearing, which takes place in an open courtroom. Here the defense attorney seeks flaws in the woman's story and may, in some states, pry into her past sexual activity.[18] If the case finally goes to a trial, it may again be in open court and this time the defense attorney will be prepared. In addition, the defense often seeks and is granted an extended trial. Throughout the ordeal there is often publicity and there is always the possibility that the jury may find the defendant not guilty. Although being a prosecution witness when you are a rape victim is not easy, you can get people who are willing and able to help you, and prosecution with conviction *is* the way to get the rapist off the streets.

Emotionally

If you are raped, don't try to deal with your emotions alone. Consult friends and family if you feel they are a good resource (responses vary from support to rejection and accusations, so be careful), a trained crisis or rape center counselor, or both. Whomever they are, they should be sensitive and concerned with restoring your self-respect and personal strength.

The full range of the feelings you are dealing with may be illusive, even to you, for a while. You may appear calm and speak rationally, be hysterical with rage, or show other equally normal reactions to stress. In fact, you may

[15]Many police stations in larger cities now assure rape victims they will be interviewed by trained, female police officers.

[16]A number of states are now enacting laws to better protect rape victims from potential embarrassment when testifying, such as preventing defense attorneys from inquiring into the victim's past sexual activity.

alternate between drastically differing moods. Some women become depressed and others report feeling nothing at all, almost numb. The particular circumstances of the rape, your personality, and the support you get from others will affect what you feel.

A sense of guilt develops in many rape victims as they decide that somehow it is their fault that they were raped. Even though statistics discount this probability, the misconception still persists. Just as there is no shame in being robbed, there should be no shame in being raped. You are the victim, not the criminal, but realizing that is difficult for some women.

Another reaction commonly described by rape victims is tremendous fear. This may not be proportionate to actual dangers, but that does not make it any less crippling. The sense of dread or panic sometimes persists for a long time, affecting the ordinary daily lives of the victims.

Women who have been raped sometimes become confused about people around them. If they knew the rapist, they may wonder if they can trust any one again. For a while, they may lose confidence in their ability to handle other difficult situations that might arise. Security and confidence will usually return in time, but, meanwhile, self-doubts and feeling distrustful of others may be very upsetting.

All these reactions (severe mood swings, guilt feeling, fear, uncertainty, and suspicion) that raped women report experiencing will be faced in different ways by different people, but it is important to have help from as many sources as you wish for as long as you need it.

CONCLUSION

When you plan for your safety, hopefully you will place your greatest effort and emphasis on preventing the occurrence of a potential rape situation. The next largest preparation will be dealing with any encounter that occurs despite those efforts. Your last concern is what to do if you are indeed raped; not last because it is unimportant, but because the main objective is never to end up in that situation. Take care.

BIBLIOGRAPHY

AMIR, MENACHIM, *Patterns in Forcible Rape.* Chicago: The University of Chicago Press, 1971.

The Boston Health Collective, *Our Bodies Ourselves.* New York: Simon and Schuster, 1973, pp. 92-98.

CSIDA, JUNE BUNDY, AND JOSEPH CSIDA, *Rape: How to Avoid It and What To Do About It if You Can't*. Chatsworth, Calif.: Books For Better Living, 1974.

MACDONALD, JOHN M., *Rape Offenders and Their Victims*. Springfield, Ill.: Charles C. Thomas, 1971.

MCCLARY, CATHERINE, *Freedom From Rape*. Ann Arbor, Mich.: The Women's Crisis Center of Ann Arbor, 1974.

MEDEA, ANDRA, AND KATHLEEN THOMAS, "How Much Do You Really Know About Rapists?" *Ms. Magazine* (July 1974), pp. 113-115.

RENNIE, SUSAN, AND KIRSTEN GRIMSTAD, *The New Women's Survival Catalogue*. New York: Coward, McCann & Geoghegan, Inc./Berkley Publishing Corporation, 1973, pp. 145-161.

STORASKA, FREDERIC, *How To Say No To A Rapist And Survive*. New York: Random House, Inc., 1975.

When Premaritally Pregnant

Ursula S. Myers

This is not a "how to" chapter. If you are already pregnant, you know how to; if you're not, you know how not to. What follows is the here and now of being single and being pregnant, and dealing with those facts.

A good starting point is to define your situation. Yours, now—not the one you prefer, or your friend's, or the events leading up to your situation. Where are you right now? Are you really pregnant? If so, is it a problem? To whom—the father (be he friend, casual acquaintance, lover, fiance), your family, society, the school, peers? If there is no problem with others, you still have to deal with the practical aspects of being pregnant and being single, if you plan to stay that way.

ARE YOU REALLY PREGNANT?

Any woman engaging in sexual intercourse without consistently using a high reliable form of contraception runs a very good chance of becoming pregnant, especially if the frequency of contact is high and the pattern is

This article was especially written for this book.

regular. If you have missed a menstrual period and have been regularly engaging in sexual intercourse, odds are that you're pregnant. However, there is always the outside chance that you have a physical disorder or, more likely, are under emotional stress, either of which could cause a delay (or even cessation) in your menstrual cycle. Whatever the precipitating factor, you must have a medical diagnosis confirming or denying pregnancy before you can engage in any decision making.

Reports abound on do-it-yourself pregnancy test kits and early diagnostic techniques soon to be available for pregnancy testing. However, these methods are, at least at present, still in the experimental, if not hopeful rumor, stage. The best resource, if you have one in your area, is either a Planned Parenthood Clinic or a Women's Free Clinic. An obstetrician-gynecologist will perform these tests, as will a medically supervised abortion clinic. (Go only to a medically supervised center if you are thinking about an abortion, which we will discuss later.) If you are on or near a college campus, there are usually Free Clinics in the area that do pregnancy and venereal disease tests. Call the campus switchboard for information. College and university medical centers and infirmaries are now testing for pregnancy and venereal disease on a routine basis, as are local health departments.

A few states still have laws prohibiting a minor from receiving medical attention without prior permission from a parent or guardian. If you are a minor and your parent(s) is aware of your concern, be sure you meet the permission procedure of whatever facility you are using. If you do not want them to know, for whatever reason, you will have to find facilities willing to ignore the law or located in another state. A good source of information is either your area National Organization of Women (NOW) group or the nearest Planned Parenthood Center. Some County Departments of Social Services have resource information as well as counselors to help you in this area, as do Clergy Consultation Services and Women's Counseling Centers.

The tests themselves are fairly simple. The one involving the least trouble is done with a urine sample and is generally recommended for just that reason—not much hassle. The other is a pelvic examination of the female reproductive organs. If you are going to have the latter, and are very young, it is a good idea to have someone (the nurse, doctor, or your counselor) explain the procedure to you beforehand. There are also some good, self-educating books, such as *Our Bodies, Ourselves,*[1] that are available at most bookstores or can be ordered.

If your test result comes back negative, or if the examining physician tells you you are not pregnant, and you haven't started menstruating within a week, you better have the procedure repeated just to be sure. If it still comes

---

[1]Boston Women's Health Book Collective, *Our Bodies, Ourselves* (New York: Simon and Schuster, 1973).

back negative, then it might be a good idea to check with your physician to see what else might be the trouble. If the result comes back with pregnancy confirmed, then you have other things to think about.

Some of you will get married and resolve the premarital part of your pregnancy that way. If you do, you will have lots of company as it is suspected that about one-third of all brides are pregnant at the time of marriage. Just be as sure (as anyone getting married can be) that this is what you really want to do and is not a desperation move. Too many teen-age marriages, for instance, end up in the divorce court — about 50 percent. Those of you choosing that alternative may still wish to read on since you may change your mind or fate may change your plans for you.

YES, YOU'RE REALLY PREGNANT

The only thing that makes you different from most other women right now is that you are pregnant. You are not per se abnormal, bad, deviant, exceptional, unusual, neurotic, or maladjusted — at least not necessarily because of your pregnancy. But if you did not plan or want to be pregnant, then you may be ignorant, uninformed, naive, misinformed, or living out the fantasy that it-couldn't-happen-to-me. If one or more of the above apply, do something about that before you find yourself on a not-so-merry-go-round of repeated pregnancies.

You are not trapped, despite what studies of premarital pregnancies may indicate. You *do* have choices (some tough ones) and you *can* determine the quality of your life and that of others important to you. It is a matter of accepting your situation, making choices, knowing what you can do, and planning accordingly. It is also a matter of using your head in making those choices. Getting irrationally, emotionally bound up in your circumstances will not help you to make the decision that is best for you. Keep a cool head.

A part of the process of doing something about it has already begun; you've read this far. Now let's get into the things that still need doing. To begin with, you might wish to be more planful with your life — run it instead of letting it run you. That means planning ahead, and I don't mean with those funny Plan Ahead signs. That you didn't do this before is pretty obvious. The stages in planning just about anything, including your life, are specific:

1. Define your problem.
2. Define the alternatives.
3. Make out a pro/con list on each alternative.
4. Evaluate.
5. Decide; what is the most viable alternative for you in your present situation and in terms of your long-range goals?

The most basic decision you must make early in your pregnancy, and once you have it confirmed, is whether to have it terminated by abortion or carry it through full term. We will discuss the details of abortion later, but the decision cannot be put off. Decide to have or not have as early as possible, for if you opt for an abortion, it is safer and simpler when done during the first 12 weeks of pregnancy. If you decide against it, you have plenty of planning time ahead. Your decision on abortion or not depends on you and all the things that make you unique; your age, your physical health, your personal beliefs and ethics, your psychological strengths and weaknesses, your short- and long-term life goals, your financial resources, and, whether we admit it or not, how much validity the important persons in your life have to you. All of these affect your decision. But you do have a choice to make.

The next step is to find a professional counselor who will help you expedite the decision you just made, who can help you sort out your feelings, help you be a planful person, and who will provide you with information and support.

In the meantime, if you are in high school, stay there! Your pregnancy need not affect your education. (If your school district tells you that you cannot stay in regular classes because of your pregnancy, contact the State Department of Public Instruction at your State Office Building—usually where it is located—in your state capitol. If there are regulations barring you from classes, check with your local or state unit of the American Civil Liberties Union to find out what recourse you have. Others have done so, and have won their lawsuits.)

Counselors specializing in social services to the premaritally pregnant are usually located in your public social service agencies (some people still call them welfare departments), private agencies (such as Children's Service Society, Catholic Social Services, Lutheran Social Services, Family Service Association) and Community Action Centers, Women's Centers and Clinics, Student Counseling Centers, and Maternal Health Centers. Some communities have an Information and Referral telephone number listed in the telephone book for just such inquiries. Your community may also have a hotline number you can call to find the nearest location of a counseling agency. The yellow pages of any phone book should have resources listed under either Social Services or Marriage and Family Counselors.

Check the credentials of the agency you have chosen and also the credentials of your counselor. A counselor in a private agency should have a degree in his or her specialty from an accredited university or college, be licensed by the state in which he or she operates, and be willing to discuss this matter and show you his or her credentials. State and county agencies have merit system (Civil Service) employees, and these counselors are required to have college degrees. They are also regulated by the state in terms of professional standards.

Several private organizations also regulate their members as to practice, skills, and knowledge. Some of these include the National Association of Social Workers (and their Academy of Certified Social Workers), the American Association of Marriage and Family Counselors, the Child Welfare League of America, and the Family Service Association of America. You can and should be particular about your choice of counselor, just as you would be about your doctor or dentist.

Telling your parents is a decision that hinges on a lot of factors. (Unless they are unusual parents, however, it is not an easy task at best.) How old are you, and what do you plan to do about the pregnancy? If you are 23, premaritally pregnant, and plan to have an abortion, perhaps you would choose to keep this a very private matter. If you are 20, in college, planning to complete your education, and keep the baby, it might be wise to involve them in your plans, depending on your involvement with them as your family.

If you are 17, pregnant, and thinking about getting married when you're 18 to solve the "unwed mother" part of the problem, it would certainly be to your advantage to discuss your pregnancy with your parents, especially since they may well be paying your medical bills — and you will probably need their approval before you can be treated by a physician or admitted to a hospital. (State laws vary so check with your local health department. An anonymous phone call will supply you with the answer quickly.) Each state also varies in its laws governing marriages of, or between, minors, so check that out with your counselor.

If you are 14 and pregnant, parents need to know. You are still a dependent child in the eyes of the law and in many other respects.

In all these situations, and where there is reluctance and uncertainty in going it alone or telling one's parents, a professional counselor specializing in unmarried parent counseling can help, either by advising you, or by going with you and actually facilitating the whole process.

Let's assume, then, that at this point you have made the basic decision as to early termination versus a full-term pregnancy. Since a full-term pregnancy has long-term implications, which will need separate consideration, let's look first at some aspects of early termination procedures.

ABORTION

A pamphlet distributed by the Abortion Rights Association spells out the current status of legal abortions in the United States:

Since the Supreme Court decisions (January 1973) which override all state laws, any woman is eligible for a legal abortion anywhere in the United States. Up to about the first 12 weeks of pregnancy the only legal requirement is that the abortion must be performed by a licensed physician. From the 13th through the 24th week a state may regulate only the procedure in ways related to maternal health. This means that through the first six months of pregnancy you may have an abortion for any reason.[2]

And the *Wall Street Journal* carried a page one item noting that:

Nearly 900,000 legal abortions were performed in 1974, compared with 750,000 in 1973 and 600,000 in 1972, the year before the Supreme Court barred states from prohibiting abortions early in pregnancy. The figures were reported by Planned Parenthood Federation's journal, which said public hospitals were slow to respond to the court decision.[3]

If you are 18 and over (21 in some states), you can elect early termination of your pregnancy by choice. If you are under 18, some states allow minors the decision rights but others do not. (You can ask your counselor or Planned Parenthood staff.) If your parents will not consent to your having an abortion, and this is your choice, or you for some reason do not wish to make them aware of your pregnancy and you live in a restrictive state, then you should discuss this with your counselor. If you don't have a counselor, contact some of the organizations listed earlier in the section on pregnancy testing.

To locate a legitimate abortion clinic in good (some are not!) medical standing, check with your counselor, contact any of the resources listed that specializes in services to the premaritally pregnant, or call a college-affiliated chapter of NOW if you don't have a local group. Ask about the clinic's credentials.

In a well-organized, thoughtful clinic, the atmosphere is quiet and pleasant, individual counseling is provided, and the procedure is carefully explained to the client. Pregnancy tests are taken, as are thorough medical histories, and Rhogam shots are available for RH-negative persons. Routine tests for VD are also generally performed. An abortion in the first trimester (up to the 12th week) does have the advantage of outpatient treatment and a certain simplicity in procedure if the uterine or vacuum aspiration method is used. During this procedure, the opening to the uterus is stretched to allow passage of a small tube. Suction is applied through the tube and the uterus is emptied of its contents, usually under local anesthesia but sometimes under general. Some women, following an abortion, have indicated pain with local anesthesia. The cramps are like hard menstrual pains and sometimes are in the back as well as in the abdomen. The bleeding after a therapeutic abortion is similar to a heavy period. If it is much heavier than that, if you run a fever

---

[2]"Abortion: A Physicians's Rights and Responsibilities," Abortion Rights Association pamphlet, New York, N.Y.

[3]*The Wall Street Journal*, February 3, 1975, p. 1.

(over 100°) or have extremely severe cramps, or a combination of any of these, contact the clinic or physician who performed the abortion. Be sure either to make an appointment for a follow-up exam before you leave or with your local ob-gyn if you live some distance from the location of your abortion.

Some clinics and hospitals prefer the D & C, or dilatation and curettage method. In this procedure, the cervix is dilated and the uterus is scraped, or curetted, with a spoon-shaped instrument. You may be asked to stay overnight as a precaution against complications. If you have time to check into the procedure and if you have a choice of settings, it is suggested that you use the vacuum aspiration method. It is easier on you physically and mentally.

There is another early procedure being done in some parts of the country called menstrual extraction, which is just that. The uterus contents are extracted shortly after what may have been an incident of conception, usually within two weeks. You never really know whether you may have been pregnant, but since you obviously didn't want to be anyway, it is somewhat irrelevant. This procedure is often used in cases of rape when the victim has not immediately been given other therapeutic medication.

Abortions performed during the fourth month of pregnancy (12 to 16 weeks) are not much more complicated, but, because they could be, are normally performed in the hospital. You will have a choice of either dilatation and curettage or vacuum aspiration, the former more frequently used during this period. The stay in the hospital may be only overnight, but that is up to the attending physician and your own special circumstances.

An abortion performed after the 16th week is called a "saline" and requires hospitalization. In this procedure, a needle is inserted into the uterus under local anesthetic and some of the amniotic fluid is replaced with a saline, or salt solution. The procedure should be done only by an experienced obstetrician-gynecologist. The ensuing miscarriage will occur after you have contractions and within one or two days.[4] How long you will stay in the hospital afterward depends on you and your doctor.

There are a few precautions you will need to observe after any abortion. You will not have intercourse or douche until after your postabortion medical checkup. You will watch for any signs of physical problems mentioned earlier. And, most important, you will decide on a contraceptive device best suited to your needs, and you will use it. Your abortion clinic or hospital may provide this counseling and also the devices, but if they do not, ask them for the names of birth control clinics nearby or near where you live. Get a method of birth control and use it. Some clinics even include this in their fee.

---

[4]"Abortion: A Physician's Rights and Responsibilities," Abortion Rights Asociation pamphlet, New York, N.Y.

Speaking of fees, you can expect to pay anywhere from $100 to $400 for an abortion, depending on the medical procedure followed. If you have medical insurance, it may well cover all, or part, of the fee. If you are on Medicaid, your medical card will probably cover it all. There may, however, be some states with a flat fee Medicaid schedule for abortions and, if you go to a clinic that charges more, you may have to pay the difference. However, many clinics and hospitals have a sliding fee schedule for cases of demonstrated need, so if you are financially down and out and can substantiate it, you may pay from $50 to nothing.

Some final words on abortions: First, the choice of having one, if you are in your early months of pregnancy, is *up to you alone*. Second, we need to say a bit about *feelings*. If you had your head together when you made your decision on whether or not to have the pregnancy terminated, and worked through the process (as previously suggested) in a calm, rational manner, you will probably have a perfectly normal emotional response. In other words, some of you will feel relieved, some elated, some a little dejected, some as though you have the big three-day blues, and some almost nothing. For those who are overly concerned about depression after the abortion, "a John Hopkins study of several hundred patients has found no greater depression or emotional stress among women who had abortions than among a match group that delivered healthy babies."[5] So you see, some of the stories you've been hearing about guilt and depression aren't necessarily so. And third, practice *common sense* (it's never too late) *and contraception* consistently after your abortion. Given the alternatives, contraception is a lot easier than repeated abortions. It does, however, require some responsible mature decision making. If you're not up to that one, you had better be up to the other.

TO HAVE

You've decided to have the baby. And once *that* decision is made, that's it. Or is it?

That word "responsibility" starts creeping in again. Responsibility to yourself, to the fetus you are carrying, to the person that mass of cells will soon become, to your family if you have one, to the father of the child (the term for him is "alleged father," and it stays that way until the court adjudicates him the father of the child), and, I expect, to your world.

And decisions. They still must be made. Even though you have made the decision to carry your child to full term, you have one more to deliberate —

[5]EMKO *Newsletter*, St. Louis, Mo. (June 1974), p. 4.

will you keep the child or will you give him or her up for adoption. Counselors call it "terminating parental rights," but it is much more than that. It is deciding whether you want to, and are *prepared* to above all, be a responsible, loving, and caring parent to this child. If you are 15 and are reading this chapter, please think about what I am saying. If you are 24 and are reading this chapter, please think about what I am saying. If you are the mother, the father, or the "involved male" who is reading this chapter, please think about what I am saying. Each child coming into this world is a gift, and we must decide whether we are the ones who will best nurture it.

You will normally have nine months to decide. Sometimes physical disabilities in the mother or child will shorten the time you have, but even then your obstetrician will be able, except for unusual situations, to give you an idea of the time frame in which your decision-making processes will take place. At the same time, you must also attend to the many other needs you have relating to your pregnancy. First of all, to yourself—your physical health, your education if you are still in school, and your future.

Your obstetrician is probably the best person to talk to in regard to prenatal health care. If you are afraid to ask him or her questions, write them down as you think of them and take the list with you when you go for your regular checkup. The doctor is used to questions, answering them is his or her job, and, after all, unless you are going to a free clinic, he or she is getting paid by you. Don't be shy about asking—it took the doctor over 20 years to gain the knowledge to practice that specialty, and he or she doesn't expect *you* to know all the facts it took that long to learn. You also have a good resource in your county and city health departments as well as the prenatal clinics attached to many hospitals, especially those that are teaching hospitals. Some of these hospitals have special miniprograms that help prepare young mothers for labor, delivery, and child care.

Those of you 18 and under and pregnant automatically fall into what the medical profession calls the "high-risk" pregnancies. That is pretty logical when you think about it, and should not rattle you too much. After all, women under that age have a lot of activity going on within themselves. They are changing physically during puberty, their neurological system is still in the developmental stage until somewhere between 16 and 18, and their personality and emotional makeup is loaded with developmental task demands. (Erik Erikson has some fine books on just this subject.[6]) Small wonder, then, that the system does not just overload and blow the circuit.

---

[6]For example, see Erik Erikson's *Identity, Youth and Crisis* (New York: Norton, 1968); *Dimensions of a New Identity* (New York: Norton, 1974); and *Childhood and Society*, 2nd ed. (New York: Norton, 1963).

Well, sometimes it does. And that is why you will find professional counselors of help. They can help you to find ways to defuse your situation, if it needs defusing.

Educational needs and desires may present difficulties for the teen-age unmarried girl, depending on the state in question. According to the Consortium on Early Childbearing and Childrearing, Washington, D.C., in 1970 less than one-third of the 17,000 school districts in the United States had any program for the education of a pregnant girl.[7] A great deal of activity has taken place since then in terms of changing that statistic, so it would be wise for any girl wishing to stay in school, in the regular classroom structure, to question seriously any move to change her educational program merely because of her pregnancy.

My theme of planning sensibly for the future should be very obvious. It is something most premaritally pregnant women have not done, need to think about, and need to do.

IF I KEEP THE BABY

You think you want to keep the baby. Then there are some things you probably should know, or take into consideration, besides all that we have already covered.

Parenting a child means more than just loving that child or saying "it's mine because I *had* it." (Counselors hear that over and over.) A person more learned and expert than most of us has already spelled that out very well. His name in Bruno Bettelheim and his book is called *Love is Not Enough*. Read it — it's worth the time! Good parenting doesn't just happen, it takes effort. (It can also be fun.)

Classes in effective parenting are presented by many groups, such as local YWCAs and YWHAs, social service agencies, college and university Child Development Centers, and community-oriented churches. Comprehensive care programs for young or new mothers may be provided by some or all of these organizations:

City, County or State Public Health Departments.
County and State Social Service Departments.
Maternal Health Centers.
Planned Parenthood Centers.

---

[7]Marion Howard, "A Discussion of State Laws and State and Local Policies as They Relate To Education of Pregnant School-Age Girls," Consortium on Early Childbearing and Childbearing, Washington, D.C. (1972), p. 5.

Vocational Schools.

Community Action Programs.

If you don't have these facilities or programs available to you, ask your librarian to help you locate a good resource book.

Another consideration is the father of the baby. How *much* of an emotional consideration depends on your relationship with him. But one fact does not depend on anything but the current laws of your state regarding the rights of the alleged father, and that fact is just that, his rights. Each state varies, but more and more of them have laws spelling out the rights of the alleged father. Whatever your involvement with him, do discuss your position and your state's laws with your counselor. You will need to know them whether you keep the baby or decide to terminate your parental rights, for important matters such as Social Security benefits for the child and support payments, which hinge on the establishment of paternity on behalf of the baby. The procedure is initiated by your local district attorney's office, so you should discuss this with your counselor as well, especially in terms of who does what. So much is happening in the courts in the area of rights of the alleged father that the benefit of discussing this carefully and thoroughly with your counselor cannot be overemphasized. If the counselor is unsure, ask for specific information, who should have it or know where to obtain.

The matter of support payments brings us head-on into money matters. If you are a minor and your parents are willing and able to pay for all the costs of your pregnancy and beyond, or have medical insurance coverage, you are lucky. If you are a minor and your parents are up against it financially, then you and one of your parents should check out the financial aid programs administered under the State Department of Health, Education and Welfare. If you are not a minor, apply on your own behalf. In some areas these agencies are County Social Service agencies; in others they are called Welfare Departments. In any case, they do have financial aid programs available to persons of demonstrated eligibility.

Each state (and locality) has its own level of assistance under Maternity Aid, or Aid to the Unborn, so check that out as well as Medicaid benefits. In some states the amount of paperwork and form-filling-out is mind-boggling, but if you are broke and really need financial help, it will be worth the patience and effort. Most agencies try hard to do their job well and quickly, but there are always exceptions. If you have too much hassle, write your local congressperson, or your state representative, but first contact the director of the agency to see if matters can be settled at the local level. If not, appeal the decision higher up.

There are many programs directly related to financial aid, and one of those having positive future impact is the provision of child care monies to minors regularly attending school for the cost of baby-sitters. There are certain requirements that must be met by the person who provides the child care before that person can be certified, which simply means that they are qualified for the job. The whole idea is to help you complete your education—for obvious reasons.

For girls and women who cannot or do not wish to stay in their own community during their pregnancy, a maternity home can be the answer. Your counselor would be aware of the homes in your area, or even far away—their qualifications, special programs, costs, and services. Some states cover the cost of these homes through their Medicaid benefits, but others do not. Check that out. Some homes, depending on their affiliation, have a sliding fee schedule. All of them under consideration should be licensed by the state in which they operate. Another option, especially for a minor who cannot stay in her own home, is that of foster home placement. This option, however, requires careful planning and evaluation, and is such an in-depth and involved subject fraught with legal and emotional ramifications that it might well be considered the last possible option. It should be discussed very carefully with licensed, professional counselors. (If the writer seems overly concerned with involving you with qualified career counselors, it is because her own professional experience has shown her how badly some women need someone else to get from one side of the mountain to the other. There are so many pitfalls and unknowns in between—at least for some—that it seems reasonable, and even easier, to involve one who knows the pitfalls and how to avoid them.)

Those of you who are minors and plan to keep your babies have some homework to do. First of all, you will have some heavy responsibilities (which exist whether you are 14 or 17). So whether you dream lovely dreams or not during your pregnancy, you *are* responsible for real life matters, such as maintaining your own good health, becoming aware of the special needs of the fetus, learning about labor and delivery, continuing your education if you are in school, learning about child care, and, most importantly, finding out who you really are and what human sexuality is all about. Your rights are those of any parent (and so are your obligations). You do have the right to decide whether you are going to keep, or terminate your rights to, your child (and so does its father). You do have the right to certain financial support, both from public welfare agencies as well as from the alleged father of the baby. You do have the right to continue your education, be it high school or college. (As indicated, many states provide child care funds for just such needs.) You do have the right to medical care under the Federal Medicaid programs, at least for your baby if you yourself are not eligible for some reason.

You also have the problem of finding out, deciding, knowing—whatever you may wish to call it—what you are going to do in the way of living after the baby arrives. Are you going to be staying at home? Do your parents want another child in their home? Should they have to be faced with that decision or that child? Would it be better for you to go into a foster home that will provide a stable environment for both you and the baby? Are you having some really bad times mentally and emotionally—and would you be better off if you and your baby were in a good residential treatment center that would have a program for both of you? You are the only one who can answer these questions.

One thing that is often helpful is to look at the whole situation from the baby's point of view. Is your baby going to have the chance to be a whole person more readily by having you as its lifetime mother, or by giving someone else this opportunity? Are you at a point in your life where you are ready to be the nurturing mother that child will need for years to come? Perhaps you are—and perhaps not. You are really the only one to decide.

And decide you will, whether consciously or not. You will either be there when the child needs you or you will not; you will concern yourself with its normal developmental needs or you will not; you will maintain your home in a warm, loving, secure manner or you will not; you will provide nourishing food and good health standards or you will not; you will stay at home when your friends are having a big "do" or you will not; you will change the diapers, clean up the vomit, switch the formula, keep on nursing the baby, or you will not. What you will do is decide for yourself whether you are going to be a mother—or not. You will make the decision, and concerned others will act on it, one way or another. Most of all, they will really try to be of help to you, whatever your decision.

IF I GIVE IT UP

The legal term for giving up your baby is "termination of parental rights." In most states both parents must go through the prescribed legal procedure before the child can be placed with adoptive parents. Again, the decision-making process may be a very resolute one, or it may be openly traumatic and vacillating. Whichever way may be yours, that counselor you talked to early in the game is going to be worth her or his weight in gold, and even more than money can buy. So many human needs, wants, terrors, and hopes come into play in these moments, and you will have your own way of managing a very difficult, intimate time. Some of you will weep for days and months; some of you will reject all thoughts of giving up your child until a precipitous incident occurs, and then you will make the decision quickly and be firm about it; some of you will be stoic and determined that you will terminate parental rights, and survive. Some of you will be curious about the whole process of having a baby but still detached from the idea of being a mother; some of you will be relieved that the whole process will be over at birth and that you will be able to get on with your lives; some of you will initially keep your baby, but after six or nine months of being a parent decide to give it up. Any of these reactions and behaviors, and those in between, are normal—as long as they are honest and you are honest with yourself about them. No one is asking you to be a perfect anything, but your baby and most of us in counseling are asking you to be an honest someone.

In almost all cases, a social worker is involved in the legal procedure of termination of parental rights as well as in the adoptive study, child placement, and supervision of the adoptive home. The Children's Code (or Child Welfare Statutes) of each state spells out specifically what steps must be taken. If you want to see this document, ask your counselor or your library for a copy.

It is probably a good idea to make the decision before you have your baby, but you don't have to. You can prepare yourself mentally for the separation just a bit more effectively if you plan ahead. Many of you will go through the classic grief processes of rejection and denial, guilt, hostility, and eventually acceptance. Some of you will not. Some of you will want to discuss the process of termination with your counselor in every detail and some of you will just want to get it over with. Some of you will want to see your newborn infant after delivery to be sure that it is a healthy, normal human being, and some of you will prefer to have the baby be an anonymous person. Whatever you opt for, it is okay if it is really the way you want it and it works best for you in your time and your world.

Now, about delivery. If you do know what your plans are, let your doctor know and ask him to tell the maternity staff of your decision. And if you are concerned that they might be confused, tell them yourself. Spell out the little details, too. They are there to help you, and they cannot operate in the dark, so to speak. If you want to see your baby after delivery, tell them. If you do not, tell them. If you change your mind, tell them. If you have trouble telling them, ask your counselor to help. They, too, have had many years of training in their profession and can often get past the real, or perceived, roadblocks between you and what you want and/or need. Some of you might want some help just physically getting out of the hospital without the baby.

You have or have not seen the baby. You are going home, or to a friend's place, or back to college, or to a foster home, perhaps. The baby will leave the hospital with someone else, generally to a licensed foster home for infants. Then what?

Procedures in the matter of termination of parental rights differ from state to state, and so it is best to obtain specific information from your social worker as to the actual steps to be taken in your local court. It will undoubtedly require action by a juvenile court judge to make this process legal and binding on all parties. (I cannot emphasize this point enough—do not participate in adoption schemes that promise money, or other benefits, or that are finalized through any procedure other than due process of law.) A part of the process is initiated by your counselor when he or she requests an appointment with the juvenile judge in whose jurisdiction you live. How quickly you are able to get a hearing date depends on the court calendar— sometimes the judge is faced with a heavy calendar and the hearing will not take place for about two months. No one likes to have this long a delay, but if that is the situation, understand that it is probably inevitable. Most court calendars are overcrowded.

Be prepared for two things. The judge will no doubt question you thoroughly in regard to your decision to terminate your rights. He or she will want to be assured that you have not been coerced or unduly influenced when making your decision, that it is yours and yours alone. And the judge will also involve the alleged father, if paternity has been established (or any possible putative father, if not). In other words, the rights of both parents must be terminated before the child of issue can be placed with adoptive parents. The details of this procedure—legal matters such as declarations of parental interest, adjudication of the natural father, waivers of parental rights, notice of hearing, transfer of guardianship and legal custody, and so on—vary from state to state and indeed from court to court. It is therefore very important that you have someone you trust, and who knows the requirements as they exist in your court district, to help you through the maze of hearing procedures. The whole process sounds confusing and obfuscatory to the person who is not a part of the system on a day-to-day basis, but it can be dealt with quite simply with the help of your counselor.

The physical process of separating yourself from your baby is one thing; the emotional separation may be quite another. How you feel about giving up your baby will be predicated on how you relate to the situation as a whole. In other words, how do you feel about yourself as a person, as a premaritally pregnant woman, and as a mother? How do you feel about the alleged father and how does he relate to your pregnancy and the baby? Is your family supporting you in your decision or are they against giving up something they consider partially theirs? Are you living totally in the present, or are you also future-oriented? Do your friends support your decision to terminate, or do they think you are some kind of nut, or even a bit sick "to give up your baby"? "You gotta be crazy!" Well, you're not.

It is really best to rely primarily on your counselor to help you sort out your feelings and get your life back in order. Too many cooks really do spoil the broth, and, in this case, you can't possibly meet everyone's expectations or satisfy their demands. For some women, having a baby is life's big experience—giving up the baby will most likely be one of the most difficult things with which they have ever had to deal. They may change their minds. And you can change your mind, you know, up to the very last minute. No one is going to think any less of you if you do.

You will not be able to change it, however, after the legal termination procedure takes place, at least not in most states. This is reasonable from the child's standpoint, for he or she also has rights, and they would certainly be violated if legal parentage could be changed at whim.

One fact may give you comfort and assurance in moments of doubt—adoptive parents who register with state licensed adoption agencies are evaluated very thoroughly and sensitively. In fact, they are scrutinized infinitely more carefully than are natural parents as to their qualifications for parenthood. Your baby will be placed with parents who most resemble it physically and mentally, in most circumstances. The adoptive parents will receive the child with enormous excitement and anticipation, for most of them have been waiting a long time for this moment.

AND AFTERWARDS[8]

After such an experience, you may say you will have nothing more to do with sexual intercourse. You may consciously avoid having intercourse until you think you are ready to become involved in a responsible way. Or you may self-talk that it wasn't any fun anyway and you're not going to do it again, so you aren't going to waste your time on birth control. But suppose you meet someone who does make it seem like fun? Some of you may feel that birth control is not natural and whatever is not natural is bad. But spend some time with a woman who has had 14 children in almost as many years and is physically, mentally, and emotionally a wasteland, or see the ravages of uncontrolled waters, the desolation of overworked and worn-out farmlands, and realize that some "natural" happenings are not per se good either. And there are those of you who have had a baby as a result of a rich, satisfying relationship, but were just a bit irresponsible about your sexual activities.

[8]See also Chapter 12 in this text, "Protecting Yourself From Unwanted Parenthood."

Now is the time to be more responsible. You can make a conscious effort either to use contraceptive methods to avoid another pregnancy or to avoid intercourse. The latter is more easily said than done. Birth control information and counseling is available to you from many resources. Actual contraceptive devices, however, other than vaginal spermicidal jellies, tablets, foams, and condoms, must be prescribed by a physician and include the pill, the intrauterine device, and the diaphragm. The others can be purchased across the counter at the pharmacy. Some states permit vending machine sales of condoms in places normally frequented by men — men's rooms, bars, and the like.

Some of the centers offering contraceptive information, referral, and counseling services are Women's Counseling Centers and Clinics, Planned Parenthood Centers, Community Action Family Planning Centers and Clinics, County Departments of Social Services, University or College Student Clinics, Teen Clinics, VD Clinics, Municipal and County Public Health Departments, and hospital-affiliated clinics. There are also, especially in university and college towns, private or government-funded projects such as traveling clinic buses, which outpost themselves in the community, usually on a regularly scheduled route. It is important for you to remember, however, that the most effective means of contraception for women to choose from are those that may be obtained by medical prescription only — the Pill, the IUD, and the diaphragm, so do ask your obstetrician-gynecologist for a prescription or an IUD.

The condom is equally effective when used as directed and when combined with vaginal spermicidal foam or jelly. It also has another plus — it curtails the spread of VD. That alone, what with the epidemic spread of venereal diseases these days, is enough to make most counselors encourage its use by all premaritally or extramaritally sexually active males of any age. However, the only control you as a female have over the use of the condom is to insist on it, and if your partner refuses, then you can say "no!"

The other item that decidedly needs attending to is determining why you got pregnant, which is more than just a matter of having sexual intercourse. This is probably one of the most vital pieces of information you will need to pry out of your psyche, especially in terms of where you are heading in your life. When all of the what-to-do-now counseling is done with, when you've made your decision as to what to do and when to do it about this pregnancy, and carried through on your planning — you still must come to grips with that basic, often deeply submerged question. Why did I get pregnant? And answering that may take some doing, or it may not. You may just like sex, got careless, and got pregnant. One solution would be just to be more careful; use contraceptives. Or you may, on the other hand, be a very needful person. You may need the pregnancy and the baby for your own gratification. (What about that baby as a *person?*) What is the answer for you? It is time you worked on that matter.

The reality of being premaritally pregnant, is, then, more than a matter of medical data. It is a reality that may well determine your role for life, not just here and now. However you will decide to handle your pregnancy, whatever your choice, the impact of this decision on you and your future depends on your ability to evaluate yourself, your needs, and your goals, in your life space. It depends on planning sensibly and realistically. How about it?

How to Tell Children They Are Adopted

Laurie Lytle

"Are you going to tell him?" "Does she know?" These are questions that adoptive parents are frequently asked. Fortunately, most adoptive parents today answer with an emphatic "Yes!" As an adoptive parent you should know that if your child is to have the foundation for a sound personality, he or she must be told that he or she is adopted, because sooner or later the child is almost certain to find out, no matter how carefully you think you have kept the secret. It is almost always a traumatic experience for an older child, or even an adult, to find out suddenly that he or she is adopted, and the damage to his or her sense of security and to your relationship with the child could be beyond repair. Your child has the right to know that he or she is adopted and should be given this information as soon as he or she is old enough to understand it. Adoption workers and child psychologists feel very strongly about this, and many adoption agencies hold postplacement group meetings for adoptive couples to discuss their own ideas about telling a child that he or she is adopted.

Since there is really no question of "whether" or not to tell, have you considered the question of "how" to tell? If when you tell your child that he or she

This article was especially written for this book.

is adopted, you feel so uncomfortable with the situation that from then on you try to ignore it and evade all discussion of it, you may do just as much harm as the parents who try to conceal the adoption. You may endanger the future happiness of your child by instilling the idea that adoption is something for which he or she should feel guilty or ashamed. It is far better to start preparing yourself now to discuss adoption openly, honestly, with warmth and understanding, and most of all with love.

In the beginning, all that your baby needs to know about the word "adopted" is that it is something good to be. When you are talking to the child while dressing, or feeding, or playing with him or her, you might occasionally use the word or you might say something such as, "We're so glad we adopted you!" When you begin reading to the child and telling stories, you might occasionally tell the story of his or her adoption in the simplest terms: "Daddy and mommy wanted a baby but didn't have any. We looked all over for the right one; finally we found you and we're happy that we did." It isn't so much what you say, but how you say it that matters. A happy relaxed manner will not only reinforce the child's feelings that "adopted" is good, but it will also help you to get over any feelings of self-consciousness as you get used to talking freely about adoption.

This does not mean that you should use every conceivable opportunity to remind your child that he or she is adopted, nor should you feel obligated to explain to every stranger who makes a comment on your child's family resemblance that the child is adopted. In fact, if the child constantly hears that he or she is adopted, he or she may begin to wonder what it is that makes him or her so different, and instead of feeling accepted the child may feel alienated.

Now that the easy part is over — your child knows he or she is adopted — we come to the difficult part — explaining what adoption is. How old is "old enough to understand?" Children vary so much that it is impossible to give a definite answer. By the time a child is three or four, however, you will want to prepare yourself for the question "Where do babies come from?" It is best to answer this question honestly, but simply enough so that the child can easily understand. You may feel some of the constraint that almost all parents feel in talking about sex with their children. This may be difficult enough for ordinary parents, but for adoptive parents it is doubly hard. First, you have to explain that a baby grows inside its mother; then sooner or later you have to tell the child that he or she did not grow inside you, but inside another mother before he or she was adopted. This may confuse the child for a while, but eventually it will be clear.

One thing that you should realize is that your child's questions will never come in exactly the form or at the moment you expect. He or she is just as apt to ask them when you have dinner guests or are in the middle of the supermarket as when you are alone. If the child does not ask questions, a good opportunity for you to open the subject may be the pregnancy of a friend or relative, or your cat or dog who is about to have a litter. Don't make too much of an occasion of it. Answer in an easy way that gives the child the feeling that it is the most natural thing in the world.

You can explain that a baby grows in a special place inside its mother and that when it is big enough it is born. This may satisfy the child. If it does, you do not have to say any more for the time being. But eventually the child will ask, "Did I grow inside you, Mommy?" You are not going to lie to your child, nor do you want to postpone the discussion, thereby implying that this is something that embarrasses you and is difficult to talk about. When the child asks that question, the time has come for him or her to learn the meaning of adoption.

An excellent book to have on hand is *And Now We Are A Family* by Judith C. Meredith. Written by an adoptive mother, it is meant to be read aloud to young adopted children. It explains beautifully and sensitively what adoption is, how babies are adopted, why parents adopt, and why some children are given up for adoption.

Remember that even if this subject is charged with feeling and embarrassment for you, it is a matter of simple curiosity to your child. Again, remember that it is not so much what you say, but how you say it. Let your love and joy shine through as you explain that for some reason you and Daddy did not grow a baby, and so you went to see someone who helps to find babies for people who don't grow any. You had to wait a long time while she looked and looked, and finally she found *him* (or *her*)! And Mommy and Daddy came to see the baby, and you loved him or her right away, and you took him or her home to love and be yours forever.

This makes a good beginning. It breaks the ice for you as well as for the child. It emphasizes the positive side of adoption, that you really wanted a baby and that you were so glad when you found the one. The story will delight the child and he or she will want to hear it many times—also, children tend to forget. A child learns a little at a time and comes back with the same questions until he or she feels sure of the answer. So be prepared to repeat this story over and over again.

Perhaps at the same time, maybe later, the child will want to know how the baby gets inside the mother. Your explanation of the father's contribution will lead to understanding that your child had *two* other parents before he had you. Of course, you must never imply that the other parents did not *want* the child. This might also be a good time to tell him or her which of your friends' children are adopted (if there are any) or of any adults that you know are adopted, so that the child does not feel that he or she alone is adopted.

Eventually, the child will ask why the "other mother" didn't keep him or her. Perhaps the best answer and nearest to the truth might be, "I don't know, but I'm sure she loved you and would have kept you if she could." You must not let the child sense any resentment or disapproval on your part of the biological mother. Let the child know that his or her biological mother loved the child enough to want him or her to be part of a family that would love him or her too. This will probably be enough to satisfy the child for the time being.

Sooner or later you will have to decide on the terminology that you are going to use when referring to the child's biological parents. Some parents prefer to use the term "biological," but that is a rather difficult word for young children to use. Other parents use the term "natural parents," but that somehow implies that the adoptive parents are "unnatural." Some use "other mother," but "other" seems to imply that the child has two sets of parents, which is not really true because *you* are the people doing all the parenting. It is best not to use the term "real mother" or "real father" because you are your child's "real" parents in every sense but the biological one. I prefer the term "first mother" (or father) or "first parents," because the word "first" does not seem to have any disturbing connotations.

If your child is older and already knows the story of his or her adoption, you may be anticipating the time when he or she will ask specific questions about the biological parents: what their names were, who they were, where they are now. Some adoption agencies always give the parents a certain amount of information to use or not at their discretion. Other agencies ask the adoptive parents just how much, if any information, they want. And, of course, in the case of a private adoption, adoptive parents may know a great deal about the biological parents.

Maybe you have decided to tell your child that you do not know anything about the first parents. This may be the easiest way out for you, but it is very unfair to your child. He or she has a right to know about the people who gave him or her birth. Knowledge of the background rightfully belongs to him or her and is a part of the "child's identity and heritage". It is your responsibility to find out as much as you can about the child's background so that you have the information ready and available when he or she wants it.

There really is no reason for you to feel apprehensive when your child asks questions about his or her biological parents. The child is not challenging your right to be his or her parents. He or she is simply trying to satisfy the same natural curiosity about heritage that any of us may have. And you should be proud that he or she has enough faith in you to ask these questions.

What you say and how much you say is up to you, of course, but answer truthfully and naturally so that the child has no reason ever to feel hesitant or ashamed about wanting to know about him- or herself.

Since the majority of adopted children are born out of wedlock, it is highly likely that your adopted child was also. It will be easier to answer his or her questions about this if you remember two things: first it is possible for two people to love each other very much even though they are not married, and second, morality is not inherited. It is fortunate that in today's society the stigma of illegitimacy has been greatly diminished, if not totally eliminated.

Some time when your child is older, he or she may want to see the court records of the adoption, and he or she should know that you would consent to this. The child has a right to know all about his or her past, including the names of biological parents. But the child should be reminded that they have rights too, especially the right to privacy. When they released the child for adoption, they deliberately limited their role to giving birth and they might not be happy with the child's sudden reappearance in their lives so many years later.

Your child is adopted. This is a fact of his or her existence and the child must learn to accept it. There is not one thing that you can do to change this fact nor to make up for it—and there is no reason for you to try. Your child will accept his or her adoption fully and happily if you yourself have fully and happily accepted it.

Bankruptcy:

Alternative Methods for Financial Crisis

Kirk Y. K. Kim

Practically every person is a debtor at almost any particular moment of his or her existence since everyone customarily accepts something of value before making payment. Everyone becomes a debtor, for instance, when he or she consumes all the utilities from day to day until the monthly bill is paid. Usually the great majority of debts are eventually repaid. However, not everyone can pay off his or her debts.

Do you know the most common cause of financial crisis for an individual like yourself? The easy availability of credit is the one thing that encourages many young people to borrow beyond their ability to repay. Three-fifths of all heads of households under the age of 54 are paying on an installment purchase or loan. Credit is so easy to obtain from so many different sources that it sometimes seems endless. Increasing numbers of people borrow money to make payments on money borrowed earlier. Credit is like a disease. You think it will get better, but it never does. The credit card, indeed, has become a dangerous source of problems for people in our society.

Americans have said "charge it" with increasing frequency since the 1950s. In 1950, Americans owed $3.4 billion for purchases with a credit card, but at

This article was especially written for this book.

the end of 1974, they owed $26.5 billion, nearly a 700 percent increase in a quarter of a century (according to the Federal Reserve figures). Furthermore, these charge accounts represent only a little over 14 percent of the total loan outstanding for that year. Consequently, Americans spend a greater portion of their disposable personal income for the payment of debt. The ratio of credit outstanding to disposable personal income was 20.5 percent in 1973, as compared to 10.4 percent in 1950, according to the Statistical Abstract of the United States. Inevitably, this led to increasing payment delinquencies and bankruptcies. A record number of Americans fell behind in their home payments in the final quarter of 1973, according to the Mortgage Bankers Association of America. Furthermore, the Association said that the delinquency rate rose to 4.70 percent of all residential mortgages, with late payments on federally subsidized housing rising to 14.71 percent. The total number of bankruptcy cases filed with the Federal Bankruptcy Courts was 201,352 during 1971 as compared to 33,392 in 1950, according to the Statistical Abstract of the United States.

If you are not overwhelmed by these figures and facts, the story of my friend John might convince you how easy it is to get into financial trouble. John is a 26-year-old schoolteacher with a wife and two children. He is over his head in debt. He owes more than 10 creditors, more than $8,000, more than half of his annual salary. This is John's account of his financial crisis.

"It started about three years ago when my wife and I wanted to refurnish our home. We took out a loan for $1,200 from a bank. About the same time, we received a Master Charge and a BankAmericard in the mail. The first time I used one was when I needed $25 and didn't have any money in my pocket. It was so easy to say "charge it," just like saying, "Hi." We also got four different department store credit cards. Soon each account showed a balance of $200 or $300 without anything tangible to show for it. A few months later, we needed a car because the old one started to give us problems. So I bought a new car. Since the old car was not worth the down payment needed for the new one, I borrowed $500 from a private loan company and got a loan from my Credit Union for the remainder. I knew I was getting ripped off, but I needed a car. At the same time I picked up a couple of credit cards for gasoline. A few months later my father-in-law passed away in Idaho. So we borrowed another 500 bucks to take a trip out there to attend his funeral. During this trip the kids came down with an infection, and the medicine and doctor's fee during that month were running me $25 a week.

"I was taking home more than $850 a month, yet I did not have any money left over after making monthly payments on these accounts. Finally, I began to miss a payment on one of my loans. But I figured I could get a loan to cover my past dues and catch up. However, I got deeper and deeper in debt.

"It began with written reminders to pay up, and soon it was followed by threatening phone calls. About this time the home problems set in. My wife was upset most of the time and we fought often. What do I do now? Where should I go?"

It will never happen to you? Probably not. However, it *can* happen to anybody. This "buy now, pay later" philosophy has helped John, and many others, to enjoy a standard of living far beyond what they can afford. Unfortunately, the "pay later" time has arrived at a bad time for most Americans, including John. As inflation forces prices up and the recession takes jobs away, families have enough trouble just paying for necessities. The rising costs force one suddenly to rearrange the budget and make it difficult to juggle things to offset a higher cost of one good by using other inexpensive substituted goods. As they are forced to spend a large portion of their income for necessities, such as food and fuel, much less covers outstanding debts. What all this adds up to is a nightmare for many people like John. Everything is about to come due at once, and one cannot borrow from anybody anymore. Whatever the cause, it is the breaking point. When all things come crashing down, what should you do?

Aside from divorce, suicide, or running away from the country, there are a couple of alternative courses of action that a debtor like John can take— bankruptcy or a long, hard road back to solvency. For solvency, a plan for bailing out of debt must be developed. This plan can be developed by either the debtor him- or herself, based on what he or she knows of his or her needs and capabilities, or a credit counselor. The plan is usually developed based on some method of gaining time and facing austerity.

Remember that any creditor will listen to almost any plan that sounds even remotely like a solution. After all, what seems to be personal tragedy to you is a business problem to the creditors. They will feel that they must take whatever steps are open to them. This means repossession of the property, even forced bankruptcy, if such a course yields some hope of recovery. But the creditors will use these weapons only as a last resort because the above courses of action by the creditors are not only a nasty piece of business, but are generally unprofitable. Hence, creditors will listen to any feasible plan out of self-interest, if for no other reason.

One of the arrangements a debtor can make is a consolidation loan that involves a new loan from one lender, such as a bank, to pay off other debts. One large debt is often preferable to several small ones, even when they total the same amount, because it usually means smaller monthly payments with an extended repayment period. Also the interest rate on a single bank loan may well be less than those on the overdue debts. It is essential, however, to be certain that the terms of any consolidation loan are really an improvement, that is, it must not add any more financial burden.

Usually, creditors will have more trust in a plan developed by a third party, such as a community counseling agency. Caution in seeking advice from professional counseling services is necessary, however. Going to an unscrupulous debt counselor may mean adding another fee to an already unmanageable financial burden. By far the safest arrangement is one made with a community-supported, nonprofit counseling agency, such as the Consumer Budget Counseling Service, a nonprofit division of Family Service, or Financial and Debt Counseling Service, which offers free debt counseling.

One of the arrangements that budget counselors can make is a debt pooling arrangement, which requires a plan to pay off the debt. Usually, a debt counselor examines the family's living pattern first and will decide how much income is needed to keep the family going. The counselor then puts the rest to work paying off the debts. In this process, a counselor may find that the debtor's rent is too high and may suggest a move to a less expensive place. Usually, however, there are two items on which typical debtors are spending too much—entertainment and impulsive buying. Hence, a debt counselor will suggest either to cut down entertainment or to substitute less expensive forms. After setting up a budget for a debtor, a debt counselor will arrange, if necessary, for companies or financial institutions that have extended credit to reduce the amount of the monthly payments. Sometimes the counselor can arrange with them to prorate the debts and get the lender to agree to a smaller settlement for cash. Most of the creditors will go along with such a plan only if they can get an assurance that the debtor will stick to it. Therefore, it may be necessary for a counselor to plan and administer the payments.

Since the first step in a financial plan is to find out exactly how much money you have to work with and information on where the money is going, a debt counselor will persuade those deeply in debt to keep a record of every expenditure, because what seems like a nickel and dime is really $10 or $20.

Although community-supported counseling agencies offer free services, commercial budgeting services can charge 9 percent, or a maximum of $30 a month, for bill paying services. If there are no community-supported, free debt counseling agencies in your area, you may wish to consult with someone who can provide you a similar service, perhaps at a local college or university (generally faculty members either in economics, home economics, finance, or management departments).

You also have another alternative of getting out of debt by going to court, although you may have to spend more money, as well as risk losing some of your property, in doing so. This debt pooling arrangement is a form of bankruptcy known as "Chapter 13," based on Chapter 13 of the Federal Bankruptcy Law. This form of debt pooling involves a judge of one of the federal district courts that handles bankruptcies. Under the judge's direction, debtor, creditors, and a referee get together to work out a way for the debtor to settle up on an installment basis. This requires a $15 filing fee in the beginning and $15 when the plan is approved. In addition, there is normally a lawyer's fee, plus 9 percent for the trustee.

For the last alternative, there is the voluntary petition for straight bankruptcy. This requires a list of all assets and liabilities and a $50 filing fee, plus a $5 reporter's fee, and normally the services of a lawyer. Ordinarily, the rest is routine. All assets, except for clothing, tools, and some household goods, will be liquidated, and the proceeds from them will be distributed among the creditors.

Although the purpose of bankruptcy legislation is to distribute the debtor's assets among creditors equitably, and to release a debtor from debts and enable him or her to start fresh, the bankruptcy record will hound the person for years to come, if not for the rest of his or her life. Re-establishing a good credit rating will be very difficult, since the computer's memory is notorious for causing problems in re-establishing credit ratings, even for people who become very successful years later.

It is easier and less expensive to avoid the financial crisis than to cure it once it has already occurred. Often an affluent life-style lures many unsuspecting individuals to the brink of financial disaster. An increasing number of families have been forced into personal bankruptcy as a result of trying to "keep up" with the Joneses next door or from impulsive buying habits.

A life-style should satisfy the needs and wants of the individual, but one has to be pragmatic about his or her financial picture. Decisions on such things as housing, automobiles, vacations, and credit must take into consideration their economic impact. After having hard facts about how much you have and where the money is going, ask yourself the following questions: Can I (or we) afford it? Do I want it enough to spend that much for it instead of for something else? Is it the most economical way to get it? Sensible answers to these questions will lead to an enjoyable and manageable spending pattern.

Last, everyone needs a plan for handling a financial emergency. For this, one has to look at savings as an obligation and take it off the top of take-home pay. By having such a cushion, a debtor can stay out of trouble.

REFERENCES

MANDELL, LEWIS, *Credit Card Use in the United States.* Ann Arbor, Mich.: The University of Michigan Press, 1972.

MEYER, MARTIN J., *Credit-Cardsmanship: How to Survive the Credit Card Nightmare and Turn Plastic Into Gold.* New York: Farnsworth Publishing Company, Inc., 1971.

MOORE, GEOFFREY H., AND PHILIP A. KLEIN, *The Quality of Consumer Installment Credit*. New York: National Bureau of Economic Research, 1967.

RAIHALL, T., ed., *Money Management for the Consumer*. Boston: Little, Brown and Company, Inc., 1973.

SMITH, LEN YOUNG, AND G. GALE ROBERSON, *Business Law*. St. Paul, Minn.: West Publishing Company, 1966.

Dignity and Welfare

Your Right to Both

Ralph G. Navarre

The process of applying for public welfare is a situation that brings about a great deal of internal conflict and distress. The application process is often seen as impersonal, degrading, and vindictive. There is no doubt that for most people who need welfare, having to apply for it is a major problem. This chapter will attempt to give an understanding of the welfare system and the resources available within it. With this information, you and your family can move through the system if the need arises, without psychological damage, loss of dignity or pride.

The welfare systems toward which most people feel negatively include Aid to Families with Dependent Children (AFDC), general relief, food stamps, Social Security Supplemental Income, and Medical Assistance. In addition, some people also hesitate to apply for federal and state insurance benefits (even though they prepaid part of the cost), such as Social Security and unemployment and disability benefits.

The first step in the welfare application process occurs before you ever decide to apply for welfare benefits. *You* must look at and clarify your ideas about receiving help from someone. Remember that your attitudes about

This article was especially written for this book.

welfare were learned from your parents, brothers and sisters, friends, teachers, and others you grew up with, plus the people you now see every day. If these people were lucky (mainly middle class, stable jobs, happy homes, educated), your ideas about welfare are probably very negative. In fact, applying for welfare may be a blot on the family record, or seen as your fault or your failure.

If some of the people around you have been on welfare, your ideas of it may be of a system designed to strip you of dignity, pride, and the right to make decisions. Also many people's attitudes on welfare are shaped by the ideas of the Judeo-Christian ethic about work, family relationships, and asking for help.

What are the facts about welfare? Government-sponsored welfare programs were set up to serve all people in need, regardless of race, religion, or national origin. Each program has specific eligibility requirements that may vary from state to state, county to county, or even township to township. All programs that receive any federal money as partial payment for the costs of service have eligibility rules clearly spelled out with court cases to support decisions made in the past. Welfare from private agencies and from local levels of government is often not clearly spelled out, and there is often disagreement as to who is eligible.

The point to remember is that welfare is clearly a *right* if the program receives federal reimbursement. However, you must apply, and often you may have to prove that you are eligible. Access to welfare programs and social services in private agencies is often limited to certain religious, ethnic, or specialized groups, such as the handicapped. These programs may not be open to all citizens of a community.

General relief is the oldest local government-supported welfare program and the one that creates the most problems. Each state controls general relief differently and the laws governing eligibility vary widely. General relief is a program of last resort. If you have no other eligibility, no large amounts of money, and no other resources, you should apply for general relief.

YOUR ATTITUDE

How does your attitude affect the application process? Because of personal attitudes, some people who apply for welfare see themselves as being harrassed, humiliated, or discriminated against in many of their dealings with welfare department officials. In some cases, discriminatory or inappropriate actions have been made by welfare personnel. In far too many cases, however, clients have been unable, unwilling, or ashamed to ask for explanations of what was happening or why a certain action was taken. The welfare application process is made up of hundreds of judgments. The workers must decide what eligibility questions to ask and how to apply the answers.

If you act as if you don't belong or are trying to hide something, the worker will try to discover what is wrong. For example, your anxiety about eligibility may be related to your need or your embarrassment, but you mistakenly may be convincing the worker that you have additional income, which you are not reporting.

Since eligibility is based on documented evidence and not your attitude, it may sound strange to emphasize your attitude so strongly, but time after time when the applicant is dissatisfied with the decision, part of the problem is related to his or her attitude.

What type of an attitude should you have as an applicant? Most importantly, you are a person with dignity and worth who has to ask society for help at this point. In federally reimbursed programs, you have a legally defined right to this help if you meet certain eligibility requirements. In addition, you have the right to receive a specific explanation as to why you are not eligible and the right to know what steps you can take to become eligible. In the entire application process, your attitude should be one of an interested participant who, as a reasonable adult, knows his or her rights. You should impress people that you will follow through, even to the formal appeal process if necessary.

Suppose your attitude is good but you are stuck with a "bad" interviewer? First, try to find out why the interviewer seems "bad." Here is where your being interested in the interviewer can pay off in a good long-term relationship. Is this the interviewer's tenth or twentieth interview today? Is the interviewer carrying over feelings from the last interview? This is not your problem, but it surely will affect your interview. If your interviewer is relaxed and not filled with stress, he or she should do the job better, faster, and with less negative impact on you.

WORKING WITH THE SYSTEM

Many programs may require a variety of evidence or proofs before eligibility can be decided. In many cases, you can collect and sort these items before you are required to submit them as evidence. You can ask what proofs are necessary when you first contact the agency. Often you will find that one or more items needed to verify your claim or application may be lost, stolen, or misplaced. Remember that this same thing happens to thousands of people each year. Do not become defensive, angry, or upset with the interviewer. Instead, explain the loss and ask for the interviewer's help or advice on how to establish the needed record or fact. Often the interviewer can verify, with a few phone calls or letters, records that could take you weeks to prove. In all cases, there is no record that cannot be established in some way or another. Dates of births, marriages, and divorces all have been proven even when all records have been lost or destroyed.

Many personal questions that are asked in the interview process also create problems for the person trying to make a claim or to establish eligibility for welfare benefits. Questions of age, racial or religious background, legitimacy of children, and personal or sexual relationships are often seen as prying or even immaterial to the approval of a claim or application for benefits. In all cases, you have the right to refuse to answer questions that you consider offensive or prying. However, be aware that such refusal may result in the denial or rejection of your claim or application. In addition, the refusal to answer questions or, even worse, the giving of false information again raises the question of what it is that you are trying to hide.

The questions of age, racial and religious background, and legitimacy of children are often required by law, and although they may be personally offensive, they should be answered if there is a logical connection to the claim or application being made. Again, remember that thousands of people are asked these questions each week and most interviewers have no personal interest in your replies. The interviewer by law may not discuss your responses with anyone not connected with processing your claim or application.

A few interviewers may express personal or moral judgments to you or to others in your presence. In such a situation, you can ask to talk to a supervisor and, after explaining the situation, request a new interviewer.

Questions about your personal and sexual relationships are much harder to deal with since some of the information may be necessary to your claim or application while other information is not. Only you can decide if you wish to talk about this information. If you decide that the information is not necessary, ask the interviewer to show you in the manual why he or she considers it necessary. If you still disagree, tell the interviewer that you plan to appeal the case if your application is denied.

APPEALS

In any case where your needs have not been met adequately or appropriately, you have the right to appeal the decisions being made concerning your claim or application. There are at least five different routes to appeal any decision the agency makes concerning you. These appeal routes include:

1. Appeal within the agency for supervisory or administrative correction of a wrong decision.
2. Appeal to the governing or administrative board of the agency for a policy or administrative ruling to change how the agency operates.
3. Appeal through the courts for a legal change in the operation or inter- pretation of a rule or guideline.
4. Appeal to community pressure by making your story known via newspapers, radio, and television.
5. Appeal to your state and federal legislature to change laws and the in- terpretation of laws so that you are eligible for the program.

It is important to remember that once you set the appeal process in motion, you set up an adversary relationship of you against THEM. It is always better to resolve an issue without an appeal if possible.

If it is not possible to settle an issue at the interviewer level, talk to the inter- viewer's supervisor. Supervisors have more experience and usually can give you written proof as to why the worker reached a certain decision. You are en- titled to know why you were denied. If no documentation or evidence is pro- vided, begin to ask questions about the appeal process at this level. If the superivsor is right and has clear evidence of his or her correct decision, he or she will probably encourage you to appeal if you think the agency is wrong. Remember, the supervisor looks good if the agency is supported as correct in the appeal process. The supervisor may also urge you to appeal if he or she has no clear guidelines. Your appeal may set agency policy for other cases on his or her desk. If the supervisor thinks you have a legitimate argument that raises a new policy issue, he or she may involve the division supervisor or even the agency director. A calm rational discussion will often get your claim or application accepted by someone in the administrative system.

If the top administrator does not accept your argument, you must file a formal appeal or give up. A formal appeal is the quasi-legal process in which a hearing examiner listens to both sides of an issue and makes a decision. This is a formal process with a legal secretary, who makes a complete record of everything that takes place. You can usually bring a lawyer and witnesses to this appeal hearing. Remember that the agency will use this record in court if you challenge the decision through the court system. If your claim is a large one, you should involve an attorney *before* you file a formal appeal. Often an attorney will help you word the appeal so that you get a judgment in your favor. If you do not have money for an attorney, legal aid societies or local bar associations often will provide lawyers at reduced rates or free, if your case has merit.

Even if your formal appeal before the hearing examiner is denied, you can still make an appearance before the agency's governing board to ask them to change the rules that affect you. If the formal appeal process and the appeal to the board both fail, you have the right and privilege to carry the case to the courts. This is long, expensive process and must involve a lawyer.

Two other appeal routes are still open. You can take your story to news reporters who may or may not think your case has merit. For example, the agency may be correct in its interpretation of the law, but perhaps that law needs to be improved to serve better those in need. Community pressure may force the agency to accept your case and help you, even though you are not technically eligible.

Finally, if all else fails you should work with your state and federal legislators to change the law.

THE PROGRAMS THAT CAN HELP

In the following paragraphs we will look at some of the major welfare and insurance programs and give you some of the general guidelines that the agencies use in providing services or money. Since many agencies and insurance programs are state or locally operated, and therefore have a range of eligibility requirements that you must meet, *you* must apply at the agency or agencies where you think you are eligible for services and money.

AFDC

If you are a single parent (unmarried, divorced, widowed) or a two-parent family where one parent cannot work because of young children at home, you may be eligible for AFDC (Aid to Families with Dependent Children). The program is directed primarily for the child's benefit, with the adults being provided for as the child's caretakers. Each state has its own eligibility requirements and they vary widely as to resources you may possess and money and services that are available.

Although there is controversy about this program, most clients do not abuse it and actually are on aid for less than one year. Most clients use the program as a bridge between an old life and the resettling necessary to begin a new one.

Food Stamp Program and Medical Assistance

Two other programs that are often sponsored by the same agency handling the AFDC program are the Food Stamp Program and the Medical Assistance

Program. If income or resources make you ineligible for AFDC or you just do not want it, you may be eligible for these two very specifically directed programs.

The Food Stamp Program is federally regulated under the Department of Agriculture but administered locally by welfare departments. You can buy food stamp coupons at a discount, which your grocer will redeem for food at full face value. The less money you earn, the greater the discount. The major problems in this program are that you must buy all of your coupons for each month at one time and you must have sufficient money to pay for these coupons at the time of purchase. Also, only nutritional foods are redeemable for food stamps.

The Department of Agriculture also regulates the local school hot lunch program. If you have a low income, your children may be eligible for reduced cost or even free school lunches. See your local school principal about this.

The Medical Assistance Program is aimed at providing care and treatment of your children's medical problems. It is directed at those major or catastrophic illnesses or accidents that can deplete a family's resources. You will be required to pay a share of the expenses, with the amount the program will pay based on your income, number of family members, and other verified expenses and bills.

Social Security Supplemental Income Programs

These programs are administered by the Social Security Administration. They serve the blind, disabled, and people over 65 who have very low or no Social Security benefits. Check with your local Social Security office to see if you may be eligible for these programs.

Old Age, Survivors, and Disability Insurance Programs

The insurance programs our society provides often are either ignored or misused.

The OASDI (Old Age, Survivors, and Disability Insurance) programs, also called the Social Security Program, is often described as a welfare program and so it is not used as much as it could be. You must remember that most people who work for others pay a tax for this income protection from their paycheck each payday. More than 80 percent of all workers are now covered by either the OASDI program or some equivalent, such as the Railroad Retirement Benefits or Armed Forces Benefits. Your OASDI benefits are built up over the time that you work. The amount of benefits available are determined by the number of three-month periods worked. This work record is recorded in terms of "covered quarters." Records are kept by computer, using your Social Security number as the reference. Keep all family Social Security numbers safe and use the benefits you paid for when you become eligible.

You should also be aware that minor children, young adults in college, and mentally retarded children and adults whose parents cannot support them may be eligible for coverage under the OASDI. Check at the Social Security office for eligibility. You may be eligible as early as age 55 for some benefits and are eligible for benefits at any age if totally and permanently disabled.

Workman's Compensation and Unemployment Compensation

The Workman's Compensation programs are federally required, state-operated programs that employers pay for and that are designed to protect you. If you are injured or disabled on the job or in a job-related accident, you may be eligible for Workman's Compensation benefits. Since a large number of claims raise the employer's insurance rates, each employer will work hard to avoid being found negligent or at fault. These claims must be pressed diligently or benefits will be lost.

Another program funded by the employer is the Unemployment Compensation program. Benefits are paid if your employer lays you off or in other ways terminates your employment. Again, rates go up if the employer has large numbers of claims, so you must press claims actively if you are to be successful.

In both the Workman's Compensation and Unemployment Compensation programs, there are literally thousands of specific rules and guidelines made over the years. You may have to file legal challenges and wait months to receive benefits. If you are declared eligible, however, the wait is worthwhile. Also remember that in times of high unemployment, it may take several months to receive benefits. Apply as soon as you think you may be eligible.

SUMMARY

The most important factor when you apply for any type of public welfare program is simply yourself. You must have a good attitude and a positive image of yourself, your family, and the program that may best serve you.

You must always keep in mind that you may be eligible for a number of different programs at any single point. You will only find out what programs you are eligible for if you ask. One of the problems of being human is that it is very hard to ask for help. The reality is, however, that unless you are willing to ask for help, you will never receive the benefits that you are entitled to and that you have paid for.

Finally, remember that this chapter touched on only a few of the largest programs that provide resources and services to people. No matter what problem you have, there is an agency, a program, or a person who is able and willing to help you.

How to Avoid
Becoming a Crime Victim

Dae H. Chang

Crime is our nation's biggest problem. It has become so serious that the President of the United States, as well as the Attorney General, has called crime our "number one enemy" and said that "we must declare war against it." In 1975 there were nearly 10 million Crime Index[1] offenses reported to law enforcement agencies. From the mid-1960s to the mid-1970s, crime has increased annually between 5 to 10 percent. Particularly alarming are the statistics on violent crime—murder, forcible rape, aggravated assault, and armed robbery.

Since 1969, violent crimes as a group have increased 47.3 percent and property crimes 37.5 percent. In 1974 there were 20,600 murders, 55,210 forci-

This article was especially written for this book.

[1]Crime Index offenses include the following: (1) criminal homicide, (2) forcible rape, (3) robbery, (4) aggravated assault, (5) burglary-breaking or entering, (6) larceny-theft (except auto theft), (7) auto theft, (8) other assaults, (9) arson, (10) forgery and counterfeiting, (11) fraud, (12) embezzlement, (13) stolen property, buying, receiving, possessing, (14) vandalism, (15) weapons, carrying, possessing, and so on, (16) prostitution and commercialized vice, (17) sex offenses (except forcible rape, prostitution, and commercialized vice), (18) narcotic drug laws, (19) gambling, (20) offenses against the family and children, (21) driving under the influence, (22) liquor laws, (23) drunkenness, (24) disorderly conduct, (25) all other offenses, (26) suspicion, (27) curfew and loitering laws, and (28) runaway (juvenile). For further detailed information, see *Crime in the United States 1973: Uniform Crime Report,* Federal Bureau of Investigation, U. S. Department of Justice, Washington, D. C.: Government Printing Office, 1975, pp. 6-7.

ble rapes, 441,290 robberies, 452,720 aggravated assaults, 3,020,700 burglaries, 5,227,700 larceny-thefts, and 973,800 auto thefts.

It appears that there is no safe haven for people to live. People are told not to walk alone on the street at night or even in daylight in certain sections of larger cities. People are told to lock their houses, businesses, bicycles, and autos. Schools and cars are vandalized, traffic signs are ripped off, banks are robbed, and planes are hijacked. Purse snatching is prevalent in shopping centers, and older people are often victimized. Between 1969-1974, nighttime residence burglary was up 60 percent and daytime residence burglary was up 67 percent. Nonresidence burglaries were also up. During the same period, purse snatching was up 3 percent and shoplifting 76 percent. During 1965-1974 there were altogether 947 police officers killed in the line of duty.

If we are to compute the occurrence of crime according to time:

1. Serious crimes — 19 each minute.
2. Violent crimes such as murder, forcible rape, and so on — 1 every 33 seconds.
3. Murder — 1 every 26 minutes.
4. Forcible rape — 1 every 10 minutes.
5. Aggravated assault — 1 every 70 seconds.
6. Robbery — 1 every 71 seconds.
7. Burglary — 1 every 10 seconds.
8. Larceny-theft — 1 every 6 seconds.
9. Auto theft — 1 every 32 seconds.

How can these crimes occur while we contend that we are "educated," "civilized," and "humane," and still crime increases every year? The above statistics are only reported cases. There are literally millions of Americans who commit crimes but are never reported or arrested and therefore never prosecuted. These people are either called "hidden criminals" or "social criminals." There are also many "white collar" crimes that are never detected and prosecuted.

Research shows that much crime — and by far the greatest portion of street crime and burglary — is the result of opportunity and luck rather than of careful and professional planning. Someone sees an "opportunity" — in an open window, an empty house, a person alone in a dark alley — and acts on it. Muggers look for likely victims, not specific individuals; burglars, for a house they can enter, not a particular address. Preselected targets frequently are chosen precisely because they are seen as "easy marks."

Who is the victim of a crime? What causes crime? Who causes crime? There are some startling answers to these questions. In the majority of cases, the victim contributes, and in some cases is a major cause, of a criminal act. All of us are potential victims. We frequently present the criminal or an individual with an invitation to commit a crime. We entice him (or her), advertise to him, coax him, give him the opportunity, and even implant the idea into his head. Through our carelessness, open disregard for our personal possessions, forgetfulness, attitudes, vanity, or whatever, we frequently invite someone to commit a criminal act either directly at ourselves or to our possessions. We also invite bodily harm upon ourselves by our actions in public and private. Our habits, attitudes, dress all are signals to the people who would be enticed into crime. In fact, we might commit crimes ourselves, although we would not look at them as crimes, but they nevertheless are. The things we do are witnessed by others and may send them an incorrect message as to our intentions. A prime example of this is the C.B. (citizen's band radio) phenomenon. It can be presumed that the major use of the C.B. in recent years by the operator is to escape from receiving a speeding ticket while speeding. This behavior, therefore, implies a message of legitimate disobedience to the law. Although this message may not be intentional, it is nevertheless the one received by the operator's significant others, thereby portraying an incorrect message.

Strictly speaking, we are all potential criminals and at the same time potential *victims* of a crime. In almost all crime cases, there are victims. Offenders have a choice as to whom they wish to victimize, what houses to burglarize, and what banks they choose to rob. Even though we do not wish to admit it readily, we are in some sense patronizing crime and organized crime syndicates. In many of the larger cities one can easily obtain a "catalogue" that contains many stolen "hot" items, ranging from brand new color televisions, expensive Japanese-made cameras, diamonds, watches, any-make automobiles, antiques, hi-fi sets, electric typewriters, and a host of other household goods. Why pay more to buy the same in legitimate stores when one can obtain the same brand and quality goods at the price of one-fifth of the retail store price? Thus, we are continuing to keep the criminal population operating in large cities because we make criminals know that "crime does pay."

CRIME AGAINST PERSONS

Generally speaking, crimes against persons are known as crimes of "violence." They include: (1) criminal homicide, (2) rape, (3) assault, and (4) robbery. Murder is commonly known as a "crime of passion," because the majority of homicide cases are directed at persons known to each other as lover, friend, wife/husband, business associate, relative, neighbor, roommate, and so on. Homicide is usually the highest during the summer; the same for forcible rape and aggravated assault. About 67 percent of murders involve handguns, rifles, and shotguns.

The circumstances of murder can be divided into the following categories: (1) spouse killing spouse, 12.1 percent, (2) parent killing child, 2.7 percent, (3) other family killing, 8.0 percent, (4) romantic triangle and lover's quarrels, 6.2 percent, (5) other arguments, 43.2 percent, and (6) known felony (or suspected felony) type, 27.8 percent. A felony is a major crime for which state or federal statute provides a greater punishment (generally a minimum of one year) than for a misdemeanor (generally a maximum of one year). The penalty for a felony conviction is usually imprisonment in a state or federal penitentiary.

With the exception of murder by professionals, the majority of homicides involve intense emotions and a sense of determination. Small arguments gradually escalate to heated debates and culminate in "eliminating" the opponent. Arguments on political, social, religious, philosophical, and personality problems enter into homicide incidences. Sometimes gossip triggers homicide. There are millions of reasons why people take certain problems too seriously. Most of the daily problems can be resolved and understood simply by remaining calm and objectively analyzing the "issue."

The usual sequence for homicidal impact follows like this: at first an "issue" arises and then emotionally becomes encased in "rightness-wrongness" arguments. Most issues, arguments, or discussions should be stopped at the preemotional level—in fact, a word "issue" means there is no readily acceptable solution to the problem. When one persists on a given issue and continues arguing on the issue, the issue becomes a "moral" issue, which seems to break down into "good" and "bad" or "black" and "white." Once this point is reached, the argument becomes "personalized," and emotions will set into the discussion. Naturally then, "good" and "bad" becomes the central issue at which a "breakdown" of logic, rationality, and objectivity occurs. Finally, there is a "breakdown of communication," and those arguing no longer speak to each other. Unless the arguers agree to enter into a compromise, or mutually agree not to discuss the matter further, or one side gives in and becomes a "loser," or a third party provides an opportunity for mutual concession, or the arguers mutually agree to "laugh it off" as a mere joke, the situation will not lead to a solution. In summary, most serious arguments start with people you know and frequently involve alcohol. Arguments often "hurt" one's ego or pride. A person does not like to admit defeat; in fact, after a few drinks he or she may become upset, and daily frustrations with job, neighbors, peers, wife (husband) or lover, debts, and the like may end up being directed at one person.

In our industrial, urbanized society, every person may at some time become frustrated by monotonous jobs, job insecurity, competition, a sense of helplessness, impersonal relationships, and the like. Those who feel they no longer can solve their problems, which they may have largely created, may attempt to take their own lives or prey on someone else as a means to end their problems "once and for all." Murderers are, to a large extent, taking the law into their own hands as a means to solve problems. Of course, they are not solving their problems; in fact, they are compounding their difficulties.

The so-called aggravated assault (an unlawful attack by one person upon another for the purpose of inflicting severe bodily injury, often accompanied by the use of a weapon) is on the rise throughout the United States. It is estimated that about a half million assaults occur annually, which constitutes 5 percent of the Crime Index offenses and 48 percent of the crimes of violence. Most aggravated assaults occur within the family and among neighbors or acquaintances. The victim-offender relationship, as well as the nature of attack, makes this crime similar to murder.

Another crime of violence is forcible rape, defined as the carnal knowledge of a female through the use of force or the threat of force. Assaults to commit forcible rape are also included; however, statutory rape (without force) is not counted in this category. During 1974, there were an estimated 55,210 forcible rapes—numerically, the volume increased by 3,980 offenses over 1973, about an 8 percent increase. In 1974, 74 percent of all forcible rape offenses were actual rape by force; the remainder were attempts to commit forcible rape. Most police agencies, as well as medical and social welfare agencies, recognize this offense as probably one of the most underreported crimes, due to fear and/or embarrassment on the part of the victims.

The age grouping of males 16 to 24 years of age constituted the greatest concentration of arrests for forcible rape in 1974. Sixty percent of the arrests for forcible rape were under the age of 25.

Victim-offender relationships are divided half and half. Some have known each other previously and some are complete strangers. There need not be any plans or preparations on the part of an offender to commit rape. The offender may simply find the situation "ripe for rape."

In our world of commercialism, mass media excites sexual passions in many ways. Television commercials, movies, and magazines make full use of "love," "passion," and "sex" to deliver their messages to audiences. Women must become more cautious and aware of possible rape situations. They must avoid places or situations where rape is possible or likely (see Chapter 31).

It has been theorized that the legalization of prostitution might reduce the number of rapes. Whether legalized or not, prostitution flourishes in large cities (and elsewhere) in the United States (or for that matter throughout the world). Legalization of prostitution is a political issue for which there is no quick answer. This section emphasizes that precautionary measures must be taken not to become an offender or a victim of rape.

CRIME AGAINST PROPERTIES

Robbery

Robbery is a vicious crime when it takes place in the presence of the victim to obtain property or a thing of value from a person by use of force or threat of force. Robbery is classified by the FBI as a violent crime because robbery frequently results in injury to the victim. More frequently, robbers use some sort of arms or weapons. Each year approximately 440,000 robbery offenses occur in the United States, which make up between 4 to 5 percent of the total crime index and comprise about 46 percent of the crimes of violence.

Robbery offenses occur most frequently during the month of December, which can be attributed to the winter season. As the nights get longer and the air gets colder, people restrain their out-of-doors activities, thereby giving the robber greater freedom to roam around unnoticed. The physical environment is in favor of the criminal. These conditions combined with the financial pressures of the holiday season partly account for the increase in crime during this month.

The heaviest volume of robbery offenses occurs in the northeastern states. Suburban areas surrounding the large core cities reported a 23 percent increase and rural areas recorded an upward trend of 22 percent. The FBI disclosed that half of the robberies were committed in the street. The average bank robbery dollar loss decreased from $4,653 in 1973 to $3,598 in 1974. The 1969-1974 trends indicate gas or service station holdups have decreased 20 percent; chain store robberies increased 184 percent; street robberies 29 percent; robberies in residences 63 percent; and holdups of other commercial or business establishments rose 42 percent.

Burglary

Burglary is defined as the unlawful entry of a structure to commit a felony or theft. The use of force to gain entry is not required to classify the crime as a burglary. It is estimated that a total of 3,020,700 burglaries occurred in 1974. This represents about 30 percent of the total volume in property crime index. The southern states reported the highest percentage of burglary (31 percent), in 1974, the western and north central states followed with 24 percent each, and the northeastern states with 21 percent. Viewed monthly, the highest volume of burglaries, like robberies, occurred in December.

Burglary is generally accepted as a crime of stealth and opportunity. It is committed by both amateurs and professionals. Viewed as a group, nighttime burglary represents 61 percent of all burglaries. Economically, the offense of burglary represents a substantial sum. Victims suffered a loss of $1.2 billion in 1974. During the same period, residential losses amounted to $758 million. The average dollar loss per burglary was $391 in 1974.

Larceny-Theft

Larceny-theft is the unlawful taking or stealing of property or articles without the use of force, violence, or fraud. It includes crimes such as shop lifting, pocket picking, purse snatching, theft from autos, thefts of auto parts and accessories, bicycle thefts, and so on. In 1974, there were 5,227,700 offenses of larceny-theft, which means a 21 percent increase compared to the previous year. Nationwide, this offense has increased 35 percent since 1969.

The average value of property stolen in each larceny in 1974 was $156, up from $111 in 1969 and $74 in 1960. When the average dollar value is applied to the estimated crime in this category, the total dollar loss was $816 million. The average value of goods and property reported stolen from victims of pickpockets was $117, by purse snatchers $75, by shoplifters $32, by theft from autos $180, and by miscellaneous thefts from buildings $271.

Auto Theft

Auto theft is defined as the unlawful taking or stealing of a motor vehicle, including attempts. In 1974, 973,800 motor vehicles were reported stolen, an increase of 5 percent compared to 1973. Auto theft is primarily an urban, large city phenomenon. Across the nation, 1 out of every 129 registered automobiles was stolen. The average value of stolen automobiles was $1,246 at the time of theft.

As in prior years, most persons arrested for auto theft were young people. In 1974, 55 percent of all persons arrested for this crime were under 18 years of age. When persons under 21 are included in the computation, the proportion of arrests rises to 74 percent. Females under 18 years of age recorded an increase of 4 percent in arrests for auto theft over 1973.

RECOMMENDED SOLUTIONS

There are many ways to avoid becoming a crime victim. The following suggestions are not necessarily listed in the order of importance; however, the individual should study his or her own situation before choosing the proper recommendation that would benefit most.

1. It may sound silly, but the majority of Americans do not know exactly what they own and where these properties are located. An inventory should be taken every year, not only for tax and insurance purposes, but also for protection of personal belongings. Many people report thefts, then find the missing item later in a forgotten place.

2. Survey your residence structure, including proper functioning of doors, knobs, locks, and exits. Consult private security organizations for obtaining security checkup recommendations. Consider installing a burglar alarm system (see the Yellow Pages for further information and call a security company for free estimates and security planning). Burglar alarm systems have proven to be a very effective, although somewhat expensive approach to curbing break-ins. Guard dogs have become popular in recent years (mainly for businesses).

3. Private residence dwellings (as well as commercial, apartment, and industrial) should not keep important papers, expensive jewelries, antiques, and other permanent items. Rent a local bank security deposit box. Such measures not only protect valuables from burglars but also protect them in case of fire or flood.

4. When you are going on an extended vacation, or even if the house is to be empty overnight, leave telephone numbers, addresses, including a rough itinerary, to trusted neighbors, just "in case." Let your neighbors check your mail daily (do not leave a mailbox full of mail or newspapers to inform burglars that you are away from home). Inform the post office and police department when you are leaving and when you are returning. The post office will hold your mail, and the police will patrol your neighborhood if you ask them. This is a public service without cost.

5. Sometimes residential burglars, knowing you are away from home, approach neighbors, pretending that your house needs repair work, such as plumbing, television repair, or carpet cleaning. Burglars make it appear that they are on a legitimate business mission. If something needs to be done in the home while you are away, be sure to let someone supervise at all times. Don't trust strangers! Tell your neighbors to call the police if repair trucks remain in the driveway.

6. When you are away from home, either one room or two should be lighted at night. Burglars do not like visibility. Don't accumulate milk bottles on the door step. Let someone mow your lawn. The shades should be half open while you are away.

7. If you own a car with all sorts of flashy equipment on it, you are inviting theft. Mag wheels, slicks, fancy wheel covers, chrome or expensive carburetors, chrome heads, special and expensive gadgets draw attention to your car. In fact, burglars do not just steal fancy equipment either. They often take ordinary items such as batteries, tires, or rearview mirrors. The very place a person leaves or parks his or her car can be an invitation for it to be either stolen or robbed. Particular caution must be exercised if you have an expensive item such as a stereo tape player, two-way radio, or other valuables kept in the car. Be sure to lock your car; never leave the key in the ignition. Put any valuables in the trunk of the car.

8. Do not leave home while you are expecting someone to visit you. If you do have to leave, do not leave any notes or messages outside. People sometimes leave a note on their door: "Will be home at 5 P.M. Door is unlocked. Walk in and make yourself at home." Burglars often do.

9. Inspect your house every night and lock all doors. You are inviting crime if you leave a lawn mower in the yard, a bicycle or wagon, power tools, and bar-b-que grill in the driveway.

10. Be cautious about inviting door-to-door salesmen into your house. Many communities and city governments (or police departments) require salesmen to carry a certain identification card. Some of these people are doing nothing more than making a quick survey of an area and will come back later and steal things they have seen while posing as salesmen. Don't sign any papers until you contact the local Chamber of Commerce or Better Business Bureau to check the authenticity of the products.

11. Are you one of those people who still leave the key under the doormat, in the mailbox, on top of the door ledge, or behind a shingle? If you are, you are asking to become a victim.

12. Do not carry a large sum of cash. If you do, don't go to congested areas such as a bus station, shopping center, airport terminal, or subway where a large number of people are constantly on the move. Pickpockets do their best business in busy crowds. Place your wallet in a safe place, not your back pocket. A man or woman with a large open-topped bag or purse is a prime target for a purse snatcher. Do not leave your purse unattended while looking for some sale items or trying on clothes in the store. It could invite a bystander to become a criminal and you to become the victim.

13. No one should stand along the highway hitchhiking alone. Frequently, a free ride may cost much more than bus fare. In fact, you could become a victim of rape, assault, robbery, or even murder.

14. In the middle of the night, occupants may detect intruders (burglars) entering the house. Be cautious and never take drastic action trying to chase

away intruders. Your manner of handling the situation, including your reaction, might endanger your life. Take note of the following: (a) never make yourself known when burglars are in your house, (b) never shout, scream, or show panic, (c) don't try to telephone the police while a burglary is in progress, (d) never take out a weapon to scare an intruder, (e) if an intruder tells you to do something, follow instructions faithfully and calmly—if you don't, more serious consequences may follow, such as kidnapping, assault, serious injury, or even loss of life. Most burglars want to conceal their identity. Most burglars carry some kind of weapon. Even though they do not like to use them, you, as a victim, may force the use of a weapon. Never take any overt action against intruders. When they have gone, call the police. Try to remember, as far as possible, physical characteristics, weapon held, escape route and method, and so on. Also survey what has been taken and provide any clues, including serial numbers of the items. Cooperate with the police, otherwise they will not be able to recover your property.

15. Research has demonstrated that increased street lighting is an effective crime prevention technique. Where bright lights have been installed, violent street crimes (such as assault and robbery) have been sharply reduced, along with the frequency of burglaries, auto thefts, and other crimes.

16. Bolt-locking doors and windows and extensive exterior lighting are usually sufficient to frustrate most burglary techniques.

17. Keeping only essential cash or convertible securities on the premises is recommended, and engraving identification numbers on possession curbs fencing of stolen property. Remember—burglary is a crime of opportunity.

CONCLUSION

In this chapter, it has been pointed out that police, courts, and correctional agencies alone cannot control crime effectively. Former Attorney General William Saxbe stated:[2]

Somehow, the people in this country have come to think that the courts and the police and the prisons are the instruments with which we can solve the criminal problem in this country. That's a mistake that should be set right. . . . Every citizen and every family has a responsibility.

The author agrees fully with William Saxbe. To reduce crime, we all must utilize every available means and preventive precaution. To do an effective job, substantial monies and time will be required. Taking special caution, as suggested above, would result in increased civil peace in the home, communi-

[2]*NEAA Newsletter*, Vol. 4, No. 3, August-September 1974, U.S. Department of Justice, Law Enforcement Assistance Administration, Washington, D.C., p. 10.

ty, and nation. Federal and state crime prevention agencies are increasingly recognizing the merits of this approach and are engaging in extensive efforts to inform citizens on how to avoid becoming victims.

The victim-avoidance approach will be successful when people develop the awareness of continually asking themselves, "Are my current actions or carelessness inviting crime, and what precautions should I take right away?"

How to
Hire, Fire, and Pay
an Attorney

Joseph K. Kuemmel

Attorneys come in all sizes, shapes, ages, and prices. Size, shape, and age are not important; skill, price, and experience are. The first thing to consider in choosing an attorney is what kind of attorney you are going to need. Most attorneys handle general problems, such as wills, traffic tickets, real estate matters, small disputes. Other problems may require an attorney familiar with the area of law governing your case. If you are charged with a criminal offense, you should hire an attorney who specializes in criminal matters. Criminal, corporate, patent, tax, maritime, and labor law are areas that require a specific kind of experience to be aware of the latest changes in the law, as well as knowing exactly how the court system in your particular county or area functions. This means that the attorney who drew up your will may not be the same attorney you will need to represent you if you are charged with a crime or desire to patent an invention. There are times when your problem does not fall into a clearly defined category. You should then ask yourself what type of skill your attorney will need. Should he or she be a trial lawyer, that is, someone who tries cases in courtrooms or in front of juries? Many at-

This article was especially written for this book.

torneys do no courtroom work and have no desire to. Will your attorney have to be aggressive? Will he or she have to be especially skillful in negotiating with difficult or emotional people, perhaps an important consideration in divorce or child custody cases. Will the attorney have to have experience or knowledge of the law and procedures of states other than the one in which he or she resides?

Once you determine what area of law governs your problem, the next step is to choose an attorney who handles your type of case on a regular basis. Several county bar associations have what are called "Lawyer Referral Systems." Often there is a phone number listed in the Yellow Pages under the heading of "Attorneys," which a person can call to obtain a name. The problem with this type of system is that usually the person answering the telephone has an alphabetical list of local attorneys' names. The operator just goes down the list and whatever name is next on the list is given to the caller, with no attempt to isolate or match the caller's problem to the attorney's specialty. You may end up with the name of some attorney who does not handle your type of case and does not want to.

Many people will look through the telephone book until they find the name of an attorney that sounds good to them. Others try to find an attorney whose office is close to their home. These methods are not recommended. You might get lucky and find a good attorney this way, but then again you might not.

The best way to choose an attorney is to start asking people about the attorneys they or their friends employ. Ask what the particular problem was that the attorney handled for that person. Did he or she do a good job? What did the attorney charge? How did the attorney charge? Did the attorney do the work on time? Was he or she easily accessible? Was the attorney easy to communicate with? Also ask what attorneys in the firm (if it was a firm rather than a sole practitioner) worked on the person's case. Usually you will find that the good attorneys or firms will have satisfied clients. Since attorneys have only recently been given the right to advertise on a very limited basis, they must rely on their clients' spreading the word about their skill and ability to increase the size of their business. Don't settle for the name of only one attorney, try to get two or three names to choose from.

The next thing to consider is whether to hire an attorney who practices law alone or to hire a law firm comprised of several attorneys. Usually, the law firm can offer the advantages of the combined skills of the attorneys of that firm. Attorneys in law firms will discuss the cases they are handling with other attorneys in the firm to attempt to arrive at the best solution. Law firms can also offer the advantage of having another attorney present to handle emergency situations that arise in the event the attorney handling your case is not in or cannot be reached. If you have to choose between a young attorney and one who is quite a bit older, you may find the older attorney more experienced, but the younger attorney may be more eager or assertive in handling your case. Perhaps the younger attorney is trying to build a clientele and has fewer clients, and if so may be able to give you faster service. However, a good reputation should be considered before age or experience.

Assuming that you have now decided to see a certain attorney you have selected, the next step is to call the attorney's office and set up an appointment. If your problem is an emergency, let the secretary know and ask that the secretary connect you with the attorney or arrange an appointment with you as soon as possible. If you are in doubt as to whether or not you need an attorney, you are probably wiser to make an appointment with the attorney and have the attorney advise you. An initial meeting with an attorney, not longer than one-half hour, costs anywhere from $20 to $35 in most parts of the country, and can often result in peace of mind. If the meeting is very short, some attorneys will not even charge you, thinking that if they make a good impression, you will hire them in the future.

It is important to understand how attorneys charge. There are 10 factors that attorneys consider when determining their fees. Some attorneys do not tell you that these are the factors they consider, but nearly all do. The factors are: (1) the time required to do your work, (2) the skill required to perform the task, (3) the ability and reputation of the attorney or firm, (4) the importance of the work to the client, (5) the result obtained, (6) the customary charge for performing the work, (7) whether you are a regular client or a "one-shot customer," (8) the urgency of the task, (9) the novelty of the task, and (10) the pleasantness or unpleasantness of the work.

Many offices, including the author's own, summarize the above factors and inform clients that their fee is based upon three things: (1) an hourly rate of so much per hour, (2) how hard the work is, and (3) the end result obtained. In many cases, law firms have "standard fees" for doing certain types of work, such as simple wills, bankruptcies, divorces. The firm or attorney's "standard fee" is set after considering the 10 factors listed above, the office-incurred expenses, the prices that other attorneys in the community charge for similar work, and the firm's desire to do work like your case.

Some attorneys will handle certain types of cases, such as personal injuries, malpractice, and negligence cases, on a contingent or percentage-of-recovery basis. This means that if the attorney sues someone for you and recovers money, he or she is paid a percentage of the amount. If the attorney sues and loses, he or she gets no money. The client will usually have to pay the out-of-pocket expenses incurred in processing the case, win or lose. Do not think that an attorney will jump at a chance to take your case on this basis. Most attorneys will have to believe first that you will win your suit and that the attorney's share of this recovery will be enough to justify the time and effort the attorney will have to expend.

How can you make sure that you are being charged fairly by your attorney? There are several things you should do when you hire an attorney. At your first meeting, make sure to discuss how he or she will charge you. Next, ask if the attorney will provide you with an itemized list showing the charges and time spent on your case. Ask the attorney to give you an estimate of the cost of handling your case. After your visit, send a letter to the attorney confirming what your agreement is regarding the fee and payment of that fee. How will your attorney expect you to pay the agreed-upon fee? Some lawyers will allow you to pay a set amount per month toward their total charge until the bill is paid. Most will request that you pay a down payment or "retainer" toward their fee and the costs of your case before they will start work on your case. In some instances, the attorney will expect to be paid in full before accepting your case. Banks, credit unions, and finance companies are often willing to loan money for attorney's fees. Some attorneys accept certain credit cards in certain cases.

If the quoted fee or fee arrangement seems high to you, or if you are not satisfied with the attorney for any reason, just tell the attorney that you want to think it over and will let him or her know your decision. Attorneys are used to this and will not think less of you for not making a snap decision. Make sure when you agree on a fee to find out how much of your case will be handled by the attorney you are talking to and how much of your case will be handled by another associate, if you are dealing with a firm. It is common practice for your initial interview to be handled by a senior partner, and then later to find yourself dealing exclusively with a junior member of the firm. This delegation to a junior lawyer is one of the most common complaints that attorneys hear when clients switch attorneys.

The next problem you may encounter, but hopefully will not, is the problem of firing the attorney you hired if you become dissatisfied with his or her work. It is amazing how hard it seems to be for some people to fire their attorneys. This is probably because most people deal on a one-to-one basis with an attorney and find it hard to tell the attorney to his or her face that they are dissatisfied with the work or the firm. Never be afraid to change attorneys if you are unhappy. The outcome of many lawsuits can greatly affect the lives of the people involved. No attorney is going to live or die because a client decides to switch from his or her firm to another law firm. Most attorneys have hundreds of clients, and it is only natural that some clients may be unhappy for some reason or another. You hired the attorney, and you can fire the attorney. I usually advise my clients that if they are unhappy about my work for any reason, to tell me so immediately. I further advise them that if at any time they wish to switch attorneys, they should do so, and I will understand.

There are two methods generally used to fire an attorney or to switch law firms. The first, and least used, method is to call or visit the attorney and tell him or her that you are dissatisfied with the handling of your case and, therefore, are dismissing the attorney and requesting your file. The second method, which is the most commonly used, is to decide who you are going to hire as your new attorney; see the new lawyer and give him or her a written authorization to pick up your file and dismiss your old attorney. This method enables you to avoid a face-to-face meeting with your old attorney. Usually, your new attorney will help you make arrangements with your old attorney to pay his or her bill. Many attorneys will not turn over your file to your new attorney until you pay their bill.

One final point about switching attorneys—many people do not understand that their case is not the only one that their attorney is handling. An attorney may be working on 100 cases besides yours, and that new attorney you want to hire, because you think your old attorney is too slow, may also have 100 other cases in progress, in addition to beginning work on your case. The message, in short, is "be patient"—most good attorneys are very busy, and the legal process and court systems are very slow. One other point on switching attorneys is, simply, attorneys work best when they are paid. Very often I will have clients come into my office complaining about the way their old attorney is handling the case. Often when I ask if they have paid their attorney as agreed upon, they say no. Attorneys are just like everyone else, they want to be paid for their work. The clients who pay the fastest usually get their work done first.

PART SIX
IDENTITY

Who Am I?

The Quest for Identity

Charles Zastrow

What kind of a person are you? What do you want out of life? What kind of person do you want to be? Who are you? These questions are probably the most important you will have to face. Without answers, you will not be prepared to make such major decisions as selecting a career, deciding whether, when, or whom to marry, deciding whether to have children, deciding where to live, deciding what to do with your leisure time. Unfortunately, many people muddle through life and never arrive at answers to these questions. Those who do not arrive at answers may be depressed, indecisive, anxious, and unfulfilled. All too often, their lives are carbon copies of Stan Sinclair's.

At age 18, Stan graduated from high school. Unable to find a job, he enlisted in the army for a three-year hitch. At 20, he started dating Julia Johnson while stationed in Illinois. He liked Julia. She became pregnant and they decided to get married. Money was tight and Julia wanted to live near her relatives. Two months after his discharge, Stan became a father. Needing a job in the area, he became a gas station attendant since it was the only employment he could find. Two and a half years later, an opening occurred in an auto assembly plant. The pay was better, so Stan applied and was hired.

This article was especially written for this book.

The job was relatively easy, but monotonous. Stan faithfully attached a muffler to a new car, over and over for 40 hours a week. During the next eight years, Stan and Julia had three more children. The pay and fringe benefits, combined with his family/financial responsibilities, locked Stan into this assembly line job until he retired at age 65. The morning after he retired, he looked into the mirror and began asking, finally, the key questions. Was it all worth it? Why did he feel empty and unfulfilled? What did he want out of the future? Never having in the past figured out what he wanted out of life, his only answer was a frown.

Identity is having a sense of who we are, a knowledge and a feeling of the ways in which we are separate, distinct persons.

GOAL VS. ROLE IDENTITY

William Glasser[1] points out that the need for identity is the single most important and basic psychological need faced by everyone. According to Glasser, for the past 10,000 years, almost everyone established an identity that was goal directed; that is, their sense of self was largely centered on survival (subsistence needs), or at best achieving economic security. To be more concrete, goal-directed persons when asked "Who are you?" would probably respond in terms of career/occupation: "I am a farmer," "a nurse," "a barber," and so on. With this perception of themselves, their sense of identity would be determined largely by the role prescriptions and expectations of their position/career. Since meeting subsistence needs (or achieving economic security) took most of their time, very few hours were available to devote to other identity questions, such as what kind of person they would like to be or what they find enjoyable in living.

In contrast to older goal-oriented society, the younger generation, during the past 20 years, is more role directed; that is, more concerned with fulfilling themselves as human beings, with the kind of persons they are, with doing the kind of things they feel are enjoyable, with the quality of life. To illustrate, a goal-directed person's main concern in seeking a job would be the economic security it would provide; a role-directed person would be mainly concerned about the potential for human satisfactions on the job. According to Glasser, this shift from "goal" to "role" identity has occurred because of: (1) affluence, (2) increased recognition of the importance of civil rights, and (3) the mass media, particularly television, which increasingly has emphasized the importance of fulfilling and enjoying oneself.

[1] William Glasser, *The Identity Society* (New York: Harper & Row, 1972).

This difference in identity orientation often has led to a cultural gap between parents and children—parents urge their children to subordinate themselves to a job; children assert that unless the job promises to be personally fulfilling, they will not apply.

Idealistically, the shift from goal to role identity may be more appealing from a humanitarian perspective. On the other hand, establishing an identity in terms of one's career/occupation was simpler and considerably less traumatic. The search for role identity involves a number of more complicated questions, including: "What do I find enjoyable?" "Who am I?" "What values and mores should I have?" "What kind of person do I want to become?" "How do I come across to other people?" "What changes should I make in the way I present myself?" "What kind of career would best suit the way I want to live my life?"

THE FORMATION OF IDENTITY

Identity development is a lifetime process. It begins during the early years and continues to change throughout one's lifetime. During the early years, one's sense of identity is largely determined by the reactions of others. A long time ago, Cooley[2] coined this labeling process as resulting in the "looking-glass self," that is, persons develop their self-concept (who and what they are) in terms of how others relate to them. For example, if a neighborhood identifies a youth as being a "troublemaker," a "delinquent," they are apt to relate to the youth as if he were not to be trusted, may accuse him of delinquent acts, and will label his semidelinquent and aggressive behavior as being "delinquent." This labeling process, the youth begins to realize, also results in a type of prestige and status, at least from his peers. In the absence of objective ways to gauge whether he is, in fact, a "delinquent," the youth will rely on the subjective evaluations of others. Thus, gradually, as the youth is related to as being a "delinquent," he is apt to begin to perceive himself in that way and will begin to enact the delinquent role.

A useful perspective for viewing identity is in terms of a success versus failure orientation. Glasser[3] points out that those who develop a success identity (a self-concept of generally being successful) have two traits: love and self-worth. To feel that one is a success in the world, Glasser asserts that one must feel that at least one other person loves him or her and that he or she also loves another person. He or she must also feel that at least one person "out

[2]C.H. Cooley, *Human Nature and the Social Order* (New York: Scribner's, 1902).
[3]William Glasser, *Schools without Failure* (New York: Harper & Row, 1967).

there" feels that he or she is a worthwhile human being, and he or she, him- or herself, must also feel worthwhile.

If a person does not feel loved or does not have a sense of self-worth, that person is apt to establish a failure identity (a feeling of being relatively unsuccessful). People with failure identities are apt to be lonely, depressed, anxious, indecisive, and reluctant to face everyday challenges. Withdrawal, escape through drugs, loneliness, or the development of emotional problems are common.

Fortunately, since identity development is a lifetime process, positive changes are probable even for those with serious failure identities.[4] A key principle to remember is: *Although we cannot change the past, what we want out of the future, along with our motivation to achieve what we want, is more important (than our past experiences) in determining what our future will be.*

HOW TO DETERMINE WHO YOU ARE

The most important decisions you make in your life may well be in answering the following questions:

1. What do I want out of life?
2. What kind of person am I?
3. What kind of person do I want to be?
4. Who am I?

Answers to these questions are not easy to arrive at. They require considerable contemplation and trial and error. But if you are to lead a gratifying, fulfilling life, it is imperative to arrive at answers to give direction to your life and to have a chance of living the kind of life you find meaningful. Without answers, you are apt, like Stan Sinclair, to muddle through life by being a passive responder to situations that arise, rather than a continual achiever of your life's goals.

To determine who you are, you need to arrive at answers to the following more specific questions:

1. What do I find satisfying/enjoyable?
2. What is my moral code? (One possible code is to seek to fulfill your needs and to seek to do what you find enjoyable, doing so in a way that does not deprive others of the ability to fulfill their needs.)
3. What are my religious beliefs? (see Chapter 27).

---

[4]Guidelines for reversing a failure identity are presented in Chapter 4 of this book.

4. What kind of a career do I desire? (Ideally, you should seek a career in which you find the work stimulating and satisfying, that you are skilled at, and that earns you enough money to support the life-style you want.)

5. What are my sexual mores? (All of us should develop a consistent code that we are comfortable with and that helps us to meet our needs without exploiting others. There is no one right code—what works for one may not work for another, due to differences in life-styles, life goals, and personal values.)

6. Do I desire to marry? (If yes, to what type of person and when; how consistent are your answers here with your other life goals? See Chapter 2.)

7. Do I desire to have children? (If yes, how many, when, and how consistent are your answers here with your other life goals?)

8. What area of the country/world do I desire to live in? (Variables to be considered are climate, geography, type of dwelling, rural or urban setting, closeness to relatives or friends, and characteristics of the neighborhood.)

9. What do I enjoy doing with my leisure time?

10. What kind of image do I want to project to others? (Your image will be composed of your dressing style and grooming habits, your emotions (see Chapter 1), personality, degree of assertiveness (see Chapter 25), capacity to communicate (see Chapter 26), material possessions, moral code, physical features, and voice patterns. You need to assess your strengths and shortcomings honestly in this area, and seek to make improvements at times; seeking counseling in problem areas may be desirable.)

11. What type of people do I enjoy being with, and why?

12. Do I desire to improve the quality of my life and that of others? (If yes, in what ways, and how do you hope to achieve these goals?)

13. What type of relationships do I desire to have with relatives, friends, neighbors, with people I meet for the first time?

14. What are my thoughts about death and dying (see Chapters 6 and 7).

15. What do I hope to be doing 5 years from now, 10 years, 20 years? What are my plans for achieving these goals in these time periods?

To have a fairly well-developed sense of identity, you need to have answers to most, but not all, of these questions. Very few persons are able to arrive at rational, consistent answers to all the questions. Having answers to most of them will provide a reference for developing your views to the yet unanswered areas.

Honest, well-thought out answers to these questions will go a long way toward defining who you are. Again, what you want out of life, along with your motivation to achieve these goals, will primarily determine your identity. The above questions are simple to state, but arriving at answers is a complicated, on-going process. In addition, expect some changes in your life goals as time goes on. Environmental influences change (for example, changes in working conditions). Also, as personal growth occurs, changes are apt to occur in activities that you find enjoyable and also in your beliefs, attitudes, and values. Accept such changes, and if you have a fairly good idea of who you are, you will be prepared to make changes in your life goals so that you will be able to give continued direction to your life.

Be honest about your strengths and shortcomings. For practically any shortcoming, there are specific intervention strategies to bring about improvement. This book has focused on specifying approaches for a number of personal shortcomings/problems, including undesirable emotions, controlling feelings of romantic love, depression, a sense of failure, loneliness, death and dying, sexual dysfunctions, sexual identity, smoking, overeating, excessive drinking, mental illness, racial and sex discrimination, broken romances, shyness, communication problems, religious concerns, grooming habits, rape, suicide attempts, premarital pregnancies, and financial crisis.

Your life is shaped by different events that are the results of decisions you make and decisions that are made for you. Without a sense of identity, you will not know what decisions are best for you, and your life will be unfulfilled. With a sense of identity, you will be able to direct your life toward goals you select and find personally meaningful.

List of Contributors

CHARLES ZASTROW is an associate professor and chairperson of the social welfare department at the University of Wisconsin-Whitewater. Prior to this faculty appointment, he was employed in counseling positions in a variety of public and private social service agencies. He has a Ph.D. degree in social welfare and an M.S. in social work.

DAE H. CHANG is a professor and chairperson of the administration of justice department at Wichita State University. He is the author of four other books, and has a Ph.D. degree in sociology.

RONALD J. BARTA is a psychiatric social worker at Lakeland Counseling Center in Wisconsin. He is also an ad hoc instructor for the University of Wisconsin-Extension, where he has developed and taught courses on counseling alcoholics and their families. He has a M.S. degree in social welfare.

WANDA L. BINCER is a psychiatrist in private practice with Madison Psychiatric Associates in Wisconsin. She received her M.D. degree in Ireland.

JANE K. BURGESS is an associate professor of sociology at the University of Wisconsin-Waukesha. She has a Ph.D. degree in sociology, and is the author of several papers on death and dying.

BERNARD I. CESNIK is the manager of emergency services (primarily suicide counseling) at Dane County Mental Health Center in Wisconsin. He is also a clinical instructor of psychiatry at the University of Wisconsin-Madison, and has an M.S. degree in social work.

ROGER CONANT is an illustrator/author with the College for Human Development at Syracuse University in New York.

MARLENE A. CUMMINGS is the human relations coordinator for Madison Public Schools in Wisconsin. She is also a producer-hostess of some local television specials in Madison, a columnist on human relations for the *Wisconsin State Journal,* and a consultant on human relations for the Indianapolis public school system.

WAYNE W. DUNNING is an assistant professor of criminalistics and criminal investigation in the administration of justice department at Wichita State University. He has a Ph.D. degree in chemistry.

SOL GORDON is a professor of child and family studies at Syracuse University, New York. He has written a number of papers, including educational comic books on human sexuality. He has a Ph.D. degree in human sexuality.

MWALIMU IMARA is director of the Boston Center for Religion and Psychotherapy, Inc., and is also a therapist for the Brandeis University Psychological Counseling Center in Waltham, Massachusetts. He has had extensive training and experience in counseling the terminally ill and the bereaved. He has a Doctor of the Ministry degree.

JANE R. JAMES is a sex therapist at the Midwest Sexual Counseling Center in Madison, Wisconsin, and is a lecturer at the University of Wisconsin-Whitewater where she teaches courses in human sexuality and sexual counseling.

CATHY JENSEN is attending the University of Wisconsin-Whitewater, and is a former bunny for the Playboy Club.

KIRK Y. K. KIM is an associate professor and chairperson of the economics department at the University of Wisconsin-Whitewater. He has a Ph.D. degree in economics.

JOSEPH K. KUEMMEL is an attorney at law and a member of the Wisconsin law firm of Klein, Kuemmel & Schmidt in Madison. He has a Juris Doctor degree.

FRANK E. LADWIG is a clinical associate professor in social work at the University of Wisconsin-Madison. Prior to this appointment, he was director of the Drug Abuse Treatment Program at the University of Wisconsin. He has an M.S. degree in social work.

LAURIE LYTLE is the mother of three children, two of whom are adopted. She is attending the University of Wisconsin-Whitewater.

MERLIN J. MANLEY is a professor of education and is the education outreach coordinator at the University of Wisconsin-Whitewater. He has an Ed. D. degree in educational psychology.

MAXIE C. MAULTSBY, JR., is an associate professor of psychiatry and director of Psychiatry Outpatient Services in the college of medicine at the University of Kentucky. He is the founder and president of the Association of Rational Thinking, and is the author of several books on rational self-counseling. He has an M.D. degree in psychiatry.

JEAN MAYER is professor of nutrition at Harvard University. He has a Ph.D. degree, and for the past several years has been a columnist for *Family Health Magazine.*

PATRICIA H. MEWALDT is director of research for effectiveness training in Solana Beach, California, which is the center for parent effectiveness training programs. She has had prior extensive experience in direct counseling, and as a lecturer in counselor education. She has an Ed. M. degree in counseling from Boston University.

URSULA S. MYERS is the supervisor of the single parent and family services unit at Rock County Department of Social Services in Wisconsin. She has an M.S. degree in social work.

RALPH G. NAVARRE is an assistant professor in the department of social welfare at the University of Wisconsin-Whitewater. Prior to this appointment, he was a supervisor of social services in a county welfare department for a five-year period. He has a M.S. degree in social work and a M.S. degree in public administration.

SUZANNE K. NIXON is the manager of adult outpatient services for the Dane County Mental Health Center in Madison, Wisconsin. She has a Ph.D. degree and has had three years of postdoctoral training in psychology.

CATHRYN M. WAGNER is a high school physical educator for Appleton Public Schools in Wisconsin. Prior to this appointment, she was a physical educator at the University of Wisconsin-Whitewater, where she was an instructor of a self-defense course for women and the coordinator of a rape prevention workshop for educators.

HYLDA M. ROBERTS is the coordinator of the Reach to Recovery Program in Rock County, Wisconsin, which provides recovery services for women who have had a mastectomy. She has also been a board member and resource person for the American Cancer Society.

WARREN SHIBLES is an assistant professor of philosophy at the University of Wisconsin-Whitewater. He is the author of several books, including one on emotions. He has an M.A. in philosophy, and has completed his course work for a Ph.D.

LLOYD G. SINCLAIR is a sex therapist for the Midwest Sexual Counseling Center in Madison, Wisconsin, and is a lecturer of a course in human sexuality at the University of Wisconsin-Whitewater. He has a M.S. degree in social work.

LETICIA M. SMITH is director of the program services bureau for the State of Wisconsin Equal Rights Division. She is also the director and vice-president of the Women's Research Institute of Wisconsin. She has a Ph.D. degree in sociology.

GEORGE C. THOSTESON is a syndicated medical columnist for the Field Newspaper Syndicate in Chicago. He has an M.D. degree, and is the author of two books.

RICHARD L. TIMMERS is the director and a sex therapist for the Midwest Sexual Counseling Center in Madison, Wisconsin. He has an M.S. degree in social work, and also is a clinical associate professor for the school of social work at the University of Wisconsin-Madison.

JANET GREGORY VERMANDEL is a full-time author and has written six widely published suspense novels.

STEVEN E. WEBSTER is the convenor of the Task Force on Gay Ministries of United Methodist Gay Caucus. Previously, he has been an interim director and the director of counseling at the Madison Gay Center in Wisconsin.

Index

Aase, J.M., 179*fn*
Abnormal Personality, The, 31*fn*
Abortion, 162, 312, 313-16
Abortion Rights Association, 313
Abstinence syndrome (*See* Withdrawal
    illness)
Academy of Certified Social Workers, 313
Acceptance, feeling of, 72
Active listening, as skill, 246-47
Activity, as relief from depression, 31-32
Addiction; definition, 171
Addictive smoking, 144
Adolescent rebellion, analysis, 9-18
Adoption: 327-31
Aggravated assault, 351
Aggressive style, of interaction, 237
Aid to Families with Dependent Children
    (AFDC), 338, 343-44
Alberti, Robert E., 237, 237*fn*, 238*fn*
Alcohol, 273*fn*
Alcohol, 187
    American abuse of, 188
    facts and effects, 172-73
Alcohol abuser, definition, 189-90
Alcoholic, definition, 189

Alcoholics Anonymous, 190*fn*
Alcoholics Anonymous, 34, 192
Alcoholism:
    confrontation, 192-93
    definition, 189
    education, 191-92
    intervention, 193
    stages in planning help for, 191
    steps in drinking behavior, 190
Alcoholism: Behavioral Research
    Therapeutic Approaches, 193*fn*
Alibi structure, of alcoholic, 189-91
Allport, Gordon W., 77, 79, 199, 199*fn*
Altschule, M.D., 177*fn*
American Association of Marriage and
    Family Counselors, 313
American Association of Sex Educators and
    Counselors, 96
American Cancer Society, 135, 140, 147,
    149, 158, 159
American Civil Liberties Union, 312
American Institute of Public Opinion, 175*fn*
American Medical Association, 182
American Psychiatric Association, 122, 129,
    164

American Psychological Association, 122, 122*fn*, 129

Ames, F.A., 174*fn*

Amir, Menachim, 291*fn*, 292*fn*, 293*fn*

Amphetamines, facts and effects, 175-76

Analysis of Human Sexual Response, An, 85*fn*

And Now We Are a Family, 329

Andrews, J.C., 178*fn*

Antisocial acts, as emotional disorders, 164-65

Anxiety:
  and delaying orgasm, 105
  and discrimination, 199-200

Application forms, and discriminatory practices, 210

Armed Forces Benefits, 344

Ashley, Richard, 179*fn*

As-If RSA, example, 9-18

Assertive style, of interaction, 237

Assertiveness:
  examples of behavior, 240-41
  guidelines, 242-43
  helping someone toward, 241-42
  range of problems, 236-37

Assertiveness training:
  approaches, 239-40
  design of, 237
  and discrimination, 226
  steps in, 238-40

Association for Rational Thinking (ART), 9*fn*

Attorneys:
  choosing, 359
  determining need for, 358-59
  fees, 360-61
  firing and/or switching, 361-62
  firm or single practice, 359-60

Attractive, how to be more, 258-64

Auto theft, 353

Baer, Jean, 238*fn*

Bankruptcy:
  alternatives to, 334-36
  case history, 333-34
  voluntary petition for, 336

Barback, Lonnie, 108*fn*

Barbituates, facts and effects, 177, 186

Beck, Aaron T., 277*fn*

Behaviors, in failure analysis, 40-41

Being Mentally Ill, 165*fn*

Belief:
  need for in accepting death, 61-62
  "wrong" and "right," 3-4

Bell, Thomas, 68

Belliveau, Fred, 107*fn*

Ben-Arie, O., 180*fn*

Bender, L., 178*fn*

Bettleheim, Bruno, 318

Beow, Robert, 256*fn*

Berlin, C.M., 179*fn*

Bewley, T.H., 180*fn*

Birth control (*See also* Contraception), 325

Bisexuality (*See also* Homosexuality), 126

Body posture, in assertiveness training, 238

Bogdanoff, B., 179*fn*

Brain deterioration, as disorder, 165

Brand, S.N., 174*fn*

Braun, John R., 165*fn*

Breast cancer, 156-57

Brecher, Edward M., 85*fn*, 180*fn*

Brecher, Ruth, 85*fn*

Brockopp, Gene W., 288*fn*

Brown, Roscoe C., 197*fn*

Buber, Martin, 51, 51*fn*

Bulbar squeeze technique, 101, 102 (*fig.*), 103

Bureaucracy, learning rules of, 226-29

Burglary, 352

"Business necessity," interpretation of, 211

Calorie counting, 152, 153

Cancer, and cigarette smoking, 136-37

Carkhuff, Robert, 39, 39*fn*, 44, 45*fn*

Carpenter, Linda, 8*fn*

Chafetz, Morris E., 188

Cherubin, Charles, 180*fn*

Children, marijuana and drug use in, 184-87

Child Welfare Statutes, 322

Childhood and Society, 317*fn*

Cholesterol, and dieting, 154

Cigarettes, 187

Cigarette smoking:
  approaches to giving up, 150
  approaching Q-Day, 140-41
  case histories of quitters, 138-40
  cutting down, 141-42
  effects of stopping, 136
  four styles, 143-44
  keeping a track record, 142-43
  Q-Day action, 145-47
  questions and answers, 147-50
  reasons for stopping, 136-38
  score card, 142, 143
  week before Q-Day, 144-45

Civil Rights Act (1964), 201, 202, 211, 222

Civil Rights Act (1968), 201, 202

Civil Rights Bill (1867), 198

Clinical Psychology in Transition, 165*fn*

Clitoris, function of and possible adhesions, 107

Cocaine, facts and effects, 181

"Coming out," as identity crisis, 123-25

Commerce Clearing House (CCH), 225

Commercial budgeting services, 335

Commitment:
  as necessary to solving failure, 38
  various levels of, 72-77

Communication (*See* Effective communication)

Community Action Centers, 50, 312, 325

Community counseling agency, use of in financial crisis, 335

Complaints:
  of discrimination, 227, 228
  filing procedures, 203-204

Conditions of work, definition, 216-17

Condoms, purchase and use of, 119-20

Conflicts (*See* Problems)

Confrontation process, as motivation for alcoholic, 192-93

Consenting Adult, 127*fn*

Consciousness-raising groups, 50

Consolidation loan, 334

Consortium on Early Childbearing and Childrearing, 318

Consumer Reports, Licit and Illicit Drugs, 180*fn*

Contraception, information available, 325

Contraceptive foams, 117, 118, 120

Conversation, as commitment, 74-75

Cooley, C.L., 367, 376*fn*

Corey, M.J., 178*fn*

Corney, R.T., 161, 161*fn*

Corsini, Raymond, 32*fn*

Counseling:
  building a relationship, 268-69
  in cases of depression, 33-34
  explore alternative solutions, 272-74
  exploring problems in depth, 269-72
  general concerns, 67
  phases, 267-68
  and problem pregnancies, 312
  suicidal persons, 277-88

County Social Service agencies, 319

Crash dieting, 151-52

"Crazy," as label, 163

Credit, ease of obtaining, 332

Credit cards, use of, 332-33

Crime:
  as national problem, 347
  opportunities and victims, 348-49
  vs. persons, 349-52

vs. properties, 352-53

recommended solution for avoiding victimization, 353-56

rising incidence of, 347-48

Crime Index, list of offenses, 347*fn*

Crime in the U.S. 1973: Uniform Crime Report, 347*fn*

Csida, Joseph, 292*fn*

Csida, June Bundy, 292*fn*

Current Psychotherapies, 32*fn*

Danto, Bruce L., 287

Death:
  anxiety about, 63
  case study, 69-72
  denial of, 68
  empathy and grief, 55-56
  expression of emotion, 59-60
  fears of, 54-55
  and need for belief, 61-62
  needs for coming to terms with, 56
  and needs of others, 61
  realistic acceptance of, 57-59
  religion and growth, 72-80
  self-identity, 56-57
  as stage of growth, 66-69

Death and Dying Seminar, 69, 71

Death: The Final Stage of Growth, 66*fn*

Debt pooling, 335-36

De facto discrimination, 200-201

De jure discrimination, 201-203

Delerium tremens (DTs), 173

Depression:
  causes, 29-31
  guidelines for resolving mild, 31-34
  post-mastectomy, 159
  in suicidal persons, 282-83
  symptoms, 29-30

Diaphragm, as contraceptive device, 117, 118-19, 325

Dictionary of Words About Alcohol, A, 189*fn*

Diet, and health, 258-59

Dieting:
  calorie counting, 152-53
  and cholesterol confusion, 154
  cooking lean, 153
  crash, 151-52
  and exercise, 154-55
  nonfattening foods, 152
  and portion size, 152-53
  and protein intake, 153-54
  and sugar intake, 154
  water and salt, 154

Dieting (*continued*)
   and "wet" calories, 153
Dimension of a New Identity, 317*fn*
Direction, as channel of meaning, 76-79
Dishotsky, N.I., 178*fn*
Don't Say Yes When You Want to Say No,
   238*fn*
Door openers, as listening skill, 246
Douching, 118
Douglass, Frederick, 201
Dress requirements, as discriminatory
   practice, 218-19
Drinking problem (*See* Alcoholism)
*Drug Abuse: Proceedings of the
   International Conference*, 178*fn*
Drug dependence, definition, 171
Drugs:
   abuse of, 171
   as aid for depression, 33, 34
   alcohol, 172-73
   American orientation toward, 170, 171
   amphetamines, 175-76
   background on use and abuse, 185-87
   barbituates, 177
   cocaine, 181
   consultation with drug programs, 187
   definition, 170-71
   hallucinogens, 177-79
   marijuana, 173-75
   opiates, 179-81
   ways to combat problems, 182-83
   what to do when children use, 184-85

Edison, G.R., 175*fn*
Education:
   about alcohol, 191-92
   about death, 55
   and minorities, 206
Effective communication (*See also*
   Counseling)
   and conflict with others, 248-50
   feeling accepting, 245
   helpful attitude, 245-46
   identifying problems, 244-45
   listening skills, 246-47
   No-Lose Problem Solving, 249-50
   and values collision, 250-51
   what to do when you have a problem,
      247-48
Efron, Vera, 189*fn*
"Ego-extension," 79
Ehrmann, Max, 50, 50*fn*
Ejaculation, 97-105
Ellinwood, Everett Jr., 176*fn*

Ellis, Albert, 32*fn*
Emergency Psychiatric Care, 380*fn*
Emmons, Michael L., 237, 237*fn*, 238*fn*
Emotion, 27*fn*
Emotional disorders, types, 164-65
Emotional problems, and labeling, 165-66
Emotions:
   learning new facts about, 3-4
   love as, 19-23
   need to express when accepting death,
      59-60
   unwanted, and RSA, 6-10
Empathy, 55-56, 270
Employment Practices Guide, 225
Employment rights, laws protecting women,
   221-24
Equal Employment Opportunity
   Commission, 203, 211, 222, 223, 225,
   226
Equal Opportunity Act (1972), 222
Equal Pay Act (1963), 221-22
Equal Rights Agency, 203
Equal rights laws, 198
Erection, 89-96
Erikson, Erik, 317, 317*fn*
Ethnic prejudice, definition, 199
Everything You Wanted to Know About Sex,
   124*fn*
Executive Order 11246, 223-24
Exercise:
   and dieting, 155
   and health, 259-60
Expectations, and sense of failure, 37
Eyewitness: The Negro in American History,
   198*fn*

Facts, definitions, 3, 4
Failure:
   determinants, 36-38
   problem resolution, steps, 38-45
Failure orientation, 367-68
   analysis of, 39-40
   symptoms, 35-36
Fair Labor Standards Act (FLSA), 221
Family Service Association of America, 313
Farberon, Norman, 380*fn*
Fashion, considerations in choosing, 262-63
Federal Bankruptcy Courts, 333
Federal Bankruptcy Law, Chapter 13,
   335-36
Federal Wage and Hour Division, 227
Feedback, and failure mechanisms, 36-37
Feminine hygiene sprays, 118
Fensterheim, Herbert, 238*fn*

Financial plan, setting up, 335-36
First Reconstruction Act (1867), 198
Fischman, V.S., 176*fn*
Food Stamp Program, 343-44
Ford, Betty, 156
Fourteenth Amendment (1866), 198
Fox, Ruth, 193*fn*
Freedom from Rape, 290*fn*, 291*fn*, 292*fn*
Freedmen's Bureau, The, 198
Friedman, Maurice, 51*fn*
Foreplay, 87
For Yourself: The Fulfillment of Female Sexuality, 108*fn*
Frenulum squeeze technique, for delaying orgasm, 100, 101 (*fig.*), 103

"Gay," definition, 123*fn*
Gay Liberation Movement, 123, 123*fn*, 125
General relief, as welfare program, 339
Genital touching, 102-103
Gibran, Kahlil, 46*fn*
Gittings, Barbara, 131
Glasser, William, 366, 366*fn*, 367, 367*fn*
Glue sniffing, 186
Goal vs. role identity, 366-67
God:
    belief in and death, 61-62
    proof of existence, 256
Goff, J.T., 161*fn*
Gordon, Thomas, 86*fn*, 244*fn*
Government agencies, and discrimination, 204-205
Grief, five stages of, 72, 77, 78 (*fig.*)
Grievance procedures, 227, 228
Grimstad, Kirsten, 292*fn*
Growth, religion and, 72-80
Growth experiences, as part of life, 66-67
Gurioli, Carol, 189*fn*
Gustafson, Robert, 99*fn*

Habitual smoking, 143
Habituation, definition, 171
Hair care, 260-61
Hallucinogens, facts and effects, 177-79
Haroutunian, Joseph, 67, 69
Hart, J.B., 176*fn*
Hasleton, S., 174*fn*
Health and information services, 121
Help Yourself to Happiness, 5, 18
Heroin, facts and effects, 179-81, 187
Hinduism, 255
Hobson, Laura, 127*fn*
Homicide, 350-51

Homosexuality:
    aloneness, 126
    changing attitudes, 122-23
    courage to be yourself, 130-31
    and "cure," 128-29
    and friends, 127
    loving someone of same sex, 129-30
    meeting other gays, 130
    preferences, 125-26
    "safe" counselors, 125
    and sex, 126
    as a sin, 126-27
    stereotypes, 124
    telling parents, 127-28
    telling spouse, 128
Horton, F.T., Jr., 161, 161*fn*
Housing, and minorities, 205
How to Help Yourself, 39, 39*fn*, 45*fn*
How to Say No to a Rapist and Survive, 304*fn*
Howard, Marion, 318*fn*
Human Nature and the Social Order, 367*fn*
Human Rights Commission, 203
Human Sexual Inadequacy, 100*fn*, 103*fn*
Human Sexual Response, 109*fn*
Hypnosis, and cigarette smoking, 149

"I language," 86, 86*fn*
Identity:
    as channel of meaning, 79
    definition, 365-66
    formation of, 367-68
    goal vs. role, 366-67
    how to determine, 368-70
    through sex, 26
Identity, Youth and Crisis, 317*fn*
Impotence, definition, 89
In the Midst of Life, 68
Individual and His Religion, The, 79*fn*
Interactions, styles of, 237
Intrauterine device (IUD), 117-18, 119, 325

Jacobson, C.B., 179*fn*
Jellinek, E.M., 190, 190*fn*
Job discrimination:
    case histories, 212-14
    examples of, 209-14
    importance of knowing about, 207-208
    laws protecting women, 221-24
    promotion, 214-19
    seniority, 219-20
    sex discrimination, 208
    what women can do, 224-29
    why women should deal with, 200-21

Johnson, Lyndon B., 201, 202
Johnson, Virginia, 85, 93*fn*, 100, 100*fn*,
   103*fn*, 104, 109*fn*, 271

Kaiser, Ernest, 202*fn*, 205*fn*
Kaplan, Helen Singer, 107*fn*
Katz, Barney, 163*fn*
Katz, William, 198*fn*
Kegel, Arnold, 108*fn*
Keller, Mark, 189, 189*fn*
Kinsey, Alfred, 123*fn*, 125
Kramer, J.C., 176*fn*
Kübler-Ross, Elisabeth, 66*fn*, 69, 70, 71

Laestadius, N., 179*fn*
Larceny-theft, 353
Law, Liberty and Psychiatry, 165*fn*
"Lawyer Referral Systems," 359
Lemert, Edwin M., 166*fn*
Lesse, Stanley, 276*fn*
Lettieri, Dan J., 277*fn*
Lieber, C.S., 173*fn*
Lieberman, B.W., 174*fn*
Lieberman, C.M., 174*fn*
Lipscomb, W.R., 178*fn*
Listening skills, 246-47
Litman, Robert E., 280*fn*
Littlefield, 176*fn*
Loneliness, 53*fn*
Loneliness, 47-53
Loneliness & Love, 53*fn*
"Looking-glass self" concept, 166, 367
Loughman, W.D., 178*fn*
Love, 19-28
   rational, 24-25
   romantic, 23-24
Love is Not Enough, 318
LSD-25, 177-79, 187
Lumpectomy, 157

MacLean, J.R., 178*fn*
Maier, Norman R.F., 211, 211*fn*
Man-woman relationships, when man leaves,
   230-35
Marijuana, facts and effects, 173-75, 187
Marks, V., 180*fn*
Masked Depression, 276*fn*
Mastectomy, adjusting to, 156-59
Masters, William, 85, 93*fn*, 100, 100*fn*, 103
   103*fn*, 104, 109*fn*, 271
Masturbation, 85, 110-11
Maternity benefits, and discrimination,
   217-18

Maugh, T.H. III, 179*fn*
Maultsby, Maxie, 5, 18
Maurer, David, 181*fn*
McClary, Catherine, 290*fn*, 291*fn*, 292*fn*
McCormick, Mairi, 189, 189*fn*
McKechnie, J.L., 190*fn*
McLeod, M.J., 178*fn*
Mechanic, David, 165, 165*fn*
Medea, Andra, 292*fn*, 293*fn*
Medicaid programs, 320
Medical Assistance, 338, 343-44
Mental illness:
   case history, 167-69
   as label, 164, 166
   motivating improvement, 166-67
   steps to becoming labeled, 165
   types, 164-65
Meredith, Judith C., 329
Message content, in assertiveness training, 239
Method of Philosophical Therapy, The,
   19*fn*
Minorities, legal status of, 205-206
Miscarriage, 160-62
Mogar, R.E., 178*fn*
Montgomery Bus Boycott, 197
Morphine, facts and effects, 179-81
Mortgage Bankers Association of
   America, 333
Moustakas, Clark, 53*fn*

Narcotics and Narcotic Addiction,
   181*fn*
National Association for the
   Advancement of Colored People
   (NAACP), 198, 204
National Association of Social Workers,
   313
National Clearinghouse for Smoking
   and Health, 144
National Commission on the Causes
   and Prevention of Violence, 291
National Fire Protection Association,
   136
National Institute on Alcohol Abuse
   and Alcoholism, 188
National Organization of Women
   (NOW), 50, 226, 310, 314
Nature of Prejudice, The, 199*fn*
Needs:
   getting these met, 247-48
   in accepting death, 56-62
Negative affect smoking, 144
*Negro Almanac: The Black Experience
   in America, The*, 197*fn*, 202*fn*, 205*fn*

New Women's Survival Catalogue, The,
  292*fn*
New Sex Therapy, The, 107*fn*
Nichols, W.W., 178*fn*
No-Lose Problem Solving, steps in,
  249-50
Nonfattening foods and dieting, 152
Nongenital touching, 102

Office of Civil Rights, 198, 205
Office of Federal Contract Compliance,
  (OFCC), 223, 224, 198, 205
Old Age, Survivors, and Disability
  Insurance Programs, (OASDI),
  344-45
Opiates, facts and effects, 179-81
Orgasm, 109-13
Orgasmic behavior, definition, 106
"Original experience," capacity for, 73
Our Bodies, Ourselves, 310, 314*fn*

Page, James P., 29*fn,* 34*fn*
Parent Effectiveness Traning, 86*fn,*
  244*fn*
Patterns in Forcible Rape, 291*fn,* 292*fn,*
  293*fn*
Payne, R.J., 174*fn*
Penelhum, Terence, 256*fn*
Performance tests, 211
Personal hygiene, 263-64
Personality tests, and discrimination,
  211
Phillips, D.L., 166*fn*
Pill, contraceptive, 117, 118, 325
Planned Parenthood, 118, 120, 121, 310,
  314, 325
Ploski, Harry, 197*fn,* 202*fn,* 205*fn*
Positive affect smoking, 143
Prediction of Suicide, The, 277*fn*
Pregnancy:
  and contraception, 117-20
  premarital, 309-26
  reasons for prevention, 115-16
  and sex discrimination, 217-18
  testing for, 120-21
President's Commission on Law
  Enforcement and Administration of
  Justice, 171*fn,* 174*fn,* 176*fn,* 177*fn,*
  181*fn*
Problems:
  exploring in depth, 269-72
  identifying and listening to, 244-47
  No-Lose Problem Solving, 249-50

  what to do, 247-48
Problems of Religious Knowledge,
  256*fn*
Promotion, and discrimination, 214-19
Prostitution, 351-52
*Protect Yourself From Becoming an
  Unwanted Parent,* 117*fn*
Psychiatric Justice, 164*fn*
Psychology in Industrial Organizations,
  211*fn*
Psychology of Abnormal Behavior, The,
  163*fn*
Psychopathology, 29*fn,* 34*fn*
Psychosis, 164, 283
Public Health Service, 149
Pubococcygeus (P.C.) muscle, 107,
  108-109

Q-Day definition and approach, 140-41
Quit clinic, for smoking, 147

Racial discrimination:
  definition, 199
  de facto, 200-201
  de jure, 201-203
  fear of, 199-200
  forms of, 199-204
  government agencies, 204-205
  legal status of minorities, 205-206
  remnants from the past, 197-98
  steps to take, 203-204
Rainey, Joseph, 198
Rape:
  emotional needs, 306-307
  increased incidence, 351-52
  legal alternatives, 305-306
  medical attention, 305
  myths about, 291-93
  precautions, 293-99
  probability of, 290-91
  when precautions fail, 300-305
*Rape! How to Avoid It and What to Do
  About It if You Can't,* 292*fn*
Rational Self-Analysis (RSA), 5-10
Religion:
  children's decisions about, 254
  diversity among, 255-57
  functions of, 253-54
  and growth, 72-80
  mixed marriages, 255
  reasons for intolerance, 252-53
  toward an open-minded view, 254-57
Religion: Origin and Ideas, 256*fn*

Rennie, Susan, 292*fn*
Resnik, H.L.P., 277*fn*, 280*fn*
Reuben, David, 124*fn*
Rhythm method, of contraception, 118
Richter, Lin, 107*fn*
Rights of Women, The, 225
Robbery, 352
Rocke, L.B., 179*fn*
Roles, and "the norm," 124
Role identity, 366-67
Role-playing, 239, 241, 274
Ross, Susan Deller, 225
Rothman, D., 161*fn*
Rubin, Harvey L., 280*fn*

Sankar, Siva, 178*fn*
Scheff, Thomas, 165, 165*fn*
Schizophrenia, definition, 163-64
Schools Without Failure, 366*fn*, 367*fn*
"Self-objectification," 77, 79
Self-pleasuring (*See* Masturbation)
Self Pleasuring for Men, 99*fn*
Seman, James H., 100*fn*
Seniority, and discrimination, 219-20
Senturia, A.G., 161*fn*
Sex:
  becoming active, 116
  forget the goal, 87-88
  health and information services, 121
  and homosexuality, 126
  knowing self and partner, 84-85
  slowing down, 83-84
  talking about, 85-87
Sex discrimination (*See also* Job
    discrimination)
  dress requirements, 218-19
  in employment, 208
  promotion, cases, 214-19
  standards, cases, 212-14
  what women can do about, 224-29
Sexual Behavior in the Human Male, 123*fn*
Shibles, Warren A., 19*fn*, 27*fn*
Simon, N.M., 161, 161*fn*
Skin care, 261-62
Smith, D.W., 179*fn*
Smith, Joseph, 256
Smoker's Self-Testing Kit, 144
Smoking (*See* Cigarette smoking)
Social Pathology, 166*fn*
Social Security, 338
Social Security Supplemental Income, 338, 344
Society and the Healthy Homosexual, 127*fn*
Stand Up, Speak Out, Talk Back!, 237*fn*

Statistics on Consumption of Alcohol and on Alcoholism, 189*fn*
Stop/start technique, for delaying orgasm, 100
Storaska, Frederic, 304*fn*
Stuart, Richard B., 164*fn*, 165
Success orientation, 367-68
Suicide:
  asking questions, 277-79
  cause of death, 275
  characteristics of counselor, 276-77
  evaluating risk, 277
  intervention planning, 286-88
  plan for, 280-82
  prior behavior, 282
  resources available, 284-86
  self-reported risk, 279
  symptoms, 282-83
Suicide and Violence, 287*fn*
Szasz, Thomas, 164, 164*fn*, 165, 165*fn*

Tales of Rabbi Nachman, The, 51*fn*
Task Force Report: Narcotics and Drug Abuse, 171*fn*
Taska, R., 178*fn*
"Termination of parental rights," 321-24
Thirteenth Amendment (1865), 198
Thomas, Kathleen, 292*fn*, 293*fn*
Thorpe, Louis P., 163*fn*
Tillich, Paul, 72
Timmers, Richard L., 99*fn*
Titus, R.J., 179*fn*
Trick or Treatment, 164*fn*
"True" religion, 253, 255-56

Understanding Human Sexual Inadequacy, 107*fn*
Unemployment compensation, 345
U.S. Bill of Rights, 206
U.S. Bureau of the Census, 208
U.S. Commission on Civil Rights, 203
U.S. Department of Agriculture, 344
U.S. Department of Health, Education and Welfare (HEW), 198, 205
U.S. Department of Justice, 204
U.S. Department of Labor, 222
U.S. Equal Employment Opportunity Commission (EEOC), 198, 203, 205
U.S. Supreme Court, 197, 205, 227, 228, 313

Values collision, 250-51

Venereal disease, 314, 325
prevention of, 119-20, 121
Verbal responses, to discrimination, 225-26
Voge, Victor, 181*fn*
Voice of the Master, The, 46*fn*
Voting, and minorities, 205
Voting Rights Act (1965), 201

Wage and Hour Division, 222
Wage differential, disguising, 217
Wallace, J., 176*fn*
Warren, W.S., 179*fn*
Wasson, Wanda, 9*fn*
Weinberg, George, 127*fn*
Welfare:
  AFDC, 343
  appeals, 341-43
  attitude toward, 339-40
  Food Stamp Program, 343-44
  Medical Assistance, 343-44
  OASDI programs, 344-45
  process of applying for, 338-39
  Social Security programs, 344
  unemployment compensation, 345

working with the system, 340-41
Workman's Compensation, 345
White, Robert, 31*fn*
Whitely, R.K., 162*fn*
Wilby, W.E., 178*fn*
Withdrawal illness, 173
Women (*See also* Job discrimination)
  and man leaving, 230-35
Women's Bureau, Dept. of Labor, 225
Women's Counseling Centers, 310, 312, 325
Women's Free Clinic, 310
Working Woman's Guide to Her Job Rights, A, 225
Workman's Compensation, 345
Written responses, to discriminatory questions, 225-26

Yanoff, M., 179*fn*
You and Your Emotions, 18
Your Perfect Right, 238*fn*

Zarafenetis, C.J.D., 178*fn*